The History of Philosophical and Formal Logic

Also available from Bloomsbury

The Bloomsbury Companion to Aristotle, edited by Claudia Baracchi
The Bloomsbury Companion to Bertrand Russell, edited by Russell Wahl
The Bloomsbury Companion to Philosophical Logic, edited by Leon Horsten
and Richard Pettigrew
Philosophical Logic, George Englebretsen and Charles Sayward

The History of Philosophical and Formal Logic

From Aristotle to Tarski

Edited by
Alex Malpass and Marianna Antonutti Marfori

BLOOMSBURY ACADEMIC
LONDON • NEW YORK • OXFORD • NEW DELHI • SYDNEY

BLOOMSBURY ACADEMIC
Bloomsbury Publishing Plc
50 Bedford Square, London, WC1B 3DP, UK
1385 Broadway, New York, NY 10018, USA

BLOOMSBURY, BLOOMSBURY ACADEMIC and the
Diana logo are trademarks of Bloomsbury Publishing Plc

First published 2017
Paperback edition first published 2018

Cover design: Catherine Wood
Cover image © Dylan Griffin

A catalogue record for this book is available from the British Library.

Library of Congress Cataloging-in-Publication Data
Names: Malpass, Alex, editor. | Marfori, Marianna Antonutti, editor.
Title: The history of philosophical and formal logic from Aristotle to Tarski
/ edited by Alex Malpass and Marianna Antonutti Marfori.
Description: London, UK; New York, NY, USA: Bloomsbury Academic, an imprint
of Bloomsbury Publishing, Plc, [2017] | Includes bibliographical
references and index.
Identifiers: LCCN 2016039911| ISBN 9781472513502 (hb) | ISBN 9781472505255 (epdf)
Subjects: LCSH: Logic–History.
Classification: LCC BC15 .H57 2017 | DDC 160–dc23 LC record available at
https://lccn.loc.gov/2016039911

ISBN: HB: 978-1-4725-1350-2
PB: 978-1-3500-9484-0
ePDF: 978-1-4725-0525-5
ePub: 978-1-4725-0717-4

Typeset by Refinecatch Limited, Bungay, Suffolk

To find out more about our authors and books visit
www.bloomsbury.com and sign up for our newsletters.

Contents

Preface

Students of introductory logic courses usually encounter the fundamental concepts of formal logic – notions like *valid argument, consistency, truth in a model, soundness, completeness*, and so on – for the first time through those courses. However, these concepts are often presented in an ahistorical way, which can make them seem highly abstract, inaccessible, and set in stone, rather than the result of many centuries of conceptual development and refinement. Understanding how the current shape of these concepts is the result of their historical development can make them appear less abstract and artificial, and thus more comprehensible. Furthermore, logicians of previous centuries understood fundamental logical questions and concepts differently than we typically do now. The richness of their ideas and approaches to logic have an intrinsic interest, but they may also provide a valuable source for philosophically-minded students who seek to challenge the currently dominant approach to philosophical and formal logic.

The History of Philosophical and Formal Logic: From Aristotle to Tarski is a partial history of these fundamental questions and concepts, beginning with the work of Aristotle, the founder of the discipline, and ending with that of a modern giant, Alfred Tarski. Each chapter has been written especially for this collection and focuses on the work of a particular figure or school, with the first part ('The Origins of Formal Logic') concentrating on Ancient Greek logic (Aristotle and the Stoics), together with the logical work of the scholastics in the Middle Ages. In the second part ('The Early Modern Period') we see how Gottfried Leibniz's mathematizing approach to logic in the 17th century was followed by nineteenth century thinkers with a similar cast of mind, Bernard Bolzano and George Boole. They can be seen as initiators of the mathematical revolution in logic that took place in the late nineteenth and early twentieth centuries. The third part, 'Mathematical Logic', is concerned with figures whose work exemplifies that revolution: C.S. Peirce, Gottlob Frege, Giuseppe Peano, Bertrand Russell, and David Hilbert. The final part, 'Twentieth-century Logic', assesses the work of two key figures in the development of contemporary mathematical logic, Kurt Gödel and Alfred Tarski, who together shaped much of the course of logic in the twentieth century. Each of the aforementioned figures was surrounded by other logicians whose achievements, and their importance for the development of logic, we were unfortunately unable to explore more extensively in this book.

The History of Philosophical and Formal Logic was conceived as a way for undergraduate students with little training in formal logic to discover the roots of logical concepts. However, we also hope that it provides a starting point for anyone with an interest in this wonderful discipline to become acquainted with its history. By producing an introductory book whose chapters span the entire history of the discipline, we aim to show how the elements of the standard undergraduate logic curriculum took their current form only relatively recently, emerging from a long development by many hands whose interests and motivations varied widely. Moreover, by shedding light on a few topics that have not been given as much attention in standard histories of logic, such as the contributions of Leibniz and Bolzano, as well as the diagrammatic logics of C.S. Peirce, we hope to play a part in encouraging a broader view of the history of logic, which as a discipline surely has much to gain in being more inclusive of other figures and traditions. We only regret not having been able to contribute more in this regard ourselves.

This book was born from a series of lectures on the history of logic at the University of Bristol, organised by Alex Malpass. Aimed at undergraduates in philosophy as well as members of other departments and faculties, the lectures were given by philosophers and logicians at Bristol, together with guest lectures from researchers at other institutions. In order to bring the content of these lectures to a wider audience, the speakers in the lecture series were invited by Alex Malpass to contribute to this book. In the end, the chapters 'Bolzano' by Jönne Kriener, 'Boole' by Giulia Terzian, 'Peano and Russell' by Alexander Bird, and 'Tarski' by Benedict Eastaugh were written by speakers in the lecture series, while the other chapters were contributed by international experts invited by the editors.

Marianna Antonutti Marfori joined the project in 2014 to complete the book. The writing of the Introduction reflects the respective expertise of the two editors: the first half, from Aristotle to Boole, was written by Alex Malpass, while the second half, from Peirce to Tarski, was written by Marianna Antonutti Marfori.

Marianna Antonutti Marfori
Paris and Munich
March 2017

Introduction

Put simply, logic deals with the inference of one thing from another, such as the inference of a conclusion from the premises of an argument. An example of this would be the following:

> The emission of certain chemicals that harm the ozone layer is likely to cause global warming, and petrol-consuming vehicles emit these chemicals in large quantities; therefore, global warming is likely.

Premises can either 'succeed' or 'fail' at ensuring that the conclusion holds, and success means that whenever the premises are true, the conclusion is either also true or at least more likely to be true. In the previous example, the premises about the harmfulness of certain emissions and the fact that petrol-based vehicles emit these chemicals in large quantities supports the conclusion that global warming is likely. If the premises are indeed successful in establishing the conclusion, then we call the resulting inference *valid*. Logic can be thought of as the study, or perhaps even the 'science', of *valid inference*. In this book we will be looking at the core of this science of inference, by which we mean *deductive logic*. In a valid deductive argument, the truth of the premises ensures the truth of the conclusion, such as in the following famous argument:

> All men are mortal, Socrates is a man; therefore, Socrates is mortal.

In this example, one cannot grant the truth of the premises without also granting that Socrates is mortal – the conclusion follows deductively from the premises. Deductive logic is only one branch of logic, however, and there is also *inductive* logic. Generally, inductive logic covers arguments where the conclusion is not established conclusively from the premises, but the likelihood of its being true is supported by the premises. Consider the following argument:

> All observed swans have been white; therefore, the next swan to be observed will be white.

To illustrate the pitfalls of inductive arguments, Bertrand Russell proposed the following example: a turkey which has been fed every single day until Christmas Eve most likely thinks that it will be fed the following day too, but, unfortunately for the turkey, this is not the case. Inductive arguments are extremely useful when conducting science, and according to some philosophers inductive reasoning is characteristic of the scientific methodology. However, we will not be concerning ourselves with inductive logic, and will be focusing specifically on deductive logic.

Like most subjects in philosophy, the general notion of logical inference is familiar from everyday life, and is often used in casual conversational settings (especially if you happen to be a Vulcan on *Star Trek*); but when we reflect on it, the phenomena that once seemed so obvious can come to take on a new light and begin to seem mysterious. Consider the curious fact that deductive logic is at the same time both entirely intangible and also incredibly powerful. It is intangible in the sense that it is a completely abstract phenomenon (for instance, one cannot *see* logic, or measure it with experiments), and yet it is powerful because, in a sense, its laws come with a force stronger than any known to physics, because the conclusions of sound deductive arguments are known to be true with *absolute certainty* (Wittgenstein once referred to this phenomenon as the 'hardness of the logical must', *PI* #437).

Mysterious though this notion might seem to be, over the past 150 years logicians have made staggering advances. It is no exaggeration to say that we live in a *golden age* for logic, which has seen foundational developments in pure logic that have led to practical consequences following on from them, primarily the establishment of computer programming, but also the formalization of various branches of the arts and sciences (consider the use of game theory in economics, for example). In this book we will look at the fascinating and highly complicated story of the history of logic, from the first tentative reflections of the ancient Greeks to the development of formal languages and mathematical models familiar to the twenty-first-century philosopher, mathematician and computer scientist.

Roughly speaking, the development of logic in Europe has had three 'golden ages': the Greek period, from around 350 to 200 BCE; the high medieval period, from around 1100 to 1400; and the modern period, from around 1850 up to the present day. These classifications are, of course, generalizations that do not capture the full reality of logical developments by lone pioneers (such as Leibniz) and in other cultures (such as in the Indian, Chinese, and Arabic and Islamic worlds). For the purposes of this book, we will be focusing on deductive logic, and its development in Europe. This is not to say that developments elsewhere are not of value – quite the contrary. The work of logicians in the Islamic world and the influence of their work on logicians in Western Europe during the High Middle Ages, in particular, is a fascinating topic that has recently gained much attention from scholars, but that for limitations of space will not be treated in this book.

The first golden age of logic happened within the space of a few generations in Ancient Greece, and included great figures like Aristotle (384–322 BCE), Diodorus Cronus (*c.* 340–280 BCE) and Chrysippus (279–206 BCE). These early logicians managed to make huge progress, with very little in the way of genuine intellectual predecessors. There were forerunners to this period who used logical inferences, particularly in ethics and metaphysics, but the formalization and reflection on the general principles of validity seems to have been lacking. For instance, Zeno of Elea (*c.* 490–430 BCE) is well known to have offered various paradoxes, of motion and of length etc., in an effort to defend the metaphysical doctrines of his master, Parmenides (*c.* 500 BCE). Zeno essentially argued that motion is an illusion, because it leads to impossible consequences. Thus, he used the argument form:

If p, then q; but not-q (because it is impossible); therefore, not-p

Zeno obviously had a good intuitive grasp of logical inference, and probably had the feeling that he was arguing in a 'correct' manner. However, simply arguing logically is not sufficient to make one a logician. What is required in addition is an appreciation of the notion of valid inference in abstraction from any particular argument; and this, it seems, did not properly arrive before Aristotle.

From the beginning of the Greek golden period we get many anticipations of later developments. From Aristotle we get a wonderfully worked-out system of 'term-logic', known as the 'syllogism', which was a precursor to the first-order logic, or 'predicate calculus', and which became easily the most influential contribution in logic for two thousand years. From the Stoics we get the first formulations of elements of propositional logic, with definitions of connectives given via truth-values, but we also see many other interesting formulations of logical problems, such as proposals for the nature of implication that are very similar to some contemporary theories on subjunctive and indicative conditionals. Much of the best work form the Stoic period, notably the work of Chrysippus, has been lost to history, but we know indirectly that he wrote much on logic generally, and specifically about paradoxes, including the Liar and the Sorites. It was for a very long time thought that the Aristotelian and Stoic conceptions of logic were at odds with one another, before their reconciliation in the modern era under the umbrella of first-order logic.

Unlike the contributions of Chrysippus, Aristotle's work on logic was very widely read, especially in Europe from the twelfth century onwards, and over the course of history it has exerted an enormous influence on how philosophers have viewed logic, giving up its dominance over the discipline only in the modern period. This influence was so great that Józef Bocheński (1902–1995) wrote in the introduction to his monumental *A History of Formal Logic* (1961) that the word 'logic' can actually be *defined* in relation to Aristotle:

> [W]e find that there is one thinker who so distinctly marked out the basic problems of [logic] that all later western inquirers trace their descent from him: Aristotle. Admittedly, in the course of centuries very many of these inquirers – among them even his principal pupil and successor Theophrastus – have altered Aristotelian positions and replaced them with others. But the essential problematic of their work was, so far as we know, in constant dependence in one way or another on that of Aristotle's *Organon*. Consequently we shall denote as 'logic' primarily those problems which have developed from that problematic.
>
> Bocheński 1961: 2

Even if few would be happy with Bocheński's definition today, Aristotle's influence on the history of logic is undeniable. Given its importance, we shall now say a little about Aristotle's main logical system, known as the 'categorical syllogism' (for more see Chapter 1). As stated above, Aristotle's syllogistic logic was primarily concerned with 'general terms', which are words like 'Greeks' or 'mortals', as opposed to singular terms, such as 'Socrates' or 'Plato'. General terms generally pick out a group of objects according to their shared possession of a property; for example the term 'Greeks' picks out all those people who have the property of having been born in Greece, etc. According to Aristotle, each basic declarative sentence has a subject–predicate structure; so there is something that the sentence *is about* (the subject), and we say something *about it* (the predicate). For example, in the sentence 'Greeks are mortal', the term 'Greeks' is the subject, and 'mortal' is the predicate. Lastly, we also need to say something about the *quantity* in which the predicate term applies to the subject term. This can come in four grades:

1. **Every** Greek is mortal   (*Universal Affirmative*)
2. **Some** Greek is mortal   (*Particular Affirmative*)
3. **Not every** Greek is mortal   (*Particular Negative*)
4. **No** Greek is mortal   (*Universal Negative*)

According to Aristotle, the syllogism is a tightly defined type of argument, in which there are two premises and a conclusion, each of which is a term-based quantified subject-predicate sentence, like 1 to 4 above, and which share three terms between them. Consider the following example of a syllogism,

Premise 1:	Every Athenian is Greek
Premise 2:	Every Greek is mortal
Conclusion:	Every Athenian is mortal

In this argument, there are three terms ('Athenian', 'Greek' and 'mortal'). The terms are referred to as *minor*, *middle* and *major*, depending on their position in the argument. The minor term is that which is the subject of the conclusion (in the above example, this would be the term 'Athenian'), the major is the predicate of the conclusion (i.e. 'mortal'), and the middle term is that which is shared by both of the premises (i.e. 'Greek'). The premises each have one of the minor or major terms, and are consequently labelled as the *minor premise* and the *major premise*. For example, premise 1 is the minor premise, as, in addition to the middle term ('Greek'), it features the minor term ('Athenian'); premise 2 is accordingly the major premise.

One of Aristotle's main innovations in the course of developing the syllogism, and one of the reasons why we date the beginnings of logic to his work, was the use of letters to stand in for the terms. This simple technique provided a useful way of abstracting away from the linguistic and conceptual detail of the terms used, and allowed one to grasp the proper logical *form* of the underlying argument. Thus, the above argument is really just a particular instantiation of an *argument form*, later known as *Barbara*, which looks like this (you can find out why and how Aristotelian syllogisms were given names like *Barbara* in Chapter 1):

Every α is β
Every β is γ
Every α is γ

This syllogism is just the first of fourteen that Aristotle categorizes for us in the *Prior Analytics*. These are arranged in three 'figures', which are distinguished by the position in the premises of the shared middle term. Aristotle takes the first two syllogisms of the first figure, which includes *Barbara*, to be 'perfect' or self-evidently valid. Using some intuitive conversion rules for sentences (like: from 'Some α is β' we can derive 'Some β is α'), Aristotle shows a method according to which one can prove that each of the other twelve syllogisms is reducible to the first two, and thus that each syllogism is correspondingly valid. Although it was not presented as such at the time, his theory of syllogisms then can be viewed as a *system*, akin to that of Euclid's (*c.* 300 BCE) geometry, in which the two perfect syllogisms are the axioms, and the others are theorems, provable via the axioms and the rules of inference he advocates. Thus, Aristotle's achievement was not just the outlines of some general thoughts about logic, as one might expect from a pioneering theoretician, but a fully developed logical system and proto-proof-theory. The sheer scale of the achievement seems to have hampered later attempts at developing logic, as there seemed to be little prospect of improving on Aristotle's example. Indeed, we see Kant (1724–1804) (who seems to be unaware of the achievements of the medieval logicians) in the preface to the second edition of the *Critique of Pure Reason* saying the following:

> That logic from the earliest times has followed this sure path may be seen from the fact that since Aristotle it has not had to retrace a single step, unless we care to count as improvements the removal of some needless subtleties or the clearer exposition of its recognized teaching, features which concern the elegance rather than the certainty of the science. It is remarkable also that to the present day this logic has not been able to advance a step, and is thus to all appearance a closed and completed body of doctrine.
>
> Kant, *Critique of Pure Reason* (1781), B viii, p. 17

The fact that Aristotle's achievement was so great actually had the unexpected consequence of holding back logical progress. It turns out that there are in fact a number of additional requirements that Aristotle built in to the theory of the syllogism which if dropped would have allowed a much more general approach to be developed, but which were not fully appreciated for many centuries due to the compelling nature of the system as it stands. When a logical system was developed that could work without these restrictions, modern logic was born.

One of these features of the logic which were later dropped in the modern period was the inference from 'All *A* is *B*' to 'Some *A* is *B*'. This effectively meant that no term is empty, i.e. no terms like 'Martian' feature in the theory of the syllogism. Also, no term refers to everything. So the terms are always of greater extension than the least possible thing (nothing), and lesser than the greatest possible thing (everything). These requirements were later dropped, in the development of the modern logic by people like Charles Sanders Peirce (1839–1914) and Gottlob Frege (1848–1925). However, the personal achievement of Aristotle was so great that it took around two thousand years for these developments to take place.

The end of this Greek golden age coincided more or less with the decline of Macedonian dominance and the rise of the newly emergent Roman power. It seems that, for whatever reason, the study of logic was not something that flourished under the Roman regime. Consequently, we find few real innovations in logic in the following centuries, which were more typified by commentaries on previous works, such as those of Alexander of Aphrodisias (*fl.* 200 CE) and Porphyry (234–305 CE), rather than genuine technical developments. As with so many of the intellectual achievements of the ancient world, the study of logic gradually faded into obscurity in Europe with the decline of the Western Empire by about 450 CE. Boethius' (480–526 CE) translation of Aristotle's *Organon* in the final years of his life represents almost the last reserve of Western knowledge of Aristotelian logic, and soon even this was lost to the learned men of Europe.

While learning in the West declined, the study of logic was kept alive in the thriving Islamic world under the Abbasid Caliphate (750–1258), and reached great heights of sophistication with notable contributors including Al-Farabi (872–950), Avicenna (980–1037) and Averroes (1126–1198). From the start of the twelfth century onwards, Europe became increasingly exposed to the Arabic world, in part due to the Crusades, and with this exposure came a rediscovery of the ancient Greek texts on logic, especially those of Aristotle, along with the benefit of the sophisticated Arabic commentaries. As these texts circulated around Europe we find the beginning of our second golden age of logic, from about 1100 to 1400, the high medieval or 'scholastic' period, with notable contributors including Peter Abelard (1079–1142), William of Sherwood (1190–1249), Peter of Spain (*c.* 1250), William of Ockham (1295–1349) and Paul of Venice (1369–1429). Curiously, during this period there was a combination both innovative progress and reverence for ancient authority, most particularly that of Aristotle. The progress came in the form of greater understanding of quantification, reference and logical consequence, a more intricate treatment of semantics, and developments in modal and temporal logic.

Unfortunately, this high point for European logic was itself not to last. The precise reasons for this decline are very complicated, and still hotly debated by contemporary historians of logic. Various factors contributed to the decline of medieval logic, including the following.

Firstly, as we saw following the decline of Greek logic, the period of great novel development in the medieval period was followed by a period of commentaries and comparisons. There were many logicians working in this period, and each had their own particular way of using technical terms and of distinguishing between concepts. It is tempting to think that the task of simply comprehending and compartmentalizing the state of the art of medieval logic was such an arduous task that it became all that the later generations could manage.

Secondly, there is an argument that socio-economic factors led to changes in the education system of the universities, which in turn led to a declining focus on logic. This has been eloquently outlined by Lisa Jardine:

> In the early decades of the sixteenth century, across northern Europe, we find the introductory arts course being adapted to meet the requirements of an influx of students from the professional classes. Within this arts course, with its humanist predilection for Greek and Latin eloquence, and legal and ethical instruction, there was an acknowledged need for some rigorous underpinning of instruction in 'clear thinking'. But the meticulous introduction to formal logic and semantic theory provided by the scholastic programme came to look increasingly unsuitable for this purpose.
>
> Jardine 1982: 805

The idea is that these new 'business classes' needed to learn practical knowledge from their education, and the dusty logical and semantic distinctions of the scholastics no longer fitted the bill.

Another closely related argument is that medieval logic was swept aside by the rise of humanism, and its focus on rhetoric over logic. One figure who is notable as a passionate advocate of humanism and critic of scholasticism is Lorenzo Valla (1407–1457). In particular, Valla championed two major and distinctively humanist ideas that clashed with the medieval outlook. Firstly, he held that the great Roman authors of antiquity, such as Cicero (104–43 BCE) and Quintilian (35–100 CE), were the final authorities when deciding a point about the correct use of Latin, which is the language that discussions of philosophy and logic were conducted in during the medieval period. In contrast to the linguistic recommendations that might follow from an abstract consideration of Aristotle's logic, Valla urged that the authority of Latin grammar ought to flow from the period when it was used as a living language. So, if a certain usage was urged by Aristotle, but a contrary one was urged by Cicero, then we ought to go with Cicero. In addition to this, Valla maintained that the most important part of argument is persuasion, rather than certain proof. One can see that in practical matters, perhaps pertaining to legal cases, it is persuasion, rather than proof, that is practised. Thus, in general, one can say that, in the pedagogical priorities of the humanist period, logic gave way to rhetoric. By the time we get to Peter Ramus (1515–1572) we get a particularly drastic rejection of the Aristotelian authority which was so characteristic of the scholastic period, as Ramus is supposed to have chosen the topic of his master's thesis to be that 'everything Aristotle taught was false' (Kneale and Kneale [1962]: 301).

While the study of pure logic may have declined in the early scientific period, there were a great many advances in mathematics, in particular in algebra and geometry. By the end of the sixteenth century European mathematicians had recovered many of the works from antiquity that had been lost, and largely improved upon the Arabic algebraic developments. This period of mathematical progress arguably culminated with the creation of the infinitesimal calculus of Leibniz (1646–1716) and Newton (1642–1727). Leibniz himself was an outstanding mind who worked in many fields and, against the intellectual tide of his day, he conducted a solitary programme of innovative research in formal logic. Although the main body of Leibniz's works on logic remained relatively unknown until the turn of the twentieth century, in retrospect he is hugely significant for articulating a completely new vision of the subject – one that stressed the use of the recently developed mathematical and algebraic methods.

In classical antiquity, logic was conceived of as a tool to be used in oratory and argumentation, as exemplified by Plato's Socratic dialogues. Although early logicians such as Aristotle and Chrysippus did reflect on rules of inference and the formalization of arguments, they too saw logic first and foremost as a tool to be used in philosophical debate. This general conception of logic was also maintained by the medieval logicians, as evidenced by the distinctively medieval notion of the *obligationes*, which was an attempt to produce rules for public philosophical debate (see Chapter 3). In contrast to this, Leibniz had a vision of logic as a purely symbolic and algebraic discipline, divorced entirely from the all too human roles of respondent and interlocutor. According to the new vision, logic would be a subject matter of the highest importance in itself, not just a tool to help someone win an argument.

Leibniz's motivations for pursuing an algebraic treatment of logic were deeply rooted in his philosophical views. He conceived of a mathematically reconstructed logic as a medium that would reflect the nature of thought more faithfully than the comparatively clumsy linguistic approach of the medieval logicians. The idea was that this new logic, being symbolic rather than linguistic, would actually *improve the way that we think*, by laying out the real elements of thought with perfect clarity, and would therefore be a crucial key in advancing science generally. In his ambition, Leibniz saw the possibility for a universal language of thought based on logic; a *lingua philosophica* (or 'philosophical language'), which is something that would be recognizable to any student of analytic philosophy today. Despite the details of Leibniz's logical innovations remaining largely out of sight in the Royal Library of Hanover until the turn of the twentieth century, the general character of his vision managed to exert an influence on a number of early pioneers in the modern age of logic. For instance, Leibniz's ideal of a perfect language of thought heavily influenced two of the most important logicians of the early modern period; George Boole (1815–1864) and Gottlob Frege. This influence is reflected in the titles of their best-known works on logic – Boole's 1854 work *The Laws of Thought* and Frege's 1879 work *Begriffsschrift* (which means 'concept-script'). Although Boole and Frege differed significantly in their approaches, both were trying to realize the mathematical vision of logic that Leibniz had envisaged.

Both Boole and another important British logician, Augustus De Morgan (1806–1871), published major works on logic in the year 1847 – Boole's *Mathematical Analysis of Logic*, and De Morgan's *Formal Logic*. It is from the publication of these works that we shall date the third, and current, golden age of logic – the modern period. Boole's work was more systematic than De Morgan's, and exerted greater influence on later thinkers. In order to give an idea of Boole's main innovations, we shall say a little about his work now.

Boole's primary concern was to give an algebraic account of the laws of logic, as found in Aristotle's categorical syllogisms. However, his developments quickly went beyond this rather limited goal. As we have seen, the categorical syllogism dealt with the logic of *general terms*, such as 'Greeks' and 'mortal', and Boole followed this lead by using the more algebraic symbols x, y, z etc. to stand for terms, but he decided to find new ways of presenting the logical relations between the terms themselves. Boole used the combination of xy (the 'multiplication' of x and y) in much the same way that natural language combines predicates in expressions like 'green cars'. The result is the intersection of the green things and the car things (only those objects that are in both classes). This allowed a very simple equation to represent the universal affirmative 'All x are y': in Boole's notation it becomes $xy = x$. The class of things that are xy coincides with the class of things that are x, because all of the things that are x are also y.

One of Boole's chief innovations came was his use of the symbols '1' for the 'universe', or class of everything, and '0' for the empty class. Using this, Boole could symbolize the notion of the things which are not-x, the 'complement' of x, as $1-x$ (i.e. everything minus the x things), which allowed him to formulate an alternative expression for the universal affirmative as $x(1-y) = 0$ (i.e. the set which is the intersection of the xs and the not-ys is empty). Also, we have the translation of the universal negative, 'No x is y', as simply $xy = 0$. The translation of the particular statements was more contentious. His proposed translation of 'Some x is y' was $v = xy$, where the auxiliary letter 'v' is used to mean 'some'. He could then translate 'Not every x is y' by the equation $v = x(1-y)$.

Boole's algebraic approach to logic was further developed by Charles Sanders Peirce (1839–1914), beginning in the late 1860s. Amongst Peirce's many contributions, one of the most striking is his abandonment of the Aristotelian dictum that no term is empty. On Peirce's account, the statement 'All unicorns are white' is true, even though no unicorns exist. This change legitimated some inferences, and invalidated others: 'Some unicorn is white' could no longer be inferred from the premise 'All unicorns are white', but 'All unicorns are coloured' could be inferred from the premises 'All unicorns are white' and 'All white things are coloured'.

Peirce was a polymath whose work in logic embraced an innovative range of diagrammatic proof systems, the *Existential Graphs*. Within these, the system of Alpha Graphs corresponds to what we now know as propositional logic, and his Beta Graphs to first-order predicate logic. The Existential Graphs were largely ignored at the time, but more recent interest in the expressive power and pedagogical advantages of diagrammatical reasoning has produced a renewed focus on this aspect of Peirce's work. While less developed, his complex system of Gamma Graphs reflected Peirce's desire to extend logic beyond what we now call classical logic, and incorporate modal features such as notions of temporality and possibility. His analysis was to prove influential on A.N. Prior (1914–1969), an important figure in the development of intensional logics that treated modal notions such as possibility, necessity and tense.

Between 1870 and 1883, Peirce also created what we now know as the *calculus of relations*. The calculus of relations is the formal study of the kinds of relationships that hold between objects, such as 'larger than' or 'parent of', and not just properties that hold of single objects, such as 'is black' or 'is a horse'. The operations of intersection, union and complement which appeared in Boole's system can be extended to the relational setting, but Peirce went further, including other operations on relations such as *composition*. Consider the relations 'is the mother of' and 'is a parent of': these compose to produce the relation 'is a grandmother of', since given any three people x, y and z, if x is the mother of y and y is a parent of z, then x is the grandmother of z.

The calculus of relations was also the setting for a further Peircian innovation, namely the introduction of *quantifiers* in something like their modern form. Quantifiers are a linguistic device which allow one to specify how many things of a certain sort satisfy some property; in natural language they include locutions such as 'every', 'there exists', 'most' and 'none'. Quantifiers allow us to make general statements, such as those we can reason about syllogistically, but the quantifiers introduced by Peirce are a more flexible and expressively and deductively powerful device. They solve the following problem that De Morgan raised for Aristotle's logic. Given that a horse is an animal, it follows that the head of a horse is the head of an animal. Aristotelian syllogistic logic does not allow us to make this inference, and thus does not capture this seemingly correct and simple inference. Peirce's quantifiers, on the other hand, do allow this inference.

Extending logic with quantifiers was a major advance, and as sometimes happens with such discoveries, it was made independently by different researchers. Peirce's initial introduction of the existential and universal quantifiers, in the guise of unrestricted unions and intersections of relations, took place in his 1880 paper 'On the Algebra of Logic', but a full presentation of his quantification theory only appeared in 1885 in 'On the Algebra of Logic: A Contribution to the Philosophy of Notations'. Six years earlier, Gottlob Frege had also introduced quantifiers in his *Begriffsschrift*, and although the discovery should be credited to both logicians, Frege's logical work includes other distinctively modern features that do not appear in Peirce, and which we shall discuss in due course.

Aristotelian quantifier phrases take two predicates as arguments: they have the form 'All A are B', 'Some A is B', 'No A is B' or 'Not all A are B'. Fregean or Peircian quantifiers are unary and introduce a *bound variable*: a variable standing for an object of the domain of quantification, of which properties can then be predicated. In Peirce's system there are two kinds of quantifier: the existential quantifier $\exists$, and the universal quantifier $\forall$. Thanks to his treatment of negation, Frege only needed the universal quantifier: he could define the existential quantifier by combining negation with universal quantification. In modern notation, the statement 'All A are B' can be formalized using a universal quantifier and the connective for the conditional, as follows: $\forall x(Ax \to Bx)$. Informally this reads 'For every object x, if x has the property A, then x has the property B'. Suppose that we take the unary predicate H to denote the property of being a horse; the unary predicate A to denote the property of being an animal; and the binary predicate C to denote the property of being the head of something. We can then formalize the statement 'Every horse is an animal' as $\forall x(Hx \to Ax)$, and the statement 'The head of a horse is the head of an animal' as $\forall x[\exists y(Hx \land Cyx) \to \exists y(Ax \land Cyx)]$. Informally we can read this second sentence as asserting that for every object x, if there is some y such that x is a horse and y is the head of x, then there is some y such that y is the head of an animal (namely x). The inference from the former to the latter is a valid one in the predicate calculus, and proving it is a good exercise for a beginning student of logic.

The logic that Frege presents in the *Begriffsschrift* has a special place in history, as it draws together in a systematic way several important elements of formal systems as we now conceive of them. One way to think of Frege's system is as a predicate calculus in the modern sense: a formal language containing quantifiers, logical connectives and predicates (including both unary and relational ones), together with logical axioms and laws of inference. The system of the *Begriffsschrift* included nine logical axioms and one law of inference, namely *modus ponens*: from a conditional statement A $\rightarrow$ B and the antecedent A, infer B. It is this packaging of a formal language, axioms and laws of inference together as a coherent whole that makes Frege's work a landmark contribution to logic. Nevertheless, one should not read too much into the oft-made claim that Frege is the father of modern logic, since his system differed in important ways from those that were to follow. To begin with, Frege's logic was *second-order*: there were not only quantifiers ranging over the objects of the domain, but second-order quantifiers which ranged over functions on the domain. For example, if the first-order domain consists of students, then the second-order domain consists of groups of students, such as all those enrolled in a philosophy degree, or all students with names of one syllable. Moreover, Frege took a 'functions first' approach, casting properties and relations in terms of functions, which he called *concepts*: properties were nothing but functions from objects to truth-values. A predicate like 'is happy' was understood by Frege as a function that mapped to 'the True' all the objects which are happy, and to 'the False' all the objects which are not happy. Finally, Frege's notation was, as Russell put it, 'cumbrous' and 'difficult to employ in practice' (Russell 1903: 501).

Frege's work is also important in another sense, namely that its intertwining of logic and the foundations of mathematics represents the continuation by formal means the programme of rigorization of the calculus (and mathematics more generally) pursued by Bolzano, Weierstraß and Cantor. In *Die Grundlagen der Arithmetik* (1884) and the two-volume *Grundgesetze der Arithmetik* (1892, 1903), Frege developed a foundation for mathematics based – at least in Frege's own view – entirely on principles which were *logical* in nature. The system of the *Grundgesetze* included the powerful Rule of Substitution, which is equivalent to a comprehension principle for Frege's second-order logic, namely a scheme asserting that every set definable by a formula in the language exists. It also included the infamous Basic Law V, which in modern terminology can be defined more or less as follows: for all functions X and Y, the extension of X (the collection of all objects with the property of being X) is equal to the extension of Y if, and only if, X = Y. Bertrand Russell (1872–1970) realized that Basic Law V implied the contradiction we now know as *Russell's paradox*. The 'extension of' operator could be used to form new concepts. This means that the formation of the following concept is legitimate within the system: the concept of all concepts whose extensions are not members of themselves. Call this concept R, and call its extension E. Does E fall under the concept of R? If it does, then E does not satisfy the definition of R, and so E cannot fall under the concept of R. But if E does not fall under the concept of R, then it satisfies the definition, and so E must fall under the concept of R. We thus have a contradiction either way. Russell's paradox was seemingly already known to Cantor, as the same phenomenon appears in set theory, and indeed is closely related to Cantor's theorem itself.

While Russell's paradox was a shock to Frege, it has proved immensely fruitful for logic and the foundations of mathematics: the development of set theory and type theory, and indeed our entire understanding of the philosophy of mathematics have been shaped by responses to Frege and Russell's paradox. Two of these responses have been particularly influential, reflecting as they do two different ways of restricting logic and the foundations of mathematics to avoid Russell's paradox. The first of these is the *theory of types*, as developed primarily in the *Principia Mathematica* of Russell and Alfred North Whitehead (1861–1947). Russell and Whitehead's ramified theory of types is highly complex and we will not attempt to explain it here; instead we shall sketch the ideas behind a simpler type theory that suffices to illustrate the point at hand. The theory of types guards against paradox by imposing a hierarchy on the universe of objects defined in the theory. At the lowest level, 0, is the type of individuals. At level 1 we have the type of classes of individuals – for example, if the individuals are natural numbers, then the class of even numbers is a type 1 object. At level 2 we have classes of classes of individuals, and so on. This restriction blocks Russell's paradox because there is no way to form the class of all classes that do not contain themselves: each class can be formed only of objects of lower type, while the definition of the Russell class R ranges over *all* classes.

The second response to Russell's paradox was the axiomatic theory of sets developed by Ernst Zermelo (1871–1953). Zermelo's solution to the paradox was to restrict the comprehension principle in two ways, giving rise to his *Aussonderungsaxiom* (Separation Axiom). The first restriction was that new collections formed via this axiom could only be subsets of existing sets: given a set X already proved to exist, the set of all members of X satisfying a given property could then be formed. Secondly, only 'definite' properties were allowed to define sets. The paradoxical Russell class was thus legislated out of existence. Modern axiomatic set theories are typically based on Zermelo's system, and can thus prove that there is no set containing all and only those sets that do not contain themselves. Zermelo did give some guidance on what the 'definite' properties were supposed to be, but the notion remained vague. Hermann Weyl (1885–1955) and Thoralf Skolem (1887–1963) both proposed that the criterion of definiteness be replaced by the notion of a one-place predicate formula in first-order logic, i.e. any formula in the first-order language of set theory with only one free variable is allowed in the Separation Axiom scheme. It is Skolem's proposal, and the first-order theory of sets that resulted, that is now the dominant approach both in set theory and in the foundations of mathematics more generally.

The off-putting nature of Frege's notation meant that the field was clear for a system of logical notation that mathematicians would be more eager to adopt. Just such a system was provided by Giuseppe Peano (1858–1932), who provided, amongst other things, the symbols $\cap$ for intersection, $\cup$ for union, and $\in$ for set membership. He also introduced the backwards 'E' symbol $\exists$ for existential quantification (the upside-down 'A' symbol $\forall$ for the universal quantifier was introduced much later), and the symbol $\sim$ for negation. The rotated 'C' (for 'consequentia') that he used to denote the material implication was adapted by Russell for *Principia Mathematica* as the now-familiar horseshoe symbol $\supset$. Peano's notational improvements were important because they allowed for the more widespread adoption of a logic that took on board Frege's deeper innovations.

The algebraic tradition of De Morgan, Peirce and Ernst Schröder (1841–1902) remained important in the early twentieth century, through its influence on the area we now know as model theory, and in particular in the work of Marshall Stone (1903–1989) on Boolean algebras, and Leopold Löwenheim (1878–1957) and Skolem on the model theory of first-order logic – that is, logic where the quantifiers range only over the objects of the domain, and not over functions on the domain, as in second-order logic. First-order logic was properly isolated as a system of central importance some years later, in the work of Gödel and Tarski, but the first-order fragment of the calculus of relations – mentioned briefly in Schröder's *Vorlesungen über die Algebra der Logik* – was interesting enough to inspire Löwenheim's work on his eponymous theorem.

To understand Löwenheim and Skolem's contributions, we must return to the nineteenth century and the work of German mathematician Georg Cantor (1845–1918). In the mid-1870s, Cantor created the area of mathematics known as *set theory*, and proved a number of key results about infinite sets (or collections), the most important of which is known as *Cantor's theorem*: that there are different sizes of infinite sets; that every set is strictly smaller than its *powerset* (the set of all subsets of a given set); and in particular that the set of all real numbers is bigger than the set of all natural numbers. The notion of size at play here is known as *cardinality*, and we say that two sets have the same cardinality just in case there exists a one-to-one correspondence between them. For example, the set of all natural numbers and the set of all even numbers have the same cardinality, since we can construct a function f which takes every natural number to an even number: $f(0) = 0, f(1) = 2, f(2) = 4$, and in general $f(n) = 2n$. Sets which are either finite or have the same cardinality as the natural numbers are called *countable*. Sets which are infinite but have a greater cardinality than the natural numbers (for example, the real numbers) are called *uncountable*.

One of the fundamental insights of the algebraic approach to logic was that logical symbols are subject to interpretation, as symbols in algebra are (for example, the geometric interpretation of complex numbers). This leads naturally to the idea of a *model*: an interpretation of the vocabulary of a logical system which satisfies its axioms. We therefore come to the notion of a *Boolean algebra*: any model of Boole's axioms of logic. Such algebras consist of a set of atoms, the elements of the algebra; distinguished elements 0 and 1; and conjunction (intersection or multiplication), disjunction (union or addition) and complementation (negation or subtraction) operations on the set of elements. The study of Boolean algebras was begun by Marshall Stone, who proved a number of important results, including the representation theorem that bears his name: every Boolean algebra is *isomorphic* to (that is, has the same structure as) a Boolean algebra of sets.

We can trace the birth of model theory to Löwenheim's paper 'Über Möglichkeiten im Relativkalkül'. Working within Schröder's version of the calculus of relations, Löwenheim showed that if a first-order sentence has a model, then it has a countable model. The Norwegian mathematician Thoralf Skolem improved Löwenheim's proof in a paper of 1920, and in doing so generalized the result from single sentences to (possibly infinite) sets of sentences. The result is important because it shows that first-order logic is not, in general, able to fix the cardinalities of its models: there can, for example, be models of the theory of real numbers which are countable, or models of set theory where sets that the theory holds to be uncountable are actually (from the external, model-theoretic perspective) countable. The completeness theorem for first-order logic, later proved by Gödel in his 1929 PhD thesis, is an easy corollary of Skolem's work from the early 1920s, but this was not understood until later.

In order for model theory to grow into a mature discipline, a further ingredient was needed, namely a precise understanding of the central notion of a model. This was supplied by Alfred Tarski (1901–1983), whose landmark 1933 paper 'On the Concept of Truth in Formalized Languages' contained a definition of the satisfaction relation. This was subsequently updated to create the definition of truth in a first-order structure published in 1956 by Tarski and his student Robert Vaught, and which is very close to the standard textbook definition used today. The essential idea is that a structure M of a language L consists of a set D of elements – the *domain*, over which the quantifiers range – together with interpretations for the nonlogical symbols of the language such as constants, relation symbols and function symbols. A relation of satisfaction, or 'truth-in-M', can then be defined recursively. If every sentence of a theory T in the language L is true in M, we say that M is a model of T. Similar definitions can be constructed for other logics, and while the model theory of first-order logic is still a major part of the discipline, logicians also study models of other logics such as modal logic and infinitary logic.

Algebraic logic as an area of study in its own right was revived some decades later by Tarski, an admirer of Peirce and Schröder. In his 1941 paper 'On the Calculus of Relations', he presented two axiomatizations of the calculus of relations. Tarski was also responsible for a broader reawakening of interest in algebraic logic, and published a number of landmarks in the field including the two books *Ordinal Algebras* and *Cardinal Algebras*, as well as developing the notion of a *cylindric algebra*. Cylindric algebras stand in the same relation to first-order logic with equality that Boolean algebras do to propositional logic. In fact, they are Boolean algebras, but equipped with additional operations that model quantification and equality.

We can also see elements of the algebraic approach in the contributions of David Hilbert (1862–1943). Hilbert was one of the leading mathematicians of his era, and his contributions to logic were conceptual and methodological, as well as technical. We can identify at least three separate and substantial achievements: his pioneering of the axiomatic method through his investigations into the foundations of geometry; his programme for the foundation of mathematics on a finitist basis, which bore fruit through the creation of proof theory, and also through the limitative results of Gödel; and his formulation of the *Entscheidungsproblem* (decision problem), whose solution led to the founding of computability theory and computer science.

The roots of the axiomatic method lie in geometry, with the work of the ancient Greek mathematicians, as collated and extended by Euclid in the *Elements*. It is therefore appropriate that it is in geometry, and specifically in Hilbert's work on the foundations of geometry, that we find the first modern exemplar of this method. During the nineteenth century, figures like Gauss, Bolyai, Lobachevsky and Riemann created non-Euclidean geometry: geometrical spaces that obeyed all of Euclid's geometrical postulates save the *parallel postulate*. Hilbert provided a general axiomatic framework in which questions of consistency and independence of geometric principles could be addressed. A central plank in this programme was the idea that once a geometrical system had been axiomatized as a collection of statements in a fixed formal language, the geometrical vocabulary could be entirely reinterpreted: models of geometrical axioms no longer had to conform to spatial intuitions, but were free to take any form at all, provided that they satisfied the axioms. In this spirit, Hilbert is reputed to have said that instead of points, straight lines and planes, one must be able to say tables, chairs and beer mugs.

By using the theory of real numbers to construct models of geometry, Hilbert proved the axioms of geometry to be consistent *relative* to the theory of real numbers – that is, analysis. But then analysis itself needed to be axiomatized, and proved consistent. While Hilbert developed an axiomatization of analysis in 1900, the consistency of analysis proved to be a difficult problem, partly because the set-theoretic path to the foundations of analysis pursued by Richard Dedekind (1831–1916) seemed to rest on assumptions just as questionable as simply assuming the consistency of analysis directly. Hilbert therefore determined to pursue a *direct* consistency proof, firstly for the more basic theory of arithmetic (that is, the natural numbers) before moving on to analysis.

In his consistency proofs for geometry, Hilbert *reinterpreted* the language in order to produce models, but in the search for a consistency proof for arithmetic, Hilbert proposed leaving the arithmetical theory *uninterpreted*, so that the axioms and formal derivations could be treated as mathematical objects in their own right. This was a ground-breaking idea: formulas could be conceived of simply as finite sequences of symbols, not endowed with any intrinsic meaning, while formal proofs were 'concrete' objects which could be grasped intuitively, namely finite sequences of sentences consisting only of axioms and sentences derived by fixed rules of inference from sentences earlier in the proof. Reasoning about these simple, symbolic objects was – so Hilbert argued – obviously secure, and could provide a metatheoretic standpoint from which to prove the consistency of arithmetic, analysis and all the rest of mathematics. Things did not pan out that way, but Hilbert's finitism has been influential nonetheless, both in the direction of the discipline of proof theory he created through his research into the consistency of arithmetic, and as a foundational stance in the philosophy of mathematics.

Hilbert's lectures on mathematical logic from 1917 to 1922 are justly famous, and his assistant Wilhelm Ackermann (1896–1962) helped him to turn them into a book, published in 1928 as *Grundzüge der theoretischen Logik* and later translated into English as *Principles of Mathematical Logic*. Amongst many other things, the book contained the first complete presentation of the system of first-order predicate calculus. It also spelled out a question Hilbert had been interested in for over twenty years: 'Is it possible to determine whether or not a given statement pertaining to a field of knowledge is a consequence of the axioms?' This question was known as the *Entscheidungsproblem*, or decision problem, and a restricted form of it can be stated with more precision as follows: is there a mechanical method that can determine whether or not a formula in a first order language L is logically entailed by a theory T in the language L? There are really two problems here: one conceptual, the other technical. The conceptual problem is to determine what a 'mechanical method' is, and to give a precise mathematical account of it; the technical problem to determine whether or not such a method for deciding first-order validity exists. These problems found a solution in the work of Alan Turing (1912–1954) and Alonzo Church (1903–1995) in the 1930s. Another major part of Hilbert's work in this period was his programme of finding a finitistically-acceptable consistency proof for arithmetic. This was later thrown into disarray by the discoveries of Kurt Gödel (1906–1978), to which we now turn.

In his 1929 doctoral thesis at the University of Vienna, Gödel proved the *completeness theorem for first-order logic*, which states that every sentence which is universally valid – that is, which comes out true regardless of which domain the variables are taken to range over, and whatever interpretation is given to the relation and function symbols of the language – is in fact *provable*. The completeness theorem, however, was to be followed by a result which, while at least as profound, was far more shocking: Gödel's *incompleteness* theorems, proved in 1930 and published in 1931.

The *first incompleteness theorem* states that for any recursively axiomatized formal system containing elementary arithmetic, if the system is consistent then there is a sentence P in the language of the system such that neither P nor ~P are provable in the system. This amounts to saying that no formal axiomatic theory that meets certain minimal requirements can capture the totality of true mathematical statements. The *second incompleteness theorem* states that for any recursively axiomatized formal system containing elementary arithmetic, if the system is consistent then the consistency of the system is not provable in the system itself. Note that, despite the confusing similarity between the names of these two properties, there is a crucial difference between the *completeness of a deductive system* (which is proved in the completeness theorem), and the *completeness of a set of axioms* (which is shown not to hold in the incompleteness theorems). The former property holds when for every valid inference there is a proof verifying that inference in the deductive system in question, while the latter is true when for every statement P in the language of a set of axioms, either P or ~P is a logical consequence of those axioms. It is this latter property that Gödel showed did not hold for consistent theories that contain enough arithmetic.

In proving the incompleteness theorems, Gödel developed novel proof techniques which have since become basic tools of mathematical logic. One such technique is *Gödel coding* (also called *arithmetization* or *Gödel numbering*), a method for representing – i.e. encoding – the syntax of formal theories in the language of arithmetic. This allowed Gödel to represent statements about a given formal system within the system itself. For example, coding allows one to express, within the formal system of first-order Peano Arithmetic, the statement that Peano Arithmetic is consistent. The basic idea is the following: the coding fixes a mapping between natural numbers and the statements of a language in a way that always allows one to recover an expression from its Gödel code, and vice versa. The information encoded in digital computers by series of zeros and ones constitutes a familiar instance of a similar kind of coding. It was the possibility of representing statements about formal systems within the systems themselves that allowed Gödel to construct statements which were (provably!) unprovable in those systems.

Gödel's incompleteness theorems had profound consequences for logic and the foundations of mathematics. The second incompleteness theorem, in particular, was a devastating blow to Hilbert's programme. It meant that there could be no finitary system of arithmetic capable of proving its own consistency, let alone that of analysis or set theory. However, it also triggered many positive developments, including amongst others the development of ordinal proof theory under Hilbert's student Gerhard Gentzen (1909–1945), and the programme of relative consistency proofs in set theory. After many decades, the incompleteness theorems have found their place as one of the building blocks of mathematical logic: the field as it exists would be inconceivable without them, and they continue to inspire new research to this day.

Furthermore, the incompleteness theorems have also had an influence outside the bounds of logic. Gödel thought that the following disjunctive thesis, now known as *Gödel's disjunction*, was a consequence of incompleteness: either the human mathematical mind exceeds the power of a computer, or there are unknowable mathematical truths (or both). This idea has been the subject of much philosophical discussion and popular interest, as demonstrated by the appearance of Roger Penrose's book *Shadows of the Mind* on the *New York Times* bestseller list.

During his lifetime, Gödel made other significant contributions to many areas of logic, set theory and philosophy of mathematics, but most of his important results in logic were proved during his time in Vienna in the 1930s. Due to the worsening political climate and a sequence of events in his personal life, Gödel moved to the United States in 1940, where he took up a position at the Institute for Advanced Study at Princeton. During the decade from 1930 to 1940 Gödel had already paid two visits to Princeton (in 1933–4 and in 1935), where a number of conditions created uniquely favourable grounds for major advancements in mathematics and logic, and almost every logician who made significant and long-lasting contributions to logic passed through Princeton at some point in this period. Many notable personalities such as Albert Einstein, Hermann Weyl and John von Neumann were attracted to Princeton as a result of the increasing power gained by the Nazi Party in Germany and Austria. They joined an already outstanding group of mathematicians and physicists.

Among these, a key figure for mathematical logic was Alonzo Church, who received his PhD at Princeton in 1927 and became Assistant Professor there in 1929. In the first years of the 1930s the logicians Stephen C. Kleene (1909–1994) and J. Barkley Rosser (1907–1989) were Church's doctoral students. John von Neumann introduced Church's group to the incompleteness theorems, in a lecture given at Princeton in 1931 on Gödel's recent work whose profound consequences he was the first to understand. Together with Alan Turing and Emil Post (1897–1954), Church and Kleene contributed to the establishment of a branch of mathematical logic now known as *computability theory* (or *recursion theory*). Hilbert's collaborator Paul Bernays (1888–1977) was also in Princeton in 1935–6 as a visiting scholar, and fruitfully interacted with Church, Kleene and Turing. What follows is a brief reconstruction of the main events at Princeton that helped shape the modern form of mathematical logic.

Between 1929 and 1931 Church developed the intensional formal system of λ-calculus. This was intended to be a foundation for mathematics that avoided the known paradoxes in a different way than Russell's type theory. The system captured the notion of *effective calculability* on which Church had been focusing since at least 1934. While the λ-calculus was less than successful as a foundation for mathematics, it was extremely influential in the development of semantics for programming languages and it is still widely researched in theoretical computer science.

In an address to the American Mathematical Society in April 1935, Church first proposed the idea that 'the somewhat vague intuitive notion of effective calculability' could be characterized in terms of two precisely defined classes of functions: the notion of a *recursive function* of positive integers, or a λ-definable *function* of positive integers. This thesis first appeared in print in Church's 1936 paper 'An Unsolvable Problem of Elementary Number Theory', and came to be known as 'Church's Thesis' since Kleene (1952) referred to it by this name.

The notion of a *recursive function* had already been employed by Gödel, who refined it using a key suggestion from Jacques Herbrand (1908–1931) in 1931, the same year in which the proof of the incompleteness theorems was published. In fact, the notion of recursiveness plays a fundamental role in the proof of the incompleteness theorems. It is needed in order to formulate a precise criterion for the decidability of the proof relation, i.e. the requirement that 'x codes a proof of y' can be verified or falsified by applying a *mechanical* method in a finite number of steps. This means that given a set of formulas and an arbitrary number (e.g. the Gödel code of a proof), there is a method that 'decides' whether the number belongs to the set (i.e. whether the number in question is the Gödel code for a correct derivation). In this case, we say that the set of formulas is 'decidable' or 'recursive'. Another key property of a set of formulas in this context is the property of being *recursively enumerable*, which belongs to sets whose elements we can effectively generate by means of a mechanical method. This means that we have instructions that tell us how to list, in a mechanical way, the elements of the set. However, if a set is recursively enumerable but not recursive, we have no general mechanical method for determining whether or not a number is, or is not, a member of that set.

It is a consequence of the incompleteness theorems that the set of arithmetical statements provable from the axioms of Peano Arithmetic is recursively enumerable, but not recursive: any formal system that is powerful enough to express basic arithmetic is incomplete, in the sense that it is always possible to find a sentence expressible in the language of the system that is *true*, but not provable within the system in question. The intuitive notion of a definite method for solving problems had been used throughout the history of mathematics, but it became clear to Gödel that in order to obtain general undecidability and incompleteness results, a precise mathematical definition of this notion was necessary.

In 1936 and 1937, Church and Turing independently published their own accounts of the notion of computability. The importance of such an advance is demonstrated by the fact that, thanks to a mathematically precise definition of the notion of computability, both Church and Turing were finally able to solve Hilbert's *Entscheidungsproblem* in the negative. Their strategy was to provide a model of computation in which all the effectively computable functions can be represented, and then show that no such function could decide the set of validities of first-order logic.

As mentioned earlier, in 'An Unsolvable Problem of Elementary Number Theory', Church argued that the notion of effective calculability could be *defined* in terms of the notion of recursive function or λ-definable function (the case for the converse – that every recursive or λ-definable function is effectively computable – was much easier to make). At the time of his 1935 address, however, Church was still not completely convinced that effective calculability could be identified with λ-definability and gave his first formulation of the thesis in terms of recursive functions, even though Gödel himself was unsatisfied with the idea. Church later wrote that his proposal to identify the notions of effective calculability and recursiveness arose in response to a question from Gödel.

Church, Kleene and Rosser quickly realized that the notions of λ-definable function and recursive function were equivalent, and the proof of this equivalence was published by Kleene in 1936. Church thought that this would strengthen the argument for thinking that these two classes of functions constituted a general characterization of the intuitive notion of effective calculability. In a two-page paper also published in 1936, Church then provided a negative solution to the *Entscheidungsproblem*, thus proving what is now known as *Church's theorem*.

At the same time, in April 1936, Alan Turing – at the time a newly elected fellow of King's College, Cambridge – completed a paper in which he developed his own account of effective computability, entirely independently from Church. After being shown Church's work, Turing realized that his characterization of effective computability was equivalent to Church's (the proof of the equivalence was added to the paper as an appendix prior to publication). Turing then contacted Church, and went to Princeton as a visiting graduate student in the autumn of 1936, eventually staying – on von Neumann's advice – for a further year to complete a PhD under Church's supervision.

Turing's paper 'On Computable Numbers, with an Application to the Entscheidungsproblem' eventually appeared in print at the end of 1936. In it,

Turing characterized the notion of computation as a *mechanical procedure*, namely a procedure which manipulates finite strings of symbols (the *inputs*) according to finitely given sets of rules (the *program* or *algorithm*) through a series of steps to obtain a result (the *output*). The novelty of Turing's approach was to define computation in terms of what an idealized human agent could in principle compute in a purely mechanical fashion; that is, following instructions in a stepwise manner without the aid of insight or ingenuity. The concept of mechanical procedure is then shown to be equivalent to the concept of a *Turing machine*, a machine which is at any time in one of a finite number of states and whose behaviour is fully determined by the rules which govern the transitions between states. The thesis that every effectively computable function is Turing computable (that is, computable by a Turing machine) now goes under the name of *Turing's thesis*. Turing went on to define the notion of a *Universal Turing Machine* as a Turing machine that can take as its input the rules of another Turing machine, and execute them. Modern digital computers are, in some sense, concrete instances of this idea: they can run any program (i.e. algorithm) that is given to them as input, and thereby emulate the running of any other computer.

Turing's analysis has had a major influence on the development of logic and the philosophy of mathematics. This is shown by the reactions of Turing's contemporaries. Church wrote in a 1937 review of Turing's paper that

> It is ... immediately clear that computability, so defined, can be identified with (especially, is no less general than) the notion of effectiveness as it appears in certain mathematical problems (various forms of the Entscheidungsproblem, various problems to find complete sets of invariants in topology, group theory, etc., and in general any problem which concerns the discovery of an algorithm).
>
> Church 1937: 43

Gödel said in 1946 lecture that

> It seems to me that [the] importance [of Turing's analysis of computability] is largely due to the fact that with this concept one has for the first time succeeded in giving an absolute definition of an interesting epistemological notion, i.e. one not depending on the formalism chosen.
>
> Gödel 1990: 150

He also said in 1964 that only Turing's work provided 'a precise and unquestionably adequate definition of the general concept of formal system', as a mechanical procedure for generating theorems from a given set of axioms. Moreover, Turing's conceptual analysis of effective computability, and its definition in terms of Turing computability, marked the beginning of both theoretical computer science and artificial intelligence. His work currently finds applications in many scientific domains ranging from physics to biology and cognitive science.

References

Bocheński, J. M. (1961), *A History of Formal Logic*, Notre Dame: University of Notre Dame Press. English edition translated and edited by Ivo Thomas.

Church, Alonzo (1937), 'Review: A. M. Turing, On Computable Numbers, with an Application to the Entscheidungsproblem', *Journal of Symbolic Logic* (2): 42–3.

Gödel, Kurt (1986), 'Postscriptum (1964) to "On undecidable propositions of formal mathematical systems"', in Solomon Feferman, John W. Dawson, Jr., Stephen C. Kleene, Gregory H. Moore, Robert M. Solovay and Jean van Heijenoort (eds), *Kurt Gödel: Collected Works Vol. I*, pages 346–72, Oxford: Oxford University Press.

Gödel, Kurt (1990), 'Remarks before the Princeton Bicentennial Conference on Problems in Mathematics', in Solomon Feferman, John W. Dawson, Jr., Stephen C. Kleene, Gregory H. Moore, Robert M. Solovay and Jean van Heijenoort (eds), *Kurt Gödel: Collected Works Vol. II*, pp. 150–3. Oxford: Oxford University Press.

Jardine, Lisa (1982), 'Humanism and the teaching of logic', in Norman Kretzmann, Anthony Kenny and Jan Pinborg (eds), *The Cambridge History of Later Medieval Philosophy*, pp. 797–807, Cambridge: Cambridge University Press.

Kant, Immanuel (1999), *Critique of Pure Reason*, English edition translated and edited by Paul Guyer and Allen W. Wood, Cambridge: Cambridge University Press.

Kneale, William and Kneale, Martha (1962), *The Development of Logic*, Oxford: Clarendon Press, Oxford.

Kleene, Stephen C. (1952), *Introduction to Metamathematics*, Amsterdam: North Holland.

Russell, Bertrand (1903), *The Principles of Mathematics*, Cambridge: Cambridge University Press.

Turing, A.M. (1937), 'On Computable Numbers, With an Application to the Entscheidungsproblem', *Proceedings of the London Mathematical Society Series 2*, 442, 230–65.

Wittgenstein, Ludwig (2009), *Philosophical Investigations*. English translation by G.E.M. Anscombe with revisions by Peter Hacker and Joachim Schulte, German text on facing pages, fourth edition, Chichester: Wiley-Blackwell.

Part I

The Origins of Formal Logic

Aristotle's Logic

Adriane Rini

1 The syllogism

Aristotle is generally credited with the invention of logic. More than two thousand years ago, he noticed that good, persuasive arguments have certain kinds of shapes, or *structures*. Logic was born when he began to study those structures, which he called *syllogisms*, identifying underlying patterns of ordinary human reasoning and then devising simple methods which can be used to determine whether someone is reasoning correctly. Aristotle was aware that this was a momentous discovery, and he himself thought that all scientific reasoning could be reduced to syllogistic arguments. There are hints that Aristotle saw his syllogistic logic as providing useful practice for participants in ancient debating contests, contests which he himself would have encountered as a student in Plato's Academy. There are also hints that Aristotle might have envisioned his syllogistic logic as providing a way to catalogue facts about science. But Aristotle never fleshes out any such details. His *Prior Analytics*, the text in which he presents his syllogistic, focuses on the mechanics of the syllogistic far more than on its interpretation, and in fact the comparative lack of interpretive detail has sometimes led scholars to suppose that what we have today of Aristotle's logic is his own sometimes scrappy lecture notes or his students' notes, and not a polished, finished work. But in the end these are of course only guesses. In modern times, the main scholarly interest in Aristotle's ancient logic has focused increasingly on the proper interpretation of the mechanical methods which Aristotle invented and on their relation to his wider philosophy.

Scholars today describe Aristotle's invention as a theory of inference or deduction. Aristotle's own explanation is famous:

(Def)   A deduction [a syllogism] is an argument in which, certain things being supposed, something else different from the things supposed follows of necessity because of their being so.

Prior Analytics 24a18–20

Suppose, for example, that a friend tells us that

(∗)   'if all birds fly, and if all seagulls are birds, then it must be the case that all seagulls fly.'

In reasoning according to (∗) our friend is trying to reason deductively. But in the particular case of (∗) our friend's reasoning involves some confusion about the *facts* – facts about birds. Certainly many and perhaps even most birds fly, but not *all* of them do. So, it is not true that 'all birds fly'. Aristotle saw that one could separate general patterns of deductive reasoning from the particular subject matter that one reasons about. And once these are separated then the patterns themselves can be studied independently of their actual subject matter. There is nothing wrong with the structure of (∗). If (∗) is not persuasive it is only because it involves a factual error, a factual error *about birds*. For it is a factual matter that there are flightless birds such as the New Zealand kiwi. And because this is a factual matter it affects the truth or falsity of a statement such as 'all birds fly'.

In *Topics* 105, Aristotle describes philosophical inquiry in terms of three possible sub-fields: he argues that any philosophical question will belong either to natural science or to logic or to ethics. His point seems to be that we should regard each of these separate fields as having different subject matter. This distinction helps to explain the difference between what is good about (∗) and what is not so good about (∗), since it lets us say that it is a matter of natural science whether or not it is in fact true that all birds fly. For example, it is a matter of biology, or of animal behaviour, but it is not a matter of logic. The distinction between the subject matter of natural science and the subject matter of logic also makes it easier to distinguish the patterns of good reasoning from the particular science that one reasons about. These patterns of reasoning are themselves the subject matter of logic, and by concentrating on what is general to the patterns, we can in effect move beyond matters of fact. The natural sciences are about discovering the truth and falsity of our claims about the world – such as discovering the falsity of the claim that all birds fly. But a helpful way of understanding **(Def)** is as saying that logic takes us *beyond* the matters of truth and falsity of any natural science – the realm of logic concerns what happens 'of necessity'.

In order to describe the patterns themselves, Aristotle developed a vocabulary with which to distinguish the various components of a syllogism.

Furthermore, there is a long tradition of representing syllogistic reasoning in three-line arguments – and representing syllogisms in this way makes it easier to identify the separate logical components. Consider, for example, the following:

(1) All birds fly
     <u>All seagulls are birds</u>
     All seagulls fly

(1) is composed of two *premises*, 'all birds fly' and 'all seagulls are birds', together with a *conclusion*, 'all seagulls fly'. The two premises are the 'certain things being supposed' that are described in **(Def)**. From this we can see that **(Def)** tells us that in syllogizing according to (1) we *suppose* that 'all birds fly' and 'all seagulls are birds' are both *true*. The supposition that both of the premises are true leads us to the truth, as well, of 'something else different' from the premises – that is, the supposition that the premises are true leads us to the truth of the conclusion. Aristotle notices that in an argument such as (1) when we assume the truth of the premises, then the truth of the conclusion 'follows of necessity'. He does not say merely that the conclusion *is* also true. His claim is stronger. In a syllogism if the premises are true then the conclusion *cannot fail to be true*. Or, another way of saying the same thing: if the premises are true then the conclusion *has to be true* as well. This basic insight is at the heart of Aristotle's discovery of logic. (It is at the heart of modern logic too, since what Aristotle is describing is what today we call logical validity.) On the other hand, if the conclusion can be false even when the premises are true, then, according to Aristotle, there is no syllogism.[1] In fact Aristotle's syllogistic is very limited. He only counts as a syllogism an argument which has exactly two premises and one conclusion.

2 A lesson from Plato: Names and verbs

While syllogisms are composed of premises and conclusions, these premises and conclusions are themselves built out of still more basic components. Plato, who was Aristotle's teacher, initiated the study of these more basic components, taking them to be features of *language*. In doing so, Plato laid the foundation for a link between human reasoning and human language, a link which strongly persists in modern philosophy. Plato explains his motivation in the dialogue called the *Sophist*:

> The signs we use in speech to signify being are surely of two kinds ... One kind called 'names', the other 'verbs' ... By 'verb' we mean an expression which is applied to actions ... And by 'name' the spoken sign applied to what performs these actions ... Now a statement never consists solely of names spoken in succession, nor yet verbs apart from names.
>
> *Sophist* 261e262b

Plato, here, introduces the idea that a simple statement (something which can be true or false) is itself built out of two basic components: name (*onoma*) and verb (*rhema*). And Plato seems, at least in this passage, to take it as obvious that names and verbs are different kinds of things: one picks out the agent; the other picks out the agent's actions. Aristotle was familiar with this passage from Plato's *Sophist* and clearly carried from it the lesson that meaningful statements must involve the combination of specific *linguistic* elements, and this is reflected in Aristotle's own consideration in *Categories* of 'things that are said':

> Of things that are said, some involve combination [literally, 'inter-weaving'] while others are said without combination. Examples of those involving combination are 'man runs', 'man wins'; and of those without combination 'man', 'ox', 'runs', 'wins'.
>
> *Categories* 1a16

You do not succeed in communicating anything true (or false) if you merely utter a noun ('man' or 'ox'), or merely a verb ('runs' or 'wins'). Nouns alone do not produce truth or falsehood. Verbs alone do not either. In this *Categories* passage, Aristotle offers two examples of ordinary, meaningful statements – 'man runs', 'man wins' – each of which is the result of our 'combining' nouns and verbs and each of which *does* communicate either a truth or a falsehood. Simple sentences such as these are called *affirmatives* because they affirm something (here, running or winning) of a subject (man). And of course, such sentences can be true or false, depending on whether the world is as the sentence says. As we saw in Section 1, Aristotle regards such factual knowledge about how the world is as the subject matter of natural science.

Not only does Aristotle inherit from Plato the distinction between name and verb, but in Aristotle's *De Interpretatione* this distinction takes on what appears to be a *syntactic* importance according to which the name and the verb fulfil specific grammatical roles within a simple statement:

> A name (*onoma*) is a spoken sound significant by convention, without time, none of whose parts is significant in separation.
>
> *De Interpretatione* 16a19

A verb (*rhema*) is what additionally signifies time, no part of it being significant separately; and it is a sign of things said of something else.

De Int 16b6

These passages create some difficulty about the project right away: is Aristotle's syllogistic logic about *things* in the world (such as men and birds), or is it about the *language* we use to describe those things (such as our *words* 'man' and 'bird')? It is hard to say. In *De Int*, Aristotle's writing is careful: names and verbs 'signify', they function as 'signs of things'. On the face of it, this would seem to suggest that he thinks of logic as a study which concerns linguistic statements which are themselves made up of names and verbs. But even if Aristotle starts out this way, it becomes difficult to sustain this view, particularly in later, more sophisticated parts of the syllogistic. This lack of clarity gives rise to a tension that runs through Aristotle's syllogistic. Modern scholars often describe the difficulty as a failure to distinguish between *using* a word and *mentioning* (talking about) a word. As we shall see in later sections, questions about the precise nature of the roles of the clearly linguistic items of name and of verb become a foundational issue within the history of the development of logic.

Sometimes, in ancient Greek, as in modern English, grammar requires more than the simple concatenation of nouns and verbs. That is, we do not always produce grammatical sentences by stringing nouns and verbs together. Sometimes the nouns and verbs themselves are linked explicitly by a *copula*, a form of the verb 'to be'. In English, for example, we do not say 'cows animals' – English requires the introduction of a copula to give the grammatical statement 'cows *are* animals'.

Aristotle recognizes this feature of Greek and allows an explicit copula when needed, but scholars disagree about how much importance to attach to the copula. (See for example Geach 1972, Smith 1989, Patterson 1995, Charles 2000.)

3 Affirmation and denial

As noted above, our ability to make an affirmation provides us with a way of describing the world, and such descriptions themselves will be either true or false. But Aristotle also noticed that 'it must be possible to deny whatever anyone has affirmed, and to affirm what anyone has denied' (*De Int* 17a31). Every affirmation has an opposite denial, and every denial has an opposite affirmation. Furthermore, in just the same way that an affirmation can be either true or false,

Aristotle recognizes that so too can a denial be either true or false. When two statements 'affirm and deny the same thing of the same thing' they are opposites and they stand in *contradiction*. It is perhaps obvious that even the most basic human communication requires that affirmation must be tractable and meaningful. But Aristotle's analysis in *De Int* makes denial tractable and *meaningful* in just the way that affirmation is. To take an example, 'all birds fly' is an affirmation, while 'some birds do not fly' is a denial, and of *these* two example statements it is the affirmation which is false, and the denial which is true – though of course there will also be examples in which the denial is false and the affirmative true (e.g. 'some men are pale'; 'no men are pale'). By considering affirmation and denial together as the two components of any contradiction Aristotle avoids problems which worried his predecessors. Plato, and Parmenides before him, sought to ground philosophy in *what is*, but then struggled to provide an analysis of *what is not*. If *what is* 'exists', does *what is not* 'not exist'? How can we talk meaningfully about what is not? If truth reflects what is, then is falsity about what is not? The need for an answer led earlier philosophers to approach the notion of falsity with caution.

Following Aristotle's instructions in *De Int*, denial is not a problem and the analysis is straightforward: we can construct the following illustration.

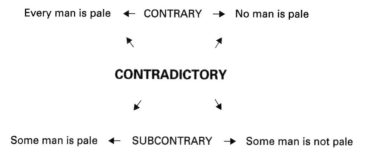

Such a diagram is called a *square of opposition*. It provides a way to represent various relations that hold between propositions. For example, when two propositions are such that one must be true when the other is false, and vice versa, Aristotle calls them *contradictories*. Reading diagonally: 'every man is pale' and 'some man is not pale' are contradictories; and 'some man is pale' and 'no man is pale' are contradictories.

That is to say, the negation of 'every man is pale' is 'some man is not pale', and vice versa; and the negation of 'some man is pale' is 'no man is pale', and vice versa. The horizontal arrows represent other relations which can hold between propositions.

When two propositions cannot both be true and cannot both be false, Aristotle calls them *contraries*. So, reading left-to-right or right-to-left: 'every man is pale' and 'no man is pale' are contraries. When two propositions cannot both be false, they are called subcontraries. Again, reading left-to-right or right-to-left, this time along the bottom of the diagram: 'some man is pale' and 'some man is not pale' are subcontraries – that is, at least one of them must be true.

The centrality of affirmation and denial to Aristotle's logic becomes obvious in the opening lines of *Prior Analytics*. When Aristotle introduces his system of syllogistic he explains that, at the most basic level, 'a premise is a sentence affirming or denying something of something' (*An Pr* 24a16). (In Aristotle's system, a conclusion, too, will always be either an affirmation or a denial.)

4 Categorical propositions

All of the example statements in the previous sections involve some subject matter. In the same way that 'all birds fly' – the first premise in (1) – is *about* birds, the statement 'some man is not pale' is *about* men. This quality of *aboutness* guides us to focus on the subject matter at hand, so that we might then assess the statements themselves for truth or falsity. But in studying logic and in distinguishing it from natural science, Aristotle takes a deliberate step away from any specific scientific subject matter. His driving concern in the syllogistic is with the structure of argument, and such structure is easier to appreciate when it is general and not bound to any specific subject matter. So since the science which guides our assessments of truth and falsity of simple statements is subject-specific, Aristotle wants to consider categorical statements generally and without regard to their specific content. He achieves this by using *term variables* – e.g., A, B and C – in place of ordinary language terms such as 'birds', 'fly', 'seagulls', 'man' and 'pale'. He begins by putting the variable letter A in place of the subject term, and the variable letter B in place of the predicate term. By this method the premise in (1), 'all birds fly', becomes 'all A are B'.

All A are B

  ↑   ↑

birds   things that fly

Aristotle's own example statement 'every man is pale' has exactly the same underlying structure as 'all birds fly'. One can see that this is so by taking Aristotle's 'every man is pale' and replacing the subject 'man' with the variable A, and replacing the predicate 'pale' with the variable B. We get 'every A is B', which is the same as 'all A are B'.

All A are B

↑   ↑

men pale

Whether we say 'every man is pale' or 'all men are pale', we are making a *universal affirmative* statement about a subject 'man' and a predicate 'pale' – and Aristotle himself recognizes similarly equivalent expressions in his Greek. He treats them just as different ways of making the very same statement.

In early chapters of the *Prior Analytics* Aristotle usually describes the predicate B as *belonging* (or *not belonging*) to the subject A, so, for example, we find affirmations and denials (i.e. affirmative and privative propositions) described as follows:

Affirmative	Privative
'B belongs to all A'	'B belongs to none of the As'
'B belongs to some A'	'B does not belong to some A'

The 'belongs to' expression reflects some of Aristotle's background science where belonging captures a certain priority of scientific terms. According to this background science, for example, man belongs to animal, but man does not belong to plant.

Through the chapters of Book 1 of *Prior Analytics*, Aristotle focuses increasingly closely on details that have more to do with his logic than with his background science, and as this happens his language shifts and the 'belongs to' expression becomes less common. So, instead of talking about how B 'belongs to' A, Aristotle begins to say simply that 'A is B'. Later in *An Pr*, when Aristotle is explaining points of special logical complexity, even this new 'A is B' expression sometimes gets still further abbreviated to the very cryptic expression 'the AB', where Aristotle leaves it to his reader to fill in the missing details. What are these further details?

As Aristotle's own examples in the square of opposition indicate, contraries and contradictories involve more than attaching subject and predicate, or name and verb. Constructing a full square of opposition requires that we add more: we must be able to signify both affirmation and denial and we must be able to indicate *quantity* – i.e. to indicate whether we are talking about 'all' or 'some' of a subject. When a premise says, for example, that 'all A are B', or that 'every A is B', or that 'none of the As are B', Aristotle calls the premise a *universal*. A premise which says that 'some A is B', or that 'some A is not B', he calls a *particular* (*An Pr* 24a17). In considering affirmations and denials which are themselves either universal or particular, Aristotle's notion of what counts as a premise is restricted to a small class of simple propositions, and scholars traditionally call this restricted class of premises *categorical propositions*. (The subject and predicate of a categorical proposition name things within the Aristotelian categories. See *Categories,* especially Chapter 4.) The four kinds of categorical propositions are frequently abbreviated according to the following convention, where A is the subject and B is the predicate:

(A) *universal affirmative* :: B belongs to every A   :: *BaA*
(E) *universal privative*   :: B belongs to no A   :: *BeA*
(I)   *particular affirmative* :: B belongs to some A   :: *BiA*
(O) *particular privative*   :: B does not belong to some A :: *BoA*

Every syllogistic premise (and conclusion) is either an A-type, E-type, I-type or O-type proposition. This notational convention is not Aristotle's own but a medieval contribution which modern scholars still use today. In *BaA*, the lower case 'a' indicates that the premise is an A-type, or universal affirmative; the upper case 'A' indicates the subject term. The logical relations of contrariety and contradiction that stand between the various categorical propositions can be expressed using a more general square of opposition than the one in Section 3, above:

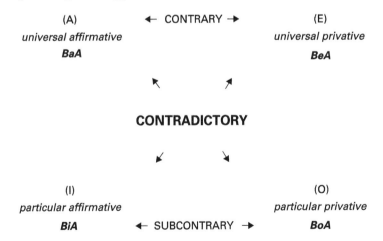

Reading left-to-right or right-to-left: A propositions and E propositions are contraries; and I and O are subcontraries. Reading diagonally: A and O are contradictories; and I and E are contradictories. So, the negation of an A proposition is its contradictory, i.e. an O proposition, and vice versa; and the negation of an E proposition is its contradictory, i.e. an I proposition, and vice versa. These contradictories get put to work when Aristotle develops methods for proving syllogisms in *Prior Analytics*.[2]

5 Further syllogisms

Aristotle takes pairs of A, E, I and O propositions which share exactly one term in common and then asks whether from some given premise pair a conclusion relating the remaining two terms must follow of necessity. For this to happen, the terms must fit one of three possible patterns: The term in common to the premises might be the subject of one premise and the predicate of the other. The term in common to the premises might be the predicate of both premises. Or the term in common might be the subject of both premises. Aristotle calls these possible combinations *figures*. Where A and B and C are variables for terms, we can represent the three figures as follows:

First figure predicate subject	*Second figure* predicate-subject	*Third figure* predicate-subject
A-B	A-B	A-C
B-C	A-C	B-C
A-C	B-C	A-B

Aristotle describes the three figures in *An Pr* Book A, chapters 4–6, and he considers possible combinations of A, E, I and O premises in each figure. The term which occurs in each of the two premises Aristotle calls the *middle term*. The middle term drops out and does not appear in the conclusion. Aristotle calls the other two terms the *extremes* – the extremes are the only terms which appear in the conclusion. (Scholars have noticed a link between Aristotle's labels for the various terms and the labels ancient geometers used in their study of proportions or harmony. Any line-segment, for example, can be divided into its extreme and its mean ratios. See Euclid Book IV, Definition 3.)

By approaching his logic in this way Aristotle places some noticeable limits on the system he develops. First, his description of the figures appears to be based solely on possible premise combinations. He gets three figures because there are only three possible combinations given that each premise must contain two terms and that the two premises must share one term in common. He also limits his system by looking for a conclusion of a particular form: in the first figure he wants a conclusion specifically relating a C subject to an A predicate; in the second figure the conclusion relates a C subject to a B predicate; and in the third figure, a B subject to an A predicate. This method rules out any other figures, but it is easy to see that there are, nonetheless, other possibilities, and Aristotle could have approached the system differently. He himself recognizes this in *An Pr* 29a21–27, where he briefly notes the possibility of a fourth figure.

Table 1 lists all of the syllogisms Aristotle establishes in Chapters A4–6 of *Prior Analytics*, using their traditional (medieval) names.[3]

Table 1.1 Non-modal syllogisms

First figure	Second figure	Third figure
Barbara	Cesare	Darapti
A belongs to every *B*	*A* belongs to no *B*	*A* belongs to every *C*
B belongs to every *C*	*A* belongs to every *C*	*B* belongs to every *C*
A belongs to every *C*	*B* belongs to no *C*	*A* belongs to some *B*
Celarent	Camestres	Felapton
A belongs to no *B*	*A* belongs to every *B*	*A* belongs to no *C*
B belongs to every *C*	*A* belongs to no *C*	*B* belongs to every *C*
A belongs to no *C*	*B* belongs to no *C*	*A* does not belong to some *B*
Darii	Festino	Datisi
A belongs to every *B*	*A* belongs to no *B*	*A* belongs to every *C*
B belongs to some *C*	*A* belongs to some *C*	*B* belongs to some *C*
A belongs to some *C*	*B* does not belong to some *C*	*A* belongs to some *B*
Ferio	Baroco	Disamis
A belongs to no *B*	*A* belongs to every *B*	*A* belongs to some *C*
B belongs to some *C*	*A* does not belong to some *C*	*B* belongs to every *C*
A does not belong to some *C*	*B* does not belong to some *C*	*A* belongs to some *B*
		Bocardo
		A does not belong to some *C*
		B belongs to every *C*
		A does not belong to some *B*
		Ferison
		A belongs to no *C*
		B belongs to some *C*
		A does not belong to some *B*

The syllogisms in Table 1.1 are called *non-modal syllogisms* – they involve premises which merely assert belonging or not belonging. For this reason the syllogisms in Table 1.1 are often called *assertoric syllogisms*. Scholars use these labels to distinguish these syllogisms from ones which do more than merely assert.[4]

Consider a syllogism with the same structure as (1) but with all true premises:

(2)   All birds are animals
      All <u>seagulls are birds</u>
      All seagulls are animals

Notice that (2) is an example of a syllogism in the first figure. In fact, it is an example of the syllogism called Barbara. Each of the categorical statements in (2) is an A-type categorical proposition. Aristotle thinks that first-figure syllogisms with A-type premises and an A-type conclusion involve the kind of basic reasoning that all rational humans can perform – even if they themselves are not conscious that such reasoning is 'syllogizing in the first figure from universal affirmative premises'.

Rational beings employ syllogistic reasoning all the time without actually reflecting on how they are reasoning, but it is the logician's job to investigate how reasoning itself works. When we have an example of Barbara, if we suppose that the premises are true, then we are guaranteed that we will *never* have a false conclusion relating a C subject to an A predicate. (The crucial difference between examples (1) and (2) is that in (2) the premises *are* both true, but in (1) they are not – however, in syllogizing according to Barbara we have to *suppose* the premises are true.)

A tension arises between what the syllogistic in *An Pr* requires and what the combination of name and verb in *De Int* requires. The *De Int* passages, cited above, make clear that Aristotle regards the combination of name and verb as providing the underlying structure of any meaningful proposition. In an I proposition of the form 'B belongs to some A', there is a special syntactic or grammatical role for each of A and B: simply, A serves as the subject and B as the predicate. Likewise for the other types of propositions. But in *An Pr*, as soon as Aristotle describes his three figures, a problem begins to become obvious. The separate syntactic roles played by name and verb turn out not to be preserved in the syllogistic figures: in the first figure the B term is the subject of one premise but the very same B term is the predicate of the other premise. In the second figure the B term is the subject of one premise but the predicate of the conclusion. In the third figure the B term is the predicate of one premise but the subject of the conclusion. So the figures themselves do not respect the earlier syntactic roles, and so the name/verb distinction which Aristotle inherited from Plato is therefore no longer a good fit. Aristotle notices this, and he clearly chooses to be guided by the demands of his logic, rather than by the demands of the syntax outlined in Plato's *Sophist*. Eventually Aristotle steps away from Plato's name/verb distinction, preferring instead to describe *onoma* and *rhema* using the more neutral label 'term' (*horos*). This move away from Plato represents a move towards the point of view of a logician because it allows Aristotle to step further away from what any particular names and verbs might mean, and allows him to focus instead on how general terms themselves, represented by variables, feature in patterns of reasoning.

This becomes particularly important in a method which Aristotle calls *conversion*. Conversion involves the transposition of subject and predicate. Consider something which is white – perhaps a flower, or a cloud, or a piece of paper. Aristotle's own example, in *Posterior Analytics* 1.22, is of a white log.

If it is true that
    (2)   some white thing is a log,
then you know that it must also be true that
    (3)   some log is white.

And more generally, if it is true that
    (2′)   some A is B,
then you know as well that
    (3′)   some B is A.

Aristotle explains that if we are given any true I-type premise with subject A and predicate B, then we also have another true I-type premise with the subject and predicate transposed, so that the A subject becomes the predicate, and the B predicate becomes the subject of the new proposition. Scholars call this I-conversion. E-type premises convert in the same way: that is, if you are given that 'no A are B' is true, then you also have 'no B are A'.[5] This is called E-conversion. Aristotle notices that he can transpose subject and predicate terms in A-type premises also, but that these A-conversions do not work exactly the same as I-conversions and E-conversions.

Consider a subject such as 'horse'. It is true that all horses are animals. It does not follow from this that *all* animals are horses, but it does follow that *some* animals are horses. And this generalizes: If 'all A are B', then 'some B are A.' Aristotle calls such A-conversion *accidental conversion*. It takes us from an A-type premise to an I-type premise – i.e. from an affirmative universal to an affirmative particular proposition. (There is no O-conversion because you cannot guarantee from an O-type premise with an A subject and B predicate anything about a premise with a B subject and an A predicate.)

One question which many twentieth-century commentators raise is: what happens to Aristotle's A-conversion if there are not any As? That is, what if the term A is 'empty'? Elsewhere in his philosophical works Aristotle does sometimes consider terms for non-existent things. His famous example is of a 'goat-stag' (*Posterior Analytics* 92b5–7), something that is part goat and part stag, and so something which, definitely, does not exist. But in his syllogistic logic he does not consider what happens if our terms are empty, and we have no direct textual evidence about his thoughts on how empty terms fare in his logic. Twentieth-century scholars, however, raise this question because modern logic does have to deal with empty terms, and this difference marks another way in which Aristotle's system is limited. It is narrower in scope than modern logic. This difference means that it is most straightforward to approach Aristotle's logic as a system which is *about things in the world*, or, as explained in Section 1, above, about what natural sciences study and discover. This way, any issues about empty syllogistic terms do not arise.

I-conversion, E-conversion, and A-conversion serve as special rules which Aristotle uses in order to construct proofs for second and third figure syllogisms. His most important proof method involves putting his conversion principles to work. This is easiest to see in an example. Aristotle offers a proof of the second-figure syllogism which has as its premises 'no B is A' and 'all C are A'. He wants to know whether these premises guarantee a conclusion linking a C subject to a B predicate. Here is how Aristotle proves the second-figure syllogism which the medievals called Cesare:

(1)	No B is A	premise
(2)	All C are A	premise
(3)	No A is B	E-conversion, (1)
(4)	No C is B	Celarent, (2)(3)

First, Aristotle converts the E-type premise (1) 'no B is A' to get (3) 'no A is B'. (3) together with premise (2) are in fact the premises of the first-figure syllogism known as Celarent (with A in place of B, and B in place of A). So, conversion lets us turn a second-figure schema into a first-figure schema, or as Aristotle describes the method, conversion 'brings us back' to the first figure. Since Celarent is a syllogism and since we can bring Cesare back to the first figure via conversion, then Cesare must also be a syllogism. The main difference, here, between Cesare and Celarent is that the validity of the first-figure Celarent is immediate and obvious, whereas the validity of second-figure Cesare is not immediate but needs to be brought out.[6] It is brought out by using conversion to turn Cesare into Celarent, thus guaranteeing that we can syllogize from (1) and (2) to a conclusion (4).

Here is how a proof in the third figure works. Take the syllogism known as Datisi, whose premises are given as follows:

(1)	All C are A	premise
(2)	Some C is B	premise
(3)	Some B is C	I-Conversion, (2)
(4)	Some B is A	Darii, (1)(3)

In the proof of Datisi, the I-type premise (2) 'some B is C' gets converted to (3) 'some C is B'. (1) and (3) are the premises of the first-figure syllogism Darii. So, again, a first-figure syllogism together with conversion guarantees that the third-figure Datisi (1)(2)(4) is a syllogism.

In each of the syllogisms in Table 1.1, a conclusion does follow of necessity from a premise pair. As noted above, Aristotle argues that in the first figure it is 'obvious' that the conclusion follows from the premises in the sense that we can grasp them immediately, without the need for any proof. The syllogisms of the first figure, therefore, function as *axioms* which ground the proofs of syllogisms in the other figures. Since the first figure is obvious, if we can bring a second-figure or a third-figure premise pair 'back to the first' by converting premises, then, even if our proof is not itself immediate and obvious, it is nonetheless something to be relied upon, something that guarantees second- and third-figure syllogisms.

6 Counterexamples: 'There is no syllogism'

The syllogisms in Table 1.1, however, do not include all possible premise combinations. There are other premise pairs from which no conclusion can be guaranteed. When a conclusion does not follow from a given premise pair, Aristotle offers instructions for constructing counterexamples, showing how in such cases the truth of any conclusion cannot be guaranteed. When there is a counterexample, Aristotle says 'there is no syllogism' – or, as modern logicians would say, there is not a *valid* schema. Here is an example of how Aristotle constructs a counterexample, in *An Pr* 26a4–9:

[N]othing necessary results in virtue of these things being so. For it is possible for the first extreme [the A term] to belong to all as well as to none of the last [the C term]. Consequently, neither a particular nor a universal deduction becomes necessary; and, since nothing is necessary because of these, there will not be a deduction. Terms for belonging are animal, man, horse; for belonging to none, animal, man, stone.

Aristotle wants to show that there is no syllogism from the first-figure premise pair 'all B are A' and 'no C are B'. He does this by showing that from true premises, first, we do not get a privative conclusion. Second, we do not get an affirmative conclusion. He gives two sets of terms for the variables A, B and C, where the terms make the premises true. His first set of terms are 'terms for belonging' which show that the conclusion cannot be privative. With animal, man and horse as A, B and C, our premises are 'all men are animals' and 'no horses are men'. We cannot have either an E-type conclusion 'no horse is an animal' or an O-type conclusion 'some horse is not an animal' because all horses are by nature animals – nothing can be a horse without also being an animal. But these E and O statements are the only possibilities for a privative conclusion, so we cannot have a privative conclusion. With the second set of terms – animal, man, stone – our premises are 'all men are animals' and 'no stones are animals'. But, in this case, we cannot have an A-type conclusion 'all stones are animals' or an I-type conclusion 'some stones are animals' – because both the A and I propositions are clearly false. A and I and E and O propositions exhaust all the possible forms of a conclusion – universal and particular, affirmative and privative.

Since our terms show that none of these is in fact available, we therefore have a proof which establishes that there is no syllogism from the initial premise pair. Some scholars describe the premise pair as *inconcludent*. Aristotle is thorough about his claims about which premise combinations yield syllogisms. He does not take it for granted that there is a syllogism or is not a syllogism – rather, in the *Prior Analytics*, he goes step-by-step through each possible premise pair, offering either a proof or a counterexample.

While his counterexamples are, of course, perfectly adequate, Aristotle does not say much about how he initially devises them or how he expects his readers to do so. This led early twentieth-century scholars sometimes to worry that Aristotle's approach must therefore be *ad hoc*, the result of mere trial and error, and not a part of a formal system. This of course is only conjecture, but Aristotle's counterexamples remain one of the least studied areas in the syllogistic.

7 Modal syllogistic

As noted in Section 5, there is more to the syllogistic than just the fourteen syllogisms in Table 1.1 together with the counterexamples against the inconcludent premise pairs. In Chapters A.8–22 of *An Pr*, Aristotle extends his syllogistic to investigate patterns of reasoning involving modal claims about necessity and possibility. It is not surprising that he is interested in patterns of reasoning involving necessity and possibility, because his general scientific and metaphysical project involves studying what *cannot-be-otherwise*. What *can* be otherwise is, according to Aristotle, not the stuff of real science. In spite of this obvious link between science and the modal notions of necessity and possibility, and in spite of the near universal praise for the invention of the syllogistic, Aristotle's modal syllogistic has not been well received. There are many reasons why scholars have struggled to interpret the modal syllogistic – too many, in fact, to cover in such a chapter as this, so that the present discussion will only concentrate on what has been perceived to be one of the most serious problems for Aristotle's modal syllogistic.

The most famous of Aristotle's modal syllogisms is a version of Barbara with one necessary premise and one premise which merely asserts:

(3) A belongs of necessity to every B
    <u>B belongs to every C</u>
    A belongs of necessity to every C

This is usually known as Barbara NXN, where N indicates a proposition involving necessity, and X indicates a proposition which merely asserts (non-modally). Aristotle argues that if we suppose such premises then we are guaranteed the truth of the conclusion. But taking Barbara NXN as a syllogism seems to commit us to one way of interpreting Aristotle's propositions about necessity. That is, (3) makes sense if the necessity is understood as attaching to the predicate A term, so that we might paraphrase the modal premise as 'every B is a necessary A', where being a necessary A is a special kind of modalized predicate. Using the modern logical symbol '$\Box$' to indicate necessity, then the premise about necessity in (3) has a structure which can be represented as follows:

(i) Every B is $\Box$A

Medieval logicians called this kind of necessity *de re* (the necessity holds of the *thing*) because it attaches to the predicate term itself. On the face of it, *de re* necessity seems to be precisely what is needed if (3) Barbara NXN is, as Aristotle insists, a (valid) syllogism. We can then represent Barbara NXN as follows:

(4) Every B is □A
     Every C is B
     Every C is □A

Most of the proofs in the modal syllogistic, like the proofs in the assertoric syllogistic, make use of conversion principles which flip-flop the order of the subject and predicate terms, and this flip-flopping now has to account for the necessity. A problem arises, here, because the modal conversion principles do not work well using *de re* necessity. Simple A-conversion takes us from 'every B is A' to 'some A is B'. So, A-conversion involving necessity (often called NA-conversion) should take us from

'every B is □A'

to

'some A is □B'

This conversion is illegitimate and is easy to falsify with a counterexample: let A be animal and B be bachelor. Then the NA-conversion would have to take us from

Every bachelor is a necessary animal

to

Some animals are necessary bachelors.

This *de re* conversion clearly does not work, because no animal is a necessary bachelor. So, the modal NA-conversion seems to require a different analysis altogether. We might try, then, to interpret an A-type premise about necessity in a different way – for example, we might suppose that, rather than the structure represented by (i), it has the following structure:

(ii) □ (B belongs to every A)

where what is necessary is the proposition 'B belongs to every A'. The medievals called the proposition 'B belongs to every A' a *dictum*, and so called the necessity in (ii) necessity *de dicto*. (It helps to think of the necessity here as being a necessary connection between two predicates neither of which need apply by necessity to a thing.) As an example, the NA-conversion would take us from, say,

By necessity every spouse is married

to

By necessity some married things are spouses.

This *de dicto* modal conversion is valid. But *de dicto* necessity does not make sense of Barbara NXN.

By necessity every spouse is married.
Every Wellingtonian is a spouse
By necessity every Wellingtonian is married.

Let's suppose that in fact everyone who lives in Wellington happens to be a spouse, but of course even in such a case no one is a spouse *by necessity*.

Since the modal syllogisms seem to demand one interpretation and the conversion rules another, it is not immediately obvious what Aristotle himself means. There is no agreement among scholars about the correct way to handle this problem, and that is why the modal syllogistic is such a controversial part of Aristotle's logic.

8 Appendix: The medieval mnemonics

The names of the syllogisms 'Barbara', 'Celarent', etc., which are found in Table 1.1, encode instructions for Aristotle's proofs. This system of mnemonics was not due to Aristotle but was rather a medieval invention. The codes work as follows:

- The vowel letters A, E, I, and O, introduced in Section 4, are used to indicate the quantity and quality of the propositions in the square of opposition and to indicate the quantity and quality of propositions in the syllogisms. The vowels tell whether the propositions are about 'all' or about 'some' of a subject, and whether the propositions are affirmative or privative. The name Barbara, with its three As, identifies the syllogism which contains three universal affirmative propositions, or A-type propositions. So, any instance of Barbara has two A-type premises and an A-type conclusion. The name Cesare describes a syllogism in which the first premise is an E-type, the second is an A-type, and the conclusion is an E-type proposition.
- The first letter of each name – always a B, C, D, or F – tells us which of the first figure syllogisms is used in the proof; for example, as we saw in

Section 5, above, Aristotle bases the proof of Cesare on the first-figure syllogism Celarent. The initial letter of Cesare is a reminder of that fact.

- Of the consonants within the names, both 'S' and 'P' indicate the need for conversion. 'S' after an E or an I indicates that the E or I premise must be 'converted' in order to complete the proof. For example, Datisi has an S occurring after an I, so we know the I premise gets converted. The need for A-conversion is indicated by a 'P' occurring in a name after an A. Aristotle's proof of Darapti, for example, requires conversion of the second A premise:

(1) A belongs to every C
(2) B belongs to every C
(3) C belongs to some B   A-Conversion (2)
(4) A belongs to some B   Darii (1)(3)

Notes

1 In modern logic, the difference between 'having a syllogism' and 'not having a syllogism' is described as the difference between having a *valid* argument and an *invalid* one. Aristotle, however, has no separate term to describe an invalid argument.

2 In more sophisticated sections of the syllogistic, Aristotle frequently uses proofs which require that we suppose the contradictory of a given proposition. The relations established by the square of opposition provide the framework required for such proofs. One famous but controversial example comes at *An Pr* A.15, 34a2–3, in what Aristotle calls proof 'through an impossibility'. It is what modern logicians call a *reductio* proof. (See Chapter 13 of Rini 2011 for a discussion of Aristotle's proof.)

3 The appendix in section 8 of this chapter explains how to decode the medieval names of the syllogisms.

4 In Aristotle's philosophy generally, he is not especially interested in mere assertion of belonging – for in his own science he is mainly interested in studying what belongs *essentially* and what *possibly* belongs. These interests are reflected in his logic also. Necessity and possibility are known as modal notions, and Aristotle develops his syllogistic to accommodate these in what is called the *modal syllogistic*. Section 7 of this present chapter includes a brief introduction to some of the interpretive issues that arise in the case of the modals.

5 Or, another way of saying the same thing: the E-type proposition 'B belongs to no A' converts to another E-type proposition 'A belongs to no B'.

6 What makes the first-figure syllogisms obvious and easy to grasp? Aristotle calls them 'perfect' or 'complete' deductions. These labels are technical terms in Aristotle's

philosophy and have attracted much attention from scholars. See for example the discussions in Patzig 1968 (43–87) and in Corcoran 1974.

References

Primary

Barnes, J. (ed.) (1984), *The Complete Works of Aristotle, The Revised Oxford Translation*, Princeton: Princeton University Press (Bollingen Series)

R. Smith, R. (1989), *Aristotle: Prior Analytics; translated, with introduction, notes, and commentary*, Indianapolis: Hackett Publishing Company.

Ross, W. D. (1949), *Aristotle's Prior and Posterior Analytics. A Revised Text with Introduction and Commentary*, (Reprinted with corrections 1957, 1965.) Oxford: Clarendon Press.

Todhunter, I. (1933) *Euclid: Elements*, London: Dent.

Tredennick, H. (1938), *The Organon, I: The Categories, On Interpretation, Prior Analytics*. Cambridge, Massachusetts: Harvard University Press (Loeb Classical Library).

White, N. (1993), *Plato: Sophist. Translated, with introduction and notes*, Indianapolis: Hackett Publishing Company.

Secondary

Charles, D. (2000), *Aristotle on Meaning and Essence*. Oxford: Clarendon Press.

Corcoran, J. (1974), 'Aristotle's Natural Deduction System', in *Ancient Logic and Its Modern Interpretations*, Dordrecht: D. Reidel, 85–131.

Geach, P. (1972), *Logic Matters*, Oxford: Basil Blackwell.

Patterson, R. (1995), *Aristotle's Modal Logic. Essence and Entailment in the Organon*. Cambridge: Cambridge University Press.

Patzig, G. (1968), *Aristotle's Theory of the Syllogism*, Translated by Jonathan Barnes. Dordrecht: D. Reidel.

Rini, A. (2011), *Aristotle's Modal Proofs, Prior Analytics A8–22 in Predicate Logic*, Dordrecht: Springer.

2

Stoic Logic

Katerina Ierodiakonou

1 Stoic logic in context

Together with the Epicureans and the Sceptics, the Stoics dominated philosophy during the Hellenistic period, i.e. during the three centuries after Aristotle's death in 322 BCE. They famously claimed that philosophy has three parts that are closely interrelated: physics, ethics and logic. Given their belief in the rationality of nature, they treated logic as inseparable from the other parts of philosophy; whereas the end of physics is knowing the world, and that of ethics is living in accordance with the natural order, logic aims at distinguishing the true from the false and thus makes it possible to find out the truths of the other parts of philosophy. In other words, the purpose of logic, according to the Stoics, was the establishment of a true and stable understanding of the cosmos that was supposed to be essential to human beings, if they were to live a well-reasoned and happy life. To show the special role of logic in the interrelation between the three parts of philosophy, the Stoics compared logic to the shell of an egg, to the surrounding wall of a fertile field, to the fortification of a city, or to the bones and sinews of a living being (e.g. Diogenes Laertius 7.40 = LS 26B; Sextus Empiricus, *Against the Mathematicians* 7.19 = LS 26D).

The Stoics did not use the term 'logic' (*logikē*) as we do nowadays. Logic for them was the study of *logos*, that is, the study of reason as expressed in all forms of articulate speech; it was meant to help people ask and answer questions methodically, argue correctly, clarify ambiguous statements, solve paradoxes. Thus understood, logic was divided by the Stoics into *rhetoric* and *dialectic*: rhetoric was defined as the art of speaking well in the form of whole, continuous speeches; dialectic, on the other hand, was defined as the art of conducting discussions by means of short questions and answers, though in a much broader sense it was also defined as the science of what is true and what is false. More specifically, Stoic dialectic was subdivided into the topics of significations and utterances, for it separately studies what is signified by our utterances and the utterances themselves. The study of utterances includes purely linguistic and grammatical phenomena; for instance, it includes a physical account of sound appropriately formed by the speech organs, a discussion of the phonemes or letters of the alphabet, an analysis of the parts of speech, an examination of the criteria for good style. The study of what is signified covers what gets said by using all sorts of utterances, but mainly by using propositions, the relations between them, the arguments composed of such propositions, and especially their validity (e.g. Diogenes Laertius 7.41–4 = LS 31A; Cicero, *On the Orator* 2.157–8 = LS 31G). Hence, the modern sense of logic was treated by the Stoics under dialectic, i.e. under the subpart of the logical part of Stoic philosophy, although they also treated under dialectic what we would nowadays call grammar, linguistics, epistemology and philosophy of language (Gourinat 2000). In what follows, I focus on the part of Stoic dialectic that corresponds to our modern sense of the term, referring to it as Stoic logic.

Chrysippus, the third head of the Stoic school, developed Stoic logic to its highest level of sophistication. It is reported that he was so renowned in logical matters that people believed that if the gods had logic, it would be no different from that of Chrysippus (Diogenes Laertius 7.180 = LS 31Q). The founder of the Stoic school, Zeno of Citium, and its second head, Cleanthes, were not logicians in the sense that they constructed a formal logical system, but they both used valid arguments of a considerable degree of complexity; given the rather standardized patterns of their arguments, they must have been aware of the logical forms in virtue of which these arguments were considered as valid (cf. Schofield 1983; Ierodiakonou 2002). On the other hand, Zeno's pupil, Aristo, fervently advocated the view that only ethics should be studied, because physics is beyond us and logic is none of our concern. He claimed that logic is not useful, since people who are skilled in it are no more likely to act well, and he compared logical arguments to spiders' webs (Diogenes Laertius 7.160–1 = LS 31 N). In general, though, the Stoics studied logic systematically and used it assiduously. They were, in fact, often criticized for being overconcerned with logical form, for elaborating empty theories, and for ignoring the useful parts of logic such as scientific proofs. Diogenes Laertius' catalogue of Chrysippus' books lists 130 titles in its section on logic, while its section on ethics contains several titles that suggest a logical content; moreover, other ancient sources offer a few supplementary titles of Chrysippus' logical treatises. But although Chrysippus was undoubtedly the authoritative figure in Stoic logic, there seem to have been divergences within the Stoa over logic, so that it is reasonable to suppose that, at least in minor ways, Stoic logic changed in the course of its long career (e.g. Sextus Empiricus, *Against the Mathematicians* 8.443 = LS 36C).

To better understand the emergence of Stoic logic, it is useful to look into the logical background out of which it historically developed (cf. Barnes 1999b). There are two philosophical schools that may have influenced Stoic philosophers in their logical endeavours: first, Aristotle and his followers, namely Theophrastus and Eudemus; and second, the Megaric or Dialectical school, namely Diodorus Cronus and Philo the Logician. There is no need to search for the influence of Epicurus, since he explicitly rejected logic, though later Epicureans did show some interest in such things as the truth conditions of conditional propositions. And there is no evidence that the philosophers in Plato's Academy, who at the time adhered to the sceptical stance, attempted to advance logic.

The established view in the nineteenth century was that Stoic logic should be considered as a mere supplement to Aristotle's logical theory; for Stoic logic, so it was alleged, does nothing more than either copy Aristotelian syllogistic or develop it in a vacuous and formal way. It is only since about the middle of the twentieth century, after the important advances in formal logic, that it has become obvious how Stoic logic essentially differs from Aristotle's (cf. Łukasiewicz 1935; Kneale and Kneale 1962). It has even been suggested that the Stoics could not have been influenced by Aristotle, since his logical treatises were not available to them and only recovered in the first century BCE (cf. Sandbach 1985). This view, however, has been extremely controversial. After all, even if the Stoics were familiar with Aristotle's works, there can still be no doubt concerning the originality of their logical system. For although it is true that Theophrastus and Eudemus published treatises on what they called 'syllogisms based on a hypothesis', which Aristotle had promised to write about in his *Prior Analytics* but never did, and these syllogisms have a great deal in common with the types of arguments discussed by the Stoics, there is no evidence that the Peripatetic logicians anticipated the outstanding feature of Stoic logic; that is, the construction of a logical system to prove the validity of a whole class of arguments of a different kind than those Aristotle focused on in his syllogistic (cf. Barnes 1999b).

As far as the Megaric or Dialectical school is concerned, the historical connections between the philosophers of this school and the Stoics are well documented. Zeno knew both Diodorus' and Philo's works well, and Chrysippus wrote treatises in which he criticized their logical theses. Although Diodorus and Philo are usually presented as mainly occupied with the study of logical puzzles or paradoxes, it is clear that they also put forward original views about, for instance, logical modalities and the truth conditions of conditional propositions (see below). But they never came close to formulating a logical calculus as elaborate and sophisticated as that of the Stoics (cf. Bobzien 1999).

2 The Stoic logical system

The reconstruction of the Stoic logical system in all its details is quite problematic, and this is for the following reasons: First, the logical treatises of the Stoics themselves are lost. Second, most of our ancient sources for Stoic logic are rather hostile and late; for instance, the Platonist Plutarch (*c.* 45–120 CE) or the sceptic Sextus Empiricus (*c.* 160–210 CE). Third, some of the available material is composed by ancient authors whose competence in the intricacies of logic is questionable; for instance, the doxographer Diogenes Laertius (*c.* third century CE). Nevertheless, on the basis of what has survived, modern scholars have provided us with a fairly reliable understanding of the fundamental features of Stoic logic, which show the logical ingenuity of Chrysippus and of the other Stoic logicians (cf. Mates 1953; Frede 1974a; Bobzien 1999, 2003; Ierodiakonou 2006).

2.1 Sayables and assertibles

The main characteristic of Stoic logic is that the inferences it studies are about relations between items that have the structure of propositions. Whereas Aristotle focused his attention on inferences that involve relations between terms, and thus introduced a logical system similar to what we nowadays call 'predicate logic', Stoic logic marks the beginning of the so-called 'propositional logic' (cf. Frede 1974b; Barnes 1999a). To say, though, that Stoic logic is propositional may be somewhat misleading; for, to start with, the Stoics have quite a different understanding of what a proposition is, or to use their own term, of what an *axiōma*, i.e. an assertible, is.

To fully grasp the Stoic notion of an *axiōma*, we first need to get some idea about another basic Stoic notion, namely the notion of a *lekton*, since *axiōmata* are defined by the Stoics primarily as *lekta* (cf. Frede 1994). The Greek term '*lekton*' is derived from the verb *legein*, i.e. 'to say', and hence it is what has been or gets said, or something that can be said, i.e. a sayable. In fact, the Stoics distinguished between what can be said, by uttering or using an expression, and the expression itself that we utter or use in saying something. For instance, they distinguished between the expression 'Socrates is walking', and what gets said by using this expression, namely that Socrates is walking. Thus the kind of item that gets said by using the appropriate expression in the appropriate way, the Stoics called a *lekton*. The Stoics also talked about a *lekton* as the state of affairs signified, i.e. the signification (*sēmainomenon*), distinguishing it from the utterance, i.e. the signifier (*sēmainon*), and from the external object which the *lekton* is about. Therefore, *lekta* are items placed between mere vocal sounds or written sentences, on the one hand, and the objects in the world, on the other (Sextus Empiricus, *Against the Mathematicians* 8.11–12 = LS 33B). Very roughly speaking, *lekta* or sayables are the underlying meanings in everything we say, as well as in everything we think; for *lekta* were also defined by the Stoics as what subsists in accordance with a rational impression, that is, as the content of our thoughts (Sextus Empiricus, *Against the Mathematicians* 8.70 = LS 33C).

But not everything that gets thought gets said, and not everything that can be said gets thought. There are indeed many things that never get thought or said, although they are there to be thought or said. In other words, Stoic sayables are not mind-dependent items; at the same time, though, they certainly do not exist in the way bodies exist in the world. The Stoics stressed that sayables are incorporeal like void, place and time (Sextus Empiricus, *Against the Mathematicians* 10.218 = LS 27D), and in order to characterize their mode of being they introduced the notion of subsistence (*huphistanai*) as opposed to that of existence (*einai*). Reality, they claimed, is not just constituted by bodies, but also by predicates and propositions true about bodies. Hence, sayables are given in Stoic ontology some status, namely the status not of bodies but of incorporeal somethings (*tina*).

The Stoics divided sayables into complete and incomplete (Diogenes Laertius 7.63 = LS 33F). Incomplete sayables include predicates, for instance what is meant by the expression 'is walking', for it is simply a thing to say about something. On the other hand, questions, oaths, invocations, addresses, commands and curses, are all complete sayables. The most important kind of complete sayables are the *axiōmata*, i.e. the assertibles. An assertible is mainly defined by the fact that it is the kind of complete sayable that when it gets said one is asserting something, and it differs from other kinds of complete sayables by the property of being true or false (e.g. Diogenes Laertius 7.65 = LS 34A; Sextus Empiricus, *Against the Mathematicians* 8.74 = LS 34B). Since they constitute a particular class of sayables, assertibles do not exist as bodies do, but they are said to subsist. Moreover, if an assertible is false it is said to merely subsist (*huphistanai*), but if it is true it is a fact and can also be said to be present (*huparchein*). In this sense true assertibles correspond to the world's having certain features, and they are available to be thought and expressed whether anyone is thinking about them or not. On the other hand, since false assertibles are said to subsist, the philosophical question of how false statements and thoughts are possible gets a reasonable answer; false assertibles are the contradictories of facts, and as such they may be said to have some ontological status.

So, Stoic assertibles and propositions, as we nowadays conceive them, share common characteristics. For instance, they are expressed by complete indicative or declarative sentences, they are either true or false, and they are incorporeal. But there are also differences between them. For instance, whereas propositions are timelessly true or false, Stoic assertibles are asserted at a particular time and have a particular tense; that is to say, an assertible can in principle change its truth-value without ceasing to be the same assertible. For example, the assertible 'If Dion is alive, Dion will be alive' is not true at all times, for there will be a time when the antecedent will be true and the consequent false, and thus the conditional will be false (Simplicius, *Commentary on Aristotle's Physics* 1299.36–1300.10 = LS 37K). Furthermore, since Stoic assertibles include token reflexive elements, e.g. 'this' or 'I', they may cease to exist and presumably also, though this is not clearly stated, begin to exist at definite times; for a Stoic assertible requires that its subject exists, otherwise it is said to be destroyed. For example, the assertible 'This man is dead' is destroyed at Dion's death, if 'this man' refers to Dion (Alexander of Aphrodisias, *Commentary on Aristotle's Prior Analytics* 177.25–178.1 = LS 38F).

Assertibles are divided into simple and non-simple assertibles (e.g. Sextus Empiricus, *Against the Mathematicians* 8.93–8 = LS 34H). Simple assertibles are those which are not composed either of a repeated assertible or of several assertibles; they are subdivided into:

(i)   Definite; e.g. 'This one is walking'.
(ii) Indefinite; e.g. 'Someone is walking'.
(iii) Intermediate; e.g. 'It is day' or 'Socrates is walking'.

In addition, the Stoics classified among simple assertibles three different kinds of negative assertibles (e.g. Diogenes Laertius 7.69–70 = LS 34K):

(i)   Negations; e.g. 'Not: it is day'.
(ii) Denials; e.g. 'No one walks'.
(iii) Privatives; e.g. 'This man is unkind'.

An interesting special case of a negation is what the Stoics called 'super-negation' or, as we would say, 'double negation'; for example, 'Not: not: it is day'. This is still a simple assertible and its truth conditions are the same as those for 'It is day'. Note that the scope of the negative particle is, according to the Stoics, the entire assertible, which means that an assertible, for instance, of the form 'It is not day' is treated as affirmative and not as negative. Hence, the negative particle 'not' was not considered by the Stoic logicians as a connective; connectives bind together parts of speech, and the Stoic negative particle does not do that.

Non-simple assertibles, on the other hand, are those which are composed either of a repeated assertible or of several assertibles which are combined by one or more connectives. The main types of non-simple assertibles studied by the Stoics are the following (e.g. Diogenes Laertius 7.71–4 = LS 35A):

(i)   A conjunctive assertible is one which is conjoined by the conjunctive connective 'both … and …'; e.g. 'Both it is day and it is light'. A conjunctive assertible is true when all its conjuncts are true.

(ii) A disjunctive assertible is one which is disjoined by the disjunctive connective 'either … or …'; e.g. 'Either it is day or it is night'. The Stoics understand the disjunctive relation as exhaustive and exclusive; that is to say, a disjunction is true when one and only one disjunct is true.

(iii) A conditional assertible is one linked by the conditional connective 'if'; e.g. 'If it is day, it is light'. A conditional, according to the Stoics, is true when there is a 'connection' (*sunartēsis*) between the antecedent and the consequent, i.e. when the contradictory of its consequent conflicts with the antecedent; for instance, the conditional 'If it is day, it is day' is true, since the contradictory of its consequent 'Not: it is day' conflicts with its antecedent 'It is day'. A conditional is false when the contradictory of its consequent does not conflict with its antecedent; for instance, the conditional 'If it is day, I am talking' is false, since the contradictory of its consequent 'Not: I am talking' does not conflict with its antecedent 'It is day'.

Chrysippus, therefore, assigned to the conditional connective 'if' a strong sense, compared to what our ancient sources attribute to Diodorus Cronus and Philo the Logician. Philo claimed that a conditional is true simply when it does not have a true antecedent and a false consequent, e.g. 'If it is day, I am talking'. This use of the conditional connective 'if' is equivalent to what we nowadays call 'material implication' and is clearly truth-functional. Diodorus, on the other hand, advocated that a conditional is true when it neither was nor is able to have a true antecedent and a false consequent. According to this view, the conditional 'If it is day, I am talking' is false, since when it is day but I have fallen silent it will have a true antecedent and a false consequent; but the conditional 'If there are no partless elements of things, there are partless elements of things' is true, for it will always have the false antecedent 'There are partless elements of things'. On the Chrysippean view, however, both the conditional 'If it is day, I am talking' and the conditional 'If there are no partless elements of things, there are partless elements of things' are false, since there is no connection in them between the antecedent and the consequent (Sextus Empiricus, *Outlines of Pyrrhonism* 2.110–13 = LS 35B).

Chrysippus' interpretation of the conditional connective 'if' has the disadvantage of rendering at least part of Stoic logic non-truth-functional. On the other hand, it is able to adequately express intelligible connections in nature and avoid cases that are counter-intuitive, such as the conditionals 'If it is day, I am talking' or 'If there are no partless elements of things, there are partless elements of things'. Similarly, the Stoics' interest in adequately expressing intelligible connections in nature shows in Chrysippus' decision not to use the conditional when discussing astrological predictions merely based on empirical observation of the correlations between astral and terrestrial events. For example, it may be that it is not the case both that Fabius was born at the rising of the dog-star and that Fabius will die at sea. Chrysippus would not express this as 'If Fabius is born at the rising of the dog-star, he will not die at sea', precisely because he was not convinced that there was a necessary causal connection between being born at that time of the year and dying on dry land. This is the reason why Chrysippus preferred in such cases the negated conjunction, i.e. 'Not: Both Fabius was born at the rising of the dog-star and Fabius will die at sea' (Cicero, *On Fate* 12–15 = LS 38E; cf. Sedley 1984; Barnes 1985).

In addition to conjunctions, disjunctions and conditionals, we find in our ancient sources more kinds of non-simple assertibles, which may have been introduced after Chrysippus. For instance, a subconditional assertible is one which is joined by the connective 'since', and it is true when the antecedent holds and the consequent follows from the antecedent; for example, 'Since it is day, the sun is above the earth' is true when said in daytime. Also, non-simple assertibles can be composed of more than two simple assertibles, either because the constituent assertibles are themselves non-simple, or because certain connectives, namely the conjunctive and the disjunctive connective, are two-or-more-place functions; for example, the Stoics used the conditional 'If both it is day and the sun is above the earth, it is light', or the three-place disjunction 'Either wealth is good or it is evil or it is indifferent'.

2.2 Modalities

The Stoics also discussed modal assertibles in their logical system. Although Stoic logic does not deal with assertibles of the form 'It is possible that it is day', simple and non-simple assertibles are standardly classified as possible, impossible, necessary and non-necessary. That is to say, the Stoic logicians regarded modalities as properties of assertibles, just like truth and falsehood. According to their view, therefore, an assertible may in principle change its modal value, since it has it at a time.

Stoic modal logic developed out of the debate over the famous Master Argument (*kurieuōn logos*), presented by Diodorus Cronus (e.g. Epictetus, *Discourses* 2.19.1–5 = LS 38A; Alexander of Aphrodisias, *Commentary on Aristotle's Prior Analytics* 183.34–184.10 = LS 38B; cf. Bobzien 1993). According to the Master Argument, the following three propositions mutually conflict: 'Every past truth is necessary'; 'Something impossible does not follow from something possible'; and 'There is something possible which neither is nor will be true'. Diodorus saw this conflict and exploited the convincingness of the first two propositions to establish the conclusion that 'Nothing which neither is nor will be true is possible'. It seems that the Stoics made various attempts to rebut Diodorus' view, reacting to the threat of a weakened form of logical determinism implied by his account of the possible as 'that which is or will be'.

Chrysippus proposed his own definitions of modalities (Diogenes Laertius 7.75 = LS 38D):

(i)   A possible assertible is that which admits of being true, and is not prevented by external factors from being true, e.g. 'Dion is alive'.
(ii) An impossible assertible is that which does not admit of being true, or admits of being true but is prevented by external factors from being true, e.g. 'The earth flies'.
(iii) A necessary assertible is that which is true and does not admit of being false, or admits of being false but is prevented by external factors from being false, e.g. 'Virtue is beneficial'.
(iv) A non-necessary assertible is that which is capable of being false, and is not prevented by external factors from being false, e.g. 'Dion is sleeping'.

(v) A plausible assertible is that which invites assent to it, e.g. 'If someone gave birth to anything, she is its mother'.

(vi) A probable or reasonable assertible is that which has higher chances of being true than false, e.g. 'I shall be alive tomorrow'.

2.3 Arguments

The Stoics defined an argument (*logos*) as a complex or a compound of premises and a conclusion. The following is a typical Stoic argument (Sextus Empiricus, *Outlines of Pyrrhonism* 2.135–6 = LS 36B2; Diogenes Laertius 7.76–7 = LS 36A1–3):

> If it is day, it is light.
> But it is day.
> Therefore it is light.

Moreover, the Stoics discussed arguments in terms of their modes (*tropoi*), which are the abbreviations of particular arguments; for instance, the mode of the previous argument is:

> If the first, the second.
> But the first.
> Therefore the second.

The ordinal numbers here stand for assertibles, though they have exactly the same role as the letters of the alphabet in Aristotelian logic which stand for terms. Finally, the Stoics also used the so-called 'mode-arguments' (*logotropoi*), in which the assertibles are given in full when first occurring, but are then replaced by ordinal numbers, obviously for purposes of simplicity and clarity:

> If Plato is alive, Plato is breathing.
> But the first.
> Therefore the second.

It was the orthodox Stoic view that an argument must have more than one premise, though it seems that some Stoics accepted single-premise arguments, like the following (Sextus Empiricus, *Against the Mathematicians* 8.443 = LS 36C7; Apuleius, *On Interpretation* 184.16–23 = LS 36D):

> You are seeing.
> Therefore you are alive.

Of arguments some are valid, others invalid. Invalid are those the contradictory of whose conclusion does not conflict with the conjunction of the premises (Diogenes Laertius 7.77 = LS 36A4); for instance, the argument

> If it is day, it is light.
> But it is day.
> Therefore Dion is walking

is invalid, because the contradictory of its conclusion, i.e. 'Not: Dion is walking', does not conflict with the conjunction of its premises, i.e. 'Both if it is day it is light and it is day'. In other words, the validity of an argument depends on the truth of the corresponding conditional formed from the conjunction of the premises as antecedent and the conclusion as consequent (Sextus Empiricus, *Outlines of Pyrrhonism* 2.137 = LS 36B3). To take again the previous argument, it is invalid because the corresponding conditional 'If both if it is day it is light and it is day, Dion is walking' is false, at least according to Chrysippus' truth conditions for conditional assertibles.

Of valid arguments, some are just called 'valid', others 'syllogistic' (*sullogistikoi*). The Stoics defined syllogistic arguments as those which either are what they called 'indemonstrables' (*anapodeiktoi*) or can be reduced to the indemonstrables (Diogenes Laertius 7.78 = LS 36A5). Indemonstrable arguments, or simple syllogisms, are those whose validity is not in need of demonstration, given that it is obvious in itself (Diogenes Laertius 7.79–81 = LS 36A11–16). The lists of indemonstrable arguments which are to be found in our ancient sources vary, but there is no doubt that Chrysippus himself distinguished five different types of such arguments. The basic logical forms of the five standard indemonstrables are described and illustrated by examples in the ancient texts as follows:

(i) A first indemonstrable argument is constructed out of a conditional and its antecedent as premises, and the consequent as conclusion, e.g.

> If it is day, it is light.
> But it is day.
> Therefore it is light.

(ii) A second indemonstrable argument is constructed out of a conditional and the contradictory of its consequent as premises, and the contradictory of its antecedent as conclusion, e.g.

> If it is day, it is light.
> But not: it is light.
> Therefore not: it is day.

(iii) A third indemonstrable argument is constructed out of a negated conjunction and one of its conjuncts as premises, and the contradictory of the other conjunct as conclusion, e.g.

> Not: both Plato is dead and Plato is alive.
> But Plato is dead.
> Therefore not: Plato is alive.

(iv) A fourth indemonstrable argument is constructed out of a disjunction and one of its disjuncts as premises, and the contradictory of the other disjunct as conclusion, e.g.

> Either it is day or it is night.
> It is day.
> Therefore not: it is night.

(v) A fifth indemonstrable argument is constructed out of a disjunction and the contradictory of one of its disjuncts as premises, and the other disjunct as conclusion, e.g.

> Either it is day or it is night.
> Not: it is day.
> Therefore it is night.

In suggesting this particular list of the five types of indemonstrable arguments, Chrysippus was obviously not trying to introduce the smallest possible number of different types of indemonstrable arguments. Rather, it seems that he included in his list all types of arguments which rely merely on the argumentative force of the different basic types of connectives known to him. In the case of the fourth and fifth indemonstrables, for instance, they just rely on what it means to use the disjunctive connective, namely to say that if one of the disjuncts holds the contradictory of the other holds too, and if the contradictory of one disjunct holds the other disjunct holds too.

2.4 Analysis

To demonstrate the syllogistic validity of any argument whatsoever, the Stoic logicians considered it necessary to reduce it to one or more of the indemonstrable arguments, which are thus regarded as the first principles of the Stoic logical system. The procedure of reducing non-simple syllogisms to indemonstrable arguments was called by the Stoics 'analysis' (*analusis*). To carry out this procedure, the Stoic logicians had at least four logical rules, the so-called *themata*, and in Latin *constitutiones* or *exposita* (e.g. Galen, *On Hippocrates' and Plato's Doctrines* 2.3.18–19 = LS 36H; Diogenes Laertius 7.78 = LS 36A5). We only know the first and the third Stoic *thema*, and it is on the basis of extremely meagre evidence that modern scholars have suggested different reconstructions of the other two.

The first *thema* is the following (Apuleius, *On Interpretation* 191.5–10 = LS 36I):

> If from two propositions a third is deduced, then from either one of them together with the contradictory of the conclusion the contradictory of the other is deduced.

The third *thema* is the following (Alexander of Aphrodisias, *Commentary on Aristotle's Prior Analytics* 278.12–14 = LS 36J):

> When from two propositions a third is deduced, and extra propositions are found from which one of those two follows syllogistically, the same conclusion will be deduced from the other of the two plus the extra propositions from which that one follows syllogistically.

As to the second and fourth *themata*, we try to reconstruct them mainly on the basis of a logical principle, the so-called 'dialectical theorem' (*dialektikon theōrēma*) or 'synthetic theorem' (*sunthetikon theōrēma*), which is most probably Peripatetic and which is supposed to do the same job as the second, third, and fourth *themata* together (e.g. Sextus Empiricus, *Against the Mathematicians* 8.231 = LS 36G4):

> When we have the premisses from which some conclusion is deducible, we potentially have that conclusion too in these premisses, even if it is not expressly stated.

To get a clearer idea of how we are supposed to apply the Stoic *themata*, and thus how Stoic analysis actually functions, let us focus on the analysis of the following non-simple syllogism (Sextus Empiricus, *Against the Mathematicians* 8.235–6 = LS 36G7):

> If things evident appear alike to all those in like condition and signs are things evident, signs appear alike to all those in like condition.
> But signs do not appear alike to all those in like condition.
> And things evident do appear alike to all those in like condition.
> Therefore signs are not things evident.

To this purpose, it would be easier to use the mode of the non-simple syllogism:

> If both the first and the second, the third.
> But not the third.
> But also the first.
> Therefore not the second.

Sextus suggests that this argument can be reduced to two indemonstrables of different types, namely to a second and a third indemonstrable argument, by going through the following two steps:

(i) By combining the first premise, which is a conditional, with the second premise, which is the contradictory of the conditional's consequent, we get a second indemonstrable which has as its conclusion the contradictory of the conditional's antecedent:

> If both the first and the second, the third.
> But not the third.
> Therefore not: both the first and the second.

(ii) By combining the conclusion of this indemonstrable, which is a negated conjunction, with the third remaining premise, which affirms one of the two conjuncts, we get a third indemonstrable which has as its conclusion the affirmation of the other conjunct:

> Not: both the first and the second.
> But the first.
> Therefore not: the second.

Hence, the dialectical theorem in this case validates the use of the conclusion of the second indemonstrable, that is to say the use of the negated conjunction, in the construction of the third indemonstrable; for according to this logical rule, the negated conjunction which is deduced from some of the premises of the argument is implicitly contained in the argument, though it is not expressly stated. And it is obvious that we may similarly use the third *thema*; for a single application of the third *thema* on the second and third indemonstrables that we have constructed, could help us deduce the non-simple syllogism whose validity we try to prove.

To summarize, Stoic analysis starts with a non-simple syllogism and continues with a series of arguments which are either indemonstrables or arguments directly derived from the indemonstrables by appropriate application of one of the Stoic *themata*. Indeed, the Stoic logicians, and in particular Chrysippus, seem to have believed that their standard list of five indemonstrables is complete in the sense of containing all that is required for reasoning. It is said, for instance, that every argument is constructed out of these indemonstrables, and that all other arguments are thought to be validated by reference to them (e.g. Diogenes Laertius 7.79 = LS 36A11). Therefore, we may infer that some claim of completeness was made by the Stoic school, but it is not at all clear what precisely the Stoics' definition of completeness was, if they ever offered one (cf. Mueller 1979; Milne 1995).

After all, the Stoics themselves admitted that we cannot apply the method of analysis to all valid arguments, that is, we cannot reduce all valid arguments to the five indemonstrables by using the four Stoic themata; for, as we have already said, there are arguments in Stoic logic which are just valid, but not syllogistic. It thus seems that, according to the Stoics, the validity of such arguments is guaranteed not by their own analysis, but by their being equivalent to syllogistic arguments. For instance, the so-called 'subsyllogistic arguments' (*huposullogistikoi logoi*) differ from syllogisms only in that one or more of their constituent assertibles, although being equivalent to those in a syllogism, diverge from them in their linguistic form (e.g. Diogenes Laertius 7.78 = LS 36A6):

'It is day and it is night' is false.
But it is day.
Therefore not: it is night.

In this example, if it were not for the first premise that slightly diverges from the linguistic form of a negated conjunction, the argument would have been a third indemonstrable. In general, what emerges from the Stoic logicians' treatment of subsyllogistic arguments is that they tried to eliminate unnecessary ambiguities by standardizing language, so that the form of a sentence would unambiguously determine the type of assertibles expressed by it; for one and the same sentence may express assertibles that belong to different classes, and equally two different sentences may express the same assertible. But if there is some agreement to fix language use in a certain way, it becomes possible to easily discern the logically relevant properties of assertibles and their compounds, by simply examining the linguistic expressions used.

Finally, a scientific demonstration or proof (*apodeixis*) is, according to the Stoics, a syllogistic argument with true premises which by means of deduction reveals, i.e. gives knowledge of, a non-evident conclusion (e.g. Sextus Empiricus, *Outlines of Pyrrhonism* 2.140–3 = LS 36B7–11). For instance, the following argument was treated by the Stoics as an example of a proof:

If sweat flows through the surface, there are ducts discoverable by thought.
But sweat flows through the surface.
Therefore there are ducts discoverable by thought.

It is exactly the revelation of this non-evident conclusion by the force of the premises that constitutes the requirement of a genuine proof, and it is this discovery to which knowledge, according to the Stoics, aspires.

2.5 Invalid arguments and paradoxes

In Stoic logic invalid arguments arise in four ways (e.g. Sextus Empiricus, *Against the Mathematicians* 8.429–34 = LS 36C1–5):

(i)   By disconnection, when premises have no connection with one another or with the conclusion, e.g.

If it is day, it is light.
But wheat is being sold in the market.
Therefore it is light.

(ii) By redundancy, when they contain premises which are superfluous for drawing the conclusion, e.g.

If it is day, it is light.
But it is day.
But also virtue benefits.
Therefore it is light.

(iii) By being propounded in an invalid schema, e.g.

If it is day, it is light.
But not: it is day.
Therefore not: it is light.

(iv) By deficiency, when they contain premises which are incomplete, e.g.

Either wealth is bad, or wealth is good.
But not: wealth is bad.
Therefore wealth is good.

For the first premise should be 'Either wealth is bad, or wealth is good, or wealth is indifferent'; and moreover, a premise is missing.

Furthermore, there is abundant evidence of the Stoics' interest in solving the following logical paradoxes (cf. Mignucci 1999).

(i) *The Liar*

Various versions of the Liar paradox were known in antiquity, but there is no single text that gives us with certainty the precise formulation of the argument. A plausible reconstruction reads as follows: 'If you say that you are lying, and you say so truly, you are lying, and if you are lying, you are telling the truth.' Presumably it was Eubulides who invented this paradox in the fourth century, but there is no doubt that it was Chrysippus who more than anyone else in ancient times tried to solve it. The peculiarity of the case of the Liar seems to be not only that we are unable to find out what the truth of the statement is, but that in this case there is no truth of the matter. Perhaps Chrysippus' view was that in cases like this the statement is neither true nor false. However, if this were the case, the solution would put the very notion of an assertible under great pressure and would force a reconsideration of its definition (Cicero, *On Academic Scepticism* 2.95 = LS 37H5; Plutarch, *On Common Conceptions* 1059D–E = LS 37I).

(ii) *The Sorites*

The name of the *Sorites* comes from the Greek noun '*sōros*', which means 'heap' or 'pile'. This paradox exploits the vagueness of certain predicates such as 'heap': Is a single grain of wheat a heap? The answer is obviously 'No'. Are two grains a heap? The answer is again 'No'. If we continue adding one grain to the previous quantity we never get a heap. Chrysippus is reported to have claimed that this paradox does not pose any real difficulty, because the wise man knows at which moment he should stop replying to questions of the form 'Are so-and-so many grains a heap?' (Cicero, *On Academic Scepticism* 2.95 = LS 37H3; Galen, *On Medical Experience* 17.1 = LS 37E3).

(iii) *The Veiled Man*

According to one version of this paradox, Chrysippus asks someone whether he knows his own father. The person replies that he does. Next Chrysippus asks him again what he would have said if a veiled man were to be placed in front of him and was asked whether he knows him. The same person replies that he would have said that he doesn't know him. Chrysippus concludes that, if the veiled man were his father, the person would have thus admitted that he both knows and does not know his own father (Lucian, *Philosophers for Sale* 22 = LS 37L).

(iv) The Horned Man

In Diogenes Laertius (7.187) we find the following formulation of this paradox: 'If you have not lost something, you have it still. But you have not lost horns. Therefore you still have horns.'

Unfortunately, there is no evidence as to the way in which the Stoics tried to solve the last two paradoxes.

3 Conclusion

In his *Introduction to Logic* the ancient physician and philosopher Galen (129– c. 200/216 CE) discussed elements of the Stoic logical system alongside Aristotle's syllogistic. He even introduced what he considered as a third kind of syllogisms, the 'relational' (*pros ti*) syllogisms; for example, 'Dio owns half as much as Theo. Theo owns half as much as Philo. Therefore Dio owns a quarter of what Philo owns.' The fact that at the end of his account Galen made reference to the late Stoic philosopher Posidonius (c. 135–51 BCE) has led some modern scholars to suggest that it was Posidonius who had previously invented relational syllogistic and further developed Stoic logic. However, the evidence is extremely scant and Posidonius' contribution to logic most probably is limited. In fact, no ancient logician seriously attempted to explore relational syllogisms or, for that matter, to combine the two major logical systems of antiquity. The Byzantine scholars who paraphrased or commented on Aristotle's logical treatises in the middle ages simply added the standard list of Stoic indemonstrable arguments to the Aristotelian syllogistic; in most cases, they did not even attribute it to the Stoics. Regrettably, the synthesis of Aristotle's predicate logic and the Stoic propositional calculus had to wait for a long time.

References

Barnes, J. (1985), '*Pithana Sunēmmena*', *Elenchos* 6, 454–67.
Barnes, J. (1999a), 'Aristotle and Stoic Logic', in K. Ierodiakonou (ed.), *Topics in Stoic Philosophy*, Oxford: Clarendon Press, 23–53.
Barnes, J. (1999b), 'Logic and Language. Introduction & Logic I. The Peripatetics', in K.

Algra, J. Barnes, J. Mansfeld and M. Schofield (eds), *The Cambridge History of Hellenistic Philosophy*, Cambridge: Cambridge University Press, 65–83.

Bobzien, S. (1993), 'Chrysippus' modal logic and its relation to Philo and Diodorus', in K. Döring and T. Ebert (eds), *Dialektiker und Stoiker*, Stuttgart: Franz Steiner, 63–84.

Bobzien, S. (1999), 'Logic II. The Megarics & III.1–7 The Stoics', in K. Algra, J. Barnes, J. Mansfeld and M. Schofield (eds.), *The Cambridge History of Hellenistic Philosophy*, Cambridge: Cambridge University Press, 83–157.

Bobzien, S. (2003), 'Logic', in B. Inwood (ed.), *The Cambridge Companion to the Stoics*, Cambridge: Cambridge University Press, 85–123.

Frede, M. (1974a), *Die stoische Logik*, Göttingen: Vandenhoeck and Ruprecht.

Frede, M. (1974b), 'Stoic vs. Aristotelian Syllogistic', *Archiv für Geschichte der Philosophie* 56, 1–32.

Frede, M. (1994), 'The Stoic Notion of a *Lekton*', in S. Everson (ed.), *Companions to Ancient Thought (vol. 3): Language*, Cambridge: Cambridge University Press, 109–28.

Gourinat, J.-B. (2000), *La Dialectique des stoïciens*, Paris: Vrin.

Ierodiakonou, K. (2002), 'Zeno's Arguments', in T. Scaltsas and A.S. Mason (eds), *The Philosophy of Zeno*, Larnaca: The Municipality of Larnaca, 81–112.

Ierodiakonou, K. (2006), 'Stoic Logic', in M.L. Gill and P. Pellegrin (eds), *Blackwell Companions: A Companion to Ancient Philosophy*, Oxford: Blackwell, 505–29.

Kneale, W. and Kneale, M. (1962), *The Development of Logic*, Oxford: Oxford University Press.

Long, A.A. and Sedley, D.N. (eds. and trans.) (1987), *The Hellenistic Philosophers*, (2 vols.), Cambridge: Cambridge University Press (=LS).

Łukasiewicz, J. (1935), 'Zur Geschichte der Aussagenlogik', *Erkenntnis* 5, 111–31.

Mates, B. (1953), *Stoic Logic*. Berkeley: University of California Press.

Mignucci, M. (1999), 'Logic III.8 The Stoics', in K. Algra, J. Barnes, J. Mansfeld and M. Schofield (eds.), *The Cambridge History of Hellenistic Philosophy*, Cambridge: Cambridge University Press, 157–76.

Milne, P. (1995), 'On the Completeness of non-Philonian Stoic Logic', *History and Philosophy of Science* 16, 39–64.

Mueller, I. (1979), 'The Completeness of Stoic Propositional Logic', *Notre Dame Journal of Formal Logic* 20, 201–15.

Sandbach, F.H. (1985), *Aristotle and the Stoics*, Cambridge: Cambridge Philological Society.

Schofield, M. (1983), 'The Syllogisms of Zeno of Citium', *Phronesis* 28, 31–58.

Sedley, D.N. (1984), 'The Negated Conjunction in Stoicism', *Elenchos* 5, 311–16.

3

Medieval Logic

Sara L. Uckelman

1 Introduction

Many people unfamiliar with the history of logic may think of the Middle Ages as a 'Dark Ages' in logic, with little development beyond Aristotelian syllogistic and full of scholastic wrangling focused on uninteresting details. This could not be further from the case. Instead, the Middle Ages, especially at the end of the High Middle Ages and into the fourteenth century, was a period of vibrant activity in logic, in many different areas – the (re)birth of propositional logic, the development of interactive and dynamic reasoning, sophisticated semantic theories able to address robust paradoxes, and more. The period can be characterized by a focus on the applied aspects of logic, such as how it relates to linguistic problems, and how it is used in interpersonal contexts.

To attempt to survey the full chronological and biographical story of medieval logic from the end of antiquity until the birth of the Renaissance in the space of a chapter would be an impossible endeavour. Instead, this chapter focuses on four topics which are in certain respects uniquely and particularly medieval: (1) the analysis of properties of terms, specifically signification and supposition; (2) theories of consequences; (3) the study of *sophismata* and *insolubilia*; and (4) the mysterious *disputationes de obligationibus*. We treat each of these in turn, giving short thematic overviews of their rise and development. First, we provide a short historical comment on the introduction of the Aristotelian corpus into the medieval West and the effects that this had on the development of logic in the Middle Ages.

2 The reception of Aristotle

In the second decade of the sixth century, Anicius Manlius Severinus Boethius decided to embark upon the project of translating from Greek into Latin all of the Aristotelian and Platonic works that he could obtain, beginning with Aristotle's logical corpus. In 523, he was sentenced to prison for treason and by his death, around 526, he had completed an admirable percentage of his task, translating Aristotle's *Categories*, *On Interpretation*, the *Prior Analytics*, the *Topics*, the *Sophistical Refutations*, and most likely the *Posterior Analytics*, as well as Porphyry's *Introduction* (to the *Categories*). He also wrote commentaries on the *Introduction*, the *Categories* and *On Interpretation*, and his own textbooks on logic, including the unique little treatise on hypothetical syllogisms (syllogisms with molecular, i.e. noncategorical, premises). These translations, the first of Aristotle into Latin, were to shape the path of medieval Western philosophy in a tremendous fashion.

After Boethius's death, many of his translations of Aristotle were lost. Only the translations of *On Interpretation* and the *Categories* remained. These two books, along with Porphyry's Introduction, formed the basic logical and grammatical corpus for the next six centuries. It was not until the 1120s that his other translations were rediscovered.[1] In the 1150s, James of Venice translated the *Posterior Analytics* (if Boethius had translated the *Posterior Analytics*, this translation has never been found), and also retranslated the *Sophistical Refutations*. The newly completed Aristotelian logical corpus was available in western Europe by the latter half of the twelfth century, though it was not until the birth of the universities in the early thirteenth century that they began to circulate widely (the exception being the *Sophistical Refutations*, which was seized upon almost immediately). These works established their place as canonical texts in logic and natural philosophy, and their effect on the development of these fields was quickly seen. The material in these new texts provided medieval logicians not only with a stronger logical basis to work from, but also proved to be a 'jumping off' point for many novel – and in some cases radically *non*-Aristotelian – developments. Aristotle long remained the authority on logic, but though most medieval logicians give the required nod to the Philosopher, they certainly felt free to explore and develop their own ideas.

3 Properties of terms

In the Middle Ages, logic was a linguistic science; it arose from a desire to understand how language is used (properly) in order to assist in textual exegesis. As a result, from an early period the study of logic was closely connected to the study of grammar (indeed, these two studies, along with rhetoric, made up the *trivium*, the branch of learning that was the core of the undergraduate's curriculum in the early universities). William of Sherwood (1190–1249) in his *Introduction to Logic* (c. 1240) explains that 'Logic is principally concerned with the syllogism, the understanding of which requires an understanding of the proposition; and, because every proposition is made up of terms, an understanding of the term is necessary' (William of Sherwood 1966: 21). Hence if we wish to become proficient in logic we must first become masters of terms, and, more specifically, their properties, the two most important of which being signification and supposition. The period from 1175 to 1250 marked the height of what is known as *terminist logic*, because of its emphasis on terms and their properties. In this section, we discuss the ideas of signification and supposition found in late terminist writers such as William of Sherwood, Peter of Spain (mid-thirteenth century), and Lambert of Lagny (mid-thirteenth century), which reflect the most mature and settled views on the issues.

3.1 Signification

According to Lambert of Lagny in his treatise on the *Properties of Terms*, the signification of a word is the 'concept on which an utterance is imposed by the will of the person instituting the term' (1988: 104). As such, signification is one of the constitutive parts of a word's meaning. Four things are required for signification:

- A thing
- A concept of the thing
- An utterance (which may be mental, spoken, or written)
- A union of the utterance and the concept (effected by the will's imposition)

A thing is any extra-mental thing, whether it be an Aristotelian substance (e.g. Socrates the man), an Aristotelian accident (e.g. the whiteness which is in Socrates) or an activity (e.g. the running which Socrates is doing right now). On the medieval view, these extra-mental things are presented to the soul by means of a concept. A term gains signification when it is used in an utterance and the utterance is connected to a concept by the will of the speaker (or thinker or writer). The concept imposed upon the term in the speaker's utterance is the signification of the term. The signification of a sentence is then built out of the signification of its terms, in a compositional fashion.

Signification served as the basis for one of the primary divisions of terms recognized by medieval grammarians and logicians, into categorematic and syncategorematic (or significative and consignificative). A categorematic term is one which signifies or has signification on its own, apart from any other word. Nouns, proper names and verbs are, for the most part, categorematic terms. (Different grammatical forms of the being verb *est* 'is' are an exception). On the other hand, a syncategorematic term is one which does not signify on its own, but only in conjunction with another word or in the context of a sentence. Now, clearly, these 'definitions' are not sufficient to uniquely identify all words as either categorematic or syncategorematic. As a result, most medieval authors illustrated the definitions of categorematic and syncategorematic terms ostensively, and different authors highlighted different syncategorematic terms. Logical connectives ('and', 'or', 'not', 'if') and quantifiers ('all', 'some', 'none') were all recognized as syncategorematic terms, but the list of syncategorematic terms is longer than the list of what are modernly recognized as the so-called 'logical constants', and many of them are perhaps surprising. For example, William of Sherwood in his *Syncategoremata* (mid-thirteenth century) (2012) discusses the following syncategorematic terms: *omnis* 'every', *totum* 'whole', *decem* 'ten', *infinita* 'infinite', *qualislibet* 'of whatever sort', *uterque* 'each', *nullus* 'none', *ni- hil* 'nothing', *neutrum* 'neither', *praeter* 'except', *solus* 'single', *tantum* 'only', *est* 'is', *non* 'not', *necessario* 'necessarily', *contingenter* 'contingently', *incipit* 'begins', *desinit* 'cease', *si* 'if', *nisi* 'if not', *quin* 'without', *et* 'and' and *vel* 'or'. Some of these words, such as *infinita*, can be used both categorematically and syncategorematically, and this fact gave rise to certain logical puzzles, or *sophismata*.

If a term has only one signification imposed upon it, then it is univocal; if it has more than one signification imposed on it, then it is equivocal, such as 'bat' (the athletic equipment) and 'bat' (the flying mammal), in English. Equivocal terms must be distinguished from each other, in order to avoid the fallacy of *quaternio terminorum* 'four terms', a type of equivocation found in syllogisms. But univocal terms must also be carefully attended to, for even though they will always have the same signification no matter the context, these terms can still be used to stand for or refer to different things, depending on the context of the sentence in which they appear. This notion of a term 'standing for', or referring to, different objects is called *suppositio* 'supposition'. While a (categorematic) term can signify in isolation from other terms, it will supposit for things only in the context of a complete sentence, in the same way that syncategorematic terms only have signification in the context of a complete sentence.

3.2 Supposition

Signification gives only an indirect way of referring to things, via the concepts which are signified. In order to refer directly to things, and not just the concepts they fall under, the mechanism of supposition is used. Lambert of Lagny defines the supposition of a term as the 'acceptance of a term for itself, for its signified thing, for some suppositum contained under its signified thing, or for more than one suppositum contained under its signified thing' (1988: 106). For example, the univocal term 'man' signifies the concept of man, but it can supposit for the word 'man', the concept man, or individual or multiple men, depending on the grammatical context in which it appears.

Every author writing on supposition divided supposition into a different number of types, and distinguished them in different ways, but three main divisions were recognized, between simple or natural supposition, material supposition, and formal or personal supposition. A word that supposits simply stands for what it signifies; for example, in 'Man is a species', 'man' supposits simply. A word that supposits materially stands for the word itself; for example, in 'Man is a three-letter word', 'man' supposits materially. Finally, a word that supposits formally or personally stands for actual things which fall under the concept signified; for example, in 'A man is running', 'man' supposits personally. Personal supposition is the most important type of supposition, since it allows us to talk about individuals.

Both simple and material supposition are not further subdivided. Personal supposition, the most common type, has many different subtypes. Of these, the ones that are most interesting are the types of supposition had by terms which, either by their nature or due to some added word such as a universal quantifier, can apply equally well to more than one thing. These two types of supposition are called strong mobile supposition and weak immobile supposition.[2] A common term has strong mobile supposition when it is preceded by a universal affirmative or universal negative quantifier (e.g. *omnis* 'every' or *nullus* 'no, none'). It has weak immobile supposition 'when it is interpreted necessarily for more than one suppositum contained under it but not for all, and a descent cannot be made under it' (Lambert 1988: 112). For example, from the sentence 'All men are running', it is possible to descend to the singular sentences 'Socrates is running', 'Aristotle is running', 'Plato is running', and so on for all (currently existing) men. Similarly, from the conjunction of the singulars 'Socrates is running', 'Aristotle is running', 'Plato is running', etc., it is possible to ascend to the universal 'All men are running'. Such ascent and descent is not possible when the universal claim is prefixed by a negation, for example 'Not all men are running.' Likewise, when the subject term has been modified by an exceptive or an exclusive, it is not possible to descend. For example, it is not possible to descend from 'Every man except Socrates is running' to a singular because, for example, 'Aristotle except Socrates is running' is ungrammatical. Likewise, from 'Only men are running', we cannot conclude of any individual man that *he* is running, since the addition of the exclusive term 'only' changes the supposition of 'man'. The basic mechanism of supposition explains how terms supposit in simple present-tensed assertoric sentences. When the tense of a sentence is past or future, or the sentence has been modified by a modal operator such as 'necessarily', 'is known', 'is thought of', medieval logicians appealed to the notions of *ampliation* and *restriction*. Lambert defines restriction as 'a lessening of the scope of a common term as a consequence of which the common term is interpreted for fewer supposita than its actual supposition requires' (1988: 134). One way that a common term can be restricted is through the addition of an adjective. For example, we can restrict the supposition of 'man' by adding to it the adjective 'white'; 'white man' supposits for fewer things than 'man' unmodified.

If the modifying word or phrase does not restrict the term's supposition but rather expands it, then we are dealing with the opposite of restriction, which is called ampliation. Ampliation is an 'extension of the scope of a common term as a consequence of which the common term can be interpreted for more supposita than its actual supposition requires' (Lambert 1988: 137). As an example, Lambert offers 'A man is able to be Antichrist' (137); in this sentence, 'man' is ampliated to stand not only for existing men but for future men. Ampliation can be caused by the addition of predicates (such as 'possible'), verbs ('can'), adverbs ('potentially') or participles ('praised'). Lambert divides ampliation into two types, ampliation 'by means of supposita' and ampliation 'by means of times'. The former is caused by 'verbs whose corresponding action is related to the subject and said of the subject but is not in the subject – such as 'can', 'is thought', 'is praised' (138). A term ampliated in this way stands for both existent and non-existent things. Ampliation by reason of times is caused by modifiers which 'cause a term to be extended to all the differences of time' (138). Examples of this kind of modifier are temporal operators such as 'always', modal operators such as 'necessarily' and 'possibly', and changes in the tense of the verb.

Theories of supposition are closely tied to considerations of temporal and alethic modalities (such as 'necessary' and 'possible') (Uckelman 2013); we cannot go further into these issues here due to reasons of space.

4 Theories of consequences

The central notion in logic, both then and now, is the concept of 'following from' or, more technically, 'logical consequence'. The question of which propositions follow from other propositions, at heart, is what all of logic is about. There is a distinct lack of any general theory of logical consequence in Aristotle. The portion of logical consequence which is studied and discussed in the Aristotelian corpus – the syllogistic – is but a fraction of the field and moving from the study of syllogisms to the study of logical consequence in general is one of the highest accomplishments of the medieval logicians.

What do we mean by '(logical) consequence'? Modern logic distinguishes different logical relationships between two propositions. There is the relationship of implication, which holds between the antecedent and the consequent of a true conditional. There is the relationship of entailment, which holds between two propositions when one cannot be true without the other one also being true. And then there is the relationship of inference or derivation, which is the relationship which arises from the process of moving from one proposition (the premise) to another (the conclusion) in an argument. While there are certainly good reasons for distinguishing between these three relationships, these distinctions were not always made in medieval logic. The Latin word *consequentia* literally means 'follows with', and it was used indiscriminately to cover implication, inference and entailment. One consequence of this is that the primary evaluative notion was not validity but 'goodness'. Whereas a conditional is either true or false, and not valid or invalid, and an argument is either valid or invalid, and not true or false, both of these can be *bona consequentiae* 'good consequences' or *bene sequiter* 'follow correctly'.

The word *consequentia* was introduced into Latin by Boethius as a literal translation of Greek κἀκολούθησις. Some scholars have argued that the roots of theories of logical consequence are to be found not in the syllogistic but instead in the theory of topical inferences (Green-Pedersen, 1984). As a result, Boethius's translation of the *Topics* and his commentary on the same were influential. Another important work of his was the short, non-Aristotelian treatise 'On Hypothetical Syllogisms'. Despite the name, this text does not focus solely on 'if . . . then . . .' statements; rather, Boethius (and others after him) used 'hypothetical' in contrast with 'categorical'. Any molecular proposition, i.e. one formed out of other propositions by means of negation, conjunction, disjunction or implication, was considered 'hypothetical', and Boethius's treatise on syllogisms or arguments using such propositions was a first step towards modern propositional logic.[3]

The study of logical consequence began in earnest in the twelfth century. The concept proved difficult to properly define and classify. In the twelfth century, the most sophisticated attempt was produced by Peter Abelard (*c.* 1079–1142), a brilliant logician who produced not one but two comprehensive theories of logical consequence. The first, in the *Dialectica* (*c.* 1116), focuses on the treatment of topics and of hypothetical syllogisms, following Boethius and Aristotle. The other, later, discussion occurs in a fragment of his commentary on Boethius's commentary on the *Topics*, which is a part of the *Logica Ingredientibus* (before 1120). Of the two discussions, that in the *Dialectica* is more complete and clear. Unfortunately, it also turns out to be inconsistent (Martin 2004).

Through the course of the next two centuries, logicians continued to wrestle with the concept of consequence. In the early part of the fourteenth century treatises devoted solely to the notion of consequence begin to appear, with the earliest being written by Walter Burley (*c.* 1275–1344) and William of Ockham (*c.* 1285–1347). These treatises define different types of consequences (e.g. formal and material, simple and 'as of now', etc.), what it means for a consequence to be good, or for one proposition to follow from another, and list rules of inferences which preserve the goodness of a consequence. These rules of inference mirror modern propositional logic very closely. For example, in Burley's *De puritate artis logicae*, which appeared in both longer and shorter versions, the following rules all appear, where P, Q and R are all atomic propositions (Boh 1982: 312–13; Burley 1951):[4]

- $P \rightarrow Q \vdash \neg\bullet\,(P \wedge \neg Q)$
- $P \rightarrow Q \vdash (Q \rightarrow R) \rightarrow (P \rightarrow R)$
- $P \rightarrow Q \vdash (R \rightarrow P) \rightarrow (R \rightarrow Q)$
- $P \rightarrow Q, Q \rightarrow R, \ldots, T \rightarrow U \vdash P \rightarrow U$
- $P \rightarrow Q, (P \wedge Q) \rightarrow R \vdash P \rightarrow R$
- $P \rightarrow Q, (Q \wedge R) \rightarrow S \vdash (P \wedge R) \rightarrow S$
- $P \rightarrow Q \vdash \neg Q \rightarrow \neg P$
- $\neg\,(P \wedge Q) \dashv\vdash \neg P \vee \neg Q$
- $\neg\,(P \vee Q) \dashv\vdash \neg P \wedge \neg Q$

The fourteenth century saw the gradual codification of two main views on the nature of logical consequence, the English and the continental, with Robert Fland (*c.* 1350), John of Holland (1360s), Richard Lavenham (d. 1399) and Ralph Strode (d. 1387) as canonical examples on one side of the channel and Jean Buridan (*c.* 1300–*c.* 1358), Albert of Saxony (1316–1390) and Marsilius of Inghen (1340–1396) on the other side.

4.1 The English tradition

The English tradition (which was taken up in Italy at the end of the fourteenth century and into the fifteenth (Maierù 1983) is characterized by an overtly epistemic definition of (formal) consequence in terms of the containment of the consequent in the antecedent. For example, Strode gives the following definition:

> A consequence said to be formally valid is one of which if it is understood to be as is adequately signified through the antecedent then it is understood to be just as is adequately signified through the consequent. For if someone understands you to be a man then he understands you to be an animal.
>
> 1493

This echoes ideas found in Abelard's views on consequences, which stress a tight connection between the antecedent and consequent, or between the premises and conclusion. It is not sufficient that a consequent be merely 'accidentally' truth-preserving; there must be something more that binds the propositions together.[5] Such a definition certainly entails necessary truth-preservation, but it goes beyond it. In stressing the epistemic aspects of consequence, Strode, and others in the English tradition, are emphasizing one of the hallmarks of the medieval approach to logic, namely the emphasis on the epistemic context of logic and the idea that logic is an applied science which must be evaluated in the context of its applications.

4.2 The continental tradition

In contrast, the defining marks of validity in the continental tradition are modality and signification. On this side of the channel, Jean Buridan's *Tractatus de consequentiis* (1330s) (Hubien 1976) provides a canonical example. The first chapter of this treatise is devoted to the definition of consequence. Buridan begins by presenting a general definition which he then revises on the basis of objections and counterexamples. The first general definition is:

> Many people say that of two propositions, the one which cannot be true while the other is not true is the antecedent, and the one which cannot not be true while the other is true is the consequent, so that every proposition is antecedent to another proposition when it cannot be true without the other being true.
>
> Hubien 1976: 21

However innocuous this definition might seem, it is problematic for Buridan, and others who follow suit, for whom the relationships of antecedent and consequent are not between propositions in the modern sense of the term – abstract entities which are necessarily existing – but rather between specific tokens of propositions, spoken, written or mental, which only have truth-values when they exist, and do not otherwise. But proposition tokens have specific properties which interfere with this definition. Buridan points out that

> Every man is running, therefore some man is running   (1)

is a valid consequence, but it does not satisfy the definition given, because it is possible for the antecedent to be true without the consequent, if someone formed 'Every man is running' without forming 'Some man is running', in which case it would be possible for the former to be true without the latter.

His second revision is to supplement the definition with the following clause 'when they are formed together' (Hubien 1976: 21), but even this is not sufficient, for consider the following:

> No proposition is negative, therefore no donkey runs.   (2)

On the second definition, this would be a consequence, since there is no circumstance under which the antecedent is true, so there is no circumstance under which the antecedent is true without the consequent. The problem with the sentence is that its contrapositive:

> Some donkey runs, therefore some proposition is negative.   (3)

is not a valid consequence, and Buridan wishes to maintain contraposition as a sound rule of inference (Hubien 1976: 22). The final revision that he gives does away with reference to truth-value altogether, and is defined in terms of signification:

> Some proposition is antecedent to another which is related to it in such a way that it is impossible for things to be in whatever way the first signifies them to be without their being in whatever way the other signifies them to be, when these propositions are formed together.[6]

The problem with a proposition such as 'No proposition is negative' is that it is a *self-refuting* proposition; it cannot be formed without its very formation making it false. Self-refuting propositions cause problems for theories of truth and consequence, and turn up as central players in treatises on *insolubilia* and *sophismata*, to which we turn next.

5 *Insolubilia* and *sophismata*

The *Sophistici Elenchi* was one of the first of the new Aristotelian works translated in the middle of the twelfth century to gain a wide readership (Dod 1982: 69). The study of fallacies and sophistical reasoning held the same draw in the Middle Ages as it did in ancient Greece and in modern times: it is not sufficient to know how to reason properly (as is taught via the syllogism in the *Prior Analytics*); in order to win in a dispute, one must also be able to recognize when one's opponent is reasoning improperly. This gave rise to the study of *insolubiliae* 'insoluble sentences' and *sophismata* 'sophisms'.

The medieval genre of *sophismata* literature developed in the twelfth century and was firmly established in both grammatical and logical contexts by the end of that century (Ashworth 1992: 518). In the context of logic, a *sophisma* or insoluble is a problematic sentence, a sentence whose analysis either leads to an apparent contradiction, or for which two equally plausible analyses can be given, one for its truth and one for its falsity.[7] Treatises on sophisms generally followed a similar framework:

1. The sophism is stated, sometimes along with a *casus*, a hypothesis about how the world is, or extra information about how the sophism should be analysed.
2. An argument for its truth and an argument for its falsity are presented.
3. There is a claim about the truth-value of the *sophisma*.
4. The apparent contradiction is resolved by explaining why the arguments supporting the opposite solution are wrong.

The result is a sentence which has a definite truth-value under the *casus* (if one is given).

Many sophisms dealt with paradoxes that arise from logical predicates, such as truth, necessity, validity, etc. Medieval logicians recognized the importance of the task of providing non-trivial and non-*ad hoc* resolutions to these insolubles and sophisms. The most productive era in the theory of insolubles was from 1320 to 1350. During this period, many treatises on *insolubilia* and *sophismata* were written, and discussions of insoluble sentences appeared in other, non-dedicated works, too. Some of the most important authors writing on the topic during this period include Thomas Bradwardine (*c.* 1295–1349), Richard Kilvington (d. 1361), Roger Swyneshed (d. 1365), William Heytesbury (*c.* 1310–1372), John Wyclif (*c.* 1330–1384) and Peter of Ailly (1351–1420). In the remainder of this section, we discuss (1) the liar paradox and related insolubles,

(2) sophisms relating to validity and logical consequence, and (3) other types of sophisms and insolubles.

5.1 The liar paradox

The most famous insoluble is the liar paradox:

This sentence is false. (4)

The earliest known medieval formulation of the paradox is in Adam of Balsham's *Ars disserendi* (1132). However, Adam 'says nothing whatever to indicate that he was aware of the very special problems they pose, that they were current topics of philosophical discussion in his day, or how one might go about trying to answer those questions' (Spade 1987: 25). It was not until the later part of the twelfth century that the problematic aspects of the liar sentence (and related sentences) were taken up in earnest. Over the course of the next two centuries, many attempts to solve the paradox were provided. These solutions can be divided into the following five families: (1) classification under the fallacy *secundum quid et simpliciter*; (2) *transcasus* theories, (3) distinguishing between the *actus exercitus* 'exercised act' and the *actus significatus* 'signified act'; (4) *restrictio* theories; and (5) *cassatio* theories.

Secundum quid et simpliciter

This is Aristotle's solution. In Chapter 25 of the *Sophistical Refutations*, Aristotle makes a distinction between 'arguments which depend upon an expression that is valid of a particular thing, or in a particular respect, or place, or manner, or relation, and not valid absolutely' (Aristotle 2013), that is, between expressions which are valid *secundum quid* 'according to something' and those which are valid *simpliciter* 'simply' (or 'absolutely'). He goes on to say:

> Is it possible for the same man at the same time to be a keeper and a breaker of his oath? ... If a man keeps his oath in this particular instance or in this particular respect, is he bound also to be a keeper of oaths absolutely, but he who swears that he will break his oath, and then breaks it, keeps this particular oath only; he is not a keeper of his oath ... The argument is similar, also, as regards the problem whether the same man can at the same time say what is both false and true: but it appears to be a troublesome question because it is not easy to see in which of the two connexions the word 'absolutely' is to be rendered – with 'true' or with 'false'. There is, however, nothing to prevent it from being false absolutely, though

true in some particular respect or relation, i.e. being true in some things, though not 'true' absolutely.

Aristotle 2013

How this solves the paradox is not entirely clear; on this view, the liar sentence can apparently be solved both ways. Many medieval logicians who adopted the Aristotelian reply argued that the liar is false *simpliciter*, and true *secundum quid*; however, it was left unspecified with respect to what *quid* it is true.

Transcasus

The Latin word *transcasus* has no straightforward translation into English. It is a literal translation of Greek μεταπτωσις 'a change, transferring'. Conceptually, it is related to the Stoic notion of μεταπιπτωντα, from the same root, which are propositions whose truth-value changes over time (Spade and Read 2009: 37). In *transcasus*, it is not that the truth-value of the liar sentence changes, but rather, what the sentence refers to (and hence how its truth-value should be evaluated). On such solutions, when someone says 'I am speaking a falsehood', the sentence is not self-referential but instead refers to what that person said immediately prior. If he did not say anything before, then the liar sentence is just false.

The *actus exercitus* and the *actus significatus*

This solution takes advantage of the fact that the liar sentence (as usually formulated in medieval treatises) involves assertion: I say, 'I am saying something false', or Plato says, 'Plato is saying something false', or similar. When such an assertion is made, it is possible to distinguish between what the speaker says he is doing (signified act) and what he is actually doing (exercised act). This view, which is not well understood, is espoused by Johannes Duns Scotus in his *Questiones super libro elenchorum* (*c*. 1295), who says that the exercised act of the liar is 'speaking the truth' and the signified act of the liar is 'speaking a falsehood' (Duns Scotus 1958). Because the liar sentence expresses something which is not true, it is false.

Restrictio

Restriction solutions are the most straightforward: by restricting the allowed grammatical/syntactic forms to disbar self-referential sentences, it is possible to rule the liar paradox as without truth-value because it is self-referential (ungrammatical). Spade (1975) discusses seventy-one different texts dealing with the liar paradox. Fourteen of these texts espouse some type of restriction theory, either explicitly or implicitly. These include a number of mid- to late-fourteenth-century anonymous treatises, as well as treatises by well-known logicians such as Walter Burley, in his *Insolubilia* (before 1320) (31) and William of Ockham, in his *Summa logicae* (1324–1327) (Ockham 1974) and his *Tractatus super libros elenchorum* (before 1328) (Ockham 1979).

Restriction solutions exist across a broad spectrum, ranging from very weak, forbidding only a small amount of self-reference, to very strong, forbidding all self-reference. On such strong restriction theories, not only does it turn out that the liar has no truth-value, but so also such insolubles as the linked liars:

$$\text{Plato: What Socrates says is false} \qquad (5)$$
$$\text{Socrates: What Plato says is false} \qquad (6)$$

as well as seemingly non-paradoxical sentences which just happen to be self-referential, such as:

$$\text{This sentence has five words.} \qquad (7)$$

Cassatio

The Latin word *cassatio* means to make null or void, or to cancel. On the view of the cassators, when you are uttering an insoluble, you are saying nothing; the paradoxicality of the sentence cancels out any meaning it might have had. Therefore an insoluble like the liar has the same truth-value as the empty utterance: none. This solution was favoured in the early period, and died out by the 1220s, though it continued to be mentioned in later catalogues of types of solutions (Spade and Read 2009, §2.5).

In addition to the liar and the linked liars, other liar-like insolubles were also considered. For example, suppose that Plato promises to give everyone who tells the truth a penny. Socrates then announces, 'You won't give me a penny'. Or similarly, Plato is guarding a bridge, and will let only those who tell the truth cross; anyone who tells a lie will be thrown into the water. Socrates approaches and says, 'You will throw me from the bridge'. Both of these present the same problems for analysis as the liar paradox, though it is clear that they cannot be solved in similar ways (for example, restriction strategies make no sense here, since there is no self- or cross-reference).[8]

5.2 Paradoxes of validity

Earlier we mentioned some of the problems that arise in the analysis of propositions such as 'No proposition is negative'. In Chapter 8 of his *Sophismata*, Buridan (2001) considers the related inferences 'Every proposition is affirmative, therefore no proposition is negative' and 'No proposition is negative, therefore some proposition is negative'. These inferences are problematic, because, on the one hand, the antecedent is either the contrary or the contradictory of the consequent, so any time it is true the consequent will have to be false, according to the rules in the Square of Opposition; and on the other hand, 'No proposition is negative' is itself a negative proposition, and any time that it exists, some negative proposition will exist, and thus some proposition will be negative. Nevertheless, it is not impossible that there be no negative propositions; as Buridan points out, 'Every proposition is affirmative' would be true if God annihilated all negatives, and then the consequent [of the first inference] would not be true, for it would not be' (2001: 953). This analysis leads Buridan to make an interesting distinction: He concludes that such a proposition 'is possible, although it cannot be true' (956); that is, he distinguishes between being 'possible' and being 'possibly-true'; a proposition can be one without being the other.

Other paradoxes of validity include self-referential propositions, but unlike the liar sentence they involve logical predicates other than truth. For example, Pseudo-Scotus offers a counterexample to Buridan's definition of logical consequence in terms of necessary truth-preservation (cf. §4.2 above) (Yrjönsuuri 2001):

$$\text{God exists, hence this argument is invalid.} \qquad (8)$$

Under standard medieval metaphysical and ontological assumptions, 'God exists' is a necessary truth.[9] Suppose, then that (8) is valid. The antecedent is not only true, but necessarily true. However, if the argument is valid, then the consequent is false, since it asserts that the argument is invalid. But then the argument is not truth-preserving, and so cannot be valid. But if the argument is invalid, then it is necessarily invalid, and as a result the consequent is necessary. But a necessary truth following from a necessary truth is necessarily a valid inference, and thus (8) is valid.

Similar paradoxes can be levelled against Buridan's final definition, in terms of signification, too. For example, the definition is adequate for the counter-example that it was designed to obviate, but would have problems dealing with the following inference:

The consequent of (9) does not signify as is the case,

therefore, the consequent of (9) does not signify as is the case.   (9)

While this precise example is not found, similar ideas are treated by Roger Swyneshed in his *Insolubilia* (*c*. 1330–1335) (Spade 1979).

5.3 Other classes of *insolubilia* and *sophismata*

In this section we briefly catalogue other common types of *insolubilia* and *sophismata*.

1. Sophisms which arise from *exponibilia* 'exponible [terms]'. An exponible term is one whose analysis requires breaking the sentence in which it appears down into a collection of sentences, each of which are simpler in form. A common example of a pair of exponible terms are *incipit* 'begins' and *desinit* 'ceases'. There are two ways that a sentence such as 'Socrates begins to be white' can be analysed:

   Socrates is not white at time t,

   and t is the last moment at which he is not white.   (10)

   Socrates is not white at time t,

   and t' is the first moment at which he is white.   (11)

   Confusing the two ways that such sentences can be expounded can result in sophisms. Such sophisms are discussed by William Heytesbury in his *Regulae solvendi sophismata* (1335) (Heytesbury 1979; Wilson 1956) and Richard Kilvington in his *Sophismata* (before 1325) (Kilvington 1990).

2. Sophisms which arise from confusing the syncategorematic and categorematic uses of terms. The most common example is *infinita est finita*, where *infinita* can be interpreted either categorematically or syncategorematically. This sentence is difficult to translate into English without losing the ambiguity; when *infinita* is used categorematically, it is taken as a substantive noun, 'the infinite', and then the sentence says that 'the infinite is finite', which is false. But syncategorematically, it is taken adjectivally, and means that 'infinite are the finite', i.e. 'there are infinitely many finite things', which is true, for example numbers. Illicit shifts between the categorematic reading and the syncategorematic reading can lead to paralogisms and sophisms. Heytesbury discusses this in his treatise *De sensu composito et diviso* (before 1335) (Heytesbury 1988).

3. Sophisms which arise from infelicities of presupposition and supposition. A typical example of these is 'Socrates promises Plato a horse' (or in some cases, a penny), and yet for any given horse (or penny), it is not the case that Socrates has promised Plato *this* horse.

4. Sophisms which arise from the re-imposition of terms, stipulating that they signify things other than their ordinary signification. We see examples of these in the next section.

Finally, we would be remiss in not mentioning (5) sophisms which illustrate that the more things change, the more things stay the same, or, more precisely, that medieval humour isn't all that different from modern humour, and that is the class of sophisms whose conclusion is *Tu es asinus* 'You are an ass'. One example of such is the paralogism: 'This donkey is yours, this donkey is a father, therefore this donkey is your father', and if your father is a donkey, then you are one as well.

6 Obligational disputations

The final area of medieval logic that we cover in this chapter is the most peculiar and the most unfamiliar. While theories of meaning and reference, systems of logical consequence, and the study of paradoxes and sophistical reasoning are all part and parcel of the modern study of logic and philosophy of language, there is no such counterpart for the uniquely medieval genre of *disputationes de obligationibus*. The earliest treatises on these disputations are anonymous, and date from the first decades of the thirteenth century. In the following two centuries, scores of treatises on obligations were written, including ones by William of Sherwood, Nicholas of Paris (*fl.* 1250), Walter Burley, Roger Swyneshed, Richard Kilvington, William of Ockham, Albert of Saxony, John of Wesel (1340/50s), Robert Fland, John of Holland, Richard Brinkley (*fl.* 1365–1370), Richard Lavenham, Ralph Strode, Peter of Ailly, Peter of Candia (late fourteenth century), Peter of Mantua (d. 1399), Paul of Venice (*c.* 1369–1429) and Paul of Pergola (d. 1455).

So what are these mysterious disputations, and why are they mysterious? An *obligatio* is a dispute between two players, an Opponent and a Respondent. The Opponent puts forward propositions (one at a time, or in collections, depending on different authors' rules), and the Respondent is obliged (hence the name) to follow certain rules in his responses to these propositions. These rules depend on the type of disputation; we give an example of one type below in §6.1 (which the reader can consult now to have a sense of what we are talking about).

Early authors distinguish six types, or species, of *obligationes*: (1) *positio* 'positing', (2) *depositio* 'de-positing' (a type of denial), (3) *dubitatio* 'doubting', (4) *petitio* 'petition', (5) *impositio* 'imposition' and (6) *sit verum* 'let it be true'. Later authors argued that some of these types could be derived from the others and so reduced the number of species, generally to three (Uckelman 2012, §4). They are mysterious because their background and their purpose is unclear. Early texts allude to Aristotle's threefold division of disputations in Book VIII, Chapter 4 of the *Topics* (cf. e.g. Walter Burley's *De obligationibus* (c. 1302) (Burley 1988). There are indications in other texts that show that the medieval authors were interested in developing *obligationes* in the tradition of disputations as described in the *Topics* – not only in motivating the genre but also in discussions concerning what type of disputations *obligationes* are (Uckelman 2012, §2). Modern scholars have advanced many hypotheses about the purpose of these disputations. In our opinion, no single answer is going to tell the whole story. It is clear – certain texts tell us so explicitly (de Rijk 1975) – that *obligationes* were used as training exercises for students. That there is a close connection between *obligationes* and *insolubilia*-literature is also clear given the use of *obligationes* -language in treatises on insolubles and sophisms (Kilvington 1990; Martin 2001). While the idea that *obligations* were developed as a type of counterfactual reasoning is not in general tenable, it can be justified in some specific contexts (Uckelman 2015).

The general procedure followed in the disputations did not vary drastically from author to author or type to type. The Respondent had three (in some cases, four) possible responses: concede, deny or doubt (some authors also allowed him to draw distinctions in the case of ambiguous propositions). Which response was the correct response depended, in part, on whether the proposition was relevant (or pertinent) or irrelevant (or impertinent). In the tradition of Walter Burley, which came to be termed the *responsio vetus* 'the old response', a proposition was defined as relevant if it, or its negation, followed from the conjunction of all the propositions conceded along with the negations of all denied. On this definition, the set of relevant sentences potentially changed with each step of the disputation. Such a definition can also be found in the works of William of Sherwood, Ralph Strode and Peter of Candia. This dynamic conception of relevance resulted in a number of consequences that later authors, particularly Roger Swyneshed, found problematic. Swyneshed, in what came to be termed the *responsio nova* 'new response', redefined relevance in his *Obligationes* (1330×1335) (Spade 1977) into a static notion, where a proposition is relevant if it or its negation follows from the *positum* (the first proposition of the disputation), and is irrelevant otherwise. It is clear that on this definition, whether a proposition is relevant or not does not change with the course of the disputation. Swyneshed was followed in this redefinition by Robert Fland, Richard Lavenham and John of Wesel, among others.

Regardless of which definition of relevance was used, the following general rules were accepted by everyone:

- A relevant proposition should be conceded if it follows, and denied if its negation follows.
- An irrelevant proposition should be conceded if it is (known to be) true, denied if it is (known to be) false, and doubted if it is neither (known to be) true nor (known to be) false.

6.1 *Positio*

Positio is the crown jewel of the *obligationes* regalia. It is the most prominently discussed, by both medieval and modern authors. *Positio* can be divided into multiple types. The first division is into possible and impossible *positio*; both divisions are further divided as to whether the proposition is simple or complex, and then further as to whether the complex propositions are formed by conjunction ('conjoined *positio*') or disjunction ('indeterminate *positio*'). In any of these types of *positio*, it is also possible that a further stipulation is added, in which case the *positio* is called 'dependent' (Burley 1988: 378). Most texts focus their discussion on possible *positio*.

	Opponent	Respondent
1	ϕ.	I admit it.
2	$\neg\phi\vee\psi$.	I grant it.
3	ψ	I grant it.

Figure 3.1 A simple example

The rules given above are, in slightly simplified form, Burley's rules for *positio*. These rules exhaustively cover all of the possibilities that the Respondent may face in the course of the disputation; how these rules play out in the context of actual disputations is made clear in Burley's examples, which are typical of thirteenth-century developments. Due to issues of space, we cannot follow this up with a discussion of the later fourteenth-century developments, but instead direct the reader to Uckelman (2012), §§4.2, 4.3.

We consider an example *positio* which appears, with slight variation, in many thirteenth-century treatises. It is fairly simple but illustrates Burley's rules nicely.

Suppose that ϕ does not imply $\neg\psi$ and ϕ is known to be false; for example, let ϕ be 'The capital of England is Paris' and ψ is 'It is raining'. Since ϕ is satisfiable (because if it were not, then it would imply $\neg\psi$), the Respondent should admit it when it is put forward as a *positum*. In the second round, the Opponent asserts $\neg\phi \vee \psi$. Now, either ϕ implies ψ, in which case the proposition follows from the *positum* and hence the Respondent should concede it, or ψ is independent of ϕ, and hence the proposition is irrelevant. In that case, we know that since ϕ is false, $\neg\phi$ is true, so the disjunction is true, and true irrelevant propositions should be conceded. But then, ϕ follows from the *positum* along with something correctly conceded, and hence when the Opponent asserts ψ, the Respondent must concede it too.

This example shows how, given a *positum* which is false, but not contradictory, the Opponent can force the Respondent to concede any other proposition consistent with it. The fact that this is possible is one of Swyneshed's primary motivations for revising the standard rules. Further formal properties, following from the assumption of a consistent *positum* (which is the definition of possible *positio*), include that no disputation requires the Respondent to concede ϕ in one round and to concede $\neg\phi$ in another round (or to concede ϕ in one round and to deny it in another); the set of formulas conceded, along with the negations of those denied, will always be a consistent set; yet, it may be that the Respondent has to give different answers to the same propositions put forward at different times.

6.2 *Depositio*

Depositio is just like *positio*, except that the Respondent is obliged to deny or reject the initial proposition (the *depositum*). A *depositio* with *depositum* ϕ will be completely symmetric to a *positio* with $\neg\phi$ as the *positum*. Nevertheless, early treatises on *obligationes*, such as that by Nicholas of Paris which dates from *c.* 1230–1250, still treat *depositio* at some length.

6.3 *Dubitatio*

In *dubitatio*, the Respondent must *doubt* the statement that the Opponent puts forward (called the *dubitatum*). While *dubitatio* was discussed in thirteenth-century texts, often at some length, later authors (both later medieval and modern authors) call *dubitatio* a trivial variant of *positio*, and thus spend little time discussing it. For example, Paul of Venice (1988) reduces *dubitatio* to *positio* (in much the same way that he, and others, reduces *depositio* to *dubitatio*);

Swyneshed, Lavenham (Spade 1978), John of Wesel (1996), Richard Brinkley (Spade and Wilson, 1995) and John of Holland (1985) do not mention *dubitatio* at all. However, such a trivializing view of *dubitatio* fails to recognize the higher-order aspects of the disputation, the mixing of both knowledge and truth, which result in a significantly more difficult type of disputation. Just as *positio* is only interesting when the *positum* is false, *dubitatio* is only interesting when the truth-value of the *dubitatum* is known (whether it is true or false) (Uckelman, Maat and Rybalko, forthcoming; Uckelman 2012). Thus, the complexity of this type of disputation partly arises from the interaction between knowledge, truth and the obligations of the Respondent, as the Respondent in many cases is required to respond *dubio* 'I doubt it' to propositions that he actually knows.

A second cause of complexity in *dubitatio* is the fact that the rules, unlike those for *positio*, are not deterministic. For example, Nicholas of Paris's rules for *dubitatio* (Braakhuis 1998: 72–6) include the following:

- Just as in *positio* a *positum* put forward in the form of the *positum*, and everything convertible to it in the time of positing is to be conceded and its opposite and things convertible with it is to be denied and just as in *depositio* a *depositum* put forward in the form of the *depositum*, with its convertibles, must be denied and its opposite with things convertible with it must be conceded; so in *dubitatio* for a *dubitatum* put forward in the form of *dubitatum* and for its convertibles and moreover for the opposite of the *dubitatum* with its convertibles must be answered 'prove!' (223).
- For everything irrelevant to the *dubitatum* the response must be according to its quality.
- For everything antecedent to the *dubitatum* the response must be 'false' or 'prove!' and never 'true' (224).
- For everything consequent to the *dubitatum* it is possible to reply 'it is true' or 'prove' and never 'it is false' (224).

Whereas there is always a unique correct response for Respondent in *positio* (in both the *responsio antiqua* and *nova*), here, the rules give Respondent a range of choices. This non-determinacy means that there is a plurality of ways that Respondent may act, and still be disputing according to the rules, a feature which no other version of *obligatio* has. However, this feature of *dubitatio* seems not to have been noticed by later authors who insisted that *dubitatio* could be reduced to *positio*.

Nicholas's *dubitatio* has similar formal properties to *positio*. Provided that the *dubitatum* is neither a contradiction nor a tautology, it can be proved that the

Respondent can *win* the disputation playing by Nicholas's rules for *dubitatio*: that is, there is never any case where he will be forced either to concede or to deny the *dubitatum* (Uckelman 2011, Theorem 24).

6.4 *Impositio/Institutio/Appellatio*

The obligation involved in *impositio*, also called *institutio* 'institution' or *appellatio* 'appellation', functions in a relevantly different manner from the obligation in *positio*, *depositio* or *dubitatio*. Whereas in these latter three, the Respondent's obligation involves how he is to respond to the *obligatum*, *impositio* involves the redefinition (re-imposition) of certain terms or phrases.[10] *Impositio* can take place in conjunction with any of *positio*, *depositio* and *dubitatio*; that is, once a new imposition is introduced, then the Respondent may also further be obliged to concede, deny, or doubt the initial *obligatum* of the disputation. Sometimes the imposition is simple and straightforward:

> I impose that 'a' signifies precisely that God exists . . . I impose that this term 'man' may be converted with this word 'donkey', or I impose that this proposition 'God exists' signifies precisely that man is donkey.
>
> Spade 1978, ¶¶2, 21

In the first example, '*a*' is being instituted as the name of a proposition that signifies that God exists; likewise in the third example, the phrase 'God exists' is instituted as the name of a proposition signifying that man is donkey; thus any time that 'God exists' is asserted in a disputation, it must be understood as meaning 'Man is donkey'. In the second example, the institution is not at the level of propositions but at the level of words; it changes the meaning of the term 'man' so that it no longer means 'man' but instead means 'donkey'. Simple impositions like these are relatively easy; the only skill they require beyond the skills needed for *positio* is the skill to remember the new imposition of the term or proposition. However, much more complicated examples can be provided, such as the following (also due to Lavenham):

> I impose that in every false proposition in which '*a*' is put down that it signifies only 'man' and that in every true proposition in which '*a*' is put down that it signifies only 'donkey', and that in every doubtful proposition in which '*a*' is put down that it signifies alternately with this disjunction 'man or non man'.
>
> Spade 1978, ¶24

Now suppose that the proposition 'Man is *a*' is put forward. The proposition is either true, false or of unknown truth-value (doubtful). Suppose it is true. Then, it means 'Man is a donkey', which is impossible; hence, contrary to supposition, the proposition is in fact false. But if it is false, it means 'Man is man' – but this is true! Thus, if it cannot be true or false, then it must be doubtful. But if it is doubtful, then it means 'Man is man or not man', which is true, and hence not doubtful! No matter which assumption is made about the value of the proposition, the Respondent is led into contradiction.

6.5 *Petitio*

In *petitio*, the Opponent asks (petitions) the Respondent to respond in a certain way, for example by conceding or denying the initial proposition. *Petitio* is rarely treated at any length, because, as a number of authors (Nicholas of Paris (Braakhuis 1998: 183), Marsilius of Inghen (1489), Peter of Mantua (Strobino 2009), Paul of Venice (1988: 38–9) argue, *petitio* can be reduced to *positio*. Thus, from the disputational point of view, there are little more than cosmetic differences between *positio* and *petitio*.

6.6 *Rei veritas / sit verum*

The sixth type, *sit verum* or *rei veritas* 'the truth of things', is rarely discussed by the medieval authors, and sometimes not even explicitly defined. As a result, it is difficult to give a precise explanation or characterization of this type. Many discussions of *sit verum* focus on epistemic aspects of the disputation (Stump 1982: 320). For instance, Paul of Venice gives the following example of *sit verum*: 'Let it be true that you know that you are replying' (1988: 45). Nicholas of Paris also gives an example of a *rei veritas* that cannot be sustained which is couched in epistemic terms (Braakhuis 1998: 166, 233). However, one cannot generalize too broadly from this, as other examples show more in common with counter-factual reasoning than epistemic reasoning (Uckelman 2015).

7 Conclusion

In this chapter we have given an overview of medieval logic which we hope is sufficient to show that the Middle Ages were, in the history of logic, not a period of darkness and crudeness, but rather one, particularly during the thirteenth and fourteenth centuries, of new insights into the nature of language and inference.

These insights, building on Aristotle's *Organon* but going far beyond him, provided a foundation for the formal education of centuries of young men, regardless of whether they intended to continue their studies in philosophy. There is much that we have not been able to address in great detail in this chapter, and still more that we have not touched on at all. (For example, we have almost completely omitted developments of the syllogistic, both assertoric and modal, as well as the interesting and complex question of how to deal with future contingents.) Nevertheless, what we have shown is that the impact of logic and the study of it in the Middle Ages therefore cannot be dismissed out of hand. Modern study of medieval logic is still, to a large extent, in its early stages, and decades to come will continue to prove the importance and sophistication of the medieval logicians.

Notes

1 Dod notes that 'how and where these translations . . . were found is not known' (1982: 46), nor indeed how and where they were lost in the first place.

2 The mobility referred to in their names is a reference to the possibility (or lack thereof) of 'descending to' or 'ascending from' singulars; see examples below.

3 It is, however, *not* modern propositional logic, since the notion of implication or conditional which he uses is neither the modern material conditional nor strict implication, but is instead based on the idea of subjects and predicates either containing each other or being repugnant to (contradictory with) each other. As a result, the logical theory in 'On Hypothetical Syllogisms' validates many theorems which are not acceptable with either material or strict implication.

4 Note that the medieval logicians did not use symbolic notation (with the exception of using letters to stand for arbitrary terms in discussions of syllogistic). Nevertheless, these are accurate and faithful representations of the rules which are found in Burley.

5 In this respect, the medieval approach to logic shares many methodological characteristics with logicians who pursue relevance logic projects nowadays.

6 Buridan is not entirely content with this definition either, but this has to do with his theory of truth, rather than any problem with the definition itself, and we do not have the space to go into these problems here. But cf. Hubien (1976) and Klima (2004).

7 In this section, we group *insolubilia* and *sophismata* in our discussion, even though historians of logic will sometimes try to bifurcate the two (cf. e.g Spade and Read 2009; Pironet and Spruyt 2011). Both of the terms are somewhat wider in scope than modern 'paradox', which implies some sort of logical contradiction. Not all insolubles are in fact unsolvable; rather, they are so named because they are difficult to solve. And not all sophisms involve the use of sophistical (i.e. fallacious) reasoning.

8 Both of these examples are adapted from Peter of Ailly's *Insolubilia* (Ailly 1980).

9 In fact, when it shows up in logical examples, it is almost always being used as a 'generic' logical truth, rather like $p \lor \neg p$. Nothing important turns on the fact that this proposition is about God.

10 For example, the anonymous author of *Obligationes Parisienses* notes that '*Institutio* is divided into certain *institutio*, and uncertain or obscure *institutio*, for example if the name 'Marcus' is fixed that it might be a name of Socrates or Plato, but you would not know of which' (de Rijk 1975: 28) and Lavenham defines *impositio* as an 'obligation by means of which a term or proposition is assigned a [new] signification'.

References

Ailly, Peter of (1980), *Peter of Ailly: Concepts and Insolubles*, ed. and trans. Paul V. Spade, Berlin: Springer.

Aristotle (2013), *On Sophistical Refutations*, trans. W.A. Pickard-Cambridge, Adelaid: University of Adelaide Library. Web edition, https://ebooks.adelaide.edu.au/a/aristotle/sophistical/.

Ashworth, E. Jennifer (1992), 'New light on medieval philosophy: The *Sophismata* of Richard Kilvington', *Dialogue*, 31:517–21.

Boh, Ivan (1982), 'Consequences', in Norman Kretzmann, Anthony Kenny and Jan Pinborg, eds, *Cambridge History of Later Medieval Philosophy*, pp. 300–15, Cambridge: Cambridge University Press.

Braakhuis, H.A.G (1998), 'Obligations in early thirteenth century Paris: the *Obligationes* of Nicholas of Paris (?)', *Vivarium*, 36(2):152–233.

Buridan, Jean (2001), 'Sophismata', trans. Gyula Klima, in *Summulae de Dialectica*, New Haven: Yale University Press.

Burley, Walter (1951), *De Puritate Artis Logicae*, ed. P. Boehner, St Bonaventure, NY: Franciscan Institute; E. Nauwelaerts.

Burley, Walter (1988), *Obligations (selections)*, in Norman Kretzmann and Eleonore Stump, eds, *The Cambridge Translations of Medieval Philosophical Texts*, vol. 1: Logic and the Philosophy of Language, pp. 369–412, Cambridge: Cambridge University Press.

de Rijk, L.M. (1975), 'Some thirteenth century tracts on the game of obligation II', *Vivarium*, 13(1):22–54.

Dod, Bernard G. (1982), 'Aristoteles latinus', in Norman Kretzmann, Anthony Kenny, and Jan Pinborg, eds, *Cambridge History of Later Medieval Philosophy*, pp. 45–79, Cambridge: Cambridge University Press.

Duns Scotus, John (1958). 'Quaestiones super libro elenchorum', in Luke Wadding, ed., *Opera Omnia*, vol. 1, pp. 268–9, Hildesheim: Georg Olms.

Green-Pedersen, Neils Jørgen (1984), *The Tradition of the Topics in the Middle Ages. The Commentaries on Aristotle's and Boethius's 'Topics'*, Investigations in Logic, Ontology, and the Philosophy of Language. Munich: Philosophia Verlag.

Heytesbury, William (1979), *On Insoluble Sentences: Chapter One of His Rules for Solving Sophisms*, ed. and trans Paul V. Spade, Toronto: Pontifical Institute of Medieval Studies.

Heytesbury, William (1988), 'The compounded and divided senses', in N. Kretzmann and E. Stump, eds and trans., *Cambridge Translations of Medieval Philosophical Texts, vol. 1: Logic and the Philosophy of Language*, pp. 413–34, Cambridge: Cambridge University Press.

Holland, John of (1985), *Four Tracts on Logic*, ed. E.P. Bos, Nijmegen: Ingenium Publishers.

Hubien, Hubert (ed.) (1976), *Iohannis Buridani: Tractatus de Consequentiis*, vol. XVI of *Philosophes Médiévaux*, Louvain: Publications Universitaires.

Kilvington, Richard (1990), *The Sophismata of Richard Kilvington*, ed. N. Kretzmann and B.E. Kretzmann, Cambridge: Cambridge University Press.

Klima, Gyula (2004), 'Consequences of a close, token-based semantics: The case of John Buridan', *History and Philosophy of Logic*, 25:95–110.

Laigny Lambert of (of Auxerre) (1988), 'Properties of terms', in N. Kretzmann and E. Stump, eds and trans., *Cambridge Translations of Medieval Philosophical Texts, vol. 1: Logic and the Philosophy of Language*, pp. 102–62, Cambridge: Cambridge University Press.

Maierù, Alfonso (1983), *English Logic in Italy in the 14th and 15th Centuries*, Naples: Bibliopolis.

Marsilius of Inghen (1489), *Obligationes*, Paris: Erroneously published under the name Pierre d'Ailly.

Martin, Christopher J. (2001), 'Obligations and liars', in M. Yrjönsuuri, ed., *Medieval Formal Logic*, pp. 63–94, Dordrecht: Kluwer Academic Publishers.

Martin, Christopher J. (2004), 'Logic', in J. Brower and K. Gilfoy, eds, *Cambridge Companion to Abelard*, pp. 158–99, Cambridge: Cambridge University Press.

Ockham, William of (1974), 'Summa logicae', in Gedeon Gál et al., eds, *Opera Philosophica*, vol. I. St Bonaventure, NY: Franciscan Institute.

Ockham, William of (1979), *Expositio Super Libros Elenchorum*, vol. 3 of *Opera Philosophica*, ed. F. Del Punta, St Bonaventure, NY: Franciscan Institute.

Pironet, Fabienne and Joke Spruyt (2011), 'Sophismata', in E.N. Zalta, ed.,*Stanford Encyclopedia of Philosophy*, Winter edition, Stanford: Stanford University Press.

Roure, Marie-Louise Roure (1970), 'La problématique des propositions insolubles au XIIIe siècle et au début du XIVe, suivie de l'édition des traités de W. Shyreswood, W. Burleigh et Th. Bradwardine. *Archives d'Histoire Doctrinale et Littérature du Moyen Âge*, 37:262–84.

Sherwood, William of (1966), *Introduction to Logic*, trans. Norman Ktetzmann, Minneapolis: University of Minnesota Press.

Sherwood, William of (2012), *Syncategoremata*, ed. and trans C. Kann and R. Kirchhoff, Hamburg: Meiner.

Spade, Paul V. (1975), 'The mediaeval liar: A catalogue of the *Insolubilia*-literature', *Subsidia Mediaevalia*, 5.

Spade, Paul V. (1977), 'Roger Swyneshed's *Obligationes*: Edition and comments', *Archives d'Histoire Doctrinale et Littéraire du Moyen Âge*, 44:243–85.

Spade, Paul V. (1978), 'Richard Lavenham's *Obligationes*: Edition and comments', *Rivista Critica di Storia della Filosofia*, 33:224–41.

Spade, Paul V. (1979), 'Roger Swyneshed's *insolubilia*: edition and comments', *Archives d'histoire doctrinale et littéraire du Moyen Âge*, 46:177–220.

Spade, Paul V. (1987), 'Five early theories in the medieval *Insolubilia*-literature', *Vivarium*, 25:24–46.

Spade, Paul V. and Stephen Read (2009), 'Insolubles', in E.N. Zalta, ed., *Stanford Encyclopedia of Philosophy*. Winter edition, Stanford: Stanford University Press, http://plato.stanford.edu/archives/win2009/entries/insolubles/.

Spade, Paul V. and Gordon A. Wilson, eds (1995), '*Richard Brinkley's* Obligationes: *A Late Fourteenth Century Treatise on the Logic of Disputation*', vol. 43 of *Beiträge zur Geschichte der Philosophie und Theologie des Mittelalters, neue Folge*. Muünster: Aschendorff.

Strobino, Riccardo (2009), 'Concedere, negare, dubitare: Peter of Mantua's Treatise on Obligations', PhD thesis, Scuola Normale Superiore, Pisa.

Strodus, Radolphus (1493), *Consequentiae cum Commento Alexandri Sermonetae et Declarationibus Getnai de Thienis*, Venice: Bonetus Locatellus.

Stump, Eleonore (1982), 'Obligations: From the beginning to the early fourteenth century', in Norman Kretzmann, Anthony Kenny and Jan Pinborg, eds, *Cambridge History of Later Medieval Philosophy*, pp. 315–34, Cambridge: Cambridge University Press.

Uckelman, Sara L. (2011), 'Deceit and indefeasible knowledge: The case of *Dubitatio*', *Journal of Applied Non-Classical Logics*, 21, nos. 3/4:503–19.

Uckelman, Sara L. (2012), 'Interactive logic in the Middle Ages', *Logic and Logical Philosophy*, 21(3):439–71.

Uckelman, Sara L. (2013), 'A quantified temporal logic for ampliation and restriction', *Vivarium*, 51(1):485–510.

Uckelman, Sara L. (2015), '*Sit Verum Obligationes* and counterfactual reasoning', *Vivarium*, 53(1):90–113.

Uckelman, Sara L., Jaap Maat and Katherina Rybalko (forthcoming), 'The art of doubting in *Obligationes Parisienses*', in C. Kann, C. Rode and S.L. Uckelman, eds, *Modern Views of Medieval Logic*, Leuven: Peeters.

Venice, Paul of (1988), *Logica Magna Part* II *Fascicule 8*, ed. E.J. Ashworth, Oxford: Oxford University Press.

Wesel, John of (1996), 'Three questions by John of Wesel on *obligationes* and *insolubilia*', ed. with an introduction and notes by Paul Vincent Spade, http://pvspade.com/Logic/docs/wesel.pdf.

Wilson, Curtis (1956), *William Heytesbury: Medieval Logic and the Rise of Mathematical Physics*, Madison: University of Wisconsin Press.

Yrjönsuuri, M. (ed.) (2001), *Medieval Formal Logic*. Dordrecht: Kluwer Academic Publishers.

Part II

The Early Modern Period

4

Leibniz

Jaap Maat

1 Introduction

Gottfried Wilhelm Leibniz (1646–1716) was a polymath who made significant contributions to a number of disciplines. In the history of mathematics, Leibniz is primarily remembered as one of the inventors of the infinitesimal calculus. In the history of philosophy, he occupies a canonical place as one of the great seventeenth-century rationalists. In the history of logic, his importance is uncontested, although the evaluation of his achievements has differed considerably from one historian of logic to another. In the present chapter, a necessarily somewhat sketchy overview of Leibniz's work on logic is provided. After considering his place in the history of logic, his efforts to systematize syllogistics are discussed. Next, a central idea that guided his work is described, namely the ideal of a philosophical language based upon an alphabet of human thoughts. Finally, several projects closely related to this ideal are examined in some detail: the arithmetization of logical inference, the creation of logical calculi, and rational grammar.

2 Leibniz as a logician

In their classic history of logic, the Kneales called Leibniz 'one of the greatest logicians of all time', while criticizing his work so severely that they admitted this epithet might seem surprising (Kneale and Kneale 1962: 336). In their view, Leibniz had gone wrong on crucial points, but his greatness as a logician was apparent in that he was the first to devise an abstract calculus that was open to several interpretations. The Kneales were echoing an evaluation of Leibniz's work first put forward by Couturat, who published a comprehensive and still valuable account of Leibniz's logic in 1901. Couturat likewise praised Leibniz for his logical ingenuity, while finding fault with many of his results: Leibniz wrongly preferred the intensional view of the proposition over the extensional one (more on this below), and failed to see that subalternation, that is, a type of inference from universal to particular propositions (e.g. 'all A are B, therefore some A are B') is invalid. These mistakes, in Couturat's view, were due to Leibniz's excessive admiration for Aristotle, which prevented him from developing the insights that later logicians such as Boole were able to formulate.

In the course of the twentieth century, several historians have evaluated Leibniz's work in logic much more positively (e.g. Rescher 1954, Kauppi 1960). Recently, Lenzen (2004a, 2004b) has argued most forcefully for the sophistication of Leibniz's logical work, and claimed that 160 years before Boole, Leibniz had worked out a full 'Boolean' algebra of sets.

There are several reasons why historians have reached such diverse conclusions not only about the merits but also about the content of Leibniz's logical work. One of these is that writers like Couturat and the Kneales were perhaps too prone to use more recent theories and achievements as a yardstick against which Leibniz's work was measured. Another reason is the rather chaotic state of Leibniz's papers. He published very little on logic, but wrote a large number of texts on the subject. Very few of these were ready, or even intended, for publication. Many papers are filled with tentative notes; others are longer pieces in which various lines of investigation are pursued. Together, these papers provide a treasure trove full of intriguing ideas and analyses, but it often requires quite some interpretative work to distil unambiguous viewpoints and results from them. Thus, it could happen that whereas some commentators found evidence of a logician vainly struggling to free himself from traditional misconceptions, others found striking results that had previously been ascribed to logicians working in later centuries.

Apart from the question to what extent modern insights and results are present in Leibniz's logical papers, it may be asked how, if at all, Leibniz's work has contributed to the development of modern logic. It is uncontroversial that Leibniz was an eminent logician, but it has often been claimed that this fact has gone unnoticed for centuries. As Parkinson remarked, Leibniz was the first symbolic logician, but 'he cannot be called the founder of symbolic logic', because most of his writings were only published after symbolic logic had been independently established by others in the nineteenth century (Leibniz 1966: lix). In fact, when Couturat edited his collection of Leibniz's unpublished logical papers in 1903, he was convinced that he had unearthed entirely unknown aspects of Leibniz's work on logic. Although Couturat had good reasons to believe this, it is certain that most logicians working in the nineteenth century, with the exception of Boole, were familiar with Leibniz's work through an edition by Erdmann (1840), which contained a limited sample of logical papers. Frege, for one, knew these papers very well, and his 'Begriffschift' (1879) derived some of its inspiration from Leibniz's ideal of a philosophical language. Yet, according to Peckhaus (2009), Leibniz's work did not exert any influence on the emergence of mathematical logic as such.

In order to understand the place of Leibniz in the history of logic, it is of course insufficient to look only at later developments, of which Leibniz could have no knowledge. It will also be necessary to put his work in the context of his own time, and compare it with that of contemporaries and predecessors. A general point about the context in which Leibniz worked is that the seventeenth century was not the most stimulating period for a logician to be working in. Logic was probably a more widely known subject than it is today, because it formed a standard ingredient of every educated man's knowledge. Textbooks on logic proliferated in the sixteenth and seventeenth centuries, but they all rehearsed roughly the same body of traditional learning, which was increasingly regarded as useless. Some of the most influential philosophers of the period, such as Bacon, Descartes and Locke, explicitly denounced the logic of the schools as obsolete, and even detrimental to clear thinking and scientific progress. Although Leibniz was not the only one to defend logic against such attacks, his view of the value of logic was quite uncommon. Against Locke's contention that little would be lost if Aristotelian logic were abolished, he maintained that the invention of the syllogistic form was among the most important ones ever made by the human mind, because it included an 'art of infallibility' (Nouveaux Essais IV, xvii, § 4).

What Leibniz perceived was that algebra, geometry and logic shared a characteristic that he considered to be of the greatest value, namely that they used formal patterns of reasoning that enabled one to draw conclusions concerning all the particular instances covered by their equations and theorems, and that this could be done in mechanical fashion once the patterns were established. Logic was the most general discipline in this regard, 'a kind of universal mathematics'. Syllogistic form, in Leibniz's view, was only one among many forms of logical inference. Convinced that the elaboration and expansion of these forms would help advance science enormously, he pursued his ideal of mathematizing logic throughout his life. As Leibniz's view of logic was shared by few if any of his contemporaries, he worked mostly in isolation. The seventeenth century was a period in which the prestige of mathematics increased, with many new developments taking place in the field, natural science being put on a mathematical footing, and philosophers such as Spinoza expounding their systems in geometrical fashion. But Leibniz was probably the only person in his time who envisaged, and worked towards, a close connection between mathematics and logic.

3 Systematizing syllogistics

Although Leibniz viewed syllogisms as only part of the grander logic he envisaged, he devoted considerable time and effort to investigating syllogistic theory. The first results of this are found in one of the few pieces on logic he ever published, in certain passages of *A Dissertation on the Art of Combinations* (DAC, 1666, G IV 27–104), written as a student thesis when he was nineteen years old. This tract was organized around a large number of 'uses' or applications of the mathematical theory of combinations and permutations. Although the uses pertained to various fields, ranging from law to geometry and logic, Leibniz described all these uses as instances of 'the logic of invention'. It is in one of the uses of this combinatorial logic of invention that a systematic treatment of syllogistics is found. The problem Leibniz set himself was to determine the number of valid types of syllogisms. In answering it, he proceeded by steps, employing combinatorics and traditional rules for the syllogism in turn.

The actual procedure he used was not the most simple, and a short description of it may serve to give an impression of Leibniz's tract on combinations. Leibniz started out by distinguishing four possible quantities a proposition may have, namely universal, particular, singular and indefinite. He combined these in groups of three, as in each syllogism three propositions occur. Next, he sorted out which of the sixty-four resulting combinations may give rise to a valid syllogism, using such rules as 'from pure particulars nothing follows', which left thirty-two 'useful' moods. Subsequently, he combined these with the useful moods with respect to the two qualities, affirmative (A) and negative (N), of which there are only three, namely A A A (both premises and the conclusion affirmative), N A N, and A N N, resulting in thirty-two times three, which equals ninety-six useful moods. He then applied rules that apply to specific figures. Of the ninety-six useful moods, eight turned out to be valid in none of the four figures. This left eighty-eight useful moods, which Leibniz further reduced by giving up the distinction of four quantities he had started out with. He now equated singular propositions to universal ones, and indefinite propositions to particular ones, so that ultimately only universal and particular propositions remained. This rather roundabout procedure resulted in the identification of twenty-four types of valid syllogisms, neatly divided into six types in each of the four figures.

That combinatorics has a role to play in determining the number of valid syllogisms was as obvious in Leibniz's time as it is now. For example, a similar, though different procedure can be found, in the Port Royal logic (Arnauld and Nicole 1662, part 3, ch. 4). However, there was no consensus on the exact number of valid syllogisms when Leibniz wrote this. Contemporary authors held different views, some wishing to exclude subalternate moods such as Barbari and Celaront (Arnauld and Nicole part 3, ch. 3, rule 2, corollary 4), and others denying that the fourth figure should be regarded as a genuine figure at all (Sanderson 1672 part 3, ch. 4; Wallis 1687, part 3, ch. 9). Leibniz insisted, also in later writings, that the fourth figure is as legitimate as the other three.

Leibniz returned to syllogistics several times in later years, since he was interested in providing it with a solid theoretical foundation. Among his papers is one that is devoted to the so-called reduction of syllogistic moods. It was a topic already treated by Aristotle, who was concerned to show that all valid syllogistic forms are reducible to the four 'perfect' syllogisms of the first figure that were afterwards labeled Barbara, Celarent, Darii and Ferio, whose validity he assumed to be self-evident. Leibniz proposed a similar way of proving the validity of syllogistic forms, but systematizing the procedure. He first showed that the four perfect syllogisms derive their certainty from an axiom of 'no less geometrical certainty than if it were said that that which contains a whole contains a part of the whole' (P 106), and which was known from scholastic times as 'the dictum de omni et nullo'. It says that whatever is affirmed or denied of the members of a class is also affirmed or denied of the members of a subclass of that class. Now this is what is expressed, as far as the affirmative part goes, by Barbara and Darii, for the whole or part of a subclass respectively, and similarly in the negative case by Celarent and Ferio. As a next step, Leibniz proved subalternation by means of Darii, and the 'identical' statement 'some A is A', assumed to be self-evidently true, as follows: 'Every A is B, some A is A, therefore, some A is B.' He proved the negative case in a similar way by means of Ferio: 'No A is B, some A is A, therefore some A is not B'. Once subalternation was proved, two further moods of the first figure could be derived: Barbari and Celaro, in which a particular conclusion replaces, by subalternation, the universal ones of Barbara and Celarent, respectively.

Having thus established six moods in the first figure, Leibniz derived from each of these a valid mood in the second, and a valid mood in the third figure, using a single principle, which he called 'regress'. It was traditionally also known as 'reductio per impossibile', and was used by Aristotle. It works by assuming that the conclusion of a valid syllogism is false and demonstrating that on this assumption one of the premises must be false as well. Thus, assuming that the conclusion of a syllogism in Barbara is false and its major premise is true, it follows that the minor must be false. Replacing the false propositions by their respective contradictories and interchanging the minor and the conclusion results in a valid syllogism of the second figure, Baroco: from 'Every C is D, every B is C, therefore every B is D' (Barbara) results 'Every C is D, some B is not D (contradictory of the conclusion), therefore some B is not C (contradictory of the minor) (Baroco). Analogously, a syllogism of the third figure Bocardo is derived by assuming the conclusion and the major premise, rather than the minor, of a syllogism in Barbara to be false. This procedure applied to each of the six moods of the first figure, so that all six valid moods in the second, and all six valid moods in the third figure could be derived.

Leibniz's point in proposing this procedure was to show that a uniform method could be used for deriving all the valid moods of the second and third figure. Furthermore, he maintained that it was the best method of proof, as it was synthetic rather than analytic, which meant that it contained 'the method by which they could have been discovered' (P 110). However, the tidy systematicity of the procedure did not extend to the moods of the fourth figure, the derivation of which requires the principle of conversion (e.g. 'No A is B, therefore no B is A') that Leibniz had been able to avoid so far. In sum, Leibniz systematized the meta-theory of syllogistics, taking the dictum de omni et nullo as an axiom, and using identical propositions, subalternation, the method of regress, which as he noted presupposes the principle of contradiction, and finally conversion as further principles to prove the validity of syllogistic moods in all four figures. All these principles were traditional, except the use of 'identical' propositions, which Leibniz employed in proving principles such as subalternation and conversion that were usually taken for granted without proof. This use of identical propositions was, as Leibniz noted, invented by Peter Ramus (Couturat 1901: 8; G IV 55).

A further example of Leibniz's efforts to investigate the theoretical basis of syllogistics is found in a paper entitled 'A Mathematics of Reason' (P 95–104). Again, he used insights that had been developed by logicians working before him, but aiming at a more rigorous treatment. In this case, it was the theory of the distribution of terms that Leibniz took as a starting point. Medieval logicians had observed that in categorical propositions some terms are 'distributed', and others are 'undistributed', meaning that only a distributed term applies to every individual belonging to the class denoted by the term. Thus, in a universal affirmative proposition such as 'All horses are animals' the term 'horse' is distributed, whereas the term 'animal' is not, since the proposition is about every individual horse, but not about every individual animal. On the basis of this criterion, it can be established that subject terms in universal propositions and predicate terms in negative propositions are distributed. The distribution of terms lay at the basis of several rules that could be used as a test for the validity of a syllogism; for example, in every valid syllogism, the middle term should be distributed in at least one of the premises. In 'A Mathematics of Reason', Leibniz called distributed terms 'universal' and undistributed terms 'particular'. He discussed the traditional rules concerning distribution, providing a justification for them: for example, if the middle term is particular (i.e. undistributed) in both premises, nothing can be concluded from the premises, because there is no guarantee that the same individuals are denoted by both occurrences of the middle term in each premise. He also enumerated and explained a series of other rules and observations, such as 'if the conclusion is a universal affirmative, the syllogism must be in the first figure', and 'in the second figure, the major proposition is universal and the conclusion negative', all of which he could justify on the basis of principles and corollaries he had proved first. It is clear, however, that, just as with the reduction of syllogistic moods, Leibniz was working within a traditional framework, and putting forward results that for the most part were already known.

By contrast, a third example of Leibniz's concern with syllogistics constituted a distinctive novelty. In a further attempt to assimilate logic to geometry, he employed diagrams of various sorts in representing the four traditional types of proposition. At first, he used circles to represent the subject and predicate terms, and made the way they did or did not overlap indicate the quality and quantity of the proposition. Similar circles are usually called Venn diagrams today, but it was Leibniz who introduced their use as a graphical representation of terms and their interrelations. A second type of diagram that Leibniz devised consisted of parallel horizontal lines representing terms, with their overlap in a vertical direction indicating how the terms were related. For example, a universal affirmative proposition was represented by a horizontal line symbolizing the predicate term, while the subject term was symbolized by a shorter parallel line drawn under it and nowhere extending beyond the longer line. Thus, it could be read off from the diagram that the subject term and the predicate term coincided in part. By adding a third line, an entire syllogism could be represented by this means, and the validity of an inference from the premises was made apparent by the resulting diagram.

4 Combinatorics, the alphabet of human thoughts and the philosophical language

Leibniz's tract on combinations contained discussion of a further logical topic that he himself considered so important that he mentioned it in retrospect as one of the main reasons why this otherwise immature work was still valuable. This topic was 'the alphabet of human thoughts' – an idea that was linked to a line of thinking that can be found with numerous philosophers from Plato to Descartes. It entailed, roughly, that everything we know and think can be broken down into smaller units. Just as sentences are composed of words, and words consist of letters or speech sounds, so is the thought expressed by a sentence composed of ideas. Ideas themselves can be analysed into components, which in their turn can be analysed. But analysis cannot go on for ever; it must stop where it reaches primitives: simple notions that have no component parts. Leibniz assumed that a class of such ideas exists, and this is what he called 'the alphabet of human thoughts'. He made it a guiding principle for many of his logical investigations.

He derived the idea from his study of logic textbooks when he was still a boy. He noticed that such textbooks were usually organized according to increasing levels of complexity: they started with the treatment of terms, presenting them as belonging to a hierarchical scheme of categories called genus and species, proceeded to propositions, i.e. combinations of terms, and concluded with syllogisms, i.e. combinations of propositions. But it did not seem to be transparent how the levels were connected; in particular, it was unclear how complex terms, i.e. propositions, were connected to syllogisms, since propositions were not divided into categories as simple terms were. On further thought, he realized that the connection between the level of terms and the level of propositions was unclear as well, and that the categories of simple terms also needed revision.

Thus, in the tract on combinations he proposed to reorganize the theory of terms altogether, using combinatorial principles for a new arrangement, so that terms were classified on the basis of the number of terms of which they are composed. There would be a first class of primitive notions, a second class containing concepts resulting from combinations of two primitives, a third class of concepts in which three primitives are involved, and so on. Supposing that such a classification is given, it would become possible to produce a list of all the terms that could be a predicate in a true proposition with the given term as subject, as well as a list of terms which could be the subject of a true proposition with the given term as predicate. To illustrate this, let us arbitrarily assume that there are only four primitive notions: a, b, c, d. Then there are four classes in all, containing the following concepts:

class I: a, b, c, d
class II: ab, ac, ad, bc, bd, cd
class III: abc, abd, acd, bcd
class IV: abcd

For every complex term, it can be determined which terms can be predicated of it so as to form a true, universal proposition. For example, the term 'ab' has 'a', 'b' and 'ab' as such predicates, for 'ab is a', 'ab is b', and 'ab is ab' are all true propositions. If the same term 'ab' occurs as a predicate, the combination with the terms 'ab', 'abc', 'abd', and 'abcd' in subject position yields a true proposition, as for example 'abc is ab' is true. Leibniz also gave rules for determining the subjects and predicates of a given term in particular and negative propositions. On analysis, these rules turn out to be inconsistent (Kauppi 1960: 143–4; Maat 2004: 281ff.). Leibniz probably saw this eventually; he did not pursue this particular idea of computing the number of subjects and predicates in later writings. But he did not give up the general principles on which it relied.

These principles are, first, that all concepts result ultimately from the combination of simpler concepts and that the entire edifice of knowledge is based upon, and reducible to a set of primitive unanalysable concepts, the alphabet of human thoughts. Secondly, it is assumed that in a true affirmative proposition the predicate is contained in the subject, as shown in the examples 'ab is a' and 'abc is ab'. This latter principle is what is called the intensional view of the proposition. On this view, a proposition expresses a relation between concepts, such that in a true proposition 'All A is B' the concept of the subject A contains the concept of the predicate B. According to the alternative, extensional, view, a proposition expresses a relation between classes or sets; a proposition such as 'All As are Bs' is true if the class denoted by B contains the class denoted by A. Leibniz preferred the intensional view, for several reasons. First, it fitted quite well with the classification of concepts according to combinatorial complexity. Thus, the truth of the proposition 'man is rational' can be proved by replacing the term 'man' by its definition, consisting of supposedly simpler concepts, namely 'rational animal'. After this substitution, the proposition reads 'rational animal is rational', which shows on the surface that the concept of the predicate 'rational' is identical to part of the concept of the subject 'man'. This type of proof relied on two principles that Leibniz later formulated explicitly in a number of papers. First, the law of substitutivity, according to which two terms or expressions are the same if they can be substituted for the other without affecting truth. Secondly, the 'law of identity', expressed as 'A is A', or in some equivalent form, which became an indispensable axiom in his logical calculi. A second reason why Leibniz preferred the intensional view is that he did not want logic to be dependent on the existence of individuals. As he put it in a paper of 1679, he rather considered 'universal concepts, i.e. ideas, and their combinations', apparently because in this way he was dealing with propositions that can be true or false regardless of whether individuals exist to which the concepts it contains are applicable.

A choice between the intensional and the extensional view of the proposition was not of particular importance in Leibniz's view, because he believed that the two were ultimately equivalent, and that results obtained within the intensional perspective could be expressed in extensional terms, and vice versa, by 'some kind of inversion' (P 20). He noted that the extension and intension of terms are systematically related: the more individuals a term is applicable to, i.e. the greater its extension, the fewer parts its concept contains, i.e. the smaller its intension. For example, the term 'animal' has greater extension but smaller intension than the term 'man'. Evaluating the proposition 'every man is an animal' can be done in two equivalent ways: either by checking whether the intension of 'animal' is contained in the intension of 'man', or by checking whether the extension of 'man' is contained in the extension of 'animal'. This relationship between the intension and extension of terms has been called the 'law of reciprocity'. It may seem a questionable principle, because it entails that if two terms have the same intension, they also have the same extension. Now this seems to be false for numerous pairs of terms, such as terms that are coextensive (have the same extension) but differ in meaning (have different intension) such as 'creature with a heart' and 'creature with a kidney'. However, Leibniz wished to consider not just individuals that in fact exist, but all possible individuals, assuming that if two terms differ in intension, there would be a possible individual to which only one of the two terms applies. Conversely, if such an individual is impossible, this proves that the two terms have the same intension after all.

Leibniz's views concerning knowledge (as ultimately derived from simple notions) and truth (as consisting in a relation between concepts and provable through analysis by means of definitions) were intimately connected with a scheme he first sketched in his tract on combinations, and which he pursued for the rest of his life. This was the construction of an artificial language that he believed would have extremely beneficial effects: it would be a reliable tool for thinking, so that by its means human knowledge and science could be enhanced at a pace previously unheard of.

Quite a few seventeenth-century philosophers were preoccupied with searching for means to advance science. They usually sought the solution in developing new methods of research. Leibniz, by contrast, believed that the construction of a new symbolism was crucial for the improvement of science. He was not altogether unique in this respect, as schemes for artificial or 'philosophical' (i.e., roughly, scientific) languages were widespread in the period, with their authors often claiming far-reaching advantages for their inventions. Two of the most fully developed schemes of this kind were created in England, by Dalgarno (1661) and Wilkins (1668), who claimed that the languages they had constructed were more logical and more philosophical than existing languages. Leibniz studied their schemes carefully, and used the vocabularies and grammar of their languages in preliminary studies for his own project. Nevertheless, he was convinced that neither Dalgarno nor Wilkins had perceived what a truly logical and philosophical language could accomplish. Such a language would not only be a means for communication, and not just an instrument for the accurate representation of knowledge, both of which characteristics were realized to some extent by the English artificial languages, but it would first of all be a tool for making new discoveries, and for checking the correctness of inferences. This logical language famously made it possible to decide controversies by translating conflicting opinions into it; for this purpose, participants in a debate would sit down together and say 'let's calculate' (G VII 200). Thus, Leibniz's scheme included the construction of an encyclopedia encompassing all existing knowledge, as well as a fully general logical calculus that would comprise all sorts of logical inferences, including but not limited to syllogistic ones. Leibniz worked towards the achievement of these goals throughout his life. He produced numerous lists of definitions, which were apparently intended for use in the encyclopedia. He also drafted many versions of a logical calculus, and he wrote a number of papers on rational grammar, investigating how existing languages express logical relationships. The next two sections provide a brief description of some of the logical calculi, and of rational grammar, respectively.

5 The logical calculi

Leibniz drafted outlines of logical calculi in a considerable number of papers, written over a long period of time. He often started afresh, and obtained results that sometimes differed from, and sometimes overlapped with previous ones. By the term 'calculus' he meant various things; he used the term to refer to a coherent series of axioms and theorems, but also to a method of providing an arithmetical model for logical inferences. We will discuss examples of both types of calculus, starting with the latter.

5.1 The arithmetization of logical inference

In a series of papers written in 1679 (P 17–32), Leibniz explored the possibility of interpreting the terms of categorical propositions by means of numbers. The purpose of this was to reduce logical inferences to arithmetical calculations, so that all reasoning would have the same perspicuity and certainty as arithmetic.

In a first attempt, Leibniz equated the combination of terms into more complex ones with multiplication; for example, just as the term 'man' results from combining the terms 'rational' and animal', so does multiplication of two and three make six. By assigning a unique, 'characteristic' number to each term in such a way that the number of a complex term is equal to the product of the component terms, determining the truth of a proposition would come down to a simple calculation: in the example just given the truth of 'man is rational' would appear from the fact that six, for 'man', is divisible by three, for 'rational'. This shows that 'rational' is part of the concept 'man', that the predicate is contained in the subject, and hence that the proposition is true. The assignment of characteristic numbers to terms would also have to be such that if of two terms neither contains the other, their respective numbers are not divisible: the truth of the proposition 'no ape is a man' would be clear, for example, if the number for 'man' would be six, and that for 'ape' would be ten.

Leibniz perceived that this system could not work, for it seemed impossible to account for particular affirmative (PA) propositions. He tried several methods of providing a model for these. First, he assumed it would be sufficient for a PA proposition to be true if either the number of the subject term were divisible by the number of the predicate term (making the universal affirmative (UA), and hence also the PA true) or the number of the predicate term were divisible by the subject term. On further thought, this did not seem satisfactory, probably because only terms related as genus and species could be accounted for in this way. Thus, he tried a second method, requiring that for a PA proposition 'some A is B' to be true, there should be numbers r and v such that the product of r and the number for A (call this A) equals the product of v and the number for B (call this B): rA = vB. This turned out to be even less satisfactory, as on this model all affirmative particular propositions are true (choose B for r and A for v), and consequently all universal negative (UN) propositions are false, rendering the model useless for Leibniz's purposes (Glashoff 2002: 174).

Leibniz soon devised a more sophisticated system, in which each term was assigned an ordered pair of natural numbers, such that the numbers were prime with respect to each other. Although each number was preceded by a plus sign or a minus sign, the system did not rely on a distinction between positive and negative numbers; the signs functioned merely as indicators of the first and second member of a pair. For a UA proposition to be true it was now required (and sufficient) that the first number of the subject term was divisible by the first number of the predicate term, and the second number of the subject term was divisible by the second number of the predicate term. On this model, a UN proposition is true if, and only if, either the first number of the subject and the second number of the predicate or the second number of the subject and the first number of the predicate have a common divisor. For example, 'No pious man is unhappy' can be shown to be true if the numbers for 'pious man' and 'unhappy' are +10 −3 and +5 −14, respectively, because 10 and 14 have 2 as a common divisor. The condition for PA propositions, which are contradictories of UN propositions, follows from this: they are true if no such common divisor exists. Similarly, PN propositions are true if the condition for the truth of the corresponding UA proposition is not fulfilled. With this model, all the problems that were connected with earlier attempts had been solved.

In the 1950s, Łukasiewicz showed that Leibniz's arithmetical interpretation of syllogistic logic is sound in that it satisfies Lukasiewicz's axioms (1957: 126–129). Leibniz intended this interpretation also to work for modal and hypothetical syllogisms, but he did not proceed to investigate this further. He knew that the arithmetical calculus was only a modest step towards his ultimate goal, the philosophical language. This was because the calculus showed that if number pairs were chosen according to certain rules, it would be possible to test the validity of inferences by means of a calculation. But the philosophical language could not be achieved until the characteristic number pairs for each term had been definitively established – and that was a colossal task he had not even begun to undertake. Recently, Leibniz's calculus has inspired logicians to do further research on arithmetical interpretations of syllogistic logic (Glashoff 2002; van Rooij 2014).

5.2 The calculus in the General Inquiries

In a lengthy piece called 'General Inquiries about the Analysis of Concepts and of Truths' (1686, P 47–87), Leibniz treated a number of subjects, which he clearly saw as all connected. Thus, he examined several ways of classifying types of terms, sought definitions of the terms 'true' and 'false', and tried to find an account of the meaning of the terms 'exist' and 'possible'. In the course of these investigations, he formulated a series of principles, which together were meant to constitute a universal logical calculus. Similar attempts at establishing such principles are found in a large number of other texts. From the 1980s onward, Lenzen has produced a number of analyses of these texts, showing that one can extract several logical calculi of diverse expressive power from them. Leibniz's 'General Inquiries' thus turns out to contain, if supplemented with a few principles expressed elsewhere, a system that Lenzen has called L1, which he has shown to be an algebra of concepts that is isomorphic to a Boolean algebra of sets. In this chapter, we can only give an impression of what this looks like, relying on Lenzen 2004a (ch. 3) and Lenzen 2004b.

The calculus that Lenzen has called L1 consists of the following main elements. The left-most column contains names of the elements given by Lenzen, and the second column Leibniz's formulation. The third column states the corresponding set-theoretical interpretation, where φ(A) denotes the set of possible individuals that the function φ assigns to the concept letter A. The fourth column contains Lenzen's notation.

Elements of L1	Leibniz	Set-theoretical Interpretation	Lenzen's Notation
Identity	A = B, coincidunt A et B	$\phi(A) = \phi(B)$	A = B
Containment	A est B, A continet B	$\phi(A) \subseteq \phi(B)$	A ∈ B
Converse containment	A inest ipsi B	$\phi(B) \subseteq \phi(A)$	AιB
Conjunction	AB, A + B, A ⊕ B	$\phi(A) \cap \phi(B)$	AB
Negation	Non-A	$\overline{\phi(A)}$	$\overline{A}$
Possibility	A est ens, A est res, A est possibile	$\phi(A) \neq \varnothing$	P(A)

Using these elements, Leibniz formulated a series of principles, which can all be interpreted as stating basic set-theoretical laws. The following is a sample of these principles (in Lenzen's notation, 'I(A)' symbolizes impossibility or inconsistency of A):

Laws of L1	Leibniz	Lenzen's Notation
(1)	B is B	$A \in A$
(2)	If A is B and B is C, A will be C	$A \in B \wedge B \in C \rightarrow A \in C$
(3)	That A contains B and A contains C is the same as that A contains BC	$A \in BC \leftrightarrow A \in B \wedge A \in C$
(4)	Not-not-A = A	$\overline{\overline{A}} = A$
(5)	If I say 'A not-B is not', this is the same as if I were to say 'A contains B'	$I(A\overline{B}) \leftrightarrow A \in B$
(6)	If A contains B and A is true, B is also true	$A \in B \wedge P(A) \rightarrow P(B)$

As Lenzen has shown (2004a, ch. 3), the principles (1) to (6) together provide a complete axiomatization of Boolean algebra. For discussion of Lenzen's results, see Burkhardt 2009.

6 Rational grammar

Leibniz's efforts in developing a formal calculus were for the most part driven by his ideal of a philosophical language, of which such a calculus would form a central element. In constructing his calculi, he usually took the traditional forms of the categorical proposition as a starting point. But he realized from an early stage onward – there is a hint of this already in the tract on combinations – that the patterns studied in traditional logic, even if not only categorical but also hypothetical, disjunctive and modal propositions were included, did not exhaust the possible forms of logically valid inference. As he put it in a piece called 'A Plan for a New Encyclopedia' (1679, A VI 4 A, 344): 'very frequently there occur inferences in logic that are to be proved not on the basis of logical principles, but on the basis of grammatical principles, that is, on the basis of the signification of inflections and particles.' In order to identify and analyse the grammatical principles involved, a thorough investigation of natural languages was called for, since these languages consist of the 'symbols that human kind in general uses in speaking and also in thinking'. Rather than rejecting existing languages as defective and illogical, Leibniz thus undertook to investigate them with a view to extracting the logical principles they embody.

Leibniz devoted a fairly large number of papers to rational grammar, none of which were published during his lifetime, and most of which were only published in full recently (A VI 4, 1999); some of them are still unpublished. In conducting his studies of language in the context of rational grammar, Leibniz understandably took traditional grammatical theory as a starting point. Thus, he investigated the 'parts of speech' or word classes, asking himself what function they have in the expression of thought.

A first result of this was that most word classes seemed superfluous. Verbs, for example, proved to be composed of a single necessary element, the copula 'is', and a noun, either adjective or substantive, or participle. Instead of 'I love' one can equivalently say 'I am loving'. In the latter expression, the verb 'love' has been resolved into the copula 'am', and the participle 'loving', which is the predicate of the proposition. This analysis of the verb was quite common among grammarians at the time, especially those concerned with philosophical or rational grammar, such as Wilkins and the Port Royal grammar. Turning to substantives, Leibniz found that they can be resolved into a combination of the single substantive 'thing, being' (res, ens) with an adjective of some sort: for example, 'gold' is 'a yellow, heavy, malleable thing'. Although adverbs are less easily reduced to other types of expressions, Leibniz observed that they often function in the same way as adjectives do. This led him to conclude that 'everything in discourse can be resolved into the noun substantive Being or Thing, the copula or the substantive verb is, adjective nouns, and formal particles.'

It is tempting to view this drastic simplification of the grammar of natural languages as an attempt to squeeze all sentence types into the mould of the subject–predicate proposition, so that they would become more manageable for both traditional logic and the logic that Leibniz was developing. Although there is some justification for this view, the importance of the last item on Leibniz's short list of indispensable types of expressions should not be overlooked, namely the 'formal particles'. These included prepositions, conjunctions, certain adverbs, and pronouns. Words of this type were called 'formal', as opposed to the 'material' words such as adjectives, as they signify operations, relations and inferences rather than concepts or things and their properties. Again, Leibniz was following a long-standing tradition in using the distinction between material and formal words. The specific approach he took to the analysis of formal particles, however, sets his rational grammar apart from his contemporaries and most of his predecessors (except for some medieval grammatical treatises), as his analysis was primarily aimed at determining the logical characteristics of these particles, such as the inferential patterns they signal.

Unlike words belonging to the other word classes, the particles required individual treatment in rational grammar. Thus, Leibniz devoted considerable effort to the description of the meaning of a large number of prepositions, (grammatical) conjunctions and pronouns, usually from the perspective of logical inference. For example, about the preposition 'with' he noted: 'if A is with B, it follows that B is with A' (A VI 4 A, 647).

About 'if . . . then' he observed: 'If I say If L is true it follows that M is true, the meaning is, that it cannot be simultaneously supposed that L is true and M is false. And this is the true Analysis of If and of It follows' (A VI 4 A, 656).

Leibniz examined not only the conjunctions that were familiar candidates for logical analysis, such as 'if . . . then', but also words like 'although' and 'nevertheless':

> Although the teacher is diligent, yet the student is ignorant. The sense of this is: the teacher is diligent, from which it seems to follow that the student is not ignorant, but the conclusion is false, because the student is ignorant . . . It is clear from this that 'although' and 'yet' involve some relation to the mind, or that they are reflexive.
>
> A VI 4 A, 656

The observation that some words, or, as he noted elsewhere, notions, or propositions, or utterances, are 'reflexive' occurs repeatedly in Leibniz's papers. Reflexivity in this sense is one of the characteristics of natural languages that showed the need for an expansion of logic. For the contexts created by 'reflexive' expressions are ones in which the law of substitutivity does not seem to hold. A word frequently used by Leibniz to indicate that such a context is present is 'quatenus' – 'in so far as'. It is used in the following example, in which substitutivity is blocked: the expressions 'Peter' (proper name of the apostle) and 'the apostle who denied Christ' can be substituted for each other, unless they occur in the context created by the reflexive word 'in so far as': the sentence 'Peter, in so far as he was the apostle who denied Christ, sinned', cannot, without affecting the truth of the sentence, be replaced by: 'Peter, in so far as he was Peter, sinned' (A VI 4 A, 552).

Reflexivity proved to be a pervasive aspect of natural languages, as it is present in all expressions containing grammatical cases (such as genitive and accusative). Cases other than the nominative were called 'oblique' cases; Leibniz accordingly called combinations of terms in which such cases are involved 'oblique'. For example, in the expression 'manus hominis', 'the hand of a man', the term 'man' enters obliquely into the expression, which is indicated by the genitive case. Such an expression is clearly different from 'direct' combinations of terms, such as 'rational animal', because unlike the latter it cannot be treated as a conjunction of the terms 'hand' and 'man'. Put differently, what 'the hand of a man' refers to is not the intersection of the set of all hands and the set of all men. Such combinations of terms thus had to be accounted for in a way different from what either syllogistics or Leibniz's own logical calculi such as the one called L1 by Lenzen (cf. section 5 above) could provide.

Leibniz's rational grammar, unsurprisingly, remained uncompleted.

References

Works by Leibniz

Gerhardt, C[arl] I[mmanuel], ed. (1875–1890). *Die philosophischen Schriften von Gottfried Wilhelm Leibniz*. Berlin: Weidemann. Abbreviated as 'G'. References are to volume and page number.

Leibniz, G.W. (1839/40). *God. Guil. Leibnitii opera philosophica quae extant Latina Gallica Germanica omnia*, 2 vols, J.E. Erdmann (ed.), Berlin: Eichler.

Leibniz, Gottfried Wilhelm (1923ff). *Sämtliche Schriften und Briefe*. Hrsg. v. der Deutschen Akademie der Wissenschaften zu Berlin. Darmstadt: Reichl (1950ff. Berlin: Akademie Verlag). Abbreviated as 'A'. References are to series, volume and page number.

Leibniz, Gottfried Wilhelm (1966). *Logical Papers*. A selection translated and edited by G.H.R. Parkinson. Oxford: Clarendon Press. Abbreviated as 'P'.

Leibniz, G.W. *Nouveaux essais sur l'entendement humain*. Translated in Remnant, Peter and Jonathan Bennett (1996). New Essays on Human Understanding, Cambridge: Cambridge University Press.

Other works

Arnauld, Antoine and Pierre Nicole (1970[1662]). *La Logique ou l'Art de Penser*. Paris: Flammarion.

Burkhardt, Hans (2009). 'Essay Review' [of Lenzen 2004a]. *History and Philosophy of Logic*, 30, 293–9.

Couturat, Louis (1901). *La Logique de Leibniz, d'après des documents inédits*. Paris: Alcan.

Couturat, Louis (1903). *Opuscules and fragments inédits de Leibniz*. Extraits des manuscrits de la Bibliothèque royale de Hanovre. Paris: Alcan. Reprinted by G. Olms Verlagsbuchhandlung (1961).

Dalgarno, George (1661). *Ars Signorum, vulgo character universalis et lingua philosophica*. London: J. Hayes. [Reprinted 1968, Menston: The Scolar Press, and edited with translation in Cram and Maat 2001: 137–289].

Glashoff, Klaus (2002). 'On Leibniz's Characteristic Numbers'. *Studia Leibnitiana*, Bd 34, H 2, pp. 161–84.

Kauppi, Raili (1960). *Über die Leibnizsche Logik*. Helsinki: Societas Philosophica.

Kneale, William and Martha Kneale (1962). *The Development of Logic*. Oxford: Clarendon Press.

Lenzen, Wolfgang (2004a). *Calculus Universalis. Studien zur Logik von G. W. Leibniz*. Paderborn: Mentis.

Lenzen, Wolfgang (2004b). 'Leibniz's Logic'. In: Gabbay, Dov M. and John Woods (eds.), *Handbook of the History of Logic*, Volume 3. Elsevier, pp. 1–83.

Lukasiewicz, Jan (1957). *Aristotle's Syllogistic from the Standpoint of Modern Formal Logic*. Oxford: Clarendon Press.

Maat, Jaap (2004). *Philosophical Languages in the Seventeenth Century: Dalgarno, Wilkins, Leibniz*. Dordrecht / Boston / London: Kluwer.

Peckhaus, Volker (2009). 'Leibniz's Influence on 19th Century Logic', *The Stanford Encyclopedia of Philosophy* (Spring 2014 Edition), Edward N. Zalta (ed.), http://plato.stanford.edu/archives/spr2014/entries/leibniz-logic-influence/

Rescher, Nicholas (1954). 'Leibniz's Interpretation of his Logical Calculi'. *The Journal of Symbolic Logic* 19(1): 1–13.

Rooij, Robert van (2014). 'Leibnizian Intensional Semantics for Syllogistic Reasoning'. In: Ciuni, R et al. (eds.), *Recent Trends in Philosophical Logic*, Springer, pp. 179–94.

Sanderson, Robert (1672 [1615]). *Logicae Artis Compendium*. Oxford.

Wallis, John (1687). *Institutio Logicae*. Oxford.

Wilkins, John (1668). *An Essay towards a Real Character and a Philosophical Language*. London: Samuel Gellibrand and John Martyn.

5

Bolzano

Jönne Kriener

1 Introduction

This chapter presents core elements of the logic developed by the Austrian mathematician and philosopher Bernard Bolzano during the first decades of the nineteenth century.* For Bolzano, logic deals with scientific reasoning quite generally. A science for him is an ordered body of true propositions. Accordingly, I will begin by explaining Bolzano's notion of proposition.

When we engage in science, our reasoning crucially involves the *derivation* of some propositions from others. Bolzano's most advanced innovation in logic is his theory of deducibility (*Ableitbarkeit*). Famously, it anticipates some aspects of the modern concept of logical consequence.

Finally we deal with a more demanding, and less well understood, way in which Bolzano took scientific truths to be ordered: his notion of *grounding* (*Abfolge*). Grounding is central to Bolzano's thinking about science, and thus an important part of Bolzano's logic.

Of course, this chapter is not a comprehensive presentation of Bolzano's logic. It is not intended to be one. I would urge you to at least have a look at some of the scholarly work I list in the bibliography, such as the *Stanford Encyclopedia* entries on Bolzano (Morscher 2012; Sebestik 2011). Bolzano's main work *Wissenschaftslehre* (1837) will be referred to as 'WL'.

Bolzano anticipated several insights of modern logic. I will focus on these innovations, and mark them clearly. Bolzano wrote in German. His technical terms have been translated into English differently by different authors. I will follow the very useful handbook entry by Rusnock and George (2004).

Before we go into details, however, let me emphasize one point. Despite being two centuries old and dealing with deep and difficult matters, Bolzano's work is a pleasure to read. Bolzano is a careful and modest thinker, and his writing is remarkably clear and well structured. Do give it a try yourself and have a look at, for instance, WL §147.

2 Life

Bernard Bolzano was born in 1781. At the age of 15, he entered university to study physics, mathematics and philosophy. In addition, from 1800 onwards he was a student of theology. Only four years later Bolzano was appointed professor of religious instruction. His chair had been created by the Austrian emperor to fight revolutionary tendencies. Threatened by Napoleon's revolutionary armies, the Habsburg monarch feared that its own subjects could want to liberate themselves from his absolutist reign. However, Bolzano's teaching did not comply with the Kaiser's intentions. Here is a quote from one of his lectures.

> There will be a time when the thousandfold distinctions of rank among men that cause so much harm will be reduced to their proper level, when each will treat the other like a brother. There will be a time when constitutions will be introduced that are not subject to the same abuse as the present one.
>
> Bolzano 1852: 19

In 1819 he was dismissed, forbidden to publish and forced to leave Prague. Friends gave him shelter at their rural estate. There, during the 1820s and 1830s, he created most of his logical and philosophical work. Eventually he was allowed to move back to Prague, and in 1842 even to become director of the Bohemian Academy of Sciences. Bolzano died in 1848.

3 Propositions and ideas

As you have read in previous chapters, traditional logic starts out from terms or ideas, and understands judgements and propositions in terms of them. Bolzano reverses this order: the basis of Bolzano's logic is his theory of *propositions*.

Recall that in present-day mainstream philosophy, a proposition is what is said by an indicative sentence. For example, the sentence 'Snow is white' expresses the proposition that snow is white. It is safe to understand Bolzano as working with a close relation of this notion. Importantly, for Bolzano a proposition is not located in space-time. In this precise sense, he takes propositions to be *abstract* entities. In particular, a proposition is not a mental entity. Thus, Bolzano refuses *psychologism* about logic, half a century before Frege and Husserl (see Chapter 8).

Innovation

Logic is *not* about judgements or thoughts as mental events, but about *abstract* propositions.

Instead of attempting an explicit definition of 'proposition', Bolzano characterizes its meaning by a number of postulates.

1. A proposition is either true or false.
2. Propositions are abstract.
3. Judgements have propositions as their content.
4. Interpreted sentences express propositions.
5. Two sentences of different structure may express the same proposition.

As compact as this characterization is, it fully suffices for Bolzano's purpose of developing a general theory of logic. Before we move on, it is worth noting the novel character of the method itself, that Bolzano uses to convey his concept of proposition. He explains his technique as follows.

> We set out various sentences in which the concept ... appears in such combinations that no other concept could be thought in its place if these sentences were to express something reasonable. By considering and comparing these sentences, the reader will gather by himself the meaning of our sign.
>
> Bolzano 1981, §9

Innovation

Bolzano deploys, and reflects on, the method of *implicit definition*.

3.1 Ideas

Given this basic theory of proposition, Bolzano proceeds to define an idea as the component of a proposition.

An idea is

> anything that can be part of a proposition ... without being itself a proposition.
>
> WL §48

Bolzano assumes that there are simple ideas, from which all other, complex ideas are built up. Bolzanian complex ideas are *structured*: it matters how they are built up from their simple parts. For example, the idea of *being allowed not to talk* is distinct from the idea of *not being allowed to talk* (WL §92). More generally, the idea i is the idea j just in case i and j are built up in the same way from the same simple ideas.

Bolzano emphasizes the distinction between an idea, which is an abstract entity, and its *objects*. Objects may be spatio-temporal, such as what falls under the idea of a table, or may not, such as the prime numbers.

Every idea i has an *extension* (WL §66), the collection of its objects. Some ideas lack any object, for example the idea of a golden mountain, or the idea of a round square (WL §67). Their extension is empty.[1]

An *intuition* is a simple idea with exactly one object, such as the idea expressed by successfully using, in a specific context, the demonstrative 'this'. A *concept* is an idea that is not an intuition nor contains any. Bolzano's prime example is the idea of being something, which is a concept because firstly it has not one but infinitely many objects, and secondly is simple and therefore does not contain any intuition (WL§ 73). All other ideas are called *mixed*.

The distinction between intuitions and concepts allows for an analogous classification of propositions. A proposition that does not contain, directly nor indirectly, any *intuition*, Bolzano calls a *conceptual proposition*. Every proposition that contains some intuition is called *empirical*. The next section will give examples.

According to Bolzano, every proposition is composed of ideas, which themselves are composed of simple ideas. However, it is crucial to his approach that the concept of a proposition is fundamental, and that the notion of an idea is defined in terms of it. Bolzano gives an identity criterion for propositions: A is B if and only if A and B are composed of the same simple ideas, in the same manner.

More precisely, every proposition immediately contains three ideas, of three distinct kinds.

1.   One subject idea,
2.   one predicate idea and
3.   the simple idea of *having*.

Thus, every proposition is of the form

   i has j

for ideas i and j.

In particular, this means that Bolzano does not have the modern notion of a logical connective. Every proposition is of the traditional subject-predicate form. For example, the proposition that

(1) either snow is white or snow is green.

is analysed as follows (WL§166):

> *The idea of a true proposition among the propositions that snow has whiteness and the proposition that snow has greenness, has non-emptiness.*

This part of Bolzano's work is still in the grip of traditional logic. However, when in the next section we turn to his logic proper, we will find that Bolzano in fact was able to analyse propositions in a much more flexible way than his official statements about their form suggest.

Exercise 5.1

Consider the following technical terms.

'intuitions', 'empirical', 'simple', 'mixed', 'propositions', 'connectives', 'ideas', 'concepts', 'complex', 'conceptual', 'judgement'

Some play a role in Bolzano's theory of propositions. Put those terms at their right place in Figure 5.1.

Truth is an abstract *idea* that applies to *propositions*. Since we identify propositions by their structure, and truth is an idea of its own, the proposition *A* is not identical with the proposition that *A* is true.

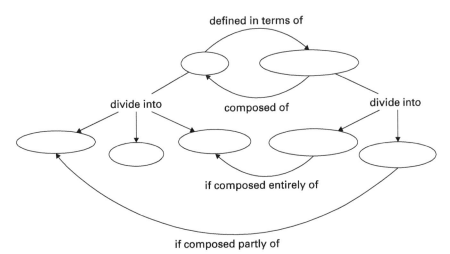

Figure 5.1 (Exercise) The key technical terms of Bolzano's theory of propositions, and how they connect

3.2 A toy Bolzanian science

Let us familiarize ourselves with Bolzano's theory of propositions by looking at a toy model. I will work with a basic science of family relations ('BF'). It contains propositions such as that every sister has a sibling, or the proposition that Fredo and Michael are brothers.

In fact, for simplicity, let us assume that there are only the Corleones (as known from *The Godfather* 1–3). That is, let us assume that as Bolzanian *intuitions* (recall: ideas that have exactly one object) we have the intuitions of Vito Corleone, Michael and the others.[2] Let the idea of being female, as well as being male, also be intuitions. These are all the intuitions we have in our toy Bolzanian science BF.

By way of simple *concepts*, we have the concepts of parenthood, marriage and the concept of sharing. Let us also treat as simple the concepts of negation, conjunction and existential quantification as well as the other concepts of first-order logic. Putting together these simple concepts we obtain *complex* ones, such as x and y being siblings (sharing a parent), x being a cousin or a parent of y and so on.

Now, we can distinguish between conceptual and empirical BF-propositions. For example, the proposition mentioned above, that Fredo and Michael are siblings, is empirical because it contains intuitions, such as the idea of Fredo.

Exercise 5.2

1.   What mixed ideas do we have? Give three examples.
2.   Give a conceptual proposition of the basic science of family relations.

4 Variation

Bolzano's conception of logic is much more inclusive than how we nowadays understand the subject. In this section, I turn to that part of Bolzano's work which corresponds to our modern, more restricted notion of logic. I turn to Bolzano's theory of consequence.

(2)   Obama is in Berlin today.

The sentence (2) expresses a true proposition on 19 June 2013, but a falsehood on 19 July.

Does this contradict Bolzano's view of truth as an idea, i.e. something independent of space and time? After all, if the sentence (2) expresses the same proposition on both days, then the truth value of this proposition would depend on time.

However, Bolzano replies, (2) does not express the same proposition at different times. The reason is that 'today' expresses distinct *ideas* on different days and therefore, when it seems to us that the proposition expressed by an utterance of (1) changes its truth value over time, we really consider *variants* of this proposition, with different ideas substituted for the idea of 19 June 2013.

This astute observation provides the basis for Bolzano's *variation logic*.

> Given a proposition, we could merely inquire whether it is true or false. But some very remarkable properties of propositions can be discovered if, in addition, we consider the truth values of all those propositions which can be generated from it, if we take some of its constituent ideas as variable and replace them by any other ideas whatever.
>
> WL §147

Innovation

Bolzano develops and makes great use of an unprecedented method of *variation*, which anticipates to some extent modern model-theoretic semantics.

For a proposition A and ideas i, j, let $A(j/i)$ be the proposition obtained from A by substituting j for every occurrence of i. Call $A(j/i)$ an 'i-variant' of A. Note that we do not assume A to contain i. If it does not, $A(j/i)$ is just A.

For example, the proposition that Anthony is Francesca's brother is a *cousin*-variant of the truth that Anthony is Francesca's cousin. Indeed, it is a false such variant, just as the proposition that he is her niece. Figure 5.2 gives one way of visualizing the replacement of the idea *is cousin of*, that is part of the proposition that Anthony is cousin of Francesca, by one or the other idea.

As indicated in the quote above, Bolzano allows not merely one but several ideas $i, j, k, \ldots$ together to be considered as variable.

4.1 Validity

It is not the case that every idea is a suitable substitution for any other. For example, the idea of being a sibling is not a good substitution for the idea of Vito Corleone. Every idea comes with its own *range of variation*: those ideas

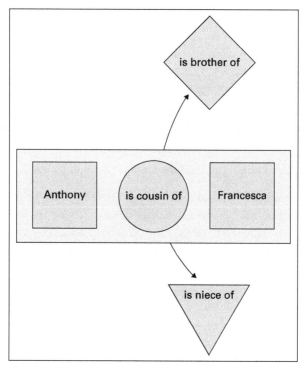

Figure 5.2 Variation

that may be substituted for it. This puts constraints on what variants we consider for a given proposition. An *i*-variant $A(j/i)$ is *relevant* if and only if:[3]

1. The subject idea of $A(j/i)$ has objects,
2. if $i \neq j$ then j and i do not have the same objects, and
3. j is in the range of variation of i.

Definition

A proposition A is *valid* (invalid) with respect to ideas $i, j, \ldots$ iff every relevant i, $j, \ldots$ -variant of A is true (false).

For example, the proposition that Michael's brother is male is valid with respect to the idea of Michael.

The variation of ideas provides Bolzano with a sophisticated tool to identify formal properties of a given proposition. It allows him to formulate a rich and very general theory of these properties. In the remainder of this section, we will get to know its most important parts. Before we do so, let me note that the power of Bolzano's variation method stems from the fact that he allows *any* idea to be varied. This effectively liberates his logic from the restrictions of the traditional subject-predicate analysis even though, officially, he clings to this received doctrine.

Definition

A is *logically* valid if A is valid with respect to all non-logical ideas in A.

Which ideas are logical? Bolzano gives examples (*and, or, not, some*) but admits that there may be distinct notions of logicality, each with its own range of logically valid propositions. Note that modern logic, too, knows such a sense of relativity. To give a famous example, Tarski acknowledged that validity (in the modern sense of truth in all models) is relative to a set of logical constants (Tarski 1956: 418f.).

Our toy science BF comprises the ideas of first-order logic, such as conjunction (*and*) and existential quantification (*some*). Let these be the *logical* ideas of our toy model.

Exercise 5.3

Give two logically valid propositions, one containing the idea of Fredo Corleone, the other containing the idea of being a female cousin.

4.2 Compatibility

We may consider variants of several propositions at once. This allows us to distinguish ways in which propositions relate to one another. Bolzano speaks of *collections* of propositions. His relevant use of this term is well viewed as anticipating how logicians today have come to use the term 'plurality', as a convenient but inessential shorthand for *plural* reference to some things (Yi 2005; Linnebo 2012).[4] Like Bolzano, I will assume a collection always to be non-empty.

Definition

A, B, ... are *compatible* with respect to some ideas i, j ... (more simply: $i, j,$ ...-compatible) just in case there are some ideas $i', j',$ ... such that $A(i'/i, j'/j, ...)$ is true, $B(i'/i, j'/j, ...)$ is true, ...

Note that the ideas $i, j,$ ... need not occur in each of A, B, ... Since we do not assume the variant of a proposition A to be distinct from A, in particular every true proposition is a true variant of itself. Hence, whenever we have some true propositions, they are compatible.

At the same time, however, a true proposition may be compatible with a falsehood. For example, the truth that Anthony is cousin of Francesca and the false proposition that Sonny is cousin of Vito are compatible with respect to the ideas of Francesca and Vito – since it is a true Francesca–Vito-variant of the latter proposition that Anthony is cousin of Vincenzo (note that variation with respect to Francesca does not have any effect).

Bolzano's compatibility resembles the modern semantic concept of *satisfiability*. However, Bolzano's notion of *having true variants* is *not having a true model*. Importantly, it is not sentences of some specified language that have variants, but propositions which exist independently of all language and interpretation.

Exercise 5.4

Give three BF-propositions compatible with respect to the idea of being a sister, and two propositions incompatible with respect to the idea of Michael.

4.3 Deducibility

Next, Bolzano considers special cases of compatibility (WL §155). Sometimes, it is not only that, say, propositions A and B each give rise to a truth if the idea j is substituted for the idea, i, but in fact every true i-variant of A corresponds to a true i-variant of B. Every way of generating a true proposition from A by replacing i is a way of turning B into a truth, too. This is Bolzano's concept of consequence, or *deducibility*.

Definition
A is deducible from $B, C, \ldots$, with respect to some *ideas* $i, j, \ldots$ ('$i, j, \ldots$-deducible') just in case $A, B, C, \ldots$ are $i, j, \ldots$-compatible, and for all $k, l, \ldots B(k/i, l/j)$, $C(k/i, l/j)$, … are true only if $A(k/i, l/j)$ is.[5]

For example, the proposition that Francesca is female is deducible from the proposition that every sister is female, with respect to the idea of being female (WL §155.20). At the same time, the false proposition that Francesca is male is *being-male*-deducible from the falsehood that every sister is male.

Exercise 5.5

Give an example to show that, with respect to the idea of Carlo, it is not deducible that Carlo is male, from the proposition that Fredo is Carlo's uncle.

A is *logically* deducible from *B* just in case *A* is deducible from *B* with respect to to all non-logical ideas in *A* and B. As with logical validity, the concept of logical deducibility is relative to a notion of logicality. I continue to identify the logical ideas of our basic science of family relations BF with the ideas expressed by the connectives, quantifiers and identity. Thus, the proposition that Francesca is female is *logically* deducible from the proposition that every sister is female together with the proposition that Francesca is a sister.

Exercise 5.6

Let us extend our basic science of family relations by the idea of admiration. Show that the proposition that Sonny admires Vito is logically deducible from the following propositions.

1. Francesca admires Michael.
2. Sonny does not admire Vito if and only if Vincenzo admires his father.
3. Vincenzo admires Sonny only if Kathryn does admire Michael.
4. No two sisters admire the same person.

How does Bolzano's notion of logical deducibility relate to the modern concept of classical logical consequence? Firstly, both deducibility and consequence are relations between sentences of formal languages; deducibility is a relation between abstract, non-linguistic entities. Secondly, Bolzano's concept of deducibility applies at least to some cases of *material consequence*. I gave an example: the proposition that Francesca is female is deducible from the proposition that every sister is female. Finally, since Bolzano requires premises and conclusion to be logically compatible, i.e. *consistent*, deducibility is more restrictive than classical consequence. For one, it is not the case that everything can be derived from inconsistent premises. In fact, nothing can be derived from such assumptions.[6]

4.4 Probability

Given Bolzano's theory of propositions, the variation of ideas is a powerful tool for logical inquiry. Bolzano discusses several other applications of it. I will focus on his theory of probability (WL §161). For propositions, $A, B, \ldots$, and ideas $i, j,$ $\ldots$ let $| A, B, \ldots |_{i,j,\ldots}$ denote the *number* of true $i, j, \ldots$-variants of. $A, B, \ldots$.

Definition

Let $A, B, \ldots$ be some compatible propositions, and let $i, j, \ldots$ be some ideas. Let M be a proposition not among but $i, j, \ldots$-compatible with them. $| M, A, B, \ldots |_{i,j,\ldots}$ divided by $| A, B, \ldots |_{i,j,\ldots}$ is called the *probability* of M conditional on $A, B,$ $\ldots$, with respect to the ideas $i, j, \ldots$.

To give an example, let us extend our basic science of family relations by the idea of someone being older than someone else.[7] Then, the probability of Michael being older than Francesca conditional on Michael being older than some cousin of hers is 8/17.

If the probability of M conditional on $A, B, \ldots$ (with respect to $i, j, \ldots$) is greater than ½, Bolzano points out, we are entitled to take M to be true if $A,$ $B, \ldots$ are (WL §161.1). Thus, Bolzano uses his concept of probability to define a notion of valid *inductive* reasoning. If M is $i, j, \ldots$-deducible from $A, B, \ldots$ then M's $i, j \ldots$-probability conditional on $A, B, \ldots$ is 1 (WL §161.3). In this precise sense, Bolzano's inductive logic includes his deductive logic as a special case.

Assume that we have distinguished a collection of ideas as *logical*.

Definition

The *logical* probability of M conditional on $A, B, \ldots$ is its probability with respect to all non-logical ideas.

As before, in the examples I will treat all and only connectives, quantifiers and identity as *logical* ideas.

Bolzano's concept of logical conditional probability satisfies, modulo his concept of logical deducibility, many of the axioms of the modern concept of conditional probability, or support functions.[8] For example, we have that if A and B are mutually logically deducible then for every M, its logical probability conditional on A is its logical probability conditional on B (WL §161.4). Thus, Bolzano's work on conditional probability anticipates to some extent modern inductive logic.

Innovation

Using his method of variation, Bolzano extends his deductive logic by a formal logic of probability. A special case of this concept anticipates modern systems of *conditional probability*.

Note, however, that what is assigned probability in Bolzano's system is not a belief, but a proposition whose existence does not depend on any subject. Further, the probability of a proposition is determined by whether or not certain other propositions are true, which itself is an entirely objective matter. Consequently, Bolzano's concept of probability is thoroughly objective. As such, unlike modern inductive logic it does not lend itself to applications in epistemology.[9]

5 Bolzano's theory of grounding

5.1 Grounding

Bolzano's logic as developed so far applies equally to true as to false propositions. However, Bolzano has more to offer: a special system for *truths*. True propositions are ordered by what Bolzano calls the relation of *Abfolge*. Let me translate it as 'grounding'. Bolzano motivates his theory of grounding from examples of the following kind (WL §198).

(3) It is warmer in Palermo than in New York.
(4) The thermometer stands higher in Palermo than in New York.

Both propositions are true. However, it is the truth of (3) that explains (4) and not vice versa. The truth of (3) grounds the truth of (4).

This relation of grounding stands out from Bolzano's system in that it is not defined in terms of variation. In particular, the fact that (3) grounds (4) and not vice versa cannot be captured by *deducibility*: (3) can be derived from (4). Therefore, a stronger concept is needed: (3) *grounds* (4).

For a long time, interpreters have found this part of Bolzano's work 'obscure' (Berg 1962: 151). Nothing in a modern logic textbook corresponds to Bolzanian grounding. Nonetheless, the concept has a long and venerable tradition. Bolzano connects with Aristotle's distinction between *why*-proofs and mere *that*-proofs (Aristotle 2006: 1051b; Betti 2010). The truth that it is warmer in Palermo than in New York is *why* the thermometer stands higher in Palermo than in New York. Generally, the *grounds* of A is *why* A. Moreover, very recently formal systems of grounding have been developed, prominently by Kit Fine, that are well viewed as resonating Bolzano's concept of *Abfolge* (Schnieder 2011; Fine 2012a; Correia 2014).

Bolzano gives further examples (WL §§ 162.1, 201).

(5) The proposition that the angles of a triangle add up to 180 degrees grounds the proposition that the angles of a quadrangle add up to 360 degrees.

(6) The proposition that in an isosceles triangle opposite angles are identical grounds the proposition that in an equilateral triangle all angles are identical.

(7) The proposition that God is perfect grounds that the actual world is the best of all worlds.

If *A* grounds *B* then it is the case that *B because* it is the case that *A*. Bolzano's grounding is a concept of objective explanation. However, it must *not* be conflated with epistemic notions, such as justification. For one, just as deducibility, grounding concerns how propositions, that do not have spatio-temporal location, are ordered independently of any subject. For another, justification suffers from the same shortcoming as deducibility, in that it does not respect the asymmetry between the truths (3) and (4). If you know that the thermometer stands higher in Palermo than in New York, then you are justified in believing that it is warmer in Palermo than in New York.

Bolzano discusses whether grounding can be defined in terms of deducibility, and possibly other notions (WL §200); his conclusion is that such a definition is not available. Therefore, Bolzano introduces grounding as a primitive concept and characterizes it by a system of principles, analogously to how he characterized his notion of proposition.

5.2 Principles of grounding

Grounding is a relation between single or pluralities of propositions. I will use Greek capital letters (those, such as 'Γ' or 'Δ', which differ typographically from capital Roman letters) as variables ranging over pluralities of propositions. Note that Bolzano assumes grounds to be always *finite* collections of propositions (WL §199). I use the symbol '◁' for grounding such that 'Γ ◁ *A*' reads: the propositions Γ ground the proposition *A*.

What stands on the left-hand side of '◁' is called the *grounds*, and that which is grounded, and stands on the right-hand side of '◁', is called their *consequence*. Officially, the consequence may also be a plurality of propositions. However, in practice Bolzano mostly uses the relation between several grounds Γ and a single consequence *A*. Therefore, many scholars have taken this to be the basic notion of grounding, and defined the relation 'Γ ◁ Δ', with multiple consequences, in terms of it (Berg 1962). I will follow them, and present Bolzano's principles of grounding as for a relation between a single consequence and its possibly many grounds.

The first principle says that only truths stand in the relation of grounding.

Factivity

If $A_0, A_1, \ldots \prec B$ then $A_0, A_1, \ldots$ and $B \ldots$ are true (WL §203).

For example, (7) is a case of grounding only if the actual world really is the best of all worlds. Generally, only true propositions stand in the relation of grounding. Turning to our toy science of the Corleones, we therefore know that

(8) Every sister is male.

does not ground

(9) Francesca is male.

The ground of A is *why* it is the case that A; it explains the truth that A. The sense of explanation at work here is objective and exhaustive. This allows us to draw two conclusions about the formal properties of grounding. Firstly, what grounds a proposition does not involve this proposition itself, neither directly or indirectly.[10]

Non-Circularity

There is no chain $A_0, \ldots, A_n$ such that for every $i < n$, A_i is among some Γ such that $\Gamma \prec A_{i+1}$, and $A_0 = A_n$. (WL §§204, 218)

Secondly, the grounds of A are *unique*.

Uniqueness

If $\Gamma \prec A$ and $\Delta \prec A$ then $\Gamma = \Delta$. (WL §206)

On the one hand, this implies that if A is grounded in Γ, then it is not grounded in Γ together with arbitrary other truths. Thus, it is ensured that every truth among Γ matters for the truth A.[11] On the other hand, the principle of uniqueness means that the truths that a proposition is grounded in, are its *complete* grounds. This captures our pre-theoretic idea of grounding as a relation of exhaustive explanation.

However, I do not include among Bolzano's formal principles of grounding that it is unique on its right-hand side. That is, I do not assume that if $\Gamma \prec A$ and $\Gamma \prec B$ then then $A = B$.

These principles describe the relation of grounding *formally*. For example, from (Uniqueness) we know that *if* the truth that

(10) Vito is Michael's male parent.

grounds that

(11) Michael is son of Vito.

then it is not the case that (11) is grounded in the truth that

(12) Sonny, Fredo and Michael are Vito's sons.

However, we would like to know more. Does (10) in fact ground (11)? More generally, what cases of grounding are there? Bolzano gives examples (such as (6) to (7)), but not many general principles. One such principle, however, is that every truth A grounds the proposition that A is true (WL §205.1). By the same principle we have that the proposition that A is true itself grounds the proposition that it is true that A is true. Recall that the proposition A is not identical with the proposition that A is true. Hence, *uniqueness* ensures it not to be the case that A grounds the proposition that it is true that A is true.

Generally, grounding is the notion of *complete, immediate* objective explanation. From it, *partial* such explanation is defined easily (WL §198): Γ *partially* ground A if there are some Δ such that Γ are among Δ, and Δ ground A.

5.3 Ascension

Bolzano does not stop at the relation between a truth and its immediate grounds. He analyses the order that it imposes on a collection of true propositions (WL §216).

> If someone starting from a given truth M asks for its ground, and if finding this in … the truths $[A, B, C …]$ he continues to ask for the … grounds, which … these have, and keeps doing so as long as grounds can be given: then I call this *ascension from consequence to grounds.*

Definition

If, ascending from M to its grounds, we arrive at some truth A, then M is said to *depend* on A, and A is called an 'auxiliary truth' for M.

Exercise 5.7

Explain that Bolzano's concept of dependence is *partial mediate* grounding.

One worry may be raised. The way Bolzano conveys his idea of ascension, and dependence, stands in tension with his declared view that, firstly, propositions are not subject to time or space (p. 000 above), and secondly, they stand in the relation of ground and consequence also independently of time and space. In the quote above, however, Bolzano uses spatial-temporal language. Indeed, the word 'ascension' suggests an upwards movement.

However, this is mere metaphor. To characterize dependence in a less metaphorical way, it helps to formulate ascension as a *game*.

Definition

Let the *ascension game* $G(M)$ for a true proposition M be played as follows. Player 1 starts by playing the true proposition A. 2 responds by playing the propositions $A, B, \ldots$ such that $A, B, \ldots \triangleleft M$. In response, 1 chooses one of $A, B,$ $\ldots,$ and so on. One player wins if the other cannot make a move. If a run continues indefinitely, 1 loses.

Such games can then be described in purely mathematical terms. For example, each play of $G(M)$ corresponds to a *tree* of true propositions whose root is M and every other node of which represents an auxiliary truth of M (see Figure 5.3). Thus, we can say that M depends on A if and only if A is represented by a node of such a tree. I say 'represents' and not 'is', since one and the same truth may be played several times during a play of $G(M)$. Bolzano himself proposes this characterization of dependence in terms of trees (WL §220).

Innovation

Having set up a sophisticated system of extensional logic, Bolzano realizes its restrictions and characterizes a more fine-grained relation of objective explanation. It anticipates, indeed partly inspired, recent work in metaphysics (Fine 2001; Rosen 2010; Fine 2012b).

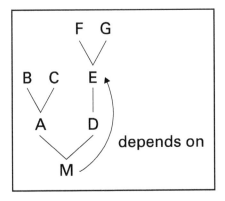

Figure 5.3 Ascension from M to its auxiliary truths

6 Conclusion

Bolzano's work on logic was ahead of his time. In this chapter, we have got to know his core innovations.

1. Logic is *not* about judgements or thoughts as mental events, but about *objective, abstract* propositions.
2. Bolzano deploys, and reflects on, the method of *implicit definition*.
3. Bolzano develops and makes great use of an unprecedented method of *variation*, which anticipates to some extent modern semantics.
4. Using his method of variation, Bolzano extends his deductive logic by a formal logic of probability. A special case of this concept anticipates modern systems of *conditional probability*.
5. Having set up a sophisticated system of logic, Bolzano realizes its restrictions and characterizes a more fine-grained relation of objective explanation: grounding.

Notes

* I thank Antje Rumberg for her constructive criticism and many helpful comments. This work was supported by the European Research Council and the University of Oslo.

1 Note that the idea of a round square necessarily lacks an object.

2 For a comprehensive list, see https://en.wikipedia.org/wiki/Corleone_family.

3 This way of bundling tacit assumptions of Bolzano's is inspired by Künne 1998, to whom the term 'relevant' is due, too.

4 However, Bolzano uses 'collection' also in other ways; see Simons (1997).

5 To improve readability, I suppress some of the remarkable generality of Bolzano's logic. As a matter of fact, Bolzano allows for derivations not only from multiple premises, but also derivations of multiple conclusions.

6 To this extent, Bolzano's logical deducibility may be viewed as anticipating *relevance* logics (Read 1988).

7 To fix matters, let us say one Corleone is older than another if and only if the former is of an earlier generation than the latter or the former is above the latter in the list at https://en.wikipedia.org/wiki/Corleone_family.

8 See e.g. Hawthorne (2012, §2.2).

9 Under the label of *formal epistemology*, recently much work has been done that connects the logic of probability with epistemological questions.

10 This formulation of non-circularity uses the notion of a *grounding chain* from Rumberg (2013).
11 To use a technical term, grounding is *non-monotone*.

References

Aristotle (2006), Metaphysics Book Θ, ed. Stephen Makin, Oxford: Clarendon Press.

Berg, Jan (1962), *Bolzano's Logic*. Stockholm, Almqvist & Wiksell.

Betti, Arianna (2010), 'Explanation in Metaphysics and Bolzano's Theory of Ground and Consequence', *Logique & Analyse* 211: 281–316.

Bolzano, Bernard (1837), *Wissenschaftslehre*, Sulzbach: Seidel.

Bolzano, Bernard (1852), 'Homily on the first Sunday of Advent, 1810', in *Erbauungsreden* Vol. 4, Prague–Vienna: Hofbuchhandlung bei Wilhelm Braumüller, 1852, p. 19.

Bolzano, Bernard (1981), *Von der Mathematischen Lehrart*, ed. Jan Berg, Stuttgart–Bad Cannstatt: Fromann-Holzboog.

Correia, Fabrice (2014), 'Logical Grounds', *The Review of Symbolic Logic* 7(1): 31–59.

Fine, Kit (2001), 'The Question of Realism', *Philosophers' Imprint* 1: 1–30.

Fine, Kit (2012a), 'The Pure Logic of Ground,' *The Review of Symbolic Logic* 5: 1–25.

Fine, Kit (2012b), 'Guide to Ground', in Fabrice Correia and Benjamin Schnieder (eds), *Metaphysical Grounding: Understanding the Structure of Reality*, pp. 37–80, Cambridge, New York and Melbourne: Cambridge University Press.

Hawthorne, James (2012), 'Inductive Logic', in Edward N. Zalta, ed., *The Stanford Encyclopedia of Philosophy*, Stanford: Stanford University Press.

Künne, W. (1998), 'Bernard Bolzano,' in *Routledge Encyclopedia of Philosophy*, pp. 824–8. London and New York: Routledge.

Linnebo, Øystein (2012), 'Plural Quantification', in Edward N. Zalta, ed., *The Stanford Encyclopedia of Philosophy*, Stanford: Stanford University Press.

Morscher, Edgar (2012), 'Bernard Bolzano', in Edward N. Zalta, ed., *The Stanford Encyclopedia of Philosophy*, Stanford: Stanford University Press.

Read, Stephen (1988), *Relevant Logic: A Philosophical Examination of Inference*, Oxford: Basil Blackwell.

Rosen, Gideon (2010), 'Metaphysical Dependence: Grounding and Reduction', in. Bob Hale and Aviv Homan (eds), *Modality: Metaphysics, Logic and Epistemology*, Oxford: Oxford University Press.

Rumberg, Antje (2013), 'Bolzano's Concept of Grounding (*Abfolge*) Against the Background of Normal Proofs', *The Review of Symbolic Logic* 6(3): 424–59.

Rusnock, Paul and Rolf George (2004), 'Bolzano as Logician', in Dov M. Gabbay and John Hayden Woods (eds), *Rise of Modern Logic: From Leibniz to Frege*, Amsterdam: Elsevier.

Schnieder, Benjamin (2011), 'A Logic for Because', *The Review of Symbolic Logic* 4 (September).

Sebestik, Jan (2011), 'Bolzano's Logic', in Edward N. Zalta, ed., *The Stanford Encyclopedia of Philosophy*, Stanford: Stanford University Press.

Simons, Peter (1997), 'Bolzano on Collections', in Mark Siebel Wolfgang Künne and Mark Textor (eds), *Bolzano and Analytic Philosophy*, pp. 87–108, Amsterdam: Rodopi.

Tarski, Alfred (1956), 'On the Concept of Logical Consequence', in *Logic, Semantics, Metamathematics*, pp. 409–20, Indianapolis: Hackett Publishing Company.

Yi, Byeong-Uk (2005), 'The Logic and Meaning of Plurals. Part 1', *Journal of Philosophical Logic* 34 (Oct./Dec.): 459–506.

Solutions to exercises

Exercise 5.1

Consider the following technical terms: 'intuitions', 'empirical', 'simple', 'mixed', 'propositions', 'connectives', 'ideas', 'concepts', 'complex', 'conceptual', 'judgement'. Some play a role in Bolzano's theory of propositions. Put those terms at their right place in Figure 5.1.

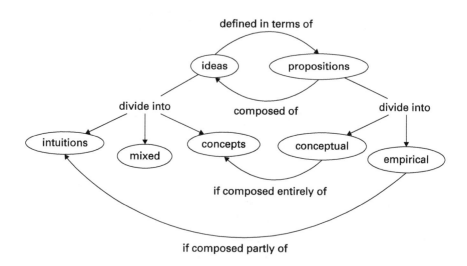

Exercise 5.2

1. What mixed ideas do we have? Give three examples.
2. Give a conceptual proposition of the basic science of family relations.

Solution

1. The idea of being a son of Vito Corleone; (b) The idea of being a sister of Sonny Corleone; (c) The idea of being a married to Michael Corleone.
2. All sisters are female.

Exercise 5.3

Give two logically valid propositions, one containing the idea of Fredo Corleone, the other containing the idea of being a female cousin.

Solution

1. Either Fredo Corleone has a sister or not.
2. If every female cousin is a sibling, then everything is a sibling if everything is a female cousin.

Exercise 5.4

Give three BF-propositions compatible with respect to the idea of being sisters, and two propositions incompatible with respect to the idea of Michael.

Solution

Three propositions compatible with respect to the idea of being sisters:

1. Fredo and Michael are sisters.
2. Francesca and Kathryn are sisters.
3. Vincenzo and Francesca are cousins.

To see that these propositions are compatible, note that the following are all true

4. Fredo and Michael share a grandmother.
5. Francesca and Kathryn share a grandmother.
6. Vincenzo and Francesca are cousins.

Two propositions incompatible with respect to the idea of Michael:

7. Michael and Sonny are sisters.
8. Michael is male.

Exercise 5.5

Give an example to show that, with respect to the idea of Charles, it is not derivable that Charles is male, from the proposition that Richard is Charles' uncle.

Solution

It is true that Fredo is Francesca's uncle, but false that Francesca is male.

Exercise 5.6

Let us extend our basic science of family relations by the ideas of admiration. Show that the proposition that Sonny admires Vito is logically derivable from the following propositions.

1. Francesca admires Michael.
2. Sonny does not admire Vito if and only if Vincenzo admires his father.
3. Vincenzo admires Sonny only if Kathryn does admire Michael.
4. No two sisters admire the same person.

Solution

Dependence is (the inverse of) partial mediate grounding, because if M depends on A, then A is among the truths that ground M, or that ground some truth that M depends on.

6

Boole

Giulia Terzian

1 Life and works

George Boole (1815–1864) was born in Lincoln, England, where he also spent more than half his lifetime working as a teacher and headmaster. From an early age, his father encouraged him to cultivate his interests in modern and ancient languages, and in mathematics. Boole senior was also 'evidently more of a good companion than a good breadwinner. [He] was a shoemaker whose real passion was being a devoted dilettante in the realm of science and technology, one who enjoyed participating in the Lincoln Mechanics' Institution; this was essentially a community social club promoting reading, discussions, and lectures regarding science' (Agazzi 1974). Boole left school at the age of sixteen in order to support his family, but also took it upon himself to continue and further his education. Thus while he was working as an assistant he taught himself several modern languages and above all mathematics. Boole opened his own school only three years later, spending the following fifteen as a schoolmaster in Lincoln.

In 1849 Boole was appointed professor of mathematics at Queen's College in Cork, becoming the first to occupy this chair. A short time later he met Mary Everest: then a student of Boole's, Everest later became a mathematician in her own right. The two married and had five daughters together. Everest shared Boole's passion for teaching as well as for mathematics; and indeed she is best known for her work and remarkably progressive ideas on the pedagogy of mathematics.[1] Boole remained in Cork until his premature death at the age of forty-nine. Different sources offer slightly varying accounts of how this came about. By piecing them together, it emerges that on a winter day Boole 'walked from his residence to the College, a distance of two miles, in a drenching rain, and lectured in wet clothes' (MacFarlane 1916: 32). By the time he got home later that day, he already had a fever which quickly developed into pneumonia. But this was the 1860s, when tragically little was known about lung infections; which explains why Mary Boole, armed only with the very best intentions, attempted to heal her husband by dousing him in ice-cold water. Boole died soon afterwards.

1.1 Boole's accomplishments

Boole was a mathematician by training, and during the course of his prolific career he contributed numerous articles to mathematics journals. But Boole's main interest was logic, and his most significant contributions lie within this field. Boole's key innovation in logic consisted in the systematic application of mathematical methods to the discipline. Indeed, according to philosopher and historian of logic John Corcoran,

> George Boole is one of the greatest logicians of all time and . . . can be, and often is, regarded as the founder of mathematical logic.
>
> Corcoran 2003: 284

More specifically, Boole's most prominent contribution to this field of inquiry is the so-called *algebra of logic*. Boole effectively gave life to what became a well-established tradition in logic, which continued to flourish long after his death. What is more, Boole's work in logic played a key role in the transition from the Aristotelian tradition in logic to the discipline we know and study today.

Boole's most important work is contained in two monographs:

MAL   *The Mathematical Analysis of Logic* (1847)
LOT   *An Investigation of the Laws of Thought, on which are founded the Theories of Logic and Probabilities* (1854)

Boole wrote MAL in response to a controversy between mathematician Augustus De Morgan (1806–1871) and philosopher Sir William Hamilton (1788–1856). De Morgan and Hamilton both demanded credit for the same idea, namely 'quantifying the predicate': this was the proposal to add the forms 'All/Some/No *A*s are All/Some/No *B*s' to the standard forms of the syllogism. Boole's MAL, an eighty-two-page-long pamphlet, already contained many of the key ideas and results later expounded and expanded upon in his magnum opus, LOT.[2]

Incidentally, De Morgan's *Formal Logic* was published in the same year as MAL; according to some sources, they even came out of press on the very same day. Nevertheless, and although there is a certain amount of overlap between the two monographs, Boole's received far greater recognition than De Morgan's. De Morgan himself later came to recognize the higher merit of Boole's work, as transpires very clearly in the following passage from Alexander MacFarlane's *Lectures on Ten Mathematicians of the Nineteenth Century* (1916: 32):

> De Morgan was the man best qualified to judge of the value of Boole's work in the field of logic; and he gave it generous praise and help. In writing to the Dublin Hamilton he said, 'I shall be glad to see his work (*Laws of Thought*) out, for he has, I think, got hold of the true connection of algebra and logic.' At another time he wrote to the same as follows: 'All metaphysicians except you and I and Boole consider mathematics as four books of Euclid and algebra up to quadratic equations.' We might infer that these three contemporary mathematicians who were likewise philosophers would form a triangle of friends. But it was not so; Hamilton was a friend of De Morgan, and De Morgan a friend of Boole; but the relation of friendship, although convertible, is not necessarily transitive. Hamilton met De Morgan only once in his life, Boole on the other hand with comparative frequency; yet he had a voluminous correspondence with the former extending over 20 years, but almost no correspondence with the latter.

Compared to both MAL and De Morgan's *Formal Logic*, however, LOT received far greater attention from logicians and mathematicians alike; for while MAL already contains the seeds of Boole's main innovations, it is in LOT that they are articulated and developed in full depth. In view of the purpose of this chapter – to provide an introduction to Boole's logic that is both comprehensive and accessible – we follow the literature by focusing mainly on LOT.

2 The laws of thought

As illustrated in earlier chapters of this anthology, during the late eighteenth and the nineteenth centuries both logic and philosophical logic had made some significant advances, most notably by the hands of Leibniz and Bolzano. Yet Aristotelian logic still dominated scholarly textbooks and articles in Boole's time. It was in this context that Boole almost single-handedly set the stage for Gottlob Frege's revolution and the transition to modern logic.

Boole was not just measuring himself against a century-strong tradition; the backdrop to his education and early work was the psychologist school in philosophy – the same that Frege was to criticize so famously and vehemently only a few decades later.

Psychologism has it that logic is really just a branch of psychology. Thus, logic is primarily a descriptive activity, the main purpose of which is to correctly understand and represent the structure and modes of our reasoning. On this view, any normative question about how we *ought* to reason should therefore defer to (and is thus dependent upon) the descriptive account. This is in stark contrast with the modern conception of logic. The latter is largely predicated on the assumption that the goal of logic is that of uncovering the principles of *correct* reasoning; and for precisely this reason it harbours a natural expectation that the descriptive question (How *do* we reason?) and the normative question (How *ought* we to reason?) would receive rather different answers. And yet things were very different just over a century ago.

Boole's assessment of psychologism was somewhat more measured than (for instance) Frege's; nevertheless, ultimately Boole distanced himself from the view altogether. However, Nicla Vassallo (1997) makes the interesting observation that Boole only did so *after* an initial period during which he was openly quite sympathetic to the view. The transition (if such it was) seems to have occurred some time between the publication of MAL – where signs of at least a weak psychologistic leaning can still be discerned – and that of LOT – where the view is more clearly and explicitly endorsed that logic is first and foremost a normative enterprise.

In LOT, Boole clearly envisions the purpose of logic as that of representing each and every component of *correct* or valid reasoning; he is also quick to see the limitations of the Aristotelian system in this respect, and the need to replace (or enrich) it with a much more comprehensive set of principles. This, in a nutshell, is what LOT sets out to achieve:

> The design of the following treatise is to investigate the fundamental laws of those operations of the mind by which reasoning is performed; to give expression to them in the symbolical language of a Calculus, and upon this foundation to establish the science of Logic and construct its method; to make that method itself the basis of a general method for the application of the mathematical doctrine of Probabilities; and, finally, to collect from the various elements of truth brought to view in the course of these inquiries some probable intimations concerning the nature and constitution of the human mind.
>
> Boole 1854: 1

Notice that in the above passage Boole is rehearsing the main steps in the construction of a formal theory. Today the concept 'formal theory' is a familiar one, so much so that this specific passage may strike readers as rather unremarkable. But place it in historical context and its significance becomes immediately apparent: aside from one or two exceptions[3] Boole's LOT contains one of the very first approximations of a formal theory in the modern sense. This fact alone would give sufficient reason to consider Boole to be a key figure in the history of logic (and philosophical logic); and at the very least it clearly identifies him as a precursor of Frege and Tarski.

In light of what has just been said, we may begin to identify two principal elements of Boole's contribution to logic: first, the resort to a *formal theory* (and associated formal language); secondly the creation and adoption of a rigorous *method* to analyse and construct arguments within such a theory. The next two subsections provide an overview of each of these in turn.

2.1 Boole's system

The first task in the construction of a formal theory is to set up a *formal language* for the theory. The 'symbolical language of a Calculus' featured in LOT comprises the following elements:

- terms $x, y, z \ldots$
  - → interpreted as *classes*
- the special class 0
  - → interpreted as the *empty class*
- the special class 1
  - → interpreted as the *universe*
- a relation symbol =
  - → interpreted as *identity* between classes
- operation symbols:
  - – addition: $x + y = v$
    - → interpreted as *union* of classes
  - – multiplication: $x \cdot y = w$
    - → interpreted as *intersection* of classes
  - – subtraction: $-x = 1 - x$
    - → interpreted as taking *complements* of classes
- no quantifiers.

The signs and operation symbols that make up the formal language just described are all borrowed from the branch of mathematics known today as *abstract algebra*: the sub-area of mathematics which studies the properties of abstract algebraic structures starting from a set of equations (which hold of the structures in question).[4]

Of course the discipline of abstract algebra was not defined in the same way (or as precisely) then as it is now; and in Boole's time it was still customary for mathematicians to refer to this discipline as *symbolical algebra* (owing to the fact that variables were then referred to as *symbols*). In modern textbooks it is common to find abstract algebra contrasted with so-called elementary algebra – the latter being 'the arithmetic of indefinite quantities or variables' (Pratt 2007) familiar from secondary school. But the two only began to be properly distinguished around the turn of the last century, when the work of several algebraists of the time – Boole being one of them – led to the inception of abstract algebra in the modern sense. Hilary Putnam writes in this regard:

> The program – the program of the 'Symbolic School' of British analysts – is today out of date, but in a certain sense it was the bridge between traditional analysis (real and complex analysis) and modern abstract algebra ... Boole was quite conscious of the idea of *misinterpretation*, of the idea of using a mathematical system as an algorithm, transforming signs purely mechanically without any reliance on meanings. In connection with logic, this very important idea appears on the opening pages of Boole's [LOT] (Putnam 1982: 293–4).

It is important to note from our historical perspective that Boole still had one foot in the old conception of algebra. Thus, for instance, he took after the algebraists of the time in treating the symbols of his algebra as coextensional with the objects symbolized. In Boole's case, the symbols were thought of as roughly akin to *mental acts*, as well as being used to represent and refer to classes:

> Let us then suppose that the universe of our discourse is the actual universe, so that words are to be used in the full extent of their meaning, and let us consider the two mental operations implied by the words 'white' and 'men'. The word 'men' implies the operation of selecting in thought from its subject, the universe, all men; and the resulting conception, *men*, becomes the subject of the next operation. The operation implied by the word 'white' is that of selecting from its subject, 'men', all of that class which are white. The final resulting conception is that of 'white men'.

Boole 1854: 31–2

It is likely owing to a perceived ambiguity between interpretation and referent of the symbols of the calculus, in fact, that some commentators were later so quick to place Boole in the psychologistic camp. But in this regard it is certainly worth noting that Boole was one of the scarce few to remain untouched by Frege's accusations of sympathizing with psychologism. On the contrary, in discussing Boole's work Frege openly expressed his interest in and respect for the ideas developed and put forward in LOT. This is all the more notable considering the fundamental disagreement, at heart, between Frege's logicist project – which sought to show that arithmetic (at least) could be reduced to pure logic – and Boole's algebraic approach – which effectively, although not as explicitly, sought to perform a reduction in the opposite direction.

After introducing the symbols of his algebra, Boole goes on to explain that the special 'universal' class (represented by the symbol 1) 'is the only class in which are found all the individuals that exist in any class' (1854: 34). Here is Corcoran on Boole's universal class:

> Boole's ... use of the symbol '1' found in [LOT], and by translation also the word 'entity', marks a milestone in logic ... In [LOT], '1' indicates not 'the universe' [in the sense of 'most comprehensive class'] but the limited subject matter of the particular discourse in which it is used, what Boole calls 'the universe of [the] discourse' which varies from one discourse-context to another ...
>
> *This is the first time in the history of the English language that the expression* 'universe of discourse' *was ever used.* In this way Boole opens up room for one and the same language to be used in many different interpretations ... *Modern logic is almost inconceivable without the concept of universe of discourse.*
>
> Corcoran 2003: 273–4; emphases added

We may now go on to present the laws of thought themselves. The list that Boole finally settled upon comprises six axioms:

Law 1 $\quad x + y = y + x$
Law 2 $\quad x \cdot y = y \cdot x$
Law 3 $\quad x^2 = x$
Law 4 $\quad z \cdot (x + y) = z \cdot x + z \cdot y$
Law 5 $\quad x - y = -y + x$
Law 6 $\quad z \cdot (x - y) = z \cdot x - z \cdot y$

Complementing these axioms are two rules of inference:

Law 7 $\quad$ Adding or subtracting equals from equals gives equals
Law 8 $\quad$ Multiplying equals by equals gives equals

The principles displayed above bring into sharper focus Boole's conception of 'algebra of logic' – or 'mathematical analysis of logic' – as a kind of *applied mathematics*. In the displayed formulas we immediately recognize familiar algebraic properties such as commutativity of addition (Law 1), multiplication (Law 2) and subtraction (Law 5); and distributivity of multiplication over addition (Law 4) and over subtraction (Law 6).

Boole was a strongly philosophically minded mathematician and logician, and as such he was sensitive to the importance of providing arguments to support his claims. That commutativity is a law of logic, for instance, is argued in the following passage:

> Now it is perfectly apparent that if the operations above described had been performed in a converse order, the result would have been the same. Whether we begin by forming the conception of '*men*', and then by a second intellectual act limit that conception to 'white men', or whether we begin by forming the conception of 'white objects', and then limit it to such of that class as are 'men', is perfectly indifferent so far as the result is concerned ... And thus the indifference of the order of two successive acts of the faculty of Conception ... is a general condition of the exercise of that faculty. It is a law of the mind, and it is the real origin of the law of the literal symbols of Logic which constitutes its formal expression ...
>
> Boole 1854: 32

Of course it is one thing to give *an* argument, and quite another to give a *good* argument. We will see in the next section that among the criticisms levelled against Boole is a complaint over the weakness of arguments such as the above.

Law 3 departs quite noticeably from the other laws: in contrast to those, it is not an axiom scheme but an ordinary algebraic equation, the (only) roots of which are $x = 0$ and $x = 1$. Partly on this account, it has received considerably more attention in the literature. Boole refers to Law 3 as the 'special law' of the algebra of thought, and to its generalized version (below) as the *index law*:

$$x^n = x^5$$

Why did Boole hail this as a general principle, and conceive of it as belonging among the 'laws of thought'? Boole's explanation is the following:

> As the combination of two literal symbols in the form *xy* expresses the whole of that class of objects to which the names or qualities represented by *x* and *y* are together applicable, it follows that if the two symbols have exactly the same signification, their combination expresses no more than either of the symbols taken alone would do. In such case [we have]
>
> $$xx = x.$$
>
> ... It is evident that the more nearly the actual significations [of *x* and *y*] approach to each other, the more nearly does the class of things denoted by the

combination *xy* approach to identity with the class denoted by *x*, as well as with that denoted by *y*.

Boole 1854: 22

Thus, the key to understanding the index law is to think of it *not* as a principle of algebra but as one of logic (where the latter is of course to be thought of as Boole did). If we place ourselves within Boole's framework and adopt his interpretation of the symbols occurring in the equation, then it is a straightforward matter to understand the rationale for Law 3. Recall that the symbol '*x*' is interpreted as the act of selecting a class of individuals within the universe of discourse (or, more concisely, '*x*' represents a class), and the multiplication symbol ('·') is interpreted as intersection (of classes). Then the logical product $x \cdot x = x^2$ represents the operation of taking the intersection of the class *x* with *x* itself; and this is of course *x* again. Thus, we have that $x^2 = x$.[6]

Boole continues:

The law which it expresses is practically exemplified in language. To say 'good, good', in relation to any subject, though a cumbrous and useless pleonasm, is the same as to say 'good'. Thus 'good, good' men, is equivalent to 'good' men. Such repetitions of words are indeed sometimes employed to heighten a quality or strengthen an affirmation … But neither in strict reasoning nor in exact discourse is there any just ground for such a practice.

Boole 1854: 23

We are now in a position to make a first (partial and provisional) assessment of Boole's project in LOT. Most prominently, it should be clear enough by now that the theory of LOT neither coincides with the theory of abstract algebra, nor is construed as such; Boole's Law 3 alone leaves no doubt about this. Nor is the claim being made that the laws of thought, the laws of logic and the laws of algebra are one and the same thing. Boole's thesis is more subtle than this, and can be broken down into two components: (i) that algebra can serve as a toolbox and a medium by which to express the laws of logic; and (ii) that the laws of *logic*, not algebra, embody the laws of thought, i.e. the laws of correct reasoning.

2.2 Boole's method

Having set up a formal language, the second task envisaged by Boole is 'upon this foundation to establish the science of Logic and construct its method …' (Boole 1854: 1). The method developed by Boole to analyse arguments is often referred to as his 'General Method' in the literature, and we follow this usage. We begin by presenting the General Method and looking at some of its applications before embarking on a more critical appraisal of Boole's work.

Boole's General Method may be reconstructed schematically as comprising the following steps:

1. Convert initial propositions (premises) into algebraic equations.
2. Apply one or more algebraic transformations to the premise equations, ultimately producing conclusion equations.
3. Convert conclusion equations into propositions (conclusions).

Rather than merely discussing the General Method in the abstract, it is much more helpful to examine a few examples of how it can be put to work (as envisaged by Boole). For a case study that is both natural and historically appropriate, let us consider the categorical propositions of Aristotelian logic. Recall from Chapter 1 that Aristotelian logic countenances eight types of propositions:

(i)   All *Y*s are *X*s
(ii)   No *Y*s are *X*s
(iii)   Some *Y*s are *X*s
(iv)   Some *Y*s are not- *X*s
(v)   All not- *Y*s are *X*s
(vi)   No not- *Y*s are *X*s
(vii)   Some not- *Y*s are *X*s
(viii)   Some not- *Y*s are not- *X*s

Now let us apply the General Method to (i). Since this is a single proposition – as opposed to a multi-line argument – application of the General Method reduces to application of (1): converting the proposition in question into an algebraic equation. But which equation? To work this out, one must examine the internal structure of (i). The proposition 'All *Y*s are *X*s' imposes a specific condition on all things *Y* and all things *X*: namely, for the proposition to hold it must be the case that the *X*s subsume *all* of the *Y*s. Put differently, if '*X*' and '*Y*' denote two classes (or subclasses of the universe class), then it must be the case that the *Y* -class is itself a subclass of *X*. In the terminology introduced in Section 2.1, let *x, y, v* denote *X*, *Y*, and the intersection of *X* and *Y*, respectively. The conversion of (i) into algebraic form then yields the following:

All *Y*s are *X*s $\sim$ $y = vx$

Take now the categorical proposition 'Some *Y*s are *X*s': in this case the relevant satisfaction condition amounts to there being a non-empty intersection of the

X-class and the *Y*-class. Let the symbols *x*, *y*, *z* be interpreted as above. The General Method then produces the following result:

Some *Y*s are *X*s   ⤳ $xy = v$

For a final example, let us look at proposition (v). When is the proposition 'All not- *Y*s are *X*s' satisfied? When *X* and *Y* are disjoint, and everything that is not a *Y* is among the *X*s. In algebraic form, this reads:

All not- *Y*s are *X*s   ⤳ $1 - y = vx$

Exercise 1

(a) Convert the remaining five types of propositions from Aristotelian logic into algebraic form.
(b) Apply Boole's method to the following argument in propositional form:

  (P1) All tigers are mammals.
  (P2) All mammals are mortal.
  (C)   Therefore, all tigers are mortal.

3 Limitations of Boole's theory

Boole had several critics, both during his lifetime and posthumously; in this section we chart some of the main worries raised against LOT. Discussion of the more widespread reception of Boole's work, and more specifically of his legacy to modern logic, will be delayed until Section 4. Here we focus on two specific charges moved against Boole. The first concerns the cogency of the arguments presented in LOT for the adoption of his General Method; the other, the logical apparatus developed in LOT itself.

3.1 Metatheory

It was mentioned earlier on that an important motivation behind Boole's project was the realization that the Aristotelian framework, which embodied the orthodoxy at the time, was too narrow in its scope to serve as a satisfactory theory of logic. A particularly prominent limitation of the Aristotelian system was its failure to account for propositions outside of the eight categories, as seen in Chapter 1.

While Boole was right about the weaknesses in Aristotle's system, it is also true that a more global comparison of LOT with Aristotle's work is not entirely favourable to Boole. There is at least one respect in which Aristotle's system still surpasses Boole's, namely its attention to *formal rigour*. More specifically, it has been noted by some commentators that Boole's system is neither sound nor complete – nor is there evidence, in LOT, that Boole was concerned with verifying whether either of these metalogical desiderata was satisfied.

Granted, the concepts of soundness and completeness as we know, define, and prove them today are both more recent than LOT, not to mention Aristotle's *Prior Analytics*. But the *ideas* were far from novel to logicians working in Boole's time. According to Corcoran, for instance,

> where Aristotle had a method of deduction that satisfies the highest modern standards of soundness and completeness, Boole has a semi-formal method of derivation that is neither sound nor complete. More importantly, Aristotle's discussions of his goals and his conscientious persistence in their pursuit make of both soundness and completeness properties that a reader could hope, if not expect, to find Aristotle's logic to have. In contrast, Boole makes it clear that his primary goal was to generate or derive solutions to sets of equations regarded as conditions on unknowns. The goal of gaplessly deducing conclusions from sets of propositions regarded as premises is mentioned, but not pursued.
>
> Corcoran 2003: 261

Exercise 2

(a) Try to think of two (or more) examples of propositions that cannot be accommodated by the Aristotelian system (for which cf. Section 2.2 above).

(b) Try to explain in your own words why examples such as these count heavily against the adoption of standard Aristotelian logic.

3.2 Language

It is well known that Gottlob Frege (1848–1925), who lived and worked a mere few decades after Boole, is almost universally credited with the invention of modern logic. It is also well known that nothing ever happens in a vacuum; and while Frege certainly deserved all the recognition he has received during his life and ever since, there is some plausibility in the conjecture that Boole's work on algebraic logic helped set the stage for the Fregean revolution.

Boole's work was firmly on the radar by the time Frege began to publish his own work; indeed, there is no doubt that Frege was very well acquainted with LOT when he started work on his *Begriffsschrift*. Evidence to this effect comes from one of Frege's earliest unpublished articles (reprinted in Frege 1979), where Boole's system is discussed on its own merits and in comparison with the theory later developed by Frege himself.

Throughout this discussion Frege maintains a largely appreciative attitude towards Boole's algebraization project. But he is also (rightly) critical of certain lingering expressive limitations in the theory of LOT, which will be mentioned briefly here. For, as Frege notes,

> Boole had only an inadequate expression for particular judgments such as 'some 4th roots of 16 are square roots of 4' ... and for existential judgments such as 'there is at least one 4th root of 16' ... apparently no expression at all.
>
> Frege 1979: 14

Aristotle's logic is inadequate to account for quantified propositions of either kind; in this instance, however, so is Boole's. For as we saw earlier in the chapter, Boole's language of thought does not include quantifier symbols, and *a fortiori* his General Method is unequipped to treat such propositions. So while Boole's algebra can accommodate a greater variety of propositions than Aristotle's logic can, LOT also does not reach quite as far in this direction as one could hope for.

Exercise 3

(a) Give two further examples of quantified propositions which cannot be adequately represented in the language of LOT.

(b) Try to explain in your own words why these examples are indeed a problem for Boole's project.

3.3 Method

Yet another worry about LOT is that Boole offers rather thin arguments in support of the adoption of the algebraic laws as the 'laws of thought'. Indeed, Boole does little more beyond claiming that the laws may be 'seen' to hold by reflecting on the operations performed by our mind:

> Sufficient illustration has been given to render manifest the two following positions, viz.:
>
> First, *that the operations of the mind*, by which ... it combines and modifies the simple ideas of things or qualities, not less than those operations of the

reason which are exercised upon truths and propositions, *are subject to general laws.*

Secondly, *that those laws are mathematical in their form,* and that they are actually developed in the essential laws of human language. Wherefore the laws of the symbols of Logic are deducible from a consideration of the operations of the mind in reasoning.

Boole 1854: 32; emphasis added

We may also note that exceptions to the applicability of the algebraic operations are easy to find:

- $x + y$ is defined *only if x, y are disjoint*
- $x - y$ is defined *only if y is a subclass of x*

On the other hand when these conditions do not obtain, the logical operation in question is labelled an *uninterpretable*. Here is Boole on this very point:

The expression $x + y$ seems indeed uninterpretable, unless it be assumed that the things represented by x and the things represented by y are entirely separate; that they embrace no individuals in common.

Boole 1854: 66

The use of just such uninterpretables attracted strong criticism among Boole's contemporaries, and most notably from William Stanley Jevons (1835–1882). Jevons, a prominent economist of his time, also cultivated an interest in logic and even published a volume (Jevons 1890) in which he developed a system of logic designed to rival – perhaps, in Jevons' intentions, to replace – Boole's LOT. But the heart of their dispute is perhaps best captured by certain extracts in the correspondence into which the two entered prior to the publication of Jevons' monograph. Thus Jevons wrote, for instance:

It is surely obvious ... that $x + x$ is equivalent only to x ... Professor Boole's notation [process of subtraction] is inconsistent with a self-evident law.

To this, Boole replied that

$x + x = 0$ is equivalent to ... $x = 0$; but [...] $x + x$ is not equivalent to ... x.

He continued,

To be explicit, I now, however, reply that it is not true that in Logic $x + x = x$, though it is true that $x + x = 0$ is equivalent to $x = 0$. If I do not write more it is not from any unwillingness to discuss the subject with you, but simply because if we differ on this fundamental point it is impossible that we should agree in others.[7]

Boole and Jevons never resolved their disagreement. Seen from Boole's perspective, this is understandable: for one thing, conceding Jevons' point would have called for quite significant revisions of the overarching framework of LOT; for another, it would have amounted to just as significant a departure from ordinary algebra. But this in turn would have meant departing from the goal of the original project, namely to show that ordinary algebra could model the laws of thought.

Exercise 4

(a) Try to produce at least two counterexamples of your own which show the limitations of Boole's method.
(b) Try to explain in your own words why these are indeed counterexamples to the universality of Boole's method.

4 Boole's algebra, and Boolean algebra

It is not uncommon to find Boole associated with – or even cited as the father of – *Boolean algebra*, and it is natural to wonder whether and to what extent the latter owes its existence to the former. This final subsection very briefly addresses such questions.

In mathematics, the term 'Boolean algebra' refers to the sub-discipline that studies the properties of two-valued logics with sentential connectives (and no quantifiers). Boolean algebra is also quite widely regarded as something of a theoretical precursor of computer science. Thus it has come to pass that Boole has sometimes been credited as no less than the grandfather of computer science itself. Now, there is no doubt that some conceptual link does exist between Boole's account of logic and the algebra of logic developed in LOT on the one hand, and the logic of Boolean algebras and computer science on the other. But such claims are historically inaccurate, at best. As several commentators have duly noted,[8] there is next to no textual evidence to support the thesis that Boole had in mind any other, and more abstract, applications of his algebra of logic.

What is in fact known about Boole's algebra of logic and about the development of Boolean algebra supports a rather weaker claim: namely, that while Boole's algebra of logic is emphatically not identical with Boolean algebra, there is a considerable amount of overlap between the principles governing the two (about which more will be said shortly). And, of course, there is little doubt that the modern mathematical discipline owes its name to the author of LOT:

The adjective 'boolean', sometimes even 'Boolean', is known to mathematicians for a powerful algebra, to electrical engineers and computing specialists who apply it widely in parts of their work, to philosophers as a component of logic, and to historically-minded people as one George Boole (1815–1864), who formed an algebra of logic from which we enjoy these modern fruits.

Grattan-Guinness and Bornet, 1997: xiii

Against the backdrop of this crucial historical disambiguation, we now move to give a brief introduction to the notion of a Boolean algebra, which will occupy what remains of this section.[9]

In mathematics, a Boolean algebra (BA) is defined as a set A together with:

- a unary operation $\neg$
- two binary operations $\vee$ (join) and $\wedge$ (meet)
- two (distinct) elements 0 and 1

such that for all $a, b, c \in A$ the following axioms hold:

- commutativity: $a \wedge b = b \vee a$

  $a \wedge b = b \wedge a$
- associativity: $a \vee (b \vee c) = (a \vee b) \vee c$

  $a \wedge (b \wedge c) = (a \wedge b) \wedge c$
- distributivity: $a \vee (b \wedge c) = (a \vee b) \wedge (a \vee c)$

  $a \wedge (b \vee c) = (a \wedge b) \vee (a \wedge c)$
- special laws I: $a \vee 0 = a$

  $a \wedge 1 = a$
- special laws II: $a \vee \neg a = 1$

  $a \wedge \neg a = 0$

It is not uncommon to find a Boolean algebra defined in terms of the closely related concept of a *ring*. In abstract algebra, a (Boolean) ring is defined as a set X with:

- a unary operation $-$
- two binary operations $+$ and $\cdot$
- two distinct elements 0 and 1.

The characteristic axioms for a Boolean ring overlap, but do not coincide with, those for a Boolean algebra:

- commutativity of addition: $a + b = b + a$
- associativity: $a + (b + c) = (a + b) + c$

  $a \cdot (b \cdot c) = (a \cdot b) \cdot c$

- distributivity:
$$a + (b \cdot c) = (a + b) \cdot (a + c)$$
$$a \cdot (b + c) = (a \cdot b) + (a \cdot c)$$

- special laws I:
$$a + 0 = a$$
$$a \cdot 1 = a$$

- special laws II:
$$a + (-a) = 1$$
$$a \cdot (-a) = 0$$

- idempotence:
$$a^2 = a.$$

Thus in talk of algebras the meet $x \vee y$ corresponds to the ring notation $x + y$ and the join $x \wedge y$ to xy.[10] From the definitions just given we also immediately see that a Boolean algebra is none other than a commutative ring – i.e. a ring in which commutativity holds for both + (ring sum) and · (ring multiplication). Indeed all other defining conditions of a Boolean ring are satisfied by a Boolean algebra and vice versa. In particular idempotence is always a property of Boolean algebras: that is, for x an arbitrary element of a Boolean algebra we have that $x \wedge x = x$.

Suppose A is a Boolean algebra as defined above. Then it is reasonably straightforward to prove the following equivalence:

$$a = b \wedge a \quad \text{iff} \quad a \vee b = b.$$

Exercise 5

Try proving the above equivalence.

Hint: the result follows from the basic properties of Boolean algebras stated earlier on in the section.

To complete this brief overview of Boolean algebras we introduce one last notion, which serves to isolate a certain special class of algebras known as *self-dual* algebras.

Let A be a Boolean algebra as before. We can then introduce a new relation $\leq$, defined by $a \leq b$ iff the above conditions hold. The relation $\leq$ defines a *partial order* on the set A, which in turn entails that the following conditions are satisfied for A:

- 0 is the least element and 1 is the greatest element
- The meet $a \wedge b$ is the infimum of $\{a, b\}$
- The join $a \vee b$ is the supremum of $\{a, b\}$

An algebra that meets all of the above conditions is termed self-dual: for, if we exchange $\wedge$ with $\vee$ or 0 with 1 within any axiom, the result is still an axiom of the algebra. Put differently, a self-dual algebra is one that is *invariant under permutation*.

It must be emphasized that the above is a sketch of the most general (and thus most basic) type of Boolean algebra which can be defined. It should hopefully be straightforward enough to see that stronger systems can be obtained by adding further conditions to the axioms listed above. There are many sources on Boolean algebras; for a conveniently compact and relatively accessible text, see for instance Halmos (1963).

Notes

1   Perhaps her most famous works are *Philosophy and Fun of Algebra* (London: C.W. Daniel, 1909) and *The Preparation of the Child for Science* (Oxford: Clarendon Press, 1904). Incidentally, Mary's uncle was Sir George Everest, after whom Mount Everest is named.

2   On the other hand, there is some controversy in the literature over the nature of the philosophical views underwriting MAL and LOT, as well as the question of whether there is a discontinuity between the former and the latter in this respect. See for instance Vassallo (1997) on this point.

3   One such notable exception, of course, is Bolzano, for which cf. Chapter 4 of this volume.

4   For a comprehensive yet accessible introduction to algebras in general, see for instance Pratt (2007).

5   Note that whereas both versions of the law are discussed in MAL, no mention of the index law is made in LOT.

6   Analogous reasoning can be applied to show that the index law holds in its generalized version also, of course.

7   All of the quotations reproduced here are extracted from Burris (2010) and Jourdain (1914).

8   Corcoran writes: '[Boole] did not write the first book on pure mathematics, he did not present a decision procedure, and he did not devise "Boolean algebra"' (2003: 282).

9   Note on terminology: in order to avoid ambiguities, Boole's will here occasionally be referred to as boolean algebra (lower case 'b'), to distinguish it from the specialist concept of Boolean algebra.

10 Although notation is not uniform everywhere: in the context of ring theory, for instance, the join is sometimes defined as $x \vee y = x + y + xy$. The lack of uniformity in notation derives from the ambiguity over the use of '+', which should be interpreted as *ring* sum.

References

Agazzi, E. (1974), 'The rise of the foundational research in mathematics', *Synthese* 27: 7–26.

Boole, G. (1847), *The Mathematical Analysis of Logic, Being an Essay Towards a Calculus of Deductive Reasoning*, Cambridge: Macmillan, Barclay & Macmillan.

Boole, G. (1854), *An Investigation of the Laws of Thought, on which are founded the Mathematical Theories of Logic and Probabilities*, Cambridge and London: Walton & Maberly.

Burris, S. (2010), 'George Boole', in Edward N. Zalta (ed.), *The Stanford Encyclopedia of philosophy*, Stanford: University of Stanford Press.

Corcoran, J. (2003), 'Aristotle's *Prior analytics* and Boole's *Laws of thought*', *History and Philosophy of Logic* 24: 261–88.

Frege, G. (1979), 'Boole's logical Calculus and the Concept-script', in Hermes, H. et al. (eds), *Posthumous Writings* (P. Long and R. White, transl.), Oxford: Basil Blackwell.

Grattan-Guinness, I., and Bornet, G. (eds) (1997), *George Boole. Selected Manuscripts on Logic and its Philosophy*, Basel: Birkhaüser Verlag.

Halmos, P. (1963), *Lectures on Boolean Algebras*, Van Nostrand Mathematical Studies (Hal- mos and Gehring, eds), Princeton and London: Van Nostrand.

Jevons, W.S. (1890), *Pure Logic and Other Minor Works*, ed. R. Adamson and H.A. Jevons, New York: Lennox Hill Pub. & Dist. Co., repr. 1971.

Jourdain, P.E.B. (1914), 'The development of the theories of mathematical logic and the principles of mathematics. William Stanley Jevons', *Quarterly Journal of Pure and Applied Mathematics*, 44: 113–28.

MacFarlane, A. (1916), *Ten British Mathematicians of the Nineteenth Century*, Mathematical monographs vol. 17 (Merriman and Woodward, eds).

Pratt, V. (2007), 'Algebra', in Edward N. Zalta (ed.), *The Stanford Encyclopedia of Philosophy*, Stanford: Stanford University Press.

Putnam, H. (1982), 'Peirce the logician', *Historia mathematica* 9: 290–301.

Van Heijenoort, J. (1967), 'Logic as calculus and logic as a language', *Synthese* 17(3): 324–30.

Vassallo, N. (1997), '*Analysis* versus *Laws*: Boole's explanatory psychologism versus his explanatory anto-psychologism', *History and philosophy of logic* 18: 151–63.

Part III

Mathematical Logic

7

C.S. Peirce

Peter Øhrstrøm

Charles Sanders Peirce (1839–1914) was a spokesman for an open and undogmatic understanding of logic. He got his inspiration first and foremost from the medieval juxtaposition of three of the seven free arts into the so-called *trivium*. The trivium consisted of the disciplines of Grammar, Dialectics (or Logic) and Rhetoric. Peirce's work from 1865 to 1903 shows a constant development of reflections on the content and application of this tripartition (see Fisch 1978). In the spring of 1865, he subdivided the general science of representations into 'General Grammar', 'Logic' and 'Universal Rhetorics'. In May the same year, he called this division 'General Grammar', 'General Logic' and 'General Rhetorics', and in 1867 it was presented as 'Formal Grammar', 'Logic' and 'Formal Rhetorics'. Twenty years later, in 1897, it had become 'Pure Grammar', 'Logic Proper' and 'Pure Rhetorics'. In 1903 Peirce – within his own now more matured framework – determined the tripartition as 'Speculative Grammar', 'Critic' and 'Methodeutic'.

Not only reflections on the trivium as such, but also several other elements of medieval logic had an impact on Peirce's analyses. One example is the tripartition of the subjects of logic into terms, propositions and arguments – a division which can be found in almost every medieval introduction to logic. It was clear to Peirce that this classification was relevant, not only within logic (in the narrow sense), but also within both grammar and rhetorics, a fact which had also been recognized by the ancients and the medievals. It should be mentioned, however, that Peirce rejected the idea of completely non-assertoric terms. In his opinion, even terms are in general assertoric (see his Collected Papers – hereafter CP – section 2.341).

Peirce's extensive knowledge of classic and scholastic logic also meant that he would not accept logic as a completely untemporal or atemporal science. He could well imagine a new development of a logic, which would take time seriously. In fact, Peirce's philosophy contains features which could be interpreted as an emergent logic for events. For example, he defined the notion of a 'Token' as applying to 'A Single event which happens once and whose identity is limited to that one happening or a Single object or thing which is in one single place at any one instant of time' (CP 4.537). However, Peirce was hesitant about advancing a formal logic of time himself, but nevertheless it is relatively easy in his authorship to find clear ideas, which can be used in a presentation of a formal logic of time. This was a great inspiration for A.N. Prior, who in the 1950s and 1960s succeeded in re-establishing the logic of time as a proper part of logic. In Prior's first great time logical work *Time and Modality* (1957), he gave a brief presentation of the history of the modern logic of time in an appendix; about a quarter of this exposition is devoted to the importance of Peirce with respect to the development of the new logic of time.

This broader view of logic is also evident in the most remarkable logical formalism suggested by Peirce, the existential graphs. His idea was that in symbolic logic 'it will be convenient not to confine the symbols used to algebraic symbols, but to include some graphical symbols as well' (CP 4.372). Peirce introduced three kinds of existential graphs: Alpha, Beta and Gamma Graphs.

The system of Alpha Graphs corresponds to what we now call propositional logic, the system of Beta Graphs corresponds to first-order predicate calculus, whereas the systems of Gamma Graphs correspond to various kinds of modal (including temporal) logic. When Peirce died in 1914 his system's Gamma Graphs were still very tentative and unfinished. In the following, we shall investigate the main structures of the axiomatic systems which Peirce suggested with his Alpha and Beta Graphs, and also some of the ideas of the Gamma Graphs he was considering. It should, however, be kept in mind that the system of Beta Graphs is an extension (or generalization) of the system of Alpha Graphs, whereas any system of Gamma Graphs will be an extension (or generalization) of the system of Beta Graphs.

1 The Alpha Graphs

In Peirce's graphs, the statements in question are written on the so-called 'sheet of assertion', SA. In fact, the empty sheet of assertion is supposed to be an axiom, essentially a sort of a constant corresponding to 'Truth'. This is the only axiom in the Peircean Alpha-system. Propositions on the SA may be enclosed using so-called 'cuts', which in fact correspond to negations (we also speak of 'negated contexts'). That is, the following combination of graphs means that P is the case, Q is not the case, and the conjunction of S and R is not the case.

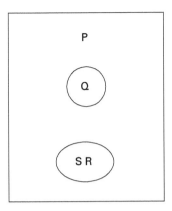

Here the box represents the SA, whereas the curved closures symbolize the cuts, i.e. the negated contexts. In terms of the established formalism of propositional logic, the above graph is equivalent to

$P \wedge \sim Q \wedge \sim (S \wedge R)$

It is obvious that such conjunctional forms are rather easy to represent in Peircean graphs. Disjunctions and implications are, however, slightly more complicated. The implication, $P \supset Q$, is represented by the following graph:

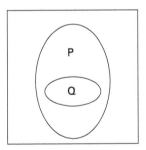

In standard formalism, this graph can be expressed as $\sim (P \wedge \sim Q)$, which is exactly the traditional definition of material implication in terms of negation and conjunction. Clearly, in this case, we have an example of nested cuts, since the Q is placed in a cut, which is inside another cut. In this way, we may in fact have very complicated systems of several nested cuts. In such cases, we may speak of sub-graphs being oddly or evenly enclosed. In the present case, we may say that Q is evenly enclosed, whereas P is oddly enclosed.

Peirce made several formulations of his logic of his existential graphs (see CP Vol. 4 book 2). In a slightly modernized form inspired by Roberts (1973: 138), the rules for the Alpha Graphs can be listed as follows:

R1. The rule of erasure. Any evenly enclosed graph may be erased.

R2. The rule of insertion. Any graph may be scribed on any oddly enclosed area.

R3. The rule of iteration. If a graph P occurs in the SA or in a nest of cuts, it may be scribed on any area not part of P, which is contained by the place of P.

R4. The rule of deiteration. Any graph whose occurrence could be the result of iteration may be erased.

R5. The rule of the double cut. The double cut may be inserted around or removed (where it occurs) from any graph on any area.

In addition to these rules, there is as mentioned above just one axiom: the empty graph (SA). It is a remarkable theoretical result that this system of Peirce's Alpha Graphs corresponds exactly to what is now called standard propositional calculus (see Sowa 1992, 2010). This means that any theorem which is provable in ordinary propositional logic (i.e. any proposition which may be shown to be a tautology using ordinary truth-tables) may also be demonstrated in Peirce's system. A few examples may be given in order to illustrate how the Peircean system of existential graphs works:

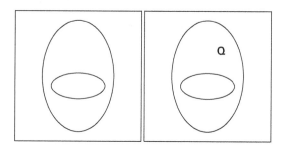

To the left a double cut is introduced (by R5). To the right the proposition Q is inserted (by R2).

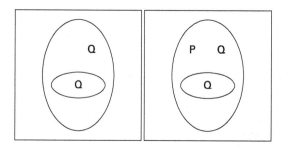

To the left the proposition Q is iterated (by R3). To the right the proposition P is inserted (by R2).

This constitutes a proof of the theorem:

$(P \wedge Q) \supset Q$

To prove a theorem corresponding to a certain graph one must transform the empty SA into the graph in question. John Sowa (1992, 2010) has argued that it is in many cases significantly easier to prove a theorem by using the graphs rather than the established logical procedures.

2 The Beta Graphs

In the Beta Graphs, Peirce introduced a predicate calculus with a quantification theory formulated in terms of what he called 'lines of identity' (ligatures). These graphs are immediately designed for existential statements. The statement which is now normally formalized as $\exists x:q(x)$ is represented by the graph:

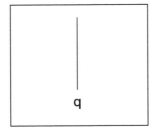

Universal statements have to be represented in a slightly more complicated way using two cuts (i.e. two negations) corresponding to the formula $\sim(\exists x:\sim q(x))$:

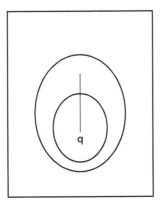

It is evident that the introduction of lines of identity (ligatures) gives rise to a number of complicated questions which Peirce had to deal with. It seems that for a longer period he was trying to find the optimal formulation of the logical rules for the Beta Graphs which should obviously be seen as an extension of the system for Alpha Graphs. Roberts (1973: 138) has suggested a reasonable exposition of Peirce's ideas and enumerates the rules for the Alpha and Beta Graphs as follows:

R1. The rule of erasure. Any evenly enclosed graph and any evenly enclosed portion of a line of identity may be erased.

R2. The rule of insertion. Any graph may be scribed on any oddly enclosed area, and two lines of identity (or portions of lines) oddly enclosed on the same area may be joined.

R3. The rule of iteration. If a graph P occurs in the SA or in a nest of cuts, it may be scribed on any area not part of P, which is contained by the place of P. Consequently, (a) a branch with a loose end may be added to any line of identity, provided that no crossing of cuts results from this addition; (b) any loose end of a ligature may be extended inwards through cuts; (c) any ligature thus extended may be joined to the corresponding ligature of an iterated instance of a graph; and (d) a cycle may be formed, by joining by inward extensions, the two loose ends that are the innermost parts of a ligature.

R4. The rule of deiteration. Any graph whose occurrence could be the result of iteration may be erased. Consequently, (a) a branch with a loose end may be retracted into any line of identity, provided that no crossing of cuts occurs in the retraction; (b) any loose end of a ligature may be retracted outwards through cuts; and (c) any cyclical part of a ligature may be cut at its inmost part.

R5. The rule of the double cut. The double cut may be inserted around or removed (where it occurs) from any graph on any area. And these transformations will not be prevented by the presence of ligatures passing from outside the outer cut to inside the inner cut.

In addition to these rules there are two axioms: the empty graph (SA) and the unattached line of identity. From these two axioms it is possible to derive a number of theorems and rules using (R1–5). For instance, the graph corresponding to the following implication

$\forall x: q(x) \supset \exists x: q(x)$

turns out to be provable, as demonstrated by Roberts (1992). The axiom of the unattached line of identity has a crucial role to play in this proof. This means that quantification cannot be empty in the logic of Beta Graphs (which is in fact also the case with Prior's quantification theory). With that restriction, it can be shown that theorems which can be proved in first-order logic can also be proved in terms of existential graphs – and vice versa. Utilizing some illustrative examples, we shall consider how some of the classical syllogisms can be handled in terms of Peirce's existential graphs.

The so-called 'Barbara' is the most famous among the Aristotelian syllogisms:

All M are P
All S are M
Therefore: All S are P

In terms of Peirce's existential graphs, it can be demonstrated that the conclusion follows from the two premises of the argument:

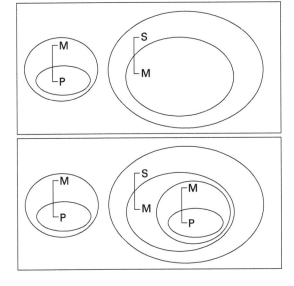

The two premises in the argument can be represented on the sheet of assertion in terms of the first diagram.

In the second diagram the graph to the left has been iterated into the interior of the graph to the right.

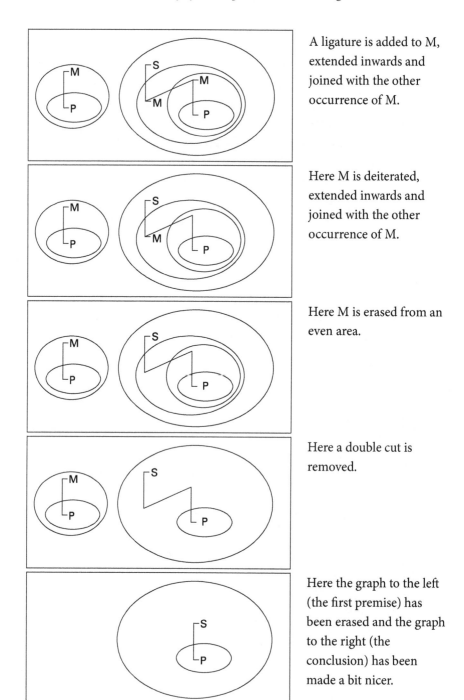

A ligature is added to M, extended inwards and joined with the other occurrence of M.

Here M is deiterated, extended inwards and joined with the other occurrence of M.

Here M is erased from an even area.

Here a double cut is removed.

Here the graph to the left (the first premise) has been erased and the graph to the right (the conclusion) has been made a bit nicer.

Another syllogistic example would be the so-called 'Ferio', which may be stated in this way:

No M are P

Some S are M

Therefore: Some S are not P

The conclusion of this syllogism may be proved from the premises in the following way using Peirce's existential graphs:

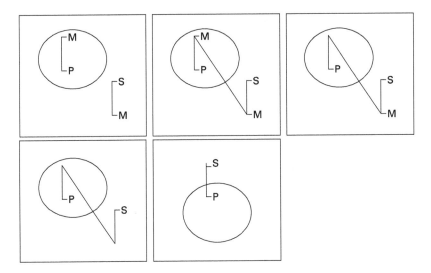

Here a ligature is added joining the two occurrences of M. Then deiteration of M and erasure of M lead to the conclusion (made a bit nicer in the last diagram). In this way the syllogism 'Ferio' in the first figure is proved.

3 The need for more than Alpha and Beta Graphs

The logic of Beta Graphs is clearly useful in many cases. They can be shown to correspond to what has later been termed first-order predicate calculus. Peirce realized, however, that the Alpha and Beta Graphs are not satisfactory in all cases. For instance, he considered the following two propositions (see CP 4.546):

1. Some married woman will commit suicide, if her husband fails in business.
2. Some married woman will commit suicide, if every married woman's husband fails in business.

Peirce argued that these two conditionals are equivalent if we analyse them in a merely classical and non-modal logic – i.e. in terms of Beta Graphs within his own logical system. For the sake of simplicity, we reformulate the problem using only predicates with one argument.

According to Peirce's rules for Beta Graphs and their lines of identity, the graphs corresponding to (1) and (2) can be proved to be equivalent, i.e.

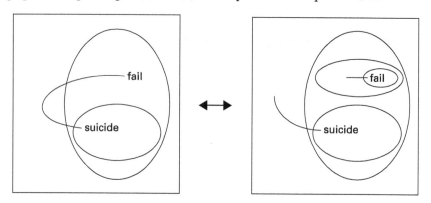

– where *fail(x)* means 'x is a woman married to a businessman who fails in business', and *suicide(x)* means 'x commits suicide'. This equivalence can be established by the rules of transformation for Beta Graphs. The two graphs respectively correspond to the following two expressions of standard predicate notation (where quantification is understood to be over the set of women married to businessmen):

(1a) $(\exists x)(fail(x) \supset suicide(x))$
(2a) $(\exists x)((\forall y)fail(y) \supset suicide(x))$

Both of these expressions are equivalent with

$(\exists x) \sim fail(x) \vee (\exists x)\, suicide(x)$

The inference from (1a) to (2a) appears rather natural. If there is a wife who will commit suicide if her husband fails in business, then it is obvious that this woman will also commit suicide in the case that all husbands fail in business. However, the opposite inference is clearly counterintuitive. Even if there is a woman who will commit suicide in the case that all husbands fail in business, it does not mean that this woman will commit suicide in the case that her own husband fails in business. Nevertheless, (1a) and (2a) turn out to be logically equivalent, as long as we are moving strictly within classical predicate logic, respectively the Beta Graphs. Therefore, as long as we are trying to represent our case within those systems, we are obliged to accept the counterintuitive inference.

However, it may be more natural to formulate the problem in terms of three predicates, so let *wife(x)* stand for 'x is the wife of a businessman'. When the statements (1) and (2) are represented with these three predicates, the crucial question will be the transition between the following graphs:

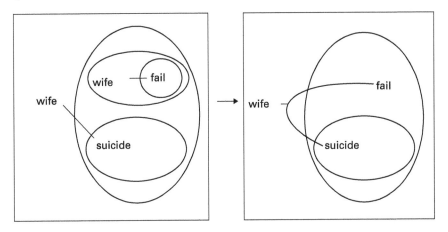

Again, these graphs can be shown to be equivalent. Essentially, their equivalence is due to the fact that the term *wife* is outside the scope of the negations. Therefore, the rules of iteration and deiteration for Beta Graphs can be applied to the inner copies. The proof using Beta Graphs could run as indicated below.

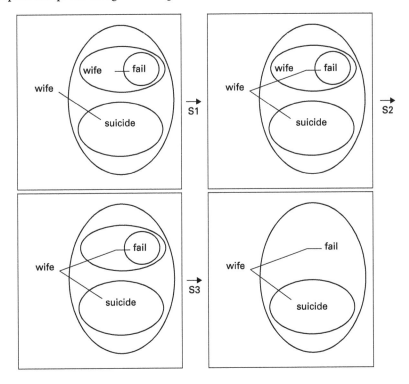

In the step (S1) a ligature is added joining to two occurrences of wife-. In step (S2), the inner occurrence of wife- is deiterated. In step (S3), a double cut is removed leading to the result.

In terms of standard formalism (1) and (2) are represented by:

(1b) $(\exists x)(wife(x) \wedge (fail(x) \supset suicide(x)))$
(2b) $(\exists x)(wife(x) \wedge ((\forall y)(wife(y) \supset fail(y)) \supset suicide(x)))$

Using fundamental equivalences from first-order logic, (1b) and (2b) can be written as disjunctions

(1b′) $(\exists x)(wife(x) \wedge \sim fail(x)) \vee (\exists x)(wife(x) \wedge suicide(x)))$
(2b′) $(\exists x)(wife(x) \wedge ((\exists y)(wife(y) \wedge \sim fail(y)) \vee suicide(x)))$

By the 'omission' of *wife(x)* in the first part of the disjunction in (2b′), it becomes evident that (1b′) follows from (2b′). If fact, it is evident that the two propositions are equivalent.

Peirce stated that the equivalence of these two propositions is 'the absurd result of admitting no reality but existence' (CP 4.546). As Stephen Read (1992) has pointed out, Peirce's analysis is a strong argument against anyone inclined to assert that conditionals in natural language are always truth-functional. But the Peircean analysis is also an argument for the need of a new tempo-modal logic. Peirce formulated his own solution in the following way:

> If, however, we suppose that to say that a woman will suicide if her husband fails, means that every possible course of events would either be one in which the husband would not fail or one in which the wife will commit suicide, then, to make that false it will not be requisite for the husband actually to fail, but it will suffice that there are possible circumstances under which he would fail, while yet his wife would not commit suicide.
>
> CP 4.546

This means that we have to quantify over 'every possible course of events'. A.N. Prior's tense-logical notation systems provide the means for doing just that. The operator suited for the problem at hand is *G*, corresponding to 'it is always going to be the case that'. Prior established a system designed to capture Peirce's ideas on temporal logic – appropriately called 'the Peircean solution'. In the Peircean system, *G* means 'always going to be in every course of events'. Using the operator in this way, we can express (1) and (2) as respectively

(1c) $(\exists x)G(fail(x) \supset suicide(x))$
(2c) $(\exists x)G((\forall y)fail(y) \supset suicide(x))$

(It should be mentioned that a linguistically more appropriate representation perhaps should take the form $N(p \supset Fq)$, where N and F stands for 'necessarily' and 'at some future time', respectively. However, (1c) and (2c) are sufficient for the conceptual considerations which are important here.)

Expression (1c) clearly means that there is some married woman w for whom the proposition, $\sim fail(w) \lor suicide(w)$, holds at any time in any possible future course of events. (2c) means that there is a married woman w for whom the proposition, $(\exists y) \sim fail(y) \lor suicide(w)$, holds at any time in any possible future course of events.

For this reason it is formally clear that (1c) entails (2c), but not conversely. And this corresponds exactly to intuition with respect to the two statements (1) and (2): the inference from (1) to (2) is valid, but Peirce was justified in maintaining that the inference from (2) to (1) should be rejected.

Generally speaking, some kind of tempo-modal logic is required for describing conditionals in natural language reasoning in a satisfactory way. Peirce's considerations on the example discussed above clearly demonstrate that he realized this. In fact, his observations served as a strong case for the development of the Gamma Graphs.

4 The Gamma Graphs

Peirce himself made some attempts at solving the problems of modality by introducing a new kind of graph. In what he called 'The Gamma Part of Existential Graphs' (CP 4.510 ff.), he put forward some interesting suggestions regarding modal logic. Some of his considerations on this topic were linked to what is now called epistemic logic, i.e. the logic of knowledge. In the following we shall describe his ideas.

In epistemic logic, the idea is that relative to a given state of information a number of propositions are known to be true. In Peirce's graph theory, propositions describing the information in question should be written on the 'sheet of assertion' SA, using just Alpha and Beta Graphs. Other propositions, however, are to be regarded as merely possible in the present state of information. Peirce represented such propositions using 'broken cuts', combined with the 'unbroken cuts', which we already know from the Alpha and Beta Graphs. A broken cut should be interpreted as corresponding to 'it is possible that not ...'. This means that 'it is possible that ...' must be represented as a combination of a broken and an unbroken cut:

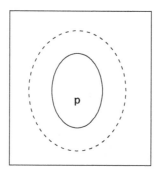

Now, consider a contingent proposition, i.e. a proposition, which is possible, but not necessary according to the present state of information. In this state, the sheet will include at least two propositions:

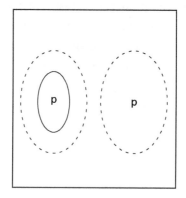

Now, suppose that *p* is contingent relative to some state of information, and that we then learn that *p* is in fact true. This would mean that the SA should be changed according to the new state of information. The graph corresponding to *Mp* ('possibly p') should be changed into the graph for 'it is known with certainty that p', i.e. ~*M*~*p*. Obviously, this means that the graph for *M*~*p* should be dropped, which results in a new (and simpler) graph representing the updated state of information. In this way, Peirce in effect pointed out that the passage of time does not only lead to new knowledge, but also to a loss of possibility. With respect to this epistemic logic, Don D. Roberts (1973: 85) has observed that the notions of necessity and possibility both may seem to collapse into the notion of truth. Roberts himself gave an important part of the answer to this worry by emphasizing how 'possibility and necessity are relative to the state of information' (CP 4.517). In the context of existential graphs, Peirce in fact established an equivalence between '*p* is known to be true' and '*p* is necessary'. In consequence, '*p* is not known to be false' and '*p* is possible' should also be equivalent in a

Peircean logic. Therefore, the kind of modal logic which Peirce was aiming at was in fact an epistemic logic, which should be sensitive to the impact of time.

5 Tempo-modal predicate logic and existential graphs

Peirce was concerned with the epistemic aspect of modality, but he also wanted to apply his logical graphs to modality in general – that is, to use them for representing any kind of modality. However, he was aware of the great complexity in which a full-fledged logic involving temporal modifications would result. This is probably the reason why Peirce's presentations of the Gamma Graphs remained tentative and unfinished. In the following, we intend to explain some of the problems he was facing, and suggest some ideas regarding the possible continuation of his project.

Our analysis of the problem from CP 4.546 suggests that the two statements should in fact be understood as follows:

(1') Some married woman will (in every possible future) commit suicide if her husband fails in business.

(2') Some married woman will (in every possible future) commit suicide if every married woman's husband fails in business.

We intend to formulate a graph-theoretical version of the tense-logical solution. So, we have to make sure that there are proper graphical representations of (1') and (2') such that the graphs are non-equivalent. In fact, it is not difficult to create graphs corresponding to the modal expressions in (1') and (2'). Obviously, a graph with a broken cut inside an unbroken cut with q would clearly correspond to the statement 'in every possible future q'. A representation of (1') and (2') could then be (omitting the SA):

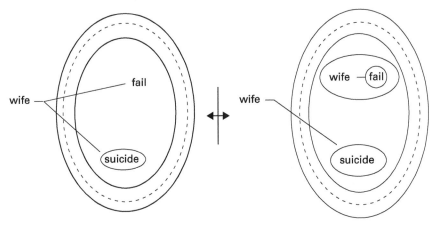

In order to treat problems like the one we have been discussing, we must be able to handle graphs involving the two kinds of cuts (broken and unbroken) as well as lines of identity. In consequence, we have to establish rules for modal conceptual graphs, specifically such that (1') and (2') would be non-equivalent. Although (2') should entail (1'), the opposite implication should not hold.

The question regarding the relation between modal operators and quantifiers is crucial for any modal predicate logic. Peirce was aware of this problem. He stated:

> Now, you will observe that there is a great difference between the two following propositions:
>
> First, There is some *one* married woman who under all possible conditions would commit suicide or else her husband would not have failed.
>
> Second, Under all possible circumstances there is some married woman or *other* who would commit suicide or else her husband would not have failed.
>
> CP 4.546

It is very likely that what Peirce had in mind was the insight that we cannot with complete generality derive $\exists x: Ns(x)$ from $N(\exists x: s(x))$ – that is, not without making some restrictions. This is in fact a very old wisdom which was also known to the medieval logicians. One cannot deduce 'there is a man who will live forever' from 'it will forever be the case that there is a man'.

The logic of Peirce's existential graphs (in particular the Gamma Graphs) turns out to be very complicated. From a modern point of view, a lot has to be carried out in order to give the system the kind of mathematical rigour which would now be expected in formal logic. Although an important contribution to this project has been made by Frithjof Dau (2006), there is still much to do in order to develop the formal and mathematical aspects of the Peircean graphs. On the other hand, enough is known already about the graphs to conclude that they present genuine and interesting alternatives to propositional logic, first-order predicate logic and various kinds of modal logic. In addition, John Sowa (1992, 2010) has demonstrated that they can be used for knowledge representation in a very illustrative and intuitively appealing manner.

References

Dau, Frithjof (2006), 'Mathematical Logic with Diagrams. Based on the Existential Graphs of Peirce', TU Dresden, http://www.dr-dau.net/Papers/habil.pdf (accessed 10 August 2016)

Fisch, Max (1978), 'Peirce's Central Theory of Signs', in Thomas A. Seboek (ed.), *Sight, Sound and Sense, Advances in Semiotics*, Bloomington: Indiana University Press, pp. 31–70.

Peirce, Charles Sanders (1931–58), *Collected Papers of Charles Sanders Peirce*, Vols I–VIII, ed. C. Hartshorne, P. Weiss and A. Burke, Cambridge, MA: Harvard University Press [CP].

Prior, A.N. (1957), *Time and Modality*, Oxford: Clarendon Press.

Read, Stephen (1992), 'Conditionals are not truth-functional: an argument from Peirce', *Analysis*, January 1992, pp. 5–12.

Roberts, Don D. (1973), *The Existential Graphs of Charles S. Peirce*, The Hague: Mouton.

Roberts, Don D. (1992), 'The existential graphs', *Computers & Mathematics with Applications*, Vol. 23, Issue 6, pp. 639–63.

Sowa, John F. (1992), 'Logical Foundations for Representing Object-Oriented Systems', *Swiss Society for Medical Informatics*.

Sowa, John F. (2010), 'Existential Graphs. MS 514 by Charles Sanders Peirce: A commentary', http://www.jfsowa.com/peirce/ms514.htm (accessed 10 August 2016).

8

Frege

Walter B. Pedriali

Introduction

Here's a neat story. After centuries of stagnation, logic was dramatically transformed, more or less at a stroke, by the appearance of Frege's *Begriffsschrift* in 1879, the *annus mirabilis* in the history of logic, the watershed year when, the story goes, modern logic was born.[1] In that epoch-changing work Frege single-handedly invented modern logic, finally breaking it free from its restrictive Aristotelian mould. His achievement is all the more extraordinary given that Frege's groundbreaking work was developed in near-complete isolation and greeted with little or no peer recognition at all. This heroic picture of Frege's solitary and unrewarded intellectual efforts is explained mostly by two circumstances: the awkward, cumbersome two-dimensional notation he employed (a notation that most readers have since found hard to decipher), and the fact that the formal system Frege later developed in *Grundgesetze* (1893) turned out to be inconsistent, thus destroying both his hope of establishing a new era for logic as a scientific discipline properly so-called as well as whatever reputation he had gained since the *Begriffsschrift* days. Frege wasn't just a heroic figure in the intellectual history of our subject, then, but a tragic one too.

The story, thus narrated, is very neat; indeed, it is a little *too* neat. It is too neat because it overlooks the importance of the work of De Morgan, Boole, Jevons, McColl, Schröder and Peirce (the *modern turn* in logic actually predates 1879). It is also too neat because it glosses over the fact that modern logic differs in important respects from that of Frege (logic became truly 'modern' a lot later than 1879).

There is, however, a sense in which the story gets things essentially right. *Begriffsschrift* is without question the first work in which we find a fairly systematic presentation of a formal system that is recognizably similar to those developed today – the modern way of *doing* logic, that is, was undoubtedly born with that slim book.

Moreover, no other single work in logic before or since contains as many wide-ranging technical innovations packed within a few pages (eighty-eight in all). Finally, it was only with *Begriffsschrift* that a unitary treatment of propositional and quantificational logic was at last provided, resolving the long-standing dispute between Aristotelian and Stoic logic by giving them a common home.

In short, while it is certainly true that the full story of the birth of modern logic is a rather complex affair, hardly reducible to a single event, it is also the case that if one nevertheless wants to single out a pivotal point for expository purposes, then the appearance of *Begriffsschrift* in 1879 is arguably the best place where to locate the watershed dividing ancient from modern approaches to logic.

My task in this chapter is to spell out the respects in which *Begriffsschrift* (and Frege's contribution more generally) marks the onset of modern logic. To that aim, I will bring out the key innovative features of Frege's pioneering work in logic, all the while indicating the ways in which that work differs from our present conception of logic (and its implementation in the various systems of logic currently being employed).[2]

I will start by giving a very brief sketch of the birth of modern logic (somewhat qualifying the standard story sketched above). In section 2, I discuss Frege's philosophical outlook, while in section 3 I lay out the system given in *Begriffsschrift*, highlighting its main novelties. In section 4 I close the chapter by briefly sketching the contradiction that arose in Frege's late work, *Grundgesetze*.

1 Locating the watershed

We start by asking: in what sense could Frege be said to have inaugurated modern logic? And what *is* modern logic anyway? Let's tackle the second question first. At a first approximation, we can say that logic became modern when it became *mathematical* logic, the study of mathematical reasoning, done by mathematical means and for mathematical purposes.

More specifically, logic became modern when a proper apparatus of quantification able to cope with the complexities of multiple generality in mathematical reasoning was developed (we'll see in a moment what all of this means). Finally, and relatedly, we can say that logic became modern when it itself became an object of mathematical study: that is, logic became modern when *meta*-logic (the study of the structural properties of logical systems) was born. And clearly, metalogic could only be developed once ways of making logical systems precise had been made available.

To sum it all up in a slogan, then, logic became distinctively modern when it became the study of *proof* rather than of argument.

With that rough sketch on board we can now ask the first question: is Frege properly regarded as *the* founder of modern logic? Well, on the standard story the answer is a resounding *yes*, and this is so because *Begriffsschrift* displays – right from its subtitle, 'a formal language of pure thought modelled after that of arithmetic' – all of the characteristic marks of modern logic that we've just reviewed, above all in its presentation of the first extended treatment of quantification.[3] Moreover, Frege made it possible pretty much for the first time to treat logic as a formal *system*. That is to say, he gave us logic as an *object* of study, an object that we could test for consistency so as to verify the good epistemic standing of our 'logical convictions'.[4]

The story, however, and as already anticipated, needs some qualification.

To finesse the story ever so slightly, then, let's first distinguish three main strands in the evolution of modern logic, namely, *i)* the algebraic tradition that went from Boole to Tarski and beyond, spawning in its wake the model-theoretic tradition that was to be developed in the 1920s and 1930s (in this tradition one studies mathematical structures, the operations that can be defined over them, and the operation-preserving mappings between those structures); *ii)* the broadly Aristotelian tradition that studied argument-schemata (in this tradition, one tries to capture with some degree of formality maximally general truth-preserving modes of reasoning irrespective of subject matter); and finally *iii)* the proof-theoretic tradition in which Frege and his formalist rival Hilbert worked (in this tradition, one sets up deductive systems, studies their formal properties, and engages in theorem proving).[5]

Now, as it happens, Frege had little inclination towards what was to become the model-theoretic approach to logic. In particular, he had no truck with the idea that a formal language could be amenable to multiple interpretations. His conception of logic was *universalist*, by which it is meant that the quantifiers would range unrestrictedly over all objects, that the domain of quantification was not variable but fixed once and for all.[6] And the task of the logically perfect language that Frege strived to construct was to capture the unique inferential relations that hold together 'the natural order of truths', an order that was immutable and of the widest generality.[7] In addition, Frege also thought that his system was a substantial improvement over those of Boole and Schröder precisely because it went *against* (or rather *beyond*) the algebraic approach to logic.[8] In particular, Frege's syntax comes with an interpretation *already* packed into it.[9] Better put: unlike Boole's, it is a language of such absolute generality as not to stand in need of interpretation (since any interpretation would represent a restriction of that generality).[10]

And now the claim that Frege is the father of modern logic begins to look a bit problematic. Why? Well, to the extent that one's conception of logic is characterized by one's conception of logical consequence, the contemporary view of consequence as truth-preservation in all models is one that is heavily shaped by the model-theoretic tradition and it is one that would have struck Frege as alien and indeed contrary to what he thought of as the proper view of logic – from his universalist perspective, it is a grave mistake to try and explain the notion of logical truth in terms of truth in all models. In short, if confronted with it Frege might well have disowned modern logic as not counting as logic at all by his lights, given its mistaken conception of logical truth.[11] This fact alone seems to somewhat weaken the claim that Frege was *the* founder of modern logic; perhaps, and to switch metaphors, we should rather see him as just one (highly striking) thread in a much wider tapestry than the one being woven in *Begriffsschrift*.[12]

And there is more. Frege's logic is higher-order (it quantifies over functions, not just objects) and it is *meant* to be that way (Frege's logicist project, of which more later, required a logic with that kind of expressive power). But on the modern conception, higher-order logic involves existential assumptions that make it controversial to claim that it *is* logic.[13] Indeed, the view that is still dominant today is that first-order logic is logic properly so called precisely because of its minimal existential assumptions – all it assumes is that its domains of quantification be non-empty. Higher-order logics, by contrast, include logical truths that make demands on the *size* of those domains, since they require infinite domains (not just non-empty ones) for their obtaining. It is, however, felt that the question of whether there are infinitely many objects is one over which logic should not adjudicate (nor is it one that logic should presuppose as settled one way or another). Furthermore, and, again, relatedly, higher-order logics lack certain key metatheoretical properties that are *now* taken to be definitive of the logical.[14]

Accordingly, the claim that 1879 is the year modern logic was born also needs qualifying with respect to *the kind of logic* that was born then.[15] Concerns about existential assumptions and desirable metatheoretical properties eventually led to a fairly stable (but not entirely uncontroversial) consensus that logic proper (i.e. the genuinely logical core of our thinking) is first-order logic, and thus only a fragment of what counted as logic for Frege. That consensus, however, arguably became truly entrenched only in the 1960s when Lindström's theorems gave it a solid formal grounding.[16] Modern logic is thus a fairly recent affair and one whose concerns are far removed from those of Frege.

And 1879's privileged status looks no less problematic when we consider Frege's influence on his more immediate successors. His work was met, almost without exception, with deep incomprehension by the few who had bothered to read it.[17] Two aspects contributed to this. First, Frege's two-dimensional notation (of which more later) left readers baffled. It was unanimously declared hard to read, and counterintuitive in the extreme. In contrast, the notation developed by Peano and Russell and Whitehead would immediately find favour with the mathematical community (in modern terms, we could say it had a friendlier interface).

Secondly, as Frege himself noted in the preface to *Grundgesetze*, the heady (and fairly seamless) mixture of mathematics and philosophy in his work meant that mathematicians were put off by the philosophy and philosophers by the mathematics.

Frege's immediate impact on the history of logic was thus fairly limited (and mostly due to Russell's highly appreciative Appendix *A* to his *Principles of Mathematics*).[18] In addition, Russell's discovery that Frege's system was in fact inconsistent did little to improve Frege's reputation but gave instead rather good copy to the story of Frege as a tragic figure who in trying to make logic ampliative, *contra* Kant, had broken its centuries-old sterility at the cost of making it engender a contradiction – to use Poincaré's rather crude jibe.[19] And indeed, if we look at the way logic and mathematics developed in the immediate post-Frege, post-paradox era, there is a good sense in which it bears very little trace of Frege's influence.[20]

All that changed in the 1950s, however, when Frege's *Grundlagen* was translated into English by J.L. Austin, and Alonzo Church published his *Introduction to Mathematical Philosophy*. Frege's importance as a *philosopher* of logic was finally recognized. His status as a classic would then be consolidated by Dummett's 1973 *opus magnum* (and all of his subsequent writings), establishing Frege's reputation as the founder not just of modern logic but of analytic philosophy as a whole.[21] And interestingly enough, the 1950s are also the time when the standard story gets established, mainly through Quine's influence.

Now, last paragraph aside, at this point you might legitimately be worried that the standard story just got things badly wrong. On closer examination, the commonly made claim that Frege is the founder of modern logic has looked more and more problematic. True, he beat everyone else to giving the first treatment of quantification.[22] But he did so in a notation that no one else adopted and from a position that was deeply hostile to ideas that were to become central to the model-theoretic tradition that informs much of the contemporary conception of logic. Finally, it is also hard to deny that his work had little immediate influence.[23]

So, in what sense, if any at all, can Frege be said to have 'discovered' the wonders of modern logic in his *Begriffsschrift*? As I said already, Frege's genuine novelty lies in the inauguration of a new way of *doing* logic and to that extent he fully deserves the accolade standardly granted him. What I want to claim, that is, is that Frege's importance is not (merely) historical: it is *operational*, as it were – Frege showed us for the first time *how* we should operate when we want to do serious logical work; he gave us the first and most powerful logical toolbox. I'll try to substantiate this claim in section 3. Before that, though, we need to take a short detour through Frege's philosophical stance.

2 Frege's philosophy of logic

As we have seen, Frege's conception of logic is in several respects significantly different to the contemporary one. And yet it is precisely Frege's idiosyncratic conception that moved him to develop the most strikingly innovative aspects of his work. So much so that the groundbreaking aspects of Frege's logic are powered precisely by those aspects of his philosophical approach that are now considered to be archaic. My task in this section is to give a brisk summary of those aspects, and to explain their peculiarities and the way in which they triggered Frege's technical innovations.[24]

Recall now the subtitle to *Begriffsschrift*: a formal language for pure thought modelled after that of arithmetic. But why should the language of pure thought be modelled on that of arithmetic, one might ask? Well, the answer, from Frege's perspective, is twofold. In the first instance, Frege's professional interests (he was a mathematician/geometer by training) put mathematical reasoning centre stage – Frege's driving concern was to make that subject-specific reasoning as rigorous as possible. But he also thought that mathematics and logic were 'reason's nearest kin'.[25] If you want to get to the roots of rationality, for Frege there's no better place to start (and end) than reasoning about mathematical objects, that is. More specifically, Frege held a thesis, later called *logicism*, whereby mathematical truths were deemed to be cleverly disguised truths of logic. And another key thesis of Frege's logicism is that mathematical objects (the objects those truths are about) are in fact (reducible to) *logical* objects.

Frege was thus a *rationalist*: the language of pure thought is the language of pure reason, the language in which the laws regulating *any* truth-oriented discourse can be stated and put to good use.[26] And the target of those laws and of thought is, as we've also already seen, what Leibniz had called *the natural order of truths* – and those truths are, of course, *a priori* truths. Frege's highly ambitious aim, then, was to show that those truths stretched a lot further into our conceptual territory than Kant had thought.

Frege's project was thus a dual one: on the one hand, it was a foundational project in the philosophy of mathematics (a project that aimed to show how arithmetical truths could be analysed away in terms of logical truths and definitions); on the other, it was an *epistemological* project that aimed to show how we are justified in taking to be true just those mathematical statements that we so take, and that, as it turns out, underscore *all* knowledge irrespective of subject matter.[27] And for Frege justification was *proof*. But not just any old notion of 'proof' would do. Rather, proper proofs had to be *gap-free*, in the sense that all assumptions underlying the proof should be made explicit and that any step taken therein could only be made in accordance with a specified rule.[28] That is, all axioms, lemmas, definitions and rules of proof appealed to in the course of the proof must be made fully manifest in the formalism itself – and this is without question *the* way in which Frege can truly be said to have inaugurated the modern way of doing logic.

A second sense in which proof had to be gap-free concerned the notion of *content*. For Frege, content is a logical notion: a proposition, or a thought, in his later terminology, is that for which the question of truth and falsity can arise (and thus the natural order of truths is a natural order of true thoughts). What individuates a given thought is its reference-determining properties, the way the thought determines its truth condition. In Frege's later terminology that means a thought is a way of naming the True, one of the two basic logical objects out of which all others are built. According to Frege's conception at the time of *Begriffsschrift*, a thought is instead individuated in terms of its inferential potential, that is, in terms of what follows from it (what other thought you can reach *from* it under the licence of logic) and what justifies it (how you can get *to* it under the licence of logic).

But in fact the two conceptions coincide: inferential properties for Frege are reference-determining properties, since it is the latter properties that ensure that in correct inference we never move from names of the True to names of the False. Furthermore, a thought is individuated in terms of its logical properties thus constituted (i.e. reference and inference-determining properties).[29]

So, in exactly the same way in which proof had to be gap-free (in the sense that the justification for a given step cannot be left to guesswork but must be precisely indicated by citing the law being applied in reaching that step and the premises on which that application rests) so content too (the inferential profile of the propositions involved in the proof) had to be gap-free (in the sense that the thoughts concerned must be taken as eternal, fully specified propositional contents whose truth-value is specified in an absolute manner).[30]

Before we can finally move to examining *Begriffsschrift*, two more features of Frege's conception deserve mention, namely his *antipsychologism* and his view that numbers are objects.[31]

Regarding the first feature, it is important to note that when we speak of mathematical reasoning or of the laws of thought, on Frege's view we must do so in complete disregard of the actual cognitive mechanisms that thinkers employ. For Frege, logic has to capture truth-preserving modes of inference between thoughts without any concern for their specific cognitive implementation by a particular reasoner. That is to say, the laws of logic hold absolutely; they prescribe how one ought to judge in a way that applies whenever anyone makes a reasoning step, irrespective of the contingent psychological make-up of the reasoner.[32] The actual psychological means whereby those movements are implemented is of no concern whatsoever to Frege. Logic, for him, is in this sense a transcendental enterprise. It is constitutive of *pure* thought and indeed of rationality. Given that perspective, the language of pure thought and the system of proof developed by Frege is not intended to model the mental processes that mathematicians go through in their proofs. The purpose of the *Begriffsschrift* is rather to bring forth the *justificatory structure* of a given theorem: a proof must make clear the structure of the reasons on the basis of which the theorem can be asserted.[33]

Regarding the second point, Frege's version of logicism was not limited to the claim that arithmetic is logic in disguise. It was also a thesis concerning the nature of number: numbers are objects, they are logical objects; that is, a particular kind of abstract objects that while not endowed with spatio-temporal properties are nevertheless fully objective, in his technical sense of *objective*, namely things about which we can issue judgements that are answerable to publicly assessable normative criteria.[34]

One very last point: Frege's antipsychologism is best seen as an expression of his strong realism about mathematical objects viewed as strongly mind-independent entities. You might then be puzzled to learn that Frege gave great importance (and indeed explanatory priority) to the notion of *judgement*. Isn't judgement something *we* do, you will immediately complain? And if so, how is that to be reconciled with Frege's Platonism about number (his view that numbers exist independently of human reflection upon them)?

Well, the tension is only apparent. While it is true that Frege gives great importance to the notion of judgement, the role played by that notion is epistemological, not ontological. Judgement, that is, is our entry point into the order of truths. To unravel that order, we start from judgement. We first entertain a thought (a putative truth) and we then come to a judgement regarding its *structure* (its inferential potential) and its truth-value. The act of judgement is simply the act of placing that thought in the order of truths (if it is false, we'll place its negation there, of course).

But why is judgement central to Frege's conception of logic? Because it is the act of judgement that generates concepts, thus making manifest a thought's inferential relations.[35] As I have just said, a judgement is not just recognition of truth-value (judgement as to whether a given thought is true or false): it is also (and perhaps above all) recognition of its *logical* structure, it is an act of understanding *why* the thought is true (or false), an acknowledgement of the inferential relations that hold that particular thought at a particular location in the order of truths.

Now, the question that you will want to ask at this point is: what kind of structure do we recognize in an act of judgement, then? This question is in fact at the heart of Frege's contribution to the history of logic. And to see how Frege answered it, we can now, at last, dip into *Begriffsschrift*, the work where logic turned truly modern.[36]

3 *Begriffsschrift*

It should by now be clear that Frege's rationalism is deeply revisionary.[37] To achieve his aim of showing that the class of truths of reason includes that of mathematical truths, he had to provide a conceptual analysis of key mathematical notions by means of exclusively logical means. In order to do that, Frege had to uncover what he took to be the real conceptual structure underlying the largely misleading surface structure both in mathematical as well as in 'natural' reasoning. Both natural and mathematical language had to be reformed, regimented, made maximally unambiguous. Let's examine how Frege set about doing so.

I said that it is through acts of judgement that we make apparent the inferential structure holding together the natural order of truths. That structure was Frege's target. What he needed was a set of tools that would allow him *to capture within a single, unified language all forms of inference* that were used in arithmetic. None of the languages that had been tried before were able to achieve that – indeed, there is a very good sense in which prior to Frege there were *no* formal languages properly so called.[38] The task he set himself with the *Begriffsschrift* was to define a formal system where the meaning of every term would be precisely specified and kept constant in all its occurrences and where *every* form of inference required for arithmetical proofs would be codified. In short, the system had to be unified and complete, accounting for all valid forms of inference within a single language.

Let's now look very briefly at the gaps left by pre-Fregean logics that Frege sets himself to close off. Here's a classic inference in Aristotelian logic:

1.   All *As* are *Bs*
2.   All *Bs* are *Cs*
∴ All *As* are *Cs*

Stoic logic would instead concerns itself with the codification of inferences of this form:

1.   If *A* then *B*
2.   *A*
∴ *B*

The contrast, then, is between a logic of *terms* (the Aristotelian) and a logic of *propositions* (the logic of the Stoics).[39] Very roughly, in Aristotelian logic one's focus is on relations between concepts, in particular relations of class-inclusion of the sort displayed in the syllogism above. In contrast, Stoic logic is designed for capturing relations between propositions.[40]

Now, while it is true that Boole had provided a framework where both forms of inference could be expressed, there was a severe limitation to the expressive power of his language. One had to switch interpretation of the language in order to capture those inferences (the symbols would be interpreted either as expressing relations between propositions or between concepts, but they could not do both at the same time, within a single interpretation). What was wanted, then, was a language that could capture both kinds of inference within the same interpretation of its symbols.

The additional problem faced by Boole's system was that there were intuitively valid 'mixed' inferences crossing the boundary between the two logics and that could not be represented in any language so far provided precisely because of the need to switch interpretation halfway through the inference. Boole himself gave one such case. Here's the example:

1) Either all As are F, or all As are G
2) All As are either F or G

The move from (1) to (2) is valid. The move from (2) to (1) isn't.

Exercise 3.1

Give a counterexample to show that the move from (2) to (1) is not a valid inference.

Boole's system was unable to give a formal account of the validity of the one move and the invalidity of the other. A related problem was that due to its rigid treatment of the subject-predicate structure of a sentence, Aristotelian logic could not deal with inferences containing premises involving quantifiers in positions other than the subject place, that is, premises such as 'Every student read some book'. Sentences of this form display the phenomenon of *multiple generality*, a phenomenon of crucial importance to mathematical discourse (e.g. 'For every number, there is some number greater than it'), and a phenomenon that also gives rise to ambiguities that one's formal language should disentangle. Frege's logic was designed to solve all of these problems.[41]

How, then, did Frege solve these issues? Clearly, the fundamental limitation in the work of his predecessors was the lack of a proper *analysis* of the genuine constituents of propositions. In modern terms, Stoic logic had concentrated on the *compositional* analysis of sentences, on how sentences are built up by means of the sentential connectives that determine a range of validities in virtue of their meaning. Aristotelian logic, instead, had concentrated on the kind of logical analysis that tries to extract relations between concepts. Frege's main groundbreaking innovation was the provision of a logic that reflected a dual-level analysis of sentential structure. On one level, the analysis reflects how sentences are assembled compositionally from their constituents (giving an *internal* analysis of their structure). On another level, the analysis disclosed the inferential relations that connect the sentence to other sentences in the language in virtue of the concepts figuring in that sentence (thus giving a kind of *external* analysis of the structure of the sentence in relation to other sentences).[42]

To make that new kind of analysis possible, Frege's first move was to abjure the subject–predicate distinction that had been at the heart of traditional logic.[43] In its place, Frege proposed a *function/argument* analysis.[44] A given thought (a given candidate for judgement, a piece of *judgeable content*) admits of (and *forces* one into acknowledging) multiple analyses whereby its location in the order of truths is disclosed.[45]

The key idea behind the function/argument analysis is that in breaking down a thought into its constituent parts (in making a judgement as to which concept is being predicated of which individual(s)) we split it into a predicate part (corresponding to the concept being predicated) and an argument part (corresponding to the entity of which the concept is being predicated). The concept part is represented by a function; the argument part is the placeholder where individuals (or rather signs denoting them) may be slotted in.[46] Incidentally, this is where another crucial advance over Boole took place, for in Boole's notation facts about individuals were expressed as facts about concepts (to say that there is an F in Boolean notation is to say that the extension of a certain concept is non-empty, not to say that an individual satisfies the corresponding property).[47]

In analysing a thought, then, we uncover its inferential relations to other thoughts. Identity of content between thoughts is settled by identity of the set of their consequences: two propositions are equivalent in *conceptual content* if they entail the same set of consequences.[48] Accordingly, conceptual content for Frege is inferential potential and the concept-script to be developed is really an inferential-script, a script representing the logical form of the inferential structure of thoughts.[49]

So, what structures both the order of truths and the logical content of a given thought is *functional structure*, as well as *compositional structure*. And indeed here we have what is arguably Frege's key insight: the linear structure of language hides away the *constructional history* of sentences.[50] So, on Frege's view you do not grasp a thought (what a sentence expresses) until you've grasped its compositional structure (the way the sentence is put together from its constituent parts) *and* its functional structure (how many concepts can be generated by decomposing the thought expressed by it). After you've done that, you've finally properly placed that thought in the order of truths. You know how to infer to and from it (according to the insight of *Begriffsschrift* §9) and you know what truth-conditions the sentence determines (according to the insight of *Grundgesetze* §32).

This was all a bit heady, so let's now look at a very simple example to see how it all works. Consider the thought that Cato killed Cato. Frege's functional analysis of its structure proceeds by *abstraction*.[51] To uncover (and indeed generate) the underlying conceptual structure, we remove *singular terms* from the expression and replace them with *variable terms* so as to obtain all possible functions that could be discerned in the thought.[52] So we might first get 'Cato killed ξ', and then 'ξ killed Cato' and finally 'ξ killed ξ', where ξ marks the *argument place(s)*, the gap(s) left in the thought after we have abstracted away the *specific* individual(s) the thought was (partly) about. In doing so, we bring out the inferential properties of the original thought (for instance, we have made apparent how we can move from 'Cato killed Cato' to 'Cato killed somebody' or to 'Somebody killed Cato', or to 'Somebody killed somebody') while simultaneously showing how we can generate concepts from a given thought.[53] Note that the thought itself remains unchanged. The possibility of multiple functional analyses of the same thought merely shows the multiplicity of inferential relations a given thought stands in. The thought itself retains a unique structure.

The other groundbreaking aspect of Frege's function/argument analysis is that the decomposition process makes available building blocks that can then be recombined to form new thoughts, new concept/object combinations. And the combinatorial process can be iterated indefinitely. To stick with our example, once we have moved from 'Cato killed Cato' to 'Cato killed ξ', it is then easy to move on and replace ξ with another singular term and obtain, say, 'Cato killed Brutus', and so on for the other patterns. This is already powerful enough, in explanatory and expressive terms, but the full power of Frege's language will become apparent when we will finally introduce the quantifiers below.

3.1 Frege's notation

It's now time to say something about Frege's (in)famous notation. It is supposedly a highly counterintuitive way of representing thoughts (and *actual* reasoning patterns). I expended much time in spelling out Frege's overarching *logico-epistemological* aims in the hope that it would be clear that, contrary to the standard story, the notation we are about to examine is a highly appropriate and indeed perspicuous way of mirroring on paper the deep structure of thought and inference. The lack of linearity of Frege's notation, that is, is not a bug but a valued feature, since it is intended to signal the *need* for a departure from the linear surface structure of standardly written linguistic strings (be they in natural language or in that of arithmetic). That is, Frege's two-dimensional notation, not unlike the generative grammarian's tree structures, makes manifest logical form in a way that *purposefully* defies linearity. It reflects *how concepts are formed* and *how the logical form of a sentence is constructed*, both eminently non-linear processes.

Let's look at the details now. Given Frege's overall framework, the first sign he needed was one that would mark judgeable content, that is, the content of possible assertions. Here it is:

——

which prefixed to the symbol for a given thought, say '*A*', gives us:

——A

This could be rendered as 'the thought that *A*' or 'the proposition that *A*'.[54] It represents the stage where a thought is merely entertained, or grasped, as Frege often put it. This horizontal stroke is called the *content stroke*. From merely entertaining a thought, we may then move to a judgement regarding its truth-value; we may, that is, move to *asserting* the thought, making the judgement that, for example, *A* is true. To signal that the thought is being asserted, Frege added a short vertical stroke to the content stroke, giving what he called the *judgement stroke*:[55]

⊢————A

Note two things here. First, the letter symbol represents that part of the content of a thought which has no logical significance in the sense that it is *logically simple* – no further decomposition in the sense above is possible. The judgement stroke instead fulfils a dual role. Its presence is essential to making an expression into a sentence of the formal language: as Frege notes, it is a predicate common to all judgements.[56] But it also makes what we could call a metalinguistic gesture: it signals that the thought that *A* is being asserted. Let me stress once again that assertion here carries no psychological connotations. It just says: there is a proof of *A*. And in fact, given Frege's axiomatic system, it says: *A* is a theorem.[57]

Frege's calculus was thus intended to be a calculus of asserted, that is, proven truths – he had no truck with the idea that we could do proofs from false statements.[58]

Note also that for Frege it was crucial that the representation of the logical structure of a thought be kept separate from those thought-components that are *logically inert*, as it were. In short, the task of the two-dimensional notation that he adopted is to vividly represent the logical form of the thought, i.e. its logical properties. That is: the letters indicated on the right-hand side represent the individual contents; the network of lines on the left-hand side represent the inferential relations holding between them. In other words, Frege's two-dimensional notation analyses the asserted thought into its constituent thoughts and the logical relations holding between them.[59]

To see how this all works, let's now look at the way Frege represents conditional statements and generality. Here's how Frege renders the thought that if *A* then *B*:

$$\vdash\!\!\!\begin{array}{c} \quad B \\ \quad A \end{array} \qquad\qquad (1)$$

Frege called the (thought expressed on the) upper line in a conditional the *supercomponent* (what we now call the consequent) and the lower line the *subcomponent* (i.e. the antecedent).[60] Note that we have a content stroke governing the entire conditional, and then two context strokes preceding the two letter symbols. The condition stroke is the vertical stroke joining up the two content strokes preceding the letter symbols. It indicates that the subcomponent is a sufficient condition for the obtaining of the supercomponent; it also signals that assertion of A logically commits you to assertion of B, that it logically *leads you up there*, as it were.[61] Note that the judgement stroke governs the entire conditional (the thought-components are *not* asserted).

The notation may well strike those of us trained in the Peano–Russell notation (say '$A \supset B$' or '$A \rightarrow B$') as counterintuitive or cumbersome, but Frege argued that his notation was in fact far more conducive to making the logical structure of thought manifest.[62] One way of unpacking Frege's claim is to say that his notation makes clear that, for example, all A-cases, all circumstances in which A obtains, are B-cases, cases in which B obtains too. The spatial representation, with A below B, is thus meant to convey the notion of *case-containment*, as it were.[63]

Now, how does Frege *define* the conditional?[64] He considers the four possible cases one could have here, interestingly enough not (yet) in terms of truth and falsity, but rather of affirmation and denial.[65] And he takes his conditional to exclude only the case in which A is affirmed and B denied.[66] Frege then immediately notes that this won't capture in full generality what we would render in natural language with *if . . ., then* because his conditional won't presuppose or convey any causal connection between A and B.[67] Causality, he notes, is something that involves generality, something he has not defined yet. A second advantage that Frege claims for his two-dimensional notation is that it affords a clearer demarcation of ambiguity of scope.

Consider a nested conditional such as:

$$\vdash\!\!\!\begin{array}{c} \quad B \\ \quad A \\ \quad \Gamma \end{array} \qquad\qquad (2)$$

It is immediately clear what the antecedent is (namely, Γ). In Peano notation, we would have to use brackets (or dots):

$$\Gamma \supset (A \supset B) \tag{3}$$

or

$$\Gamma . \supset . A \supset B \tag{4}$$

and Frege thought this introduced unneeded complexity, especially with more complex conditionals, while also masking the logical form of the thought.[68]

Let's look at negation next. Frege expresses negation by adding a short vertical stroke under the content stroke:

$$\text{---}_\top A \tag{5}$$

The asserted version is as expected:

$$\vdash_\top A \tag{6}$$

The gloss given is also as expected: the negation sign expresses the circumstances that the content does not obtain.[69]

And now it is time for some exercises.[70]

Exercise 3.2

Define conjunction using Frege's notation (i.e. write out A ∧ B in two-dimensional notation).

Exercise 3.3

Define disjunction using Frege's notation (i.e. write out A ∨ B in two-dimensional notation).

Exercise 3.4

Define exclusive disjunction using Frege's notation.

Exercise 3.5

Write out ¬(A ∧ B) in two-dimensional notation.

Exercise 3.6

State the principle of contraposition, $(\neg\psi \rightarrow \neg\phi) \rightarrow (\phi \rightarrow \psi)$, in Frege's notation.

Exercise 3.7

The set of logical connectives used by Frege, {¬, →} in modern notation, is *functionally complete*, that is, it suffices to express all (two-valued) truth-functions (functions taking truth-values as arguments and returning truth-values as values). Show that the set $\{\neg, \wedge\}$ is truth-functionally complete. (Hint: show that any formula expressible using the first set is expressible using the second set as well. Check Bostock (1997: §2.7) if you get stuck. You don't have to do this in Frege's notation but you get bonus points if you do!).

3.2 Generality

The most celebrated technical innovation introduced in *Begriffsschrift* is Frege's treatment of generality. Here we face yet another slightly paradoxical situation, for on the one hand Frege is supposed to have inaugurated the modern treatment of quantification, but on the other hand his own treatment is again highly idiosyncratic and widely divergent from the standard textbook account. Frege, that is, treated quantification as a form of predication. According to Frege, in making a quantificational statement such as 'every philosopher is smart' what we are really doing is saying that a certain property, in this case that of being smart if one is a philosopher, is satisfied by everything. In quantifying, we are thus predicating a property of a property (we say that a property has the property of being either satisfied by everything, or by something, or by nothing).[71] Actually, the real technical and philosophical advance made by Frege was in his treatment of the variable. Previously, variables were treated as being symbols that *refer* to indeterminate individuals in the sense of individuals that were taken to have indeterminate properties. Frege insisted that names and variables behave differently and that variable symbols *indicate* (*andeuten*) arbitrary individuals rather than refer (*bedeuten*) to them.[72] Let's now see how Frege rendered generality in his notation.

First, let's quickly recall the function/argument analysis we have already discussed. Let Φ denote an indeterminate function (i.e. any of a possible range of functions). We mark the argument place in a way still familiar to us by enclosing the argument in parenthesis following the function sign: $\Phi(A)$.[73] This statement lacks full generality, for 'A' indicates a specific, if arbitrary, argument.

To indicate generality, Frege used two devices. Let's first look at the simplest one:

$$\vdash X(a) \tag{7}$$

In modern terms, this is a formula with one free variable, the small Roman letter 'a'. But Frege is here taking the universal closure of this formula (he's tacitly fronting the formula with a universal quantifier binding whatever free variables there are in the formula).[74]

This approach, while efficient, is very blunt, since the scope of the generality claim coincides with the entire formula. Frege's original contribution comes with the other way of expressing generality that he proposed. What we do this time is slot a German letter in the argument place, $X(\mathfrak{a})$, and *bind* that letter by placing another token of the very same letter-type in what Frege called the *concavity* sign interposed in the content stroke. We thus obtain:

$$\vdash\!\!\!-\!\!\stackrel{\mathfrak{a}}{\smile}\!\!-X(\mathfrak{a}) \tag{8}$$

This is read as the judgement that for any argument whatever the function Φ is a fact, as Frege rather clumsily put it in *Begriffsschrift*. In his later terminology, we would say: it names the True for all arguments. In contemporary terminology: it is true under all assignment functions, i.e. no matter what individual is assigned to the variable.[75]

Now, the role of the concavity is to delimit 'the scope that the generality indicated by the letter covers'. And with this, Frege secured exactly what he needed to model the multiple generality mode of reasoning so frequent in mathematics. Here's an example:

$$\vdash\!\!\!-\!\!\stackrel{\mathfrak{a}}{\smile}\!\!\begin{array}{l} \text{------} A(\mathfrak{a}) \\ \underset{\smile}{\raisebox{0.5ex}{\rule{0.6pt}{1.8ex}}}\stackrel{\mathfrak{e}}{\smile}\!\!- B(\mathfrak{a},\mathfrak{e}) \end{array} \tag{9}$$

Exercise 3.8

Write out formula 9 in modern notation.

Here we have two quantifiers, expressing a multiple generality claim. Note how Frege's notation makes the fact that the scope of *a* is wider than that of *e* immediately apparent. More interestingly still, it also clarifies right away that the scope of *e* is more restricted than the entire formula, a flexibility that had eluded Boole's attempts. Indeed, the introduction of the concavity sign is where the watershed we talked about earlier really takes place.[76]

The crucial innovation made by Frege, then, is that his system, unlike Boole's, can express *within the same language* valid arguments in which propositional *and* quantificational inference steps occur. Adding the concavity to the content stroke simply *expands* the language, leaving the previous fragment of the language still in place.[77]

Having presented his way of dealing with generality, Frege goes on to demonstrate the interaction between negation and generality, now made possible by the concavity device, noting the contrast between:

$$\vdash\!\!\!-\!\!\!-\!\!\stackrel{\mathfrak{a}}{\smile}\!\!\!-X(\mathfrak{a}) \tag{10}$$

$$\vdash \!\!-\!\!\mathfrak{a}\!\!-\!\!\top\!\!-X(\mathfrak{a}) \qquad\qquad (11)$$

Exercise 3.9

Write out formulae 10 and 11 in modern notation.

Frege next shows how to make existential generalizations in his system using only generality and negation:

Exercise 3.10

Express the existential statement 'There is one F' in Frege's notation.

Exercise 3.11

Express in Frege's notation the classic multiple generality statement that for every natural number there is a greater one.

In rounding off Part I of *Begriffsschrift*, Frege does two more things. He first shows how causal connections may be expressed in his system:[78]

$$\vdash \!\!-\!\!\mathfrak{a}\!\!-\!\!\begin{array}{l}-P(\mathfrak{a}) \\ -X(\mathfrak{a})\end{array} \qquad\qquad (12)$$

Note here another didactic advantage of Frege's notation: it clearly represents set-subsumption (that the *Xs* are contained in the *Ps*) by having the contained set (the subordinate concept, and subcomponent of the conditional) below the container set (the superordinate set, and supercomponent of the conditional).[79]

The second thing he does is to quietly point out how the traditional Aristotelian square of opposition can be expressed in his system.[80] In effect, having already shown how he can deal with multiple generality, he's closed the first part of his groundbreaking work by showing that his formal system is a proper extension of Aristotelian logic.

It should be clear from the examples above that there is another crucial respect in which the modern turn in logic truly occurred only with *Begriffsschrift*: generality, negation and the conditional can all be *iterated* and combined without limit, thus allowing the language to keep pace with the inexhaustible nature of mathematical structures.

A crucial instrument here is Frege's unstated rule of substitution, whereby formulae can be substituted for other sentential variables in any of the theorems, without restrictions other than uniformity of replacement (the substituend must be replaced across all occurrences of the substituens).[81] Here's a quick example. In

$$
\begin{array}{c}
\vdash\!\!\!\!\begin{array}{c} \rule{2cm}{0.4pt}\ B \\ \rule{1.5cm}{0.4pt}\ A \end{array}
\end{array}
\qquad (13)
$$

we can substitute the formula itself for its subcomponent obtaining:

$$
\begin{array}{c}
\vdash\!\!\!\!\begin{array}{c} \rule{2.5cm}{0.4pt}\ B \\ \rule{2cm}{0.4pt}\ B \\ \rule{1.5cm}{0.4pt}\ A \end{array}
\end{array}
\qquad (14)
$$

The process is clearly iterable indefinitely. No system before Frege had such expressive combinatorial power. For the first time in the history of logic, mathematical (and to some extent, natural) reasoning could be captured with precision and flexibility. Moreover, no system before Frege had succeeded in *writing out* the logical structure of expressions and the iterability of the rules of formation *into* the very language used to capture logical and mathematical thoughts.

3.3 The formal system

Now that we have taken a look at some of the details of Frege's notation and its philosophical underpinnings, we can say a bit more about the system of logic presented in *Begriffsschrift*. What we find there is the first axiomatic system for a higher-order predicate calculus with identity.[82] Frege's presentation is more informal than is customary today, but it was far more precise than anything that had been done before and remained unsurpassed in rigour for quite some time.[83]

In essence, Frege's language had only two connectives, the conditional and negation, and one quantifier, the universal quantifier. His system had nine axioms and one (explicit) rule of inference, or rather, of *proof*, namely, *modus ponens* (MP).[84]

Frege had two reasons for such parsimony: first, to keep the metatheory simple; second, to make the epistemological status of the system as a whole as clear as possible (the fewer primitive notions, the clearer the assumptions on which the system rests). Unusually to modern eyes, Frege does not introduce the other standard connectives and quantifiers by means of definitions based on the primitive notions. He limits himself to noting how he can express those other connectives and quantifiers by means of his chosen ones.

All in all, the system given in *Begriffsschrift* is arguably the first system of logic that can properly be called formal. Lines of proof are numbered, axioms are numbered, formulae are numbered and cross-referenced, inference steps and conclusions of derivations are clearly marked, the axioms and rules of inference used are properly flagged.[85] There is no question at all that properly disciplined deduction starts in 1879. No step is taken without proper justification, and all moving parts of the system are up for inspection, with nothing left to guesswork, as Frege put it. This is the sense in which I have been insisting that *Begriffsschrift* inaugurated the modern way of *doing* logic.[86]

Let's now look at the axioms and the rule(s) of proof used by Frege. In part II of *Begriffsschrift*, Frege states his nine axioms, interspersed with proofs to exemplify how his system works in practice and to build up theorems that are then used in subsequent proofs as abbreviations of their proofs. Axiomatic presentations of predicate logic are seldom used in introductory courses, chiefly because of the difficulty in finding proofs within such systems.[87] On the other hand, they make it a lot neater to prove the classic metatheoretical results as well as making very clear the meaning of the connectives and quantifiers involved in the axiomatization by means of the axioms – you look at the axioms and you know exactly what system you're dealing with and what the connectives 'mean'. All such presentations find their kernel in *Begriffsschrift*. Indeed, it is now customary to call them *Frege–Hilbert systems*.[88]

In §6 Frege introduced his main rule of inference, namely *modus ponens*. The rule was introduced and justified in terms of the definition of the condition stroke already given in §5.[89] Let me stress once again that the system in *Begriffsschrift* is a *proof system*, a system where proofs always start from axioms.[90] Frege thus needed to list the axioms that he required for his purposes. He does so, albeit rather perfunctorily, in §14.

Let's look at the first three of Frege's axioms:[91]

Axiom 1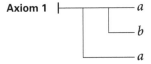

This is pretty much a direct consequence of the definition for the condition stroke. Frege gives a direct justification in terms that we might call semantic: given the meaning of the connective, the only possibility for an instance of axiom 1 to be false is the case where we affirm the antecedent (a given thought represented here by *a*) and deny the consequent, that is, the nested conditional. But in turn that conditional will only be false when its antecedent is affirmed and its consequent (the very same thought represented by *a*) is denied. And this, Frege notes, amounts to both affirming and denying the thought expressed by *a*, which, he confidently concludes, is impossible.

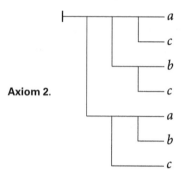

Axiom 2.

Axiom 2 is a kind of 'distributive' axiom that is very useful indeed in proofs, as we shall see in a moment. Frege's justification is similar in structure to the one given for axiom 1.

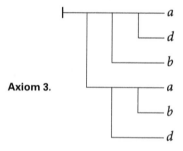

Axiom 3.

Axiom 3 states a principle that would become a rule of inference in *Grundgesetze*: the interchangeability of subcomponents. In other words, their order doesn't matter.[92]

Exercise 3.12

Transcribe axioms 1 to 3 into modern notation.

And here are three more axioms that should strike you as very familiar indeed:[93]

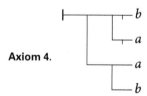

Axiom 4.

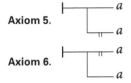

Axiom 5.

Axiom 6.

Exercise 3.13

Transcribe axioms 4 to 6 into modern notation and state their current names.

Most of part II is devoted to proofs in propositional logic. From §20 onwards, identity and quantification enter the scene, announced by the final three axioms.[94] Here are the two axioms defining identity:

Axiom 7. $f(d)$
$f(c)$
$c=d$

Axiom 8. $\vdash\!\!- c \equiv c$

Frege's treatment of identity in *Begriffsschrift* has been the object of much discussion. We don't need to enter into all its subtleties here.[95] I will just note that the treatment of identity is one of the aspects that Frege will substantially revise in his later system of logic in *Grundgesetze*. At any rate, the two axioms in *Begriffsschrift* have an obvious use in proof (for instance, axiom 7 allows that two names with the same content be interchangeable in any proof context).

Finally, Frege introduces his axiom for the quantifier:

Axiom 9. $f(c)$
$\mathfrak{a}\!\!-\! f(\mathfrak{a})$

This axiom should be self-explanatory.

Exercise 3.14

Transcribe axiom 9 into modern notation.

Exercise 3.15

Note that Frege uses German and Roman letters in the axiom. Why?

One thing to note in connection with axiom 9 is that as it stands it is a *type-neutral axiom*,[96] in that Frege took it not to be restricted to first-order variables only. The German letter could also be taken to range over functions too, that is (with the predicate letter then ranging over functions of higher order). In *Grundgesetze*, by contrast, Frege will formulate two distinct axioms, one first-order and another higher order.[97]

For the remainder of part II, Frege shows how his system can model three familiar Aristotelian syllogisms. He then leaves it as an exercise for the reader to show how this can be extended to all other valid forms.

Let's now wrap up our discussion of Frege's formal system in *Begriffsschrift* by talking a bit more about his (unstated) rule of substitution. As I said, Frege–Hilbert systems make finding proofs a notoriously hard task. The trick consists in 'spotting' how to substitute formulae into axioms so as to enable the derivation of the needed theorems by appropriate applications of *modus ponens*. There's no better way of grasping what the modern turn in logic was all about than by doing proofs. So let's look very briefly at a proof to see how it all works in practice.

We go for an easy proof. We want to prove:

$$\vdash \begin{array}{l} a \\ a \end{array} \qquad\qquad (15)$$

(15) is a way of stating the law of identity (sometimes called *reflexivity* in its metatheoretical version), so Frege's system had better be able to prove it. *Modus ponens* (MP) is the main rule of proof in our system. So the last step in the proof is going to be an application of MP that would yield (15) as the last formula in the proof. The formula on the preceding line of proof will then have to have (15) as supercomponent to be detached in the concluding line. What could the subcomponent look like? It'd better be an axiom (so that we can detach our target theorem). Well, a plausible candidate is:

$$\vdash \begin{array}{l} a \\ a \\ a \end{array} \qquad\qquad (16)$$

Is (16) an axiom? Yes it is. We have just replaced *a* for *b* in axiom 1

to obtain (16).[98] Now, if we plug (16) as subcomponent of a formula that has

(15) as supercomponent, the resulting formula doesn't look like any of our axioms:

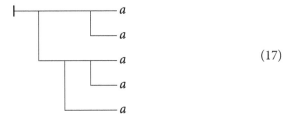

(17)

So, (17) will itself be the result of the application of another MP step. Again, by the same reasoning what we now need is a formula with (17) as its supercomponent and a subcomponent which is an axiom. You will not be surprised to hear that, once more, our friend here is the substitution rule. The following formula is an instance of axiom 1:

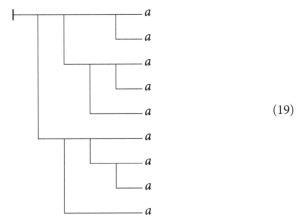

(18)

for we have simply substituted $\vphantom{}$ for b.[99] And now we can put together (18) as subcomponent and (17) as supercomponent and end up with:

(19)

The question is: have we finally reached an instance of an axiom so that we can get our proof started? Well, let's remind ourselves of what axiom 2 looks like:

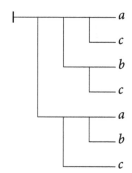

Is (19) then an instance of axiom 2? Yes it is, although it may not be easy immediately to see it is so. Let's unpack the two moves that get us there. First, we can replace c with a in axiom 2 to obtain

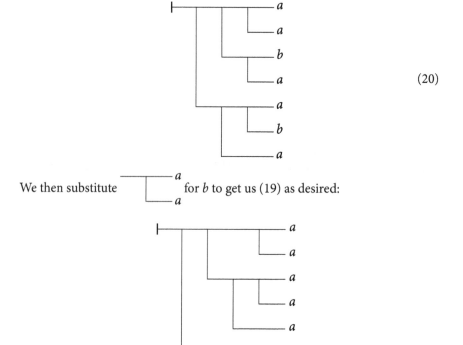

(20)

We then substitute [diagram: a over a] for *b* to get us (19) as desired:

And we're done at last! We finally got to an axiom and that will allow us to start our proof (a good rule of thumb to find proofs in this kind of system is to start from the conclusion and reverse-engineer a proof until we reach an axiom, as we have just done).

Here then is the entire proof:

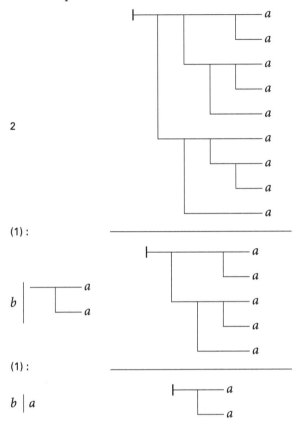

A few things to note: the '2' next to the first formula flags out which axiom it is an instance of. The horizontal line below the first formula signals that an inference has been drawn. The colon next to '(1)' signals that the inference was an MP step and that the major premise has been omitted from the statement of the proof. '(1)' signals that the omitted formula in the MP step, that is, the subcomponent of the initial formula, was an instance of axiom 1. If we had instead omitted the minor premise, we would have marked that with ':::'. The same procedure is repeated for the second step in the proof. Finally, at each step, we specify to the left of the derived formula which subformula we have replaced to derive the substitution instance of the axioms involved.

Exercise 3.16

The proof given above is the standard one given in the streamlined Frege–Hilbert system for propositional logic. The *Begriffsschrift* system, however, had more axioms, allowing for a different proof of $\vdash \begin{array}{c} a \\ a \end{array}$, one that uses axioms 1 and 3 (the one excised by Łukasiewicz), substitution and two applications of MP. Can you work out this proof? (if you can't, check the end of §16 of *Begriffsschrift* and see how Frege did it. It's a beautiful little proof, more ingenious than the one above and it will reveal much of the innovative proof-theoretic power of Frege's system. Before checking that out, do try to find the proof yourself! And remember, the key is to find the crucial substitution moves that allow you to appeal to one of the axioms.)[100]

This, then, is Frege's system in action, painstakingly precise in the conduct of proof, leaving nothing to guesswork, and establishing, when needed, the good epistemic standing for even the most commonly accepted propositions, as exemplified in our little proof.

4 The rise and fall of Frege's project

Frege's treatment of quantification was groundbreaking, as we have repeatedly noted, but it was also unusual by modern standards in that it included, without much fanfare, quantification over *properties*, not just over objects. This was of a piece with Frege's commitment to logicism. As we have seen already, Frege took mathematics to be part of logic in the sense that its statements were to be analysed by means of purely logical notions. And right at the opening of *Begriffsschrift* he had announced his first goal towards that aim, namely, to show that 'the concept of ordering in a sequence', *the* fundamental notion in arithmetic, the device that generates all numbers, could be reduced to and explained in terms of that of *logical* ordering.[101] To do so, Frege had to include properties within the scope of his quantifiers, for the notion of ordering is, in effect, the principle of mathematical induction, the principle that states the constraints under which certain properties can be inherited by all members of a particular sequence.

Frege's definition of the notion of ordering was as follows:

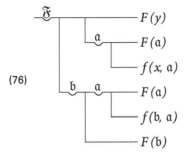

(76)

This is proposition (76) of *Begriffsschrift*, and it defines what is now called the *strong ancestral*. Frege glosses this definition roughly like this: if we can infer from the two propositions that property *F* is hereditary in the *f*-sequence and that any element that follows *x* in the *f*-sequence has property *F* that, for any *F* whatsoever, *y* has the property *F*, then we can say that *y* follows *x* in the *f*-sequence or that *x* precedes *y* in that sequence.

Exercise 4.1

Why is there no assertion stroke in front of the conceptual notation for (76)?

Exercise 4.2

Write out Frege's definition in modern notation.

There are many remarkable things about this definition and the use to which it is put in the proofs that follow.[102] For our purposes let's isolate two facts. First, in proposition (76) Frege introduces, without any comment at all, quantification over properties, not just over objects – the letter $\mathfrak{F}$ placed above the concavity that governs the entire formula in (76) quantifies over any property whatsoever, with *F* being just one arbitrary instance. Secondly, in the proofs that follow, Frege helps himself to a substitution rule in which letters that range over properties and relations are replaced by letters ranging over formulae. This practice amounts in effect to a comprehension schema (a schema pairing membership conditions to a specific set), and from there to paradox it is a very short road indeed.

The next substantive step Frege took in the pursuit of his logicist project was the introduction, in *Grundgesetze*, of a new kind of objects, namely extensions of concepts, or what he called *value-ranges* – in modern terms, something like the graph of a function, the set of ordered pairs of argument and values that characterize the function extensionally.

With concepts and extensions in his ontology and an unrestricted substitution rule (i.e. an unrestricted comprehension schema), Frege's expanded and more precisely regimented logical system in *Grundgesetze* would be proved inconsistent by Bertrand Russell's famous letter of 16 June 1902.[103]

As Frege himself presents the paradox in the *Afterword* to *Grundgesetze*, we start with the plausible assumption that there are classes that do not belong to themselves (the class of human beings, for instance). We then consider the case of the concept *class that does not belong to itself*. Under that concept fall all and only those classes that do not belong to themselves. Its extension will then be the class of all classes that do not belong to themselves. Call that class K. We now ask the question of whether K belongs to itself, and we end up with a contradiction whichever answer we give. The paradox arises because we are treating properties (classes) as entities over which the variables can range; we treat them as potential arguments for higher-order predicates, that is. Without some kind of restriction on the range of those variables in place, paradox will inevitably arise.

In *Begriffsschrift* Frege had not yet introduced extensions of concepts and therefore he did not have classes in his system. But from *Grundlagen* onwards, he wanted to define the concept of number in terms of extensions of concepts, and he therefore introduced a theory of classes into his system with catastrophic results.[104] His life's work had been all but destroyed.[105]

The irony is that Frege's mature system failed him just where he had been at his most brilliant in his early path-opening work. That is, the strikingly original proof of the property of connectedness of the ancestral, the proof that had shown the young Frege at his best, was to unleash, fourteen years later, the contradiction that scuppered his logicist ambitions.

Frege had wanted the history of logic to be the history of arithmetic. That proved to be an impossible goal to satisfy and at the end of his life he admitted as much.[106] After him, logic and the theory of classes, what we now call set theory, parted company. What is now called logic is the consistent part of Frege's system, namely the first-order fragment. Set theory, in turn, is still grappling with questions of consistency to this day.

What, then, is Frege's place in the history of logic?

Gödel (1944: 119) gave perhaps the most penetrating characterization of Frege's peculiar role in that history. On the one hand, Frege's main interest was in 'the analysis of thought'. And we could add: Boole may well have titled his treatise *The Laws of Thought* but it was Frege who first devoted at least as much effort to clarifying what thought was, from a logical point of view, as he'd spent clarifying what its laws were.[107] Indeed, that's why I gave so much space in this chapter to Frege's philosophy of thought – there is no understanding his philosophy of logic without understanding his philosophy of thought. On the other hand, Gödel also noted that Frege's progress had been unduly slowed down by his 'painstaking analysis of proof'. And we could add: it was Frege's obsessive insistence on precise definitions for the purposes of proof that had made him miss the crucial warnings about the looming contradiction in Cantor's writings and alienated the much-needed sympathy of his colleagues.[108]

In the opening section, I said that whatever qualifications one might want to add to the standard story, Frege could indeed be taken to be the founder of modern logic because he had shown us how to do logic. But arguably Frege did more than that. Logic is something *we* do. It is, again as Frege (1897a: 128) himself insisted, a normative science in its own right, directing us in our thinking and, more generally, in our lives. And logic's main concern is with truth.

In assessing Frege's unique contribution to the history of logic, then, his unremitting dedication to the cause of truth is perhaps even more remarkable and praiseworthy than his technical achievements.

There is thus no better way of closing our account of Frege's position in the history of logic than by quoting Russell's glowing tribute:

> As I think about acts of integrity and grace, I realise that there is nothing in my knowledge to compare with Frege's dedication to truth. His entire life's work was on the verge of completion, much of his work had been ignored to the benefit of men infinitely less capable, his second volume [of *Grundgesetze*] was about to be published, and upon finding that his fundamental assumption was in error, he responded with intellectual pleasure clearly submerging any feelings of personal disappointment. It was almost superhuman and a telling indication of that of which men are capable if their dedication is to create work and knowledge instead of cruder efforts to dominate and be known.[109]

Frege, then, didn't just show us how to *do* logic. He also showed us how to *be* a logician, how to put truth first, at all times, no matter what the costs may be. And that, surely, is the hardest lesson of all to learn.

Notes

1   The story is common currency in writings about Frege (e.g. from the seminal Dummett (1973: xxxiii–xxxvi) all the way to the more recent Burge (2005: 69), Potter (2010: 3) and Zalta (2013)), as well as in textbooks (e.g. from the introduction to the first two editions of Quine (1950) and his (1960: 163) to Soames (2010: 1–2)). It probably originates with a remark in Łukasiewicz (1935: 112). Putnam (1982) and Boolos (1994) strongly (perhaps a tad *too* strongly) oppose the standard account. A more balanced story is in Hodges (1983/2001: 1–4) and Sullivan (2004: §2.1).

2   A good discussion of the current conception is in e.g. Beall and Restall (2006: §2.5). On Frege's conception, see Goldfarb (2010) and Blanchette (2012).

3   There is a lively debate concerning the extent to which Frege's work may properly be said to be concerned with metatheoretical considerations. See e.g. Stanley (1996), Tappenden (1997) and Heck (2010) for the view that he was, Ricketts (1986, 1996) for the contrary view, and Sullivan (2005) for a sophisticated assessment of the controversy. Read (1997) is also useful.

4   Frege (1893/2013: xxvi). The irony is that in modern terms by this move Frege inaugurated the now common distinction between logic and logics, a distinction that he, however, would have found repugnant for the reasons I discuss in the next page and in note 6 below.

5   Very roughly, deductive systems can be divided into systems of proof properly so called (axiomatic systems that only allow axioms – or previously derived theorems – to figure as premises in proof) or deductive systems more generally, that is, systems of deduction, where assumptions other than axioms (or theorems) can figure as premises in a derivation. See Sundholm (1983/2001) and Socher-Ambrosius and Johann (1997).

6   Van Heijenoort (1967b). As Dummett (1991a: 219) observes, Frege seemed to have in mind a 'single intended interpretation' for his language, defined over absolutely all objects (or at least, all objects for which the language had names). See Blanchette (2012: ch. 3) for a recent discussion of this issue.

7   See *Grundlagen* §17.

8   See Frege (1880/1881; 1882; 1897b: 242).

9   Again, the issue is not as simple as that. See Heck (2012: 40–1) for useful qualifications.

10 Boolos (1975: 47) labels a view of this kind as 'archaic'. So much for Frege's being the founder of *modern* logic then! See Blanchette (2012: ch. 6) for further discussion.

11 It is surely not by chance that a model theorist like Hodges (1983/2001: 1) instead situates the watershed in 1847, the year Boole published his *Mathematical Analysis of Logic*. See Dummett (1959) for some powerful reasons to disagree with Hodges.

12 Just as Hilbert and Ackermann (1928: 1–2), and Putnam (1982: 260), would have it.

13 The classic criticism is in Quine (1970: 66). See Boolos (1975: 44–5) and Shapiro (1991) for critical discussion. Very roughly, the problem is that in quantifying over properties one appears to be *naming* them, and hence reifying attributes into entities, thus inflating our ontology to 'staggering' proportions.

14 That is, first-order logic is the strongest logic that can satisfy compactness, completeness and the downward Löwenheim–Skolem theorem, a result known as *Lindström Theorem(s)*. See Ebbinghaus *et al.* (1994: ch. 13) for the technical details. See also Read (1997) for a good account of the early history of logic in this connection.

15 Sure, it is true that Frege inaugurated a new way of *doing* logic, that he established new *methods* of logic, but the object (what counted as logic) and targets (what it was for) of those methods were significantly different to those that are common currency today.

16 For those theorems, see note 14. Depending on where we stand on this issue, we can say that modern logic *was* born in 1879 because Frege developed its first-order fragment then or because higher-order logic *is* logic anyway. The latter is without question a minority view. See Shapiro (1991) for the most sustained argument in its support. Interestingly, first-order logic's privileged status was consolidated when it showed itself to be the perfect tool of the model theorist, and model theory became in turn settled in the 1950s and 1960s.

17 Potter (2010: 23) quotes a remark from one of Frege's colleagues that even at his own university 'hardly anyone took Frege seriously'. Frege did not fare much better in the wider world. See Grattan-Guinness (2000: §4.5.1–2).

18 Another early exposition of Frege's system was Jourdain (1912).

19 Frege's system wasn't the only victim. Hilbert and Zermelo had been aware of the paradoxes a few years ahead of Russell (see e.g. Hilbert's last letter to Frege in Frege 1980: 51). Hilbert took the paradoxes to show that 'traditional logic is inadequate'. So, there you have it: by 1903 modern logic was already traditional!

20 Opinion is divided here. Putnam (1982) takes the view that Frege's work had a very limited impact. Defenders of the standard story (e.g. Reck and Awodey 2004: 40–1) have instead argued that Frege's *indirect* influence was nevertheless a determinant factor in the evolution of logic in that the logicians he taught, met or corresponded with (i.e. Carnap, Wittgenstein, Russell and Peano) were the lead players in the field, and in particular that Gödel's fundamental results of 1930–31 were heavily indebted to Carnap's 1928 lecture course on metalogic that Gödel had attended. For their part, Whitehead and Russell wrote in the preface to *Principia* that 'in the matter of notation' they followed Peano's lead. In 'all questions of logical analysis', however, their 'chief debt' was to Frege (p. viii). Basically, Frege's axiomatic system was rewritten into *Principia* in Peano's notation. That's how Frege's work entered the bloodstream of modern logic.

21 Dummett (1973, 1981, 1991a, 1991b, 1994).

22 It was a close shave though. See Putnam (1982: 255–59) and Goldfarb (1979) for details.

23 It's even more serious than that. In a very good sense, had Frege's peculiar approach to logic become dominant, it would have actually *hindered* the full development of modern logic. Here's just one example. Frege's notation for the quantifier, of which more later, made it completely unsuitable to the crucial treatment given by Skolem, where quantified formulae are divided into matrix (quantifier-free component) and prefix (the quantifier component), allowing the formulation (and proof) of various laws about quantifier elimination that are essential to proving fundamental metalogical results. If you're curious about this, Kelly (1997: §9.2.3) gives a very gentle introduction to the delights of Skolemization.

24 Indeed, Frege (1897b: 234, 237, 248) himself insists that we can make sense of a system of deduction only if we are fully apprised of the aims and purposes of the writer.

25 *Grundlagen*, §105. The view was of course by no means unique to Frege. Boole (1854/2009: 422) for one held that view too.

26 On Frege's original take on rationalism, see e.g. Burge (1992: 299–302; 1998), Gabriel (1996), Jeshion (2001: 969), Ruffino (2002) and Reck (2007).

27 For Frege (1879: 7) the language of pure thought captured by the *Begriffsschrift* constituted the *core* on which *any* scientific (i.e. truth-oriented) discourse would be based.

28 Frege argued convincingly that mathematicians' habits in this regard were unacceptably sloppy.

29 Note that this is why Frege's language comes with an interpretation already packed into it. It makes no sense to speak of alternative interpretation of the *Begriffsschrift* formulae because their logical properties cannot be altered without changing the thought, since those properties are determined by the position that the thoughts expressed by those formulae occupy in the order of truths.

30 Beaney (1996: ch. 6) has a penetrating discussion of the problems that Frege's conception of absolute thoughts give rise to.

31 Psychologism was, very roughly, the view that mathematical entities are essentially defined in terms of our mental acts. For instance, according to early Husserl, a set consists in a 'unifying act of consciousness'. Frege's strongest attack on psychologism is in Frege (1894). See also the preface to *Grundlagen*.

32 Frege (1893/2013: xvii).

33 See Frege (1879: §13; 1897b: 235). By contrast, Gentzen's systems of *natural* deduction were intended to model more closely the actual way in which mathematicians prove results. But it is no objection against Frege to say that his axiomatic system bears no resemblance to how mathematicians actually reason. This charge simply betrays a deep misunderstanding of Frege's project.

34 Objective, then, in the sense of mind and judgement-independent, as against
   sensations and intuitions (in Kant's sense) that are inevitably subject-relative.
35 See Frege (1879/1891: 2), (1880/1881: 16).
36 Lest this be confusing, to recap: my suggestion is that while the modern turn began
   before Frege, the new direction in logic only became firmly established in his work
   so that the modern way of doing logic was born with him. Modern *logic* (in *our*
   sense of logic) was finally codified only in the 1960s.
37 On the revisionary/descriptive contrast, see Strawson (1959: 9).
38 From Frege's perspective, the failings of the 'language' developed by Boole had been
   threefold: *i)* its expressions were given multiple interpretations within the same
   language; *ii)* the language as a whole admitted of (and required) multiple
   interpretations (roughly, a propositional and a calculus of classes interpretation); *iii)*
   the language lacked the expressive power to account for all forms of inference
   (specifically, it was unable to account for multiple generality inferences). See Frege
   (1880/1881).
39 I use the notion of proposition loosely here and interchangeably with that of
   sentence. The sense at stake is: whatever it is that the operators of so-called
   propositional logic operate on.
40 An excellent treatment of Aristotelian logic geared towards explaining the Fregean
   revolution is in Beaney (1996: ch. 1).
41 Not entirely without residue though. See Beaney (1996: §2.3–2.4) for the loss of
   some subtleties of syllogistic logic in Frege's system.
42 The contrast is between what Dummett (1981: 271ff.) has called, respectively,
   analysis proper and *decomposition*.
43 Frege (1879: §3; 1895: 120; 1897b: 239). The rejection of the *logical* significance of
   that distinction goes hand in hand with Frege's introduction of the quantifiers: e.g.
   Frege *deliberately* chose to express existential generalizations such as 'some numbers'
   as the negation of generality ('not all numbers are such that not') so as to eliminate
   the possibility of treating 'some numbers' as a *logical* subject. It is probably better to
   say that Frege did not *quite* reject the claim that all propositions are of subject–
   predicate form. Rather, his point was that the subject–predicate distinction is neither
   fixed nor properly tracked by standard grammar. Logical analysis is required to show
   what is predicated of what.
44 Very roughly, a function is an operation mapping objects (called *arguments*)
   from one set to objects (called *values*) in another (not necessarily distinct) set.
45 At the time of *Begriffsschrift*, Frege had not yet drawn his sense/reference
   distinction. The notion of judgeable content would later be split into grasp of
   thought (sense) and truth-value appraisal (judgement concerning reference, for
   according to Frege the reference of a sentence is its truth-value). See Frege
   (1893/2013: 9, fn. 2).

46 In *Begriffsschrift* Frege is a bit sloppy regarding the use/mention distinction, so he switches between talk of objects and signs fairly freely. See Stevenson (1973) for a good discussion of this issue. The point to bear in mind is that for the later Frege functional expressions refer to functions and variables to objects.

47 As Frege (1880/1881: 18) points out, this makes it impossible to distinguish between individuals and concepts under which they uniquely fall. Peirce made the same move as Frege, only a few years later. See Haaparanta (2009: §5).

48 I keep switching between thought, content and proposition. Frege changed his terminology (and his conception of these notions) over his career. To keep things simple, I slide back and forth between these notions as appropriate. No harm should ensue, as long as you keep in mind that the details of the story vary over time.

49 I mentioned the subtitle of *Begriffsschrift*. This is probably the place to point out that the title itself means *concept-script*, a conceptual calculus, a calculus of concepts, or even better: a calculus *generating* concepts. See Frege (1880/1881: 15m fn. *).

50 As argued convincingly in Dummett (1973: 2, 9, 11).

51 Note that abstraction is here a purely technical notion, not to be confused with the mental process of abstraction (i.e. introspective removal of properties) that Frege criticized in authors such as J.S. Mill and Husserl.

52 Frege's notion of function is radically general (much wider than the one standard in mathematics): the result of removing a singular term from *any* (well-formed) sentence (expressing a thought) will be a function(-name). See *Grundgesetze* I §2.

53 For Frege concepts are a subspecies of functions (see Frege 1891). They map individuals to truth-values: e.g. 'Cato killed ξ' is a function that maps all individuals such that they were killed by Cato to the True and everything else to the False (where we replace the name of an individual for ξ and evaluate the resulting thought for truth and falsity).

54 This is slightly anachronistic. At the time of *Begriffsschrift*, Frege hadn't yet drawn the sense/reference distinction. The way he put things then was that '*A*' stands for a state of affairs, a worldly entity, rather than something in the realm of sense like his later notion of *Gedanke*. I choose to speak of thought instead to stress the continuity in Frege's approach to logic (and in any case Frege himself also speaks interchangeably of thought and content in e.g. §8). 'The content that *A*' could be a more neutral way of putting matters.

55 Whitehead and Russell (1910/1997: 8) shortened the horizontal stroke and called it the *assertion sign*. It then became the standard sign for the derivability relation in a proof system. Martin-Löf (1972) will resurrect Frege's conception of a calculus of asserted proposition.

56 Frege (1879: §3). The requirement will be made more precise in *Grundgesetze* I §5.

57 Theorems are formulae provable in the system from the axioms. The axioms are treated as theorems by courtesy.

58 Frege (1918–19: 375; 1923: 261).

59 In Dummett's terminology (see fn. 42), his notation represents *both* the decomposition and the analysis of the thought.

60 There is the temptation to suggest that Frege intended this notation to represent the conceptual (or perhaps epistemological) dependency of the supercomponent on the subcomponent (see e.g. Boolos 1998: 144). The temptation should, however, be resisted. Frege's condition stroke is equivalent to the material conditional and no dependency of any kind is thereby asserted. The gloss in Landini (2012: 43) in terms of a metalinguistic conditional is equally misplaced. Frege is *very* aware his condition stroke does not characterize the natural language conditional *in full generality*. All that the stroke expresses is that the subcomponent is a sufficient condition for the obtaining of the supercomponent. See e.g. Frege (1879: 37).

61 For Frege's two senses of assertion (*Aussage*) see Ebert and Rossberg (1893/2013: xvii). Sometimes Frege seems to take the dependency expressed by the condition stroke as a stronger relation yet, as in §16 where he glosses the stroke as expressing the thought that the supercomponent is a *consequence* of the subcomponent.

62 See Frege (1897b: 236).

63 This applies even more clearly to the way Frege renders the classic concept-containment statement 'All *As* are *Bs*'.

64 I distinguish between the conditional (the formula as a whole) and the condition stroke (the vertical stroke joining up two content strokes).

65 In *Grundgesetze* he will switch to talk of naming the True or the False, because in his later philosophy he took sentences to be names of logical objects, that is, the two truth-values.

66 In effect, this is the truth-conditional definition of the conditional, first defended by Philo of Megara and currently called the *material conditional* reading.

67 Frege is also dismissing the so-called paradoxes of material implication as irrelevant precisely because he is not modelling *all* uses of *if . . ., then*.

68 Frege (1897b: 247). As we shall see, Frege used only two connectives, conditional and negation, which meant that formulae in his system often consisted of deeply nested conditionals. Most commentators have accepted the verdict of history (or of common practice) and sided with Peano. For a vigorously dissident opinion, see Cook (2013). See also Landini (2012).

69 Note that if you remove the vertical component of the judgement stroke and the content stroke preceding '*A*', you'll be left with the modern way of representing negation, '¬'.

70 The answers to most exercises are to be found in *Begriffsschrift* itself, but of course you should attempt them *before* reading Frege's work!

71 Quantifiers are *second-level* concepts, in Frege's later terminology: they take properties, rather than objects, as their arguments. There is a further twist to the

story. After work by Mostowski in the 1950s, so-called *generalized quantifiers* have become standard, especially in natural language semantics. And the inspiration for that second revolution came from Frege! See e.g. Barwise and Cooper (1981) and Peters and Westerståhl (2006: ch. 2).

72 The issue of the variable is one that looms large in early analytic philosophy (see e.g. Russell (1903/1996) and Wittgenstein's *Tractatus*). In many ways, the modern treatment of the variable was born only with Tarski (1935). Frege's treatment represents an alternative to Tarski's notion of assignment. See Heck (2012: ch. 3) for discussion.

73 It may seem a little confusing that Frege is here using the same sort of letter to denote propositions (as in the conditional formulae discussed above) and arguments of functions. But one should bear in mind that for Frege functions could take as argument just about anything, including functions themselves. Note, however, that, in his formal language, when functions figure as arguments of other functions, they are really 'feeding' the values they return to the higher-order functions (see *Grundgesetze* I, §21). Moreover, in *Grundgesetze* function names, once 'saturated' with an argument, are names of truth-values, and so what a higher-level function does is really operate on the truth-values names provided by the lower-level function which is their argument.

74 One reason why Frege adopts this variant notation is that it validates the transitivity of chains of generalized statements (i.e. the old *Barbara* syllogism) not otherwise available in his system (the concavity sign – to be explained below – would get in the way, as it were). See Frege (1893/2013: I, §17). Note that this is one more way in which Frege strived to provide a language that would give a unified treatment of all valid forms of inference. Frege also noted the need for restrictions to be in place, namely, that *a* should not occur in *X* other than in its argument places. He noted similar and now familiar restrictions in the case of inferences of the form $\vdash \begin{array}{l} \phi(a) \\ A \end{array}$, *a* must also not occur in *A*. It is in remarks like these that we recognize that the modern turn has now fully taken place: this is, notation apart, just like what *we* do in logic today.

75 In modern notation, this would be the familiar $\forall x\, F(x)$, or, in slightly more exotic textbooks, $\forall x\, \varphi(x)$. Russell (1908: 65–6) gave a similar gloss. To make Frege's awkward formulation more precise, one would say that the thought expressed by the proposition obtained by applying the function Φ to any argument is true. There is some uncertainty as to whether Frege had a substitutional conception of quantification (replacement of the variable by linguistic expressions from a given class) or an *objectual* conception (replacement of the variable by a constant denoting an object in the domain). In this context, Frege glosses the notion as 'whatever we may put in place of *a*'. The 'whatever' is not quite so unrestricted though. See Stevenson (1973: 209–10) for discussion.

76 Equally important is §9 where the function/argument analysis is introduced.

77 Think of Boole's language as a multi-use tool: you can change the head of the tool to carry out different jobs, but you can never carry out more than one job at a time. Frege's language abolishes the need for a change of head, as it were.

78 Frege had little time for modalities, but given his view of absolutely unrestricted generality (*all* substitution instances were available in his system), (12) comes pretty close to expressing a naïve view of causal connection.

79 See also Frege (1893/2013: I §12).

80 In response, early critics in the algebraic tradition such as Jevons had been crudely dismissive, saying that Frege had clothed Aristotle in mathematical dress without making any real advance over Boole. Frege (1882) gives the lie to that claim.

81 Frege puts a (vague) restriction in place, namely, that when the substituend is a function sign, this be taken into account. In *Grundgesetze*, I §48 rule 9, Frege will state his substitution principles much more rigorously but far too liberally. Indeed, those rules will be the source of the contradiction that scuppered his system. There is a good sense in which *Begriffsschrift* is consistent because it lacks the precision of *Grundgesetze* with regard to the rules of substitution. See Kamareddine and Laan (2004: §1b1).

82 The calculus happens to be complete and sound. In §13 Frege gestured towards an awareness of the need to ensure that a system satisfy those two conditions (roughly, soundness means that its axioms be true and its rule(s) of inference truth-preserving; completeness, that the system be strong enough to prove all intuitively true propositions in the subject matter at hand).

83 As Gödel (1944: 120) famously noted, Russell's and Whitehead's *Principia* represented a retrograde step in expository rigour, particularly with respect to the treatment of syntax.

84 It is a rule of proof because it takes as premises only axioms or previously established theorems. Here I assume familiarity with MP. As I have mentioned already, Frege also made recourse to a rule of substitution, not clearly stated as such.

85 Section 6 is where Frege states most of these now familiar bookkeeping conventions.

86 Frege also seems to be the first to introduce the distinctions between object and metalanguage (Frege 1923: 260) and variable and meta-variable (*Grundgesetze* I, 6, fn. 1).

87 Mendelson (1964–1997), Hamilton (1978) and Hodel (1995) are among the exceptions.

88 Most current axiomatic presentations are derived from the amendments given in Łukasiewicz (1935), where the completeness of a streamlined version of Frege's system was established. One of the things that Łukasiewicz showed was that Frege's axioms could be reduced in number (for instance, axiom 1 and 2 entail axiom 3, and

so the latter is redundant). In case you're tempted to check out that paper, be warned that the axioms are given using Polish notation!

89   As hinted already, Frege also used an unstated rule of uniform substitution, widely used in his proofs (a formula may be substituted for another uniformly throughout the containing formula). He also used the equivalence between (7) and (8) as another rule of inference (given in two variants). See §11 of *Begriffsschrift*.

90   And so strictly speaking *modus ponens* is here a rule of proof: it can be applied only to *theorems*, not to assumptions (as one would do in a Gentzen-like natural deduction system). Frege also allows that proofs be commenced from previously established theorems (see for instance the last proof in §15).

91   Strictly speaking, we should speak of *axiom schemata*: all instances of these axioms are true. Frege, however, is here using small German letters with the understanding that they are universally closed in the sense of formula (7). On this second reading, the axioms are not schematic at all. A schematic reading, however, preserves the contrast between axiom 9 that explicitly involves (and indeed defines one direction of the notion of) generality and the other eight that instead do not.

92   The interchangeability of subcomponents allows Frege to treat conditionals as having the conjunction of all their interchangeable subcomponents as a single subcomponent. Following Cook's (2013: A-9) elegant suggestion, we can thus read the condition stroke as an *n*–ary function $\displaystyle \vdash\!\!\!\overbrace{}^{\Gamma}_{\{\Delta_1, \Delta_2, \ldots, \Delta_n\}}$ where the Δs are all the formula's subcomponents.

93   Section 17, formula 28, §18 formula 31 and §19 formula 41 respectively.

94   Section 20 formula 52, §21, formula 54 and §22, formula 58 respectively.

95   If you're interested in the topic, take a look at Mendelsohn (2005: ch. 4).

96   In Sullivan's (2004: 672) useful terminology.

97   Basic Law IIa, §20, and Basic Law IIb, §25, respectively.

98   Again, depending on whether we read Frege's axioms as schemata or as universally closed formulae, we may decide to say that it *is* axiom 1. Incidentally, if you are unfamiliar with substitution techniques, you may be surprised to see that we can instantiate axioms that bear different variables by using the same variable. Nothing wrong with that at all. And Frege exploited this technique over and over again in his proofs.

99   I'm omitting quotation marks around subformulae here in keeping with Frege's cavalier attitude to the use/mention distinction!

100 Interestingly enough, in *Grundgesetze*, I, §18, Frege treats (15) as a special case of axiom 1 by appeal to his form of the contraction rule, what he called the *union of subcomponents* (two occurrences of the same subcomponent can be absorbed/contracted into one).

101 Frege's target here was again Kant, who had argued that mathematical induction can only be explained in mind-dependent terms. A purely logical explanation of the kind Frege gave was meant to falsify Kant's claim.

102 For a detailed assessment of Frege's technical achievements in Part III of *Begriffsschrift* see Boolos (1985).

103 To be precise, the form in which Russell stated the contradiction did not apply to Frege's system. Frege pointed this out in his reply, but he also immediately restated the contradiction in terms that would indeed be syntactically appropriate, and fatal, to his system.

104 See Frege's own diagnosis in Frege 1980: 191, fn. 69.

105 For good introductory accounts of Frege's life and work, see Kenny (1995), Weiner (1990) and Noonan (2001). For an account of Frege's logic in *Grundgesetze* see Cook (2013).

106 Frege (1924, 1924/1925).

107 Rather, what the laws of the laws of thought were, to adapt *Grundlagen*.

108 On the first point see Frege (1892) and Tait (1997: 246). On the second, see the increasing irritation in Hilbert's letters (Frege 1980) and Peano's doubts, expressed in his 1895 review of *Grundgesetze*, regarding Frege's 'unnecessary subtleties'.

109 Van Heijenoort (1967a: 127).

References

Barwise, John and Cooper, Robin (1981), 'Generalized Quantifiers and Natural Language'. *Linguistics and Philosophy*, 4: 159–219.

Beall, J.C. and Restall, Greg (2006), *Logical Pluralism*. Oxford: Clarendon Press.

Beaney, Michael (1996), *Frege: Making Sense*. London: Duckworth.

Beaney, Michael and Reck, Erich H. (eds) (2005), *Gottlob Frege: Critical Assessment*. London: Routledge.

Blanchette, Patricia A. (2012), *Frege's Conception of Logic*. Oxford: Oxford University Press.

Boole, George (1854/2009), *An Investigation of the Laws of Thought*. Cambridge: Cambridge University Press.

Boolos, George (1975), 'On Second-Order Logic'. In Boolos (1998), pp. 37–53.

Boolos, George (1985), 'Reading the *Begriffsschrift*'. In Boolos (1998), pp. 155–70.

Boolos, George (1994), 1879?' In Boolos (1998), pp. 237–54.

Boolos, George (1998), *Logic, Logic, and Logic*. Cambridge, MA: Harvard University Press.

Bostock, David (1997), *Intermediate Logic*. Oxford: Clarendon Press.

Burge, Tyler (1992), 'Frege on Knowing the Third Realm'. In Burge (2005), pp. 299–316.

Burge, Tyler (1998), 'Frege on Knowing the Foundation'. In Burge (2005), pp. 317–55.

Burge, Tyler (2005), *Truth, Thought, Reason. Essays on Frege*. Oxford: Clarendon Press.

Cook, Roy (2013), 'How To Read *Grundgesetze*'. In Frege (1893/2013), pp. A1–A42.

Dummett, Michael (1959), 'George Boole'. In *Truth and Other Enigmas*. Cambridge, MA: Harvard University Press, pp. 66–73.

Dummett, Michael (1973), *Frege. Philosophy of Language*. 2nd edn. London: Duckworth.

Dummett, Michael (1981), *The Interpretation of Frege's Philosophy*. London: Duckworth.

Dummett, Michael (1991a), *Frege and Other Philosophers*. Oxford: Clarendon Press.

Dummett, Michael (1991b), *Frege. Philosophy of Mathematics*. London: Duckworth.

Dummett, Michael (1994), *Origins of Analytical Philosophy*. Cambridge, MA: Harvard University Press.

Ebbinghaus, H.-D., Flum, J. and Thomas, W. (1994), *Mathematical Logic*. 2nd edn. New York: Springer.

Ebert, Philip A. and Rossberg, Marcus (1893/2013), 'Translators' Introduction'. In Frege (1893/2013), pp. xiii–xxvi.

Frege, Gottlob (1879), '*Begriffsschrift*'. In van Heijenoort (1967a), pp. 5–82.

Frege, Gottlob (1879/1891), 'Logic'. In Frege (1979), pp. 1–8.

Frege, Gottlob (1880/1881), 'Boole's logical Calculus and the Concept-Script'. In Frege (1979), pp. 9–52.

Frege, Gottlob (1882), 'Boole's logical Formula-language and my Concept-script'. In Frege (1979), pp. 47–52.

Frege, Gottlob (1891), 'Function and Concept'. In Frege (1984), pp. 137–56.

Frege, Gottlob (1892), 'On Sense and Reference'. In Beaney, Michael (ed.) *The Frege Reader*. Oxford: Blackwell, pp. 151–71.

Frege, Gottlob (1893/2013), *Basic Laws of Arithmetic*. Oxford: Oxford University Press.

Frege, Gottlob (1894), 'Review of E.G. Husserl, *Philosophie der Arithmetik I*'. In Frege (1984), pp. 195–209.

Frege, Gottlob (1895), 'Comments on *Sinn und Bedeutung*'. In Frege (1979), pp. 118–25.

Frege, Gottlob (1897a), 'Logic'. In Frege (1979), pp. 118–51.

Frege, Gottlob (1897b), 'On Mr Peano's Conceptual Notation and My Own'. In Frege (1984), pp. 234–48.

Frege, Gottlob (1918–19), 'Negation'. In Frege (1984), pp. 373–89.

Frege, Gottlob (1923), 'Logical Generality'. In Frege (1979), pp. 258–62.

Frege, Gottlob (1924), 'A New Attempt at a Foundation for Arithmetic'. In Frege (1979), pp. 278–81.

Frege, Gottlob (1924/1925), 'Numbers and Arithmetic'. In Frege (1979), pp. 275–7.

Frege, Gottlob (1979), *Posthumous Writings*. Oxford: Blackwell.

Frege, Gottlob (1980), *Philosophical and Mathematical Correspondence*. Oxford: Blackwell.

Frege, Gottlob (1984), *Collected Papers on Mathematics, Logic, and Philosophy*. Oxford: Blackwell.

Gabbay, Dov and Guenthner, Franz (eds) (1983/2001), *Handbook of Philosophical Logic*, vol. 1. 2nd edn. Dordrecht/Boston/Lancaster: D. Reidel Publishing Company.

Gabriel, Gottfried (1996), 'Frege's "Epistemology in Disguise"'*. In Schirn, Matthias (ed.) *Frege: Importance and Legacy*. Berlin: Walter de Gruyter, pp. 330–46.

Gödel, Kurt (1944), 'Russell's Mathematical Logic'. In Feferman, Solomon (ed.) *Collected Works*, vol. II. Publications 1938–1974. Oxford: Oxford University Press, pp. 119–41.

Goldfarb, Warren (1979), 'Logic in the Twenties: The Nature of the Quantifier'. *Journal of Symbolic Logic*, 44, 3: 351–68.

Goldfarb, Warren (2010), 'Frege's Conception of Logic'. In Potter and Ricketts (2010), pp. 63–85.

Grattan-Guinness, Ivor (2000), *The Search for Mathematical Roots, 1870–1940. Logic, Set Theories and the Foundations of Mathematics from Cantor through Russell to Gödel*. Princeton and Oxford: Princeton University Press.

Haaparanta, Leila (2009), 'The Relation between Logic and Philosophy, 1874–1931'. In Haaparanta, Leila (ed.) *The Development of Modern Logic*. Oxford: Oxford University Press, pp. 222–62.

Hamilton, A.G. (1978), *Logic for Mathematicians*. Cambridge: Cambridge University Press.

Heck, Richard (2010), 'Frege and Semantics'. In Potter and Ricketts (2010), pp. 342–78.

Heck, Richard (2012), *Reading Frege's* Grundgesetze. Oxford: Clarendon Press.

Hilbert, David and Ackermann, Wilhelm (1928), *Principles of Mathematical Logic*. Providence, Rhode Island: AMS Chelsea Publishing.

Hodel, Richard E. (1995), *An Introduction to Mathematical Logic*. Boston: PWS Publishing Company.

Hodges, Wilfrid (1983/2001), 'Elementary Predicate Logic'. In Gabbay and Guenthner (1983/2001), pp. 1–129.

Jeshion, Robin (2001), 'Frege's Notion of Self-Evidence'. *Mind*, 110, 440: 937–76.

Jourdain, Philip E.B. (1912), 'Gottlob Frege'. *Quarterly Journal of Pure and Applied Mathematics*, 43: 237–69.

Kamareddine, Fairouz and Laan, Twan (2004), *A Modern Perspective on Type Theory From its Origins until Today*. Dordrecht: Kluwer Academic Publishers.

Kelly, John (1997), *The Essence of Logic*. Harlow: Prentice Hall.

Kenny, Anthony (1995), *Frege*. Harmondsworth: Penguin Books.

Landini, Gregory (2012), *Frege's Notations. What they are and how they mean*. Basingstoke: Palgrave Macmillan.

Łukasiewicz, Jan (1935), 'Zur Geschichte der Aussagenlogik'. *Erkenntnis*, 5, 111–31.

Martin-Löf, Per (1972), 'An Intuitionistic Theory of Types'. In Sambin, Giovanni and Smith, Jan M. (eds), *Twenty-five Years of Constructive Type Theory*. Oxford: Clarendon Press, pp. 127–72.

Mendelsohn, Richard L. (2005), *The Philosophy of Gottlob Frege*. Cambridge: Cambridge University Press.

Mendelson, Eliott (1964–1997), *Introduction to Mathematical Logic*. 4th edn. Boca Raton: Chapman & Hall.

Noonan, Harold W. (2001), *Frege: A Critical Introduction*. Cambridge: Polity Press.

Peters, Stanley and Westerståhl, Dag (2006), *Quantifiers in Language and Logic*. Oxford: Clarendon Press.

Potter, Michael (2010), 'Introduction'. In Potter and Ricketts (2010), pp. 1–31.

Potter, Michael and Ricketts, Tom (eds) (2010), *The Cambridge Companion to Frege*. Cambridge: Cambridge University Press.

Putnam, Hilary (1982), 'Peirce the Logician'. In *Realism with a Human Face*. Cambridge, MA: Harvard University Press, pp. 252–60.

Quine, W.V. (1950), *Methods of Logic*. Cambridge, MA: Harvard University Press.

Quine, Willard V. (1960), *Word and Object*. Cambridge, MA: The MIT Press.

Quine, Willard V. (1970), *Philosophy of Logic*. 2nd (1986) edn. Cambridge, MA: Harvard University Press.

Read, Stephen (1997), 'Completeness and Categoricity: Frege, Gödel and Model Theory'. *History and Philosophy of Logic*, 18: 79–93.

Reck, Erich H. (2007), 'Frege on Truth, Judgment, and Objectivity'. In Greimann, Dirk (ed.) *Essays on Frege's Conception of Truth*. Grazer Philosophische Studien, Amsterdam and New York: Rodopi, pp. 149–73.

Reck, Erich H. and Awodey, Steve (eds) (2004), *Frege's Lectures on Logic. Carnap's Student Notes 1910–1914*. Chicago and La Salle, Illinois: Open Court.

Ricketts, Thomas (1986), 'Objectivity and Objecthood: Frege's Metaphysics of Judgement'. In Haaparanta, L. and Hintikka, J. (eds) *Frege Synthesized*. Reidel: Dordrecht, pp. 65–95.

Ricketts, Thomas (1996), 'Logic and Truth in Frege'. *Proceedings of the Aristotelian Society, Supplementary Volumes*, 70: 121–40.

Ruffino, Marco (2002), 'Logical Objects in Frege's *Grundgesetze*, Section 10'. In Reck, Erich H. (ed.) *From Frege to Wittgenstein*. Oxford: Oxford University Press, pp. 125–48.

Russell, Bertrand (1903/1996), *The Principles of Mathematics*. London: Routledge.

Russell, Bertrand (1908), 'Mathematical Logic as Based on the Theory of Types'. In Marsh, Robert C. (ed.) *Logic and Knowledge*. London: Routledge, pp. 59–102.

Shapiro, Stewart (1991), *Foundations without Foundationalism. A Case for Second-order Logic*. Oxford: Clarendon Press.

Soames, Scott (2010), *Philosophy of Language*. Princeton, New Jersey: Princeton University Press.

Socher-Ambrosius, Rolf and Johann, Patricia (1997), *Deduction Systems*. New York: Springer.

Stanley, Jason (1996), 'Truth and Metatheory in Frege'. In Beaney and Reck (2005), pp. 109–35.

Stevenson, Leslie (1973), 'Frege's Two Definitions of Quantification'. *The Philosophical Quarterly*, 23, 92: 207–223.

Strawson, P.F. (1959), *Individuals*. London and New York: Routledge.

Sullivan, Peter (2004), 'Frege's Logic'. In Gabbay, Dov M. and Woods, John (eds.) *Handbook of the History of Logic*, vol. 3. The Rise of Modern Logic: From Leibniz to Frege. Amsterdam: Elsevier, pp. 671–762.

Sullivan, Peter (2005), 'Metaperspectives and Internalism in Frege'. In Beaney and Reck (2005), pp. 85–105.

Sundholm, Göran (1983/2001), 'Systems of Deduction'. In Gabbay and Guenthner (1983/2001), pp. 133–88.

Tait, William (1997), 'Frege versus Cantor and Dedekind: On the Concept of Number'. In *The Provenance of Pure Reason. Essays in the Philosophy of Mathematics and Its History*. Oxford: Oxford University Press, pp. 212–51.

Tappenden, Jamie (1997), 'Metatheory and Mathematical Practice in Frege'. *Philosophical Topics*, 25, 2: 213–64.

Tarski, Alfred (1935), 'The Concept of Truth in Formalized Languages'. In *Logic, Semantics, Metamathematics*, 2nd (1983) edn. Indianapolis: Hackett, pp. 152–278.

van Heijenoort, Jean (ed.) (1967a), *From Frege to Gödel*. Cambridge, MA: Harvard University Press.

van Heijenoort, Jean (1967b), 'Logic as Calculus and Logic as Language'. *Synthèse*, 17, 3: 324–30.

Weiner, Joan (1990), *Frege in Perspective*. Ithaca, NY: Cornell University Press.

Whitehead, Alfred North and Russell, Bertrand (1910/1997), *Principia Mathematica to *56*. Cambridge: Cambridge University Press.

Zalta, Edward (2013), 'Frege's Theorem and Foundations for Arithmetic'. In Zalta, Edward (ed.) *The Stanford Encyclopedia of Philosophy*, fall 2013 edn, http://plato.stanford.edu/archives/fall2013/entries/frege-logic/.

9

Peano and Russell

Alexander Bird

Introduction

Gottlob Frege is customarily awarded the honorific title 'the father of modern logic'. Jean van Heijenoort (1992: 242) tells us that 'Modern logic began in 1879, the year in which Gottlob Frege (1848–1925) published his *Begriffsschrift*', while Michael Dummett (1993: xiii) regards Frege as the 'initiator of the modern period in the study of logic'. Yet, the praise so frequently accorded to the originality and quality of Frege's logic and philosophy has obscured the significance and influence of his contemporary, Giuseppe Peano. The contribution of the latter has been underestimated; indeed in terms of causal consequence, Peano's work had a greater impact on the development of logic at a crucial period surrounding the turn of the nineteenth century. Peano's influence was felt principally through his impact on Bertrand Russell (indeed, much the same can be said of Frege). In this chapter we shall examine this line of influence, looking first at Peano's logic and then at Russell's.

1 Giuseppe Peano

Giuseppe Peano was born in Piedmont, in 1858, ten years after Frege and fourteen years before Russell. He was educated in the Piedmontese capital, Turin, where he became professor of mathematics, teaching and researching in analysis and logic. As with several other mathematicians, his interest in logic was in part motivated by the need to promote rigour in mathematics. The emphasis he places on rigour can be appreciated through a debate between Peano and his colleague Corrado Segre. Segre had made important contributions to algebraic geometry, and with Peano made Turin a notable centre for geometry. Nonetheless, they had quite different attitudes towards rigour, proof and intuition. Segre felt that in order to make progress in a new area of mathematics, it would often be necessary to resort to less rigorous, incomplete procedures (Borga and Palladino 1992: 23). Peano (1891: 66) responded that 'a result cannot be considered as obtained if it is not rigorously proved, even if exceptions are not known.'

The difference between the intuitive approach and the rigorous approach is apparent in the mathematical understanding of continuity. The *intuitive* notion of a continuous curve is one that can be divided into parts, each of which is continuously differentiable. Curves of the latter sort cannot fill a space – however small a space we choose, the curve cannot go through every point in the space. Intuitively a one-dimensional thing, a continuous curve, cannot fill two-dimensional space. However, Peano shows that some continuous curves can go through every point in a finite space, indeed in infinite space. In a paper published in 1890, Peano gave a formal description of what became known as the 'Peano curve', a curve that passes through every point in the unit square. The paper gave no illustration of the curve, precisely because, Peano held, it is thinking in visual terms about geometry and analysis that leads to the use of intuition in mathematics and the breakdown of rigour.

The other influence on the Peano curve was Cantor. Peano was intrigued by Cantor's proof that the set of points in the unit interval (the real numbers between 0 and 1) has the same cardinality as (i.e. can be put into 1–1 correlation with) the number of points in the unit square. Since the cardinality of the unit interval is equal to that of the whole real line, this raises the possibility that there is a curve that proves Cantor's conclusion by going though every point in the unit square. Peano's curve does exactly that.

1.1 Peano's logical symbolism

In the year following publication of his space-filling curve, Peano instituted his 'Formulario' project, the aim of which was to articulate all the theorems of mathematics using a new notation that Peano had devised. A little earlier Peano (1888) has published a book on the geometrical calculus, following the approach of Hermann Grassmann's *Ausdehnungslehre*. According to Grassmann, geometry does not have physical space as its subject matter. It is rather a purely abstract calculus that may have application to physical space. Conceiving it this way allows for a formal approach to geometrical proof divorced from intuition and thereby allows for flaws in intuition-based reasoning (for example in Euclid) to be avoided. Moritz Pasch, in his *Vorlesungen über neuere Geometrie* (1882) tools certain terms as primitive and undefined (*Kernbegriffe* as Pasch later called them) while certain theorems (*Kernsätze*) are taken as unproved, i.e. are the axioms. Derived theorems are to be proved by pure logic alone, independently of any intuition. Pasch's approach influenced Peano's *I principii di geometria logicamente esposti* (1889). For this programme to be realized fully, Peano held, the geometrical calculus needed the framework of a logical calculus.

In 1889 Peano published his *Arithmetices principia, nova methodo exposita*. This work (in Latin) contained his famous five postulates for arithmetic – the *Arithmetices principia*. The phrase 'nova methodo exposita' refers to the new symbolism that Peano introduced for logical relations: the now familiar '∈' for set/class membership and '⊃' (a rotated 'C' for 'consequentia'). In the second volume of the *Formulaire* Peano replaced '⊃' with the now-familiar horseshoe '⊃'). Peano had already invented several other symbols central to the symbolism of logic and set theory, such as the symbols for union and intersection, '∪' and '∩', and existential quantification, '∃', and the tilde '~' for negation. Peano signified universal generalization using subscripts and his '⊃'. The familiarity of these symbols tends to mask the importance of their introduction. But the idea is also familiar that having the appropriate terminology is crucial not just to expressing thoughts clearly but often also to having the relevant thoughts at all. The development of a symbolism for logic was not just a lubricant to the accelerating vehicle that was mathematical logic, but was an essential part of its motor, as Bertrand Russell was soon to acknowledge.

2 From Peano to Russell

In the final summer of the nineteenth century, the first International Congress of Philosophy took place in Paris (it was to be followed immediately by the second International Congress of Mathematics). Peano was on the committee for the Congress and one of its leading lights. Also attending was twenty-eight-year-old Bertrand Russell. Born into the aristocracy and grandson of a Prime Minister, Russell came from quite a different background to Peano. Nonetheless, their interests converged on the intersection of mathematics, logic and philosophy. Russell went up to Cambridge in 1890, where he completed both the Mathematical and Moral Sciences (Philosophy) Triposes. Like Peano, Russell was much taken by the work of Georg Cantor. He had begun to study Cantor's work in 1896 (Grattan-Guinness 1978: 129), and had been thinking a great deal when he met Peano in August 1900. In his autobiography, Russell records the significance of his meeting thus:

The Congress was the turning point of my intellectual life, because there I met Peano. I already knew him by name and had seen some of his work, but had not taken the trouble to master his notation. In discussions at the Congress I observed that he was always more precise than anyone else, and that he invariably got the better of any argument on which he embarked. As the days went by, I decided that this must be owing to his mathematical logic ... It became clear to me that his notation afforded an instrument of logical analysis such as I had been seeking for years.

Russell 1967: 144

And thus:

I went to [Peano] and said, 'I wish to read all your works. Have you got copies with you?' He had, and I immediately read them all. It was they that gave the impetus to my own views on the principles of mathematics.

Russell 1959: 65

2.1 Burali-Forti's paradox and Cantor's theorem

Russell, who had been intending to stay for both congresses, left Paris in order to return home to study Peano's work in greater detail. He was, however, already aware of Burali-Forti's paradox and of Cantor's paradox. Cesare Burali-Forti was Peano's assistant and lectured on Peano's mathematical logic and used Peano's symbolism in his own work. In 1897 Burali-Forti had published his famous paradox concerning ordinals. In a simple terms the class of all ordinals, Ω, is an ordinal or corresponds to an ordinal. But then we can construct a greater ordinal, which is both a member of Ω (because it is an ordinal) and not a member of Ω (because it is greater than Ω). Georg Cantor had earlier (1891) published his diagonal proof that the power set of a set is always larger than the set itself, as follows.

Let us assume that there is a 1–1 correspondence between S and its power set $\mathcal{P}(S)$, which we will call f (so $f: S \rightarrow \mathcal{P}(S)$ is a bijection); for every member of x of S, $f(x) \in \mathcal{P}(S)$, and for every member y of $\mathcal{P}(S)$, there is a unique $x \in$ S such that $f(x) = y$.

Table 9.1 f is a 1–1 correlation between S and $\mathcal{P}$ (S)

S	$\mathcal{P}(S)$
x	$f(x)$

The various $f(x)$ are subsets of S. And so some members of S may be correlated by f with sets of which they are themselves members, i.e. $x \in f(x)$. Let us use 'Σ' to denote the set of such members of S, i.e. $\Sigma = \{x : x \in S \wedge x \in f(x)\}$. Now consider the remaining members of S; call this set 'Σ^*'. Σ^* contains those members of S which are not members of the sets with which they correlate under f; i.e. $\Sigma^* = \{x : x \in S \wedge x \notin f(x)\}$.

Every member of S is a member of one or other of Σ and Σ^* but not of both. Both Σ and Σ^* are subsets of S, hence they are members of $\mathscr{P}(S)$. This means, by the definition of f, there must be members of S which correlate with them. Let 'x^*' denote the member that correlates with Σ^* (i.e. $f(x^*) = \Sigma^*$).

Table 9.2 Some members of S correlate with sets they are members of; these are members of Σ. Others correlate with sets they are not members of; these are members of Σ^*.

S	$\mathscr{P}(S)$
x	$f(x)$ where $x \in f(x)$ – such sets are members of Σ
z	$f(z)$ where $z \notin f(z)$ – such sets are members of Σ^*

Table 9.3 x^* correlates with $\Sigma^* = f(x^*)$

S	$\mathscr{P}(S)$
x^*	Σ^*

Now we ask: Is x^* a member of Σ or Σ^*? If $x^* \notin \Sigma^*$ i.e. $x^* \in \Sigma$, then by definition of Σ, $x^* \in f(x^*)$ (see Table 9.2). But by definition of x^* (see Table 9.3), $f(x^*) = \Sigma^*$, so $x^* \in \Sigma^*$. So we have shown that $x^* \notin \Sigma^* \rightarrow x^* \in \Sigma^*$.

If on the other hand $x^* \in \Sigma^*$, then by definition of Σ^* (see Table 9.2), we have $x^* \notin f(x^*)$. Since $f(x^*) = \Sigma^*$ (see Table 9.3), it follows that $x^* \notin \Sigma^*$. That is, we have shown that $x^* \in \Sigma^* \rightarrow x^* \notin \Sigma^*$.

So together we have: $x^* \in \Sigma^* \leftrightarrow x^* \notin \Sigma^*$, which is a contradiction. Thus the assumption that there is a 1–1 correlation between S and $\mathscr{P}(S)$ is false.

But Russell had not initially seen the full significance of this result. He wrote: '[I]in this one point the master [Cantor] has been guilty of a very subtle fallacy, which I hope to explain in some future work' (Russell 1963: 69). Nonetheless, in due course, most probably as a result of thinking about Burali-Forti's paradox and being assisted by Peano's symbolism, he came to see the implications of Cantor's proof and of Burali-Forti's paradox. Cantor himself, had, around the same time as Burali-Forti, drawn the conclusion from his theorem that there is no largest cardinal. Russell later remarked, 'I attempted to discover some flaw in Cantor's proof that there is no largest cardinal ... Applying this proof to the supposed class of all imaginable objects, I was led to a new and simpler contradiction'. The contradiction to which he was led was that of the set of sets which do not contain themselves.

3 Bertrand Russell

In 1903 Russell published his *Principles of Mathematics*, in which he set out the logicist programme he was to pursue with Alfred North Whitehead. Although Russell had already been at work on a book with this title, he was impelled to rewrite the work completely as a result of meeting Peano, which he did in the last three months of 1900 (Russell 1959: 72–3). At this time Russell was not aware of Frege's work. Indeed Russell came across Frege by reading the works of Peano, which Peano had presented to him in Paris. On seeing Frege's *Grundgesetze der Arithmetik* (Basic Laws of Arithmetic) and *Grundlagen der Arithmetik* (Foundations of Arithmetic), Russell was struck by the philosophical significance of the latter and by the fatal flaw in the former. Because Russell engaged with Frege's work only after he had completed writing the *Principles of Mathematics*, Russell chose, in the light of its philosophical significance, to add an extended appendix in which Frege's work is discussed. Russell says:

> The work of Frege, which appears to be far less known than it deserves, contains many of the doctrines set forth in Parts I and II of the present work, and where it differs from the views which I have advocated, the differences demand discussion. Frege's work abounds in subtle distinctions, and avoids all the usual fallacies which beset writers on Logic. His symbolism, though unfortunately so cumbrous as to be very difficult to employ in practice, is based upon an analysis of logical notions much more profound than Peano's, and is philosophically very superior to its more convenient rival. In what follows, I shall try briefly to expound Frege's theories on the most important points, and to explain my grounds for differing where I do differ. But the points of disagreement are very few and slight compared to those of agreement.

The conclusion we should draw, I believe, is that despite the quality of Frege's work, it was not especially influential in the early development of modern logic. Russell is the crucial figure (perhaps with Hilbert alongside him). But although Frege's work may have sharpened Russell's subsequent philosophical thinking, there is no reason to suppose that Russell's logic would have been much different without Frege. Even if less worthy, Peano's logic was, as we have seen, seminal for Russell.

As for the fatal flaw, Russell immediately saw that Frege's axioms in his Basic Laws led to a contradiction. As Russell wrote to Frege, just as the completion of the latter was in print:

> Let *w* be the predicate: to be a predicate that cannot be predicated of itself. Can *w* be predicated of itself? From each answer its opposite follows. Therefore we must conclude that *w* is not a predicate. Likewise there is no class (as a totality) of those classes which, each taken as a totality, do not belong to themselves. From this I conclude that under certain circumstances a definable collection does not form a totality.
>
> 16 June 1902, letter to Frege, translation in van Heijenoort 1967: 125[1]

Frege's fifth axiom (V) claims that every predicate defines a set, its extension. Russell's *w* seems to be precisely a predicate that does not have an extension.

Let Fx be $x \notin x$ (def F). (Recall def $\in$: $x \in y \leftrightarrow \exists G(y = \char`\^G \wedge Gx)$.) By (V) we have an extension for F, *viz.* $\char`\^$F. We now consider whether or not F($\char`\^$F).

(1)	$\neg$F($\char`\^$F)	assumption
(2)	$\char`\^$F$\in\char`\^$F	(1, def F, double negation)
(3)	$\exists G(\char`\^F=\char`\^G \wedge G(\char`\^F))$	(2, def $\in$)
(4)	$\char`\^F=\char`\^G \rightarrow (F\leftrightarrow G)$	(Vb)
(5)	$\exists G(F\leftrightarrow G \wedge G(\char`\^F))$	(3, 4 MP)
(6)	F($\char`\^$F)	(5, simple logic)
(7)	$\char`\^$F$\in\char`\^$F	(from def $\in$)
(8)	$\neg$F($\char`\^$F)	(def F)

And so considering lines 1, 6 and 8, we have: $\neg$F($\char`\^$F) $\leftrightarrow$ F($\char`\^$F), which is Russell's paradox.

Another of the paradoxes considered by Russell was that discovered by the French mathematician Jules Richard. Russell gives it as follows: consider all decimals that can be defined by means of a finite number of words; let E be the class of all such decimals. Since the possible finite expressions of a natural language are countable, the number of members of E is countable. Hence we can order (not necessarily in order of size) the members of E as the first, second, third etc. Let N be a number defined as follows: if the nth figure in the nth decimal is p, let the nth figure in N be p+1, or 0 if p=9. Then N is different from all the members of E, since whatever finite value n may have, the nth figure in

N is different from the nth figure in the nth of the decimals in the ordering of E (i.e. N is constructed by Cantor's diagonal method). Nevertheless we have defined N in a finite number of words, and therefore N ought to be a member of E. Thus N both is and is not a member of E. (A simpler version of the paradox is this: let M = the least integer not definable in fewer than twenty syllables. M has just been defined in nineteen syllables, so M both is and is not definable in fewer than twenty syllables.)

The paradox is dissolved, according to Richard, if we hold that the definition of E, as the totality consisting of all decimals finitely definable, cannot rightly be regarded as ranging over decimals which are defined by reference to that totality. Thus given that N is defined that way, it is not a sensible possibility that N is in E.

3.1 The vicious circle principle

Richard's dissolution exemplifies the vicious circle principle formulated by Richard and by Henri Poincaré to exclude viciously circular definition.

Russell states the principle thus: '"Whatever involves all of a collection must not be one of the collection", or, conversely: "If, provided a certain collection had a total, it would have members only definable in terms of that total, then the said collection has no total".' And in a footnote he explains this last: 'When I say that a collection has no total, I mean that statements about all its members are nonsense' (Russell 1908: 30). Although the application of the principle is, as it stands, not entirely clear, it is probably unfair to claim, as Kurt Gödel did, that Russell gives us not one but three principles. There is but one principle: if a definition is to be meaningful then if the definiens refers to all of some totality the definiendum may not be part of that totality.

The aim of the vicious circle principle is to exclude impredicative definitions. The idea of impredicativity, never made entirely clear, was roughly this: a definition is not impredicative if the definiendum is defined in terms of predicates to which it is not a possible argument: i.e. the definiendum is defined in terms of totalities (the argument domains of the predicates) of which it is not a part. In impredicative definitions, the definiendum is a possible argument of the predicate and is included in the totality according to which it itself is defined.

Let us see how this works for contradictions resulting from unrestricted comprehension (essentially the same as the contradiction emanating from Frege's axiom (V)). Unrestricted comprehension says: for any predicate ϕ there is a class y of objects satisfying ϕ, i.e. for any ϕ, $\exists y \forall x (x \in y \leftrightarrow \phi x)$. The contradiction arises from taking ϕx to be $x \notin x$, i.e. there is a y such that $\forall x (x \in y \leftrightarrow x \notin x)$.

Substituting y for x (since x ranges over all classes) we have $y \in y \leftrightarrow y \notin y$. This definition of y is impredicative since y is being defined in terms of a predicate, $x \in x$, for which y is itself a possible argument. Russell takes the vicious circle principle to exclude such definitions.

The vicious circle principle is negative, pointing to one source of contradiction which must be excluded. As such it is a criterion of meaningfulness. We must construct our mathematical logic and its language in such a way that sentences which violate the principle are meaningless. On which positive principles the logic should be constructed the principle does not directly suggest. However, different interpretations of why violation leads to contradiction will encourage different approaches to a positive logic. Poincaré, on the one hand, saw the illegitimacy in talking of all of the class of finitely definable decimals as deriving from the fact that that class is infinitely large. Hence logic must be constructed in such a way as to allow quantification only over finite classes.

3.2 Russell's theory of types

Russell, on the other hand, saw the issue as turning on logical homogeneity. The things we talk about may not be all of the same logical kind or type. According to Russell, it should be improper to quantify over things of a different logical type. If one assumes that things which involve all of a collection are different sorts of thing from the members of the collection, then the requirement of logical homogeneity would forbid quantifying over members of a collection and the collection itself at the same time. The contradictions arise because the heterogeneity, the difference in kind, is hidden by the description given of the object. The hidden heterogeneity of the collections appears to license including in the collection the very entity which is defined in terms of the collection. Consequently there would be no violations of the vicious circle principle in a logic which precludes talking of heterogeneous collections, but allows quantification only over entities of the same logical type.

This is precisely what Russell and Whitehead's theory of types aims to do. How it does this is again most easily seen in connection with the abstraction axiom (naïve/unrestricted comprehension): for all ϕ, $\exists y \forall x (x \in y \leftrightarrow \phi x)$. We have seen how this axiom leads to contradiction. The theory of types, by submitting to the vicious circle principle, avoids the contradiction in two ways. Firstly, classes are not allowed to be members of themselves or of classes of the same type as themselves; formulae such as $x \in x$ and $x \notin x$ are simply ill-formed, they are not formulae of the language and hence the question of their truth or falsity does not arise. Thus they do not represent predicates that can take the place of ϕ in the above abstraction axiom. More generally our stricture prevents the universal and existential quantifiers in the axiom, the '$\forall x$' and '$\exists y$' in $\exists y \forall x(x \in y \leftrightarrow \phi x)$, from overlapping. If their ranges did overlap, as they are allowed to do in the derivation of the contradiction, we would be forced to contemplate possibilities such as $y \in y$, which I have said are excluded as being nonsense. The quantifiers are restricted each to one homogeneous type.

These logical types form a hierarchy, at the very bottom of which comes the type of individuals, which are not really classes at all. The next level up, the first type of classes, contains only those classes which contain individuals as members. The next higher type is the type of classes whose members are the classes of the first type, i.e. the type of classes of classes of individuals. The hierarchy continues in such a way that each class is assigned a particular type, and if this type is the n+1th, its elements are of the nth type, and it itself may only be a member of those classes of the type n+2.

Correspondingly we allow it to make sense to assert that one set is a member of another only if the type of the latter is one higher than that of the former. Hence quantification must be only within a single type; to be exact, in formulas such as '$\forall x F x$' we should specify which type of classes the apparent variable x ranges over.

If this is specified as n, then the gloss for '$\forall x F x$' starts 'for all classes of the nth type ...' which we might emphasize by writing: '$\forall x_n F x$'. Our axiom of comprehension then looks like this: $\exists y_{n+1} \forall x_n (x_n \in y_{n+1} \leftrightarrow \phi x_n)$.

It should be noted that our hierarchy means that it makes no sense to talk of 'class' (nor of 'cardinal' or 'ordinal' etc.) simpliciter, for the term is ambiguous, not referring to one sort of object, but many sorts. Thus use of the term 'class' must be governed by a systematic ambiguity, that is, taken as referring to classes of some one, albeit unspecified, type.

This hierarchy of classes does a nice job of excluding the set theoretic or class paradoxes: Russell's, Cantor's, Burali-Forti's. It seemed as if classes were all of one sort and that we could quantify over all of them. In *Principia Mathematica* it turns out that classes may be rather different things and that we cannot quantify over all with one variable.

3.3 Dissolving the semantic paradoxes

On the other hand, the paradox from which we first gleaned our guiding vicious circle principle, the Richard paradox, and those like it appear to be somewhat different. In the class case we applied the principle that a class which is defined in terms of some totality of classes is a different sort of class from those in that totality, hence it could not be part of that totality. But in the case of the Richard paradox we tried to define one decimal, N, in terms of a particular class, E, of decimals. In this case it could not possibly be said that N is a different sort of object from the members of E. On the contrary, N is a decimal just like the members of E, and assuming the paradox is dissolved in such a way that N does exist, there may well be classes containing N and the members of E.

It would appear that the semantic paradoxes are not to be dissolved by pointing to hierarchies of entities which differ in type. Let us return to the vicious circle principle. It warned us not to refer to illegitimate totalities. Russell's approach was then to seek in each paradox the illegitimate totality referred to. In his own paradox it was 'all classes'; in the Burali-Forti contradiction it was 'all ordinals' etc. In the case of the Richard paradox our problem is not the totality 'all decimals' but 'all definitions of decimals', for the crucial question was whether the definition of N belongs to this totality. Similarly the paradox of the least indefinable ordinal refers to all definitions. Berry's paradox refers to all names. What we must then do is to seek a hierarchy of definitions or names, which will amount to the same thing since the definitions and names are both given by description, that is, in terms of properties. And indeed, this part of Russell and Whitehead's theory, the theory of orders, proceeds precisely analogously to the theory of class-types. If a property (strictly, a propositional function) is defined in terms of some totality of properties, then the defined property is of a different sort, i.e. of a higher order. The term 'property' is itself ambiguous, requiring specification, at least in principle, of some specific order. Variables range only over properties of one order.

3.4 The no-class theory

Russell thought that if classes really did exist as objects independent of functions or of constructions then there would be no logical reason why a class might not be a member of itself. More significantly, Russell held, like Frege, that there could be no restriction on variables preventing them from ranging over all objects in the world, which would not be arbitrary. Thus if classes were real, there could be no objection to our talking of the totality of classes which do not contain themselves and other such totalities which lead to the contradictions. Thus the theory of types requires taking a non-platonist, non-realist view of classes

By making classes derivative of functions, the hierarchy of classes could be justified on the ground of the distinction between functions. The justification is most natural if functions are seen as linguistic entities constructed in terms of other functions already defined. Clearly such a view obeys the vicious circle principle as it was formulated above; contravention would be a case of circular definition, obviously giving no meaning to the sign in question. Furthermore, it coheres with Russell's logical atomism. Nonetheless there is nothing in this to prevent a function taking arguments of more than one type so long as all such types are lower than the type of the function itself, as in a cumulative hierarchy like Zermelo–Frankel set theory. In *Principia Mathematica* this possibility is excluded.

In fact Russell and Whitehead come later, in the second edition of *Principia Mathematica* (1925–7), to justify certain contentious axioms (the axioms of reducibility and infinity) abductively; that is, by virtue of their ability to generate 'true' theorems. This marks a departure from their original logicist programme of founding mathematics on evident logical axioms.

3.5 Problems with the theory of types

The theory of types does not lead to the sort of contradictions faced by Frege's logic. However, it does depend on two axioms which do not seem to be true logical principles. One is the axiom of reducibility and the other is the axiom of infinity. The former need not concern us here. The need for the axiom of infinity arises because we are not able to quantify over entities belonging to different types. Imagine that there are only a finite number of individuals in the world. Thus only a finite number of entities of type 0. The entities of type 1 will be all the possible classes of entities of type 0. The number of such entities will also be finite (2^n to be precise). Thus there will only ever be a finite number of entities of any given type. This means there will be no type with an infinite number of entities. So we will not be able to get enough classes to represent the natural numbers (which Russell does in Frege's manner: 3 = the class of three membered classes (of a certain type).) Thus we need to have as an axiom, the assertion that there are infinitely many individuals in the universe. This axiom seems to be one which cannot be a truth of logic.

Conclusion

Frege was undoubtedly an important force in the development of modern logic. But his significance can be overstated under the influence of the retrospective appreciation of the quality of both his logical and philosophical work. Frege's work was not widely read in his lifetime. But two thinkers who did read Frege were Peano and, thanks to Peano, Russell. The influence of Peano and Frege on Russell and Whitehead may be summed up in the Preface to *Principia Mathematica*:

> In the matter of notation, we have as far as possible followed Peano, supplementing his notation, when necessary, by that of Frege or by that of Schröder ... In all questions of logical analysis, our chief debt is Frege.

Note

1   It is worth remarking that in this letter Russell expresses the contradiction explicitly using Peano's notation, thus: $w = \text{cls} \cap x \, \mathfrak{s}(x \sim \varepsilon x).\supset: w \, \varepsilon w. =. \, w \sim \varepsilon w$. Russell says that he had written to Peano about this.

Further reading

Gödel, Kurt (1951), 'Russell's Mathematical Logic', in Schlipp, Paul Arthur (ed.), *The Philosophy of Bertrand Russell*, 3rd ed., New York: Tudor, 123–153. Reprinted in Benacerraf, Paul and Putnam, Hilary (eds) (1983), *Philosophy of Mathematics: Selected Readings*, 2nd ed., Cambridge: Cambridge University Press.

Grattan-Guinness, Ivor (2000), *The Search for Mathematical Roots, 1870–1940: Logics, Set Theories and the Foundations of Mathematics from Cantor through Russell to Gödel* (2000), Princeton: Princeton University Press.

Kennedy, Hubert (1980), Peano: Life and works of Giuseppe Peano. Dordrecht: D. Reidel.

Russell, Bertrand (1908), 'Mathematical Logic as Based on the Theory of Types'. Reprinted in J. van Heijenoort, ed. (1967), *From Frege to Gödel: A Source Book in Mathematical Logic, 1879–1931*. Cambridge, MA: Harvard University Press.

Russell, Bertrand (1903), *The Principles of Mathematics*, Cambridge: Cambridge University Press.

Russell, Bertrand (1919), *Introduction to Mathematical Philosophy*, London: George Allen and Unwin. Selection reprinted in Benacerraf, Paul and Putnam, Hilary (eds) (1983), *Philosophy of Mathematics: Selected Readings*, 2nd ed., Cambridge: Cambridge University Press

Sainsbury, Mark (1974), *Russell*, London: Routledge and Kegan Paul.

Shapiro, Stewart (2000), *Thinking About Mathematics*, Oxford: Oxford University Press.

Wang, Hao (1974), *From Mathematics to Philosophy*, London: Routledge and Kegan Paul.

Whitehead, Alfred North and Russell, Bertrand (1910), Introduction to *Principia Mathematica* [full reference below].

References

Borga, M. and D. Palladino (1992), 'Logic and foundations of mathematics in Peano's school', *Modern Logic* 3: 18–44.

Dummett, M. (1993), *Frege: Philosophy of Language*. London: Duckworth.

Grattan-Guinness, I. (1978), 'How Bertrand Russell discovered his paradox', *Historia Mathematica* 5: 127–37.

Peano, G. (1888), *Calcolo geometrico secondo l'Ausdehnungslehre di H. Grassmann, preceduto dalle operazaioni della logica deduttiva*. Turin: Bocca.

Peano, G. (1891), 'Osservazioni del direttore sull'articolo precedente', *Rivista di Matematica* 1: 66–9.

Russell, B. (1908), 'Mathematical Logic as Based on the Theory of Types', *American Journal of Mathematics*, 30(3): 222–62.

Russell, B. (1959), *My Philosophical Development*. London: George Allen & Unwin.

Russell, B. (1963), *Mysticism and Logic*. London: Unwin Books.

Russell, B. (1967), *The Autobiography of Bertand Russell*. London: George Allen & Unwin.

van Heijenoort, J. (ed.) (1967), *From Frege to Gödel. A Sourcebook in Mathematical Logic, 1879–1931*. Cambridge, MA: Harvard University Press.

van Heijenoort, J. (1992), 'Historical development of modern logic', *Modern Logic* 2: 242–55.

Whitehead, A. N., and Russell, B. (1910, 1912, 1913), *Principia Mathematica*, 3 vols, Cambridge: Cambridge University Press; second edn, 1925 (Vol. 1), 1927 (Vols 2, 3).

10

Hilbert

Curtis Franks

1 A mathematician's cast of mind

Charles Sanders Peirce famously declared that 'no two things could be more directly opposite than the cast of mind of the logician and that of the mathematician' (Peirce 1976: 595), and one who would take his word for it could only ascribe to David Hilbert that mindset opposed to the thought of his contemporaries, Frege, Gentzen, Gödel, Heyting, Łukasiewicz and Skolem. *They* were the logicians *par excellence* of a generation that saw Hilbert seated at the helm of German mathematical research. Of Hilbert's numerous scientific achievements, not one properly belongs to the domain of logic. In fact several of the great logical discoveries of the twentieth century revealed deep errors in Hilbert's intuitions – exemplifying, one might say, Peirce's bald generalization.

Yet to Peirce's addendum that '[i]t is almost inconceivable that a man should be great in both ways' (ibid.), Hilbert stands as perhaps history's principle counter-example. It is to Hilbert that we owe the fundamental ideas and goals (indeed, even the name) of proof theory, the first systematic development and application of the methods (even if the field would be named only half a century later) of model theory, and the statement of the first definitive problem in recursion theory. And he did more. Beyond giving shape to the various sub-disciplines of modern logic, Hilbert brought them each under the umbrella of mainstream mathematical activity, so that for the first time in history teams of researchers shared a common sense of logic's open problems, key concepts and central techniques. It is not possible to reduce Hilbert's contributions to logical theory to questions of authorship and discovery, for the work of numerous colleagues was made possible precisely by Hilbert's influence as Europe's pre-eminent mathematician together with his insistence that various logical conundra easily relegated to the margins of scientific activity belonged at the centre of the attention of the mathematical community.

In the following examination of how model theory, proof theory and the modern concept of logical completeness each emerged from Hilbert's thought, one theme recurs as a unifying motif: Hilbert everywhere wished to supplant philosophical musings with definite mathematical problems and in doing so made choices, not evidently necessitated by the questions themselves, about how to frame investigations 'so that', as he emphasized in 1922, 'an unambiguous answer must result'. This motif and the wild success it enjoyed are what make Hilbert the chief architect of *mathematical logic* as well as what continue to inspire misgivings from several philosophical camps about logic's modern guise.

2 Model theory

Hilbert's early mathematical work stands out in its push for ever more general solutions and its articulation of new, increasingly abstract frameworks within which problems could be posed and solved in the sought generality. Because of the deviation from traditional methods brought about by these ambitions, Hilbert's work engendered praise for its scope and originality as well as criticism for its apparent lack of concreteness and failure to exhibit the signs of what was customarily thought of as proper mathematics. His fundamental solution of Gordan's problem about the bases of binary forms exemplifies the trend: Hilbert extended the problem to include a much wider range of algebraic structures, and his proof of the existence of finite bases for each such structure was 'non-constructive' in that it did not provide a recipe for specifying the generating elements in any particular case. When Hilbert submitted the paper for publication in *Mathematische Annalen* Gordan himself rejected it, adding the remark 'this is not mathematics; this is theology' (Reid 1996: 34). The work was recognized as significant by other eminent mathematicians, however, and it was eventually published in an expanded form. Felix Klein wrote to Hilbert about the paper, 'Without doubt this is the most important work on general algebra that the *Annalen* has ever published' (Rowe 1989: 195).

The split reception of Hilbert's early work foreshadows an infamous ideological debate that ensued with constructive-minded mathematicians L.E.J. Brouwer and Herman Weyl in the 1920s – a debate which resurfaces in the third section of this chapter. For now it will do to focus on the pattern of abstraction and generality itself, as it arose in Hilbert's logical study of the foundations of geometry. The question of the relationship of Euclid's 'parallel postulate' (PP) to the other principles in his *Elements* had mobilized scholars since antiquity until in the nineteenth century Gauss, Lobachevski, Riemann, Beltrami and others offered examples of well-defined mathematical spaces in which Euclid's principles each are true except for PP. Whereas the classical ambition had been to derive PP from the other principles, showing it to be redundant, such spaces made evident the *independence* of PP from the others: Because one of these spaces could be read as an interpretation of the principles in the Elements, the truth of the other postulates does not guarantee the truth of PP; neither does the truth of the other postulates guarantee that PP is false, for the long familiar Euclidean plane can be viewed as an interpretation in which PP, alongside the other principles, is true. One burden shouldered by advocates of independence proofs of this sort was to demonstrate that the several interpretations described are in fact coherent mathematical structures – indeed, a favourite tactic among medieval and Renaissance thinkers was to argue indirectly for the derivability of PP by showing that any such interpretation would be self-contradictory. This burden proved to be a heavy one because of a prevailing view that a 'space' should be responsible to human intuition or visual experience so that the content of one's spatial perception was cited to undermine 'deviant' interpretations of the geometric postulates. Nineteenth-century advances in algebraic geometry helped quarantine independence proofs from this sort of objection, but some confusion persisted about whether the results were refinements of the concept of space or purely logical observations about the relationships among mathematical principles. Thus von Hemholtz said both that Riemann's work 'has the peculiar advantage that all its operations consist in pure calculation of quantities, which quite obviates the danger of habitual perceptions being taken for necessities of thought', and that the resulting geometries should be considered as 'forms of intuition transcendentally given ... into which any empirical content whatever will fit' (Helmholtz 1976: 673).

In his *Foundations of Geometry* of 1899, Hilbert provided a general setting for proving the independence of geometric principles and greatly sharpened the discussion of mathematical axioms. Along the way he offered new independence proofs of PP and of the Archimedean principle and constructed interpretations of assemblages of axioms never before thought of together. But the impact of the work lay not in any one of the independence proofs it contained nor in the sheer number of them all, so much as in the articulation of an abstract setting in which the compatibility and dependence of geometric principles could be investigated methodically and in full generality. 'It immediately became apparent', explained his close collaborator Paul Bernays, 'that this mode of consideration had nothing to do with the question of the epistemic character of the axioms, which had, after all, formerly been considered as the only significant feature of the axiomatic method. Accordingly, the necessity of a clear separation between the mathematical and the epistemological problems of axiomatics ensued' (Bernays 1922: 191).

Hilbert managed this separation by dispensing with the stricture that the models used to interpret sets of geometric principles be viewed as spaces in any traditional way. In the abstract setting of *Foundations of Geometry*, Euclid's principles were recast as collections of formal axioms (as theories, T_1, T_2, ...). Though they contained words like 'point' and 'line', these axioms no longer had any meaning associated with them. Further, Hilbert exploded the distinction between the mathematical principles being studied and the structures used to interpret collections of them. In *Foundations of Geometry*, there are only theories, and an interpretation of a collection of geometric axioms T is carried out in an algebraic theory (typically a field over the integers or complex numbers) S, so that each axiom in T can be translated back into a theorem of S.

From this point of view, Hilbert was able to articulate precisely the sense in which his demonstrations established the consistency of collections of axioms or the independence of one axiom from others. In each case the question of the consistency of T is reduced to that of the simpler or more perspicuous theory S used in the interpretation, demonstrating the 'relative consistency' of T with respect to S. For if T were inconsistent, in the sense that its axioms logically imply a contradiction, then because logic is blind to what meaning we ascribe to words like 'point' and 'line' this same implication holds also under the reinterpretation, so that a collection of theorems of S itself implies a contradiction. Because theorems of S are implied by the axioms of S, in this case S is inconsistent. So the interpretation shows that T is inconsistent only if S is. Similarly, the independence of an axiom like PP from a collection of axioms C can be demonstrated relative to the consistency of (typically two different) theories S_1 and S_2: one constructs theories $T_1 = C \cup$ PP, $T_2 = C \cup \neg$PP and demonstrates the consistency of T_1 relative to that of S_1 and of T_2 relative to that of S_2.

Of course the generality of Hilbert's methods is suited for investigations unrelated to geometry, to *metatheoretical* questions about axiom systems in general. And while some contemporaries, notably Gottlob Frege, demurred from the purely logical conception of consistency on offer, Hilbert's techniques won the day. 'The important thing', Bernays remarked, 'about Hilbert's *Foundations of Geometry* was that here, from the beginning and for the first time, in the laying down of the axiom system, the separation of the mathematical and logical from the spatial-intuitive, and with it from the epistemological foundation of geometry, was completely carried out and expressed with complete rigour' (Bernays 1922: 192). Indeed the abstract point of view Hilbert introduced, together with the idea of using interpretations of this sort to study the logical relationships among the axioms of familiar mathematical theories, are the basic setting and tool of contemporary model theory.

Amid the revolutionary turn of thought displayed in Hilbert's work on geometry are two notorious doctrines worth attention because of their influence in logic. The first is Hilbert's insistence that mathematical existence amounts to nothing more than the consistency of a system of axioms. 'If the arbitrarily given axioms do not contradict one another', he wrote to Frege, 'then they are true, and the things defined by the axioms exist' (Frege 1980: 40). As a doctrine of mathematical existence, this idea is doubly dubious: it would later be clear from discoveries of Skolem and Gödel that a consistent theory is typically not 'categorical' – its several models are not isomorphic – so the sense in which it is supposed to implicitly (partially?) define the terms that appear in its axioms is not clear. Further, the inference from the compatibility of a collection of axioms to the existence of a structure that models them is *an inference*. As Gödel would emphasize, it is careless *to define* existence in this way, because the validity of that inference depends on the completeness of the underlying logic. Among the reasons that a contradiction might be underivable from a set of axioms is the possibility that the logic used is too meagre to fully capture the semantic entailment relation. In the case of first-order theories, consistency does indeed imply the existence of a model, but the incompleteness of higher-order logic with respect to the standard semantics leaves open the possibility of consistent theories that are not satisfied by any structure at all.

A second doctrine is Hilbert's idea that his 'axiomatic method' would do more than allow a general setting for consistency and independence results but in fact provide significant advances in the ordinary mathematical theories that were subjected to axiomatization. At times, Hilbert even expressed an ambition that axiomatics would open the door to the solution of all mathematical problems, perhaps even by rendering unsolved mathematical conjectures to systematic resolution in the abstract setting of formal, uninterpreted sentences subject to combinatorial tests of derivability. Just posing this idea generated significant interest in the *decision problem*: the question whether the truth or falsity of any given sentence in the language of a formal theory can be effectively determined. By the work of Church and Turing it became known that even first-order quantification theory is undecidable, for although there is an algorithm for discovering of any valid formula of quantification theory that it is valid, there is no corresponding procedure for discovering of a formula that it is not valid (or, equivalently, that its negation has a model) in the event that it is not. Still worse, according to Gödel's first incompleteness theorem, no axiomatic theory **T** whatsoever in the signature of even basic arithmetic could ever be 'syntactically complete' in the sense that for any sentence ϕ in that signature, either $\mathbf{T} \vdash \phi$ or $\mathbf{T} \vdash \neg\phi$. One cannot, as Hilbert had hoped to do, provide a full axiomatization of number theory.

However overreaching Hilbert's ambitions may have been, his more modest prediction that, through axiomatics, symbolic logic would facilitate advances in ordinary mathematics was confirmed. In the first decade of the twentieth century, Hilbert himself applied his model-theoretical techniques to problems in algebra, geometry and mathematical physics with considerable success: already in *Foundations of Geometry* one finds the description of non-Archimedean geometries, a topological definition of the plane, and new results about continuous functions. With the further maturation of model theory, Mal'tsev, Tarksi, Robinson and others successfully proved results in group theory and the theories of algebraic classes defined via interpretations of the sort found in *Foundations of Geometry* by applying the metatheorems of classical logic (such as the compactness theorem) to these domains. Robinson's statement of the significance of this breakthrough can be read as an acknowledgement that Hilbert's vision is being realized even if the dream that logic could answer all mathematical questions has been refuted:

> [The] concrete examples produced in the present paper will have shown that contemporary symbolic logic can produce useful tools – though by no means omnipotent ones – for the development of actual mathematics, more particularly for the development of algebra and, it would appear, of algebraic geometry. This is the realization of an ambition which was expressed by Leibniz in a letter to Huygens as long ago as 1679.
>
> Robinson 1952: 694

3 Proof theory

Whereas the consistency of a geometrical theory in which the axiom of parallels fails was a pressing open question to mathematicians in the nineteenth century, the consistency of basic arithmetic and even of mathematical analysis could be doubted only by the severest sceptics. Though Kronecker had earned scorn for his repudiation of higher mathematics, Hilbert noted that 'it was far from his practice to think further' about what he did accept, 'about the integer itself'. Poincaré, too, 'was from the start convinced of the impossibility of a proof of the axioms of arithmetic' because of his belief that mathematical 'induction is a property of the mind'. This conviction, like Cantor's insistence that 'a "proof" of their "consistency" cannot be given' because 'the fact of the "consistency" of finite multiplicities is a simple, unprovable truth' (Hilbert 1922: 199) struck Hilbert as short-sighted. Why should one infer, from the fact that the consistency of a set of principles is not legitimately in doubt, the belief that the question of their consistency cannot be meaningfully posed? Opposed to this way of thinking, Hilbert proposed that a definite mathematical problem can be formulated about the consistency of any axiomatic system, and at the dawn of the Twentieth Century he set out to show just this.

A new tactic would be needed for the task, for the relative consistency proofs of Hilbert's earlier work appear to be unavailable in the case of arithmetic. The consistency of various geometric theories had been proved relative to that of arithmetical ones, but relative to what could the consistency of arithmetic be meaningfully established? 'Recourse to another fundamental discipline', Hilbert remarked, 'does not seem to be allowed when the foundations of arithmetic are at issue' (1904: 130). The consistency of arithmetical theories must be established in some sense 'directly'.

His wish to design direct consistency proofs saw Hilbert return once more to the fundamental insight of the metatheoretical perspective: the fact that the axioms of a formalized theory could be viewed as meaningless inscriptions. Rather than, as before, using this fact to construct *reinterpretations* of the axioms by changing the meanings of the terms they contain, Hilbert now proposed that the theory be left *uninterpreted*, so that each axiom, and indeed each formal derivation from the axioms, could be treated as an object for the mathematician to reason about. Mathematical proof is an activity infused with meaning, but a proof in a formal axiomatic theory is 'a concrete object surveyable in all its parts' (Bernays 1922: 195). This groundbreaking idea, which gives shape to the whole enterprise of proof theory, first appeared in Hilbert's 1917 talk at Zürich:

> [W]e must – this is my conviction – take the concept of the specifically mathematical proof as an object of investigation, just as the astronomer has to consider the movement of his position, the physicist must study the theory of his apparatus, and the philosopher criticizes reason itself.
>
> Hilbert 1918: 1115

The question of the consistency of a system of axioms can be posed formally as the question whether there are proofs in the system of two contradictory results. It is easy to see that this formulation is equivalent to the question whether there is a proof in the system of some one predesignated evident falsehood. In the case of an arithmetical theory **T**, a direct consistency proof would thus amount to an (informal mathematical) argument that it is not possible to derive the expression $1 \neq 1$ from axioms of **T** by means of the rules of inference designated for **T**.

Before describing how such an argument might unfold, a few words about the philosophical debate surrounding the whole programme are due. Hilbert emphasized in many of his early papers that the informal mathematical arguments comprising his consistency proofs do not involve reasoning more 'complex' or 'dubious' than the principles of reasoning encoded in the axioms of the theory about which one is reasoning. It is not hard to see why: if one draws from complex principles in order to show that a relatively simple theory is consistent, then it is not clear that one has demonstrated anything, for in even asking about the consistency of a theory (even if one does not literally harbour any doubts), one has presumably assumed a position from which that theory's own principles are not all available. To use them, and especially to use principles stronger than them, would seemingly be to drop the question one meant to be asking. Indeed, the proofs issued by Hilbert and his colleagues Ackermann and von Neumann were criticized on precisely these grounds, their insistence that they had avoided any such circularity notwithstanding. Interesting and heated debates ensued, fuelled in large part by Brouwer's and Weyl's allegiance to constructivist principles violated by the systems Hilbert aimed to prove consistent. By Gödel's second incompleteness theorem, it is known that the consistency of any consistent arithmetical theory of the sort Hilbert studied cannot be formalized in that very theory, that the metatheory in which the consistency proof is carried out must be in at least some ways stronger. The debate about the sense in which Hilbert's methods are circular as well as the debate about whether the epistemological gains of a consistency proof were actually of central importance to Hilbert continue to this day. To the latter issue, Kreisel's report that 'Hilbert was asked (before his stroke) if his claims for the ideal of consistency should be taken literally' and that Hilbert 'laughed and quipped that the claims served only to attract the attention of mathematicians to the potential of proof theory' is noteworthy (Kreisel 2001: 43). In any case, the mathematical and logical interest of Hilbert's style of consistency proof is completely unscathed by any defect in the epistemological motivations of Hilbert or anyone else.

In the vicinity of these issues, however, one finds Hilbert describing the logic of his proof theory as 'finitist'. As others had objected in principle to the use of non-constructive existence proofs and uses of the law of excluded middle on infinite totalities like those featured in Hilbert's solution of Gordan's problem, now Hilbert himself banned these techniques. But Hilbert's stance was certainly not based on a principled opposition to classical logic. On the contrary, his aim was to demonstrate that mathematical theories laden with non-constructive principles are consistent and conservative extensions of the finitary ones used to reason about their proofs. Again, a convincing interpretation of Hilbert's several remarks about the significance of finitism has proved to be elusive: was he hoping only to show that infinitary mathematics and non-constructive techniques are safe and efficient, though in fact meaningless, tools for discovering facts about the 'real', finitary realm? Or was he rather fully in defence of the meaningfulness of ordinary mathematics, adopting finitist restrictions in his proof theory in an attempt to avoid circularity and thereby arrive at meaningful consistency arguments? A third reading, closer to the attitude of contemporary proof theorists, is that the stipulation of restrictions in one's logic was simply a response to the constructive nature of proof transformations. Each interpretation has its textual support, but whatever Hilbert's motives were, it is undeniable that to him the logic of proof theory and the logic of ordinary mathematics are importantly different. For Hilbert there is no single 'true logic'; rather, the logic appropriate for a particular investigation is derived *a posteriori* from the details of that investigation – a position that foreshadows the contemporary notion of 'logical pluralism'.

In roughest outline, the reasoning in a direct consistency proof is the following *reductio ad absurdum*: assume that a proof in the theory **T** of $1 \neq 1$ has been constructed (so that **T** is evidently inconsistent). This object will be a finite list of formulas, the last of which is $1 \neq 1$, each of which is an axiom of **T** or the result of applying one of the rules of inference of **T** to formulas that appear earlier in the list. Following a general algorithm, first transform this object into another proof in **T** of $1 \neq 1$ containing only closed formulas, typically in some perspicuous normal form. Then transform the resulting proof into a third object (again this will be a finite list of formulas, but not necessarily a proof) consisting entirely of formulas containing only numerals, propositional connectives, and the equality sign. A recursive argument can then be used to verify that every formula (beginning with those that emerged from axioms, continuing to those that emerged from formulas that were arrived at in one inference, etc.) in this list is 'correct' according to a purely syntactic criterion (for this, Hilbert stipulated that numerals are finite strings of the symbol '1' concatenated.) This is the birth of a common proof-theoretical technique: in contemporary parlance, one has shown that the axioms each have this property and that the inference rules 'preserve' the property. After a finite number of steps, one will have verified that the formula 1 ≠ 1 is 'correct' (although the way Hilbert defined this notion it, of course, is not). From this contradiction, one concludes that no proof of 1 ≠ 1 can be constructed in **T**, so that **T** is consistent.

A special case to consider is the treatment of quantifiers ∀, ∃ in this algorithm. To facilitate the 'elimination' of quantifiers along the way to construct a list of purely numerical formulas of the sort just described, Hilbert rendered his arithmetical theories in the ε-calculus. This is an extension of quantifier-free number theory with a function symbol ε that operates on formulas $A(a)$ to form terms $\varepsilon_a A(a)$, with the intuitive meaning 'that which satisfies the predicate A if anything does'. (If this construction seems peculiar, bear in mind that $\exists x(\exists y A(y) \supset A(x))$ and $\exists x(A(x) \supset \forall y A(y))$ are first-order logical truths, the first corresponding to the ε-term, and the second corresponding to its dual τ term (that which satisfies A only if everything does.) Hilbert's arithmetical theories included the *transfinite axioms*:

1. $A(a) \supset A(\varepsilon_a A(a))$ and
2. $\varepsilon_a A(a) \neq 0 \supset \neg A(\delta \varepsilon_a A(a))$ (δ is the predecessor function)

It is not hard to see that these axioms allow one to derive the usual axioms for the quantifiers and induction.

To accommodate the ε-terms that appear in a proof, the algorithm stipulates how to substitute numerical terms for each appearance of the ε-terms: In the case that only one ε-term appears in the proof, one simply replaces each of its occurrences with the numeral 0 and each occurrence of $\varepsilon_a A(a)$ with the least n for which $A(n)$ is true. When more than one ε-term appears in the proof and especially when there are nested ε-terms, the substitution becomes far more complicated, and the algorithm loops in response to these complications.

Now, the strength of the metatheory needed to conduct such reasoning is determined by the problem of verifying that the algorithm for proof transformation eventually comes to a halt. The transformed proofs are typically much larger than the objects with which one begins, and in order to rule out the possibility that *any one* of the proofs in **T** ends in 1 ≠ 1, one effectively considers the transformation of *every one* of the proofs of **T**. For this, because of the spiralling nature of the algorithm, one must use multiply embedded inductive arguments. This comes to light especially in the consideration given to the treatment of ε-terms. When several terms are present, some falling within the scope of others, these must be indexed, and an ordering defined on the indices, in order to keep track of how the proof transformation proceeds. One then observes that verifying that the algorithm eventually halts involves 'transfinite induction' through the ordinal number used to order the indices of terms. Already in 1924, Ackermann was explicit that induction to ω^{ω^ω} was used in the proof of the consistency of a theory he considered. He wrote:

> The disassembling of functionals by reduction does not occur in the sense that a finite ordinal is decreased each time an outermost function symbol is eliminated [as in an ordinary inductive proof]. Rather, to each functional corresponds as it were a transfinite ordinal number as its rank, and the theorem that a constant functional is reduced to a numeral after carrying out finitely many operations corresponds to [a previously established fact].
>
> Ackermann 1924: 13.

This is the sense in which today one speaks of ordinals associated with mathematical theories: The 'consistency strength' of a theory is measured by the ordinal used to track the induction used to prove its consistency.

In the continuation of the passage just quoted, Ackermann claimed that the use of transfinite induction did not violate Hilbert's 'finitist standpoint'. This posture was later emulated by Gentzen, who presented his masterful consistency proof of first-order Peano Arithmetic (PA) together with a statement that although one 'might be inclined to doubt the finitist character of the 'transfinite' induction' through

$$\varepsilon_0 = \sup_{n < \infty} \omega_1^{\omega_2^{\cdot^{\cdot^{\omega_n}}}}$$

used in his proof 'even if only because of its suspect name' it is important to consider

> that the reliability of the transfinite numbers required for the consistency proof compares with that of the first initial segments ... in the same way as the reliability of a numerical calculation extending over a hundred pages with that of a calculation of a few lines: it is merely a considerably vaster undertaking to convince oneself of this certainty.
>
> Gentzen 1938: 286

The debate about the relationship between Hilbert's wish to provide a finitist consistency proof of arithmetic, Gödel's theorem to the effect that any consistency proof would have to extend the principles encoded in the theory one is proving to be consistent, and Gentzen's proof (which is carried out in the relatively weak theory PRA (primitive recursive arithmetic) together with the relatively strong principle of transfinite induction up to ε_0) is not likely to be resolved any time soon. From the point of view of logic, however, this debate is a distraction from what seems to have been Hilbert's main purpose: to show that the question of the consistency even of elementary mathematical theories could be formulated as a mathematical problem requiring new perspectives and techniques for its solution and ushering in rewarding insights along the way.

An example of such an insight can be extracted from Gentzen's achievement. By showing that transfinite induction to the ordinal ε_0 can be used to prove the consistency of PA, Gentzen demonstrated that this principle is unprovable in PA. (This follows immediately from Gödel's 'second incompleteness theorem', mentioned above). But he also showed that transfinite induction to any ordinal below ε_0 (a stack of ωs of any finite height) is provable in PA. This is the sense in which ε_0 is sometimes described as *the* ordinal of PA: no smaller ordinal will suffice. But Gentzen did more. PA has as an axiom a principle of mathematical induction over all formulas in its signature. One can also consider fragments of PA defined by restricting quantifiers to formulas with a maximum quantifier complexity (call these the theory's class of inductive formulas). Gentzen showed that the size of the least ordinal sufficient for a proof of the consistency of such a fragment corresponds with the quantifier complexity of that theory's class of inductive formulas. In effect he established a correspondence between the number of quantifiers of formulas in the inductive class and the number of exponentials needed to express the ordinal that measures the theory's consistency strength. This correspondence 'one quantifier equals one exponential' has been called the central fact of the logic of number theory and is rightly seen as the maturation of Hilbert's technique of quantifier elimination, the realization of Hilbert's idea that consistency proofs could be used to analyse quantifiers.

Though observing, in 1922, that 'the importance of our question about the consistency of the axioms is well-recognized by the philosophers', (Hilbert 1922: 201), Hilbert strove to distinguish his interests from theirs. 'But in this literature', he continued, 'I do not find anywhere a clear demand for the solution of the problem in the mathematical sense'. That, we have seen, is what Hilbert demanded, and if Gentzen can be credited with providing the solution, Hilbert must be credited for formulating the question in purely mathematical terms and for articulating a setting for its investigation.

As for the philosophical significance of the result, one must appreciate that the 'mathematical sense' of the consistency question, unprecedented and unpopular at the time that Hilbert first put it forward, is the one that commands the interest of mathematicians today as well as the one that brought logical investigations once again, in a yet different way, into the mainstream of mathematical activity. Anticipating this revolution, Bernays remarked that 'Mathematics here creates a court of arbitration for itself, before which all fundamental questions can be settled in a specifically mathematical way, without having to rack one's brain about subtle logical dilemmas such as whether judgments of a certain form have a meaning or not' (Bernays 1923: 222). In Hilbert's proof theory, he wrote elsewhere, 'mathematics takes over the role of the discipline formerly called mathematical natural philosophy' (Bernays 1930: 236).

Hilbert's influence in proof theory does not stop with these well-known accomplishments, though. We will see in the next section that in his lectures of 1917–18, Hilbert pioneered the metalogical investigation of the semantic completeness of quantification theory, asking for the first time whether all universally valid formulas of this theory could be syntactically derived. But remarkably, in his lectures from 1920, he had so modified his framework that 'questions of completeness' and 'of the relationship between the formalism and its semantics ... receded into the background'. In their place, seeking 'a more direct representation of mathematical thought', Hilbert redesigned his logical calculus for quantification theory so that the rules governing the calculus, rather than a semantic theory external to that calculus, could be thought of as directly 'defining' or 'giving the meaning' of the propositional connectives and quantifiers (Ewald and Sieg 2013: 298).

Thus one finds in Hilbert's lectures from early 1920 what is likely the earliest articulation of the concept of 'proof-theoretical semantics' that later characterized the approach to the study of logic of Gentzen, Prawitz and others: 'Diese Regel kann als die Definition des Seinszeichens aufgefassst werden' (ibid.: 323). This is remarkable not only because of how dramatically it extends the reach of Hilbert's influence. True to Hilbert's pragmatic attitude, here he once more articulates a fruitful concept deeply at odds with entire frameworks of logical investigation that he had earlier pursued.

4 Logical completeness

In the description of a 'symbolic calculus' with which he began his treatise on *Trigonometry and Double Algebra*, Augustus De Morgan listed three ways in which a formal system, even one whose 'given rules of operation be necessary consequences of the given meanings as applied to the given symbols', could nevertheless be 'imperfect'. The last sort of imperfection he considered is that the system 'may be incomplete in its rules of operation'. He explained:

> This incompleteness may amount either to an absolute privation of results, or only to the imposition of more trouble than, with completeness, would be required. Every rule the want of which would be a privation of results, may be called *primary*: all which might be dispensed with, except for the trouble that the want of them would give, may be treated merely as consequences of the primary rules, and called *secondary*.
>
> De Morgan 1849: 351

Evidently, De Morgan would fault a system, not only for our inability in principle to prove with it everything we would like to know (all the truths or valid laws in some domain), i.e. for its lacking certain primary rules, but also for being cumbersome. But in distinguishing these two weaknesses, he clearly isolated a property of logical systems converse to the first one he mentioned. To say that all a system's rules are necessary consequences of the given meanings is to say that the system is sound. To say that it has enough rules to derive each such necessary consequence is to say that it is complete.

Some years later, in a paper called 'On the algebra of logic', Peirce boldly asserted, 'I purpose to develop an algebra adequate to the treatment of all problems of deductive logic', but issued this caveat: 'I shall not be able to perfect the algebra sufficiently to give facile methods of reaching logical conclusions; I can only give a method by which any legitimate conclusion may be reached and any fallacious one avoided' (Peirce 1885: 612). The concern about efficiency had been dropped. Peirce sought only to present a sound (avoiding any fallacious conclusion) and complete (reaching each legitimate one) logic.

It is entirely mysterious why Peirce felt entitled to claim that his logical system is complete. No argument of any sort to this effect appears in his paper. De Morgan made no such boast. But the two logicians shared an appreciation of what a good logical system would be like. One wonders what the source of this commonality might have been, because outside the writing of these two, one scarcely finds a hint that the question of completeness even occurred.

One exception is Bolzano, who a half century earlier developed logical theory on two fronts. He designed one theory of 'ground and consequence' that was supposed to track the dependencies of truths and another of 'derivability' that was supposed to allow us to reason from hypotheses to their necessary conclusions. Those dependencies of truths were the things we are supposed to care about, and derivability was merely an analysis of well-regulated reason. Peculiar, though, is the fact that his theory of ground and consequence closely resembles the logical calculi of the modern era, whereas his definition of derivability is a precursor to today's notion of logical consequence. So when Bolzano asked if every ground–consequence relation is in fact derivable, he seems to have our concept of completeness, which we inherited from De Morgan and Peirce, the wrong way around. Evidently, the completeness question, which seems today so perfectly natural and central, is of recent vintage.

Bolzano despaired at not finding a way to formulate his version of the completeness question so that he would know how to answer it, which is noble compared to De Morgan and Peirce's apparent lack even of an attempt at such a formulation. The whole enterprise was rather ill-fated, and by the turn of the twentieth century, as logic began to settle into its modern guise, the question of logical completeness simply did not arise. Logicians began either to think of logical systems as primitive encodings of the principles of right reasoning, with no eye towards matters of logical truth, or not to think of them at all, focusing entirely on matters of truth, satisfaction of formulas, and such semantic notions. Those like Gentzen in the first camp could still ask if anything was missing from their systems, but the question was a matter of psychological introspection or possibly an empirical study of the types of inferences that appear in mathematical journals. Skolem and others in the second camp had no systems to ask after and pursued instead questions of decidability of classes of formulas.

In this setting, Hilbert stood alone. He was discontent equally with the idea of empirically validating a logical system and of ignoring them altogether. In an address at the Bologna International Congress of Mathematicians, Hilbert remarked: '[T]he question of the completeness of the system of logical rules [of the predicate calculus], put in general form, constitutes a problem of theoretical logic. Up till now we have come to the view that these rules suffice only through experiment' (Hilbert 1929: 140). The sentiment first appeared in Hilbert's lectures from the academic year 1917–18, in which he remarked that 'whether [the predicate calculus] is complete in the sense that from it all logical formulas that are correct for each domain of individuals can be derived is still an unsolved question', because our knowledge about this at the time was entirely 'empirical' (Ewald and Sieg 2013).

As before, it is not clear that Hilbert harboured any doubts about the completeness of quantification theory. Quite possibly, the empirical evidence that familiar systems could not be improved upon with the addition of new principles was convincing to him. But even if the evidence was conclusive, what the world did not have and what the prevailing attitudes about logic precluded was a mathematical proof of a theorem about these matters. Once again, Hilbert seemed to be motivated to transform a question from philosophy or natural science into a mathematical problem and to see what sorts of mathematical ideas would be generated in the process. The stock of fundamental insights is vast. But Hilbert's own intellectual trajectory to posing the question is subtle, and it is rewarding to trace this history before tallying the spoils.

In 1905 Hilbert defined completeness in two apparently different ways. (The exposition beginning here follows closely Mancosu, Zach, and Badesa 2009, which should be consulted for further details.) He asked first (Hilbert 1905: 13) whether or not the axioms of a formal theory suffice to prove all the 'facts' of the theory in question. On page 17 he formulated a 'completeness axiom' that he claimed 'is of a general kind and has to be added to every axiom system whatsoever in any form'. Such an 'axiom' had first appeared in *Foundations of Geometry*. Hilbert explained:

> [I]n this case . . . the system of numbers has to be so that whenever new elements are added contradictions arise, regardless of the stipulations made about them. If there are things that can be adjoined to the system without contradiction, then in truth they already belong to the system.

The first thing to notice is that Hilbert is both times speaking about axiomatic mathematical theories and is not yet asking about the completeness of a logical calculus. But the dissimilarities are also important: the completeness axiom is an axiom *in* a formal theory; the first notion of completeness is a property *of* such a theory. One wonders why the same word would be used in these two different ways.

A partial answer can be found in 1917–18 where Hilbert elided these notions together as he turned his attention to logical calculi. In this passage, he is discussing propositional logic:

> Let us now turn to the question of completeness. We want to call the system of axioms under consideration complete if we always obtain an inconsistent system of axioms by adding a formula which is so far not derivable to the system of basic formulas.
>
> Ewald and Sieg 2013: 152

Here, for the first time, the question of the completeness of a logical calculus has been posed as a precise mathematical problem. But although the question is being asked about a system of logic rather than being formulated as a principle within the system, the question bears more structural resemblance to the axiom of completeness than to the primitive question about all 'facts' (or tautologies) of propositional logic being proved: the completeness axiom says that the addition of any new element in, for example, an algebraic structure will result in a contradiction; the completeness of the propositional calculus is the conjecture that the addition of any formula to a set of theorems will result in a contradiction.

These lecture notes contain proofs both of the consistency of a calculus for propositional logic and of the completeness, in the sense just described, of that same system. To prove consistency, Hilbert used the following interpretation strategy (the system under consideration contains connectives only for disjunction and negation): let the propositional variables range over the numbers 1 and 0, interpret the disjunction symbol as multiplication and the negation symbol as the function $1 - x$. In this interpretation, every formula in the classical propositional calculus (CPC) is a function on 0 and 1 composed of multiplication and $1 - x$. Hilbert observes that the axioms are each interpreted as functions that return the value 0 on any input, and that the rules of inference each preserve this property (so that every derivable formula is constant 0). Furthermore, the negation of any derivable formula is constant 1 and therefore underivable. Thus, no formula is derivable if its negation also is, and so the system is consistent.

The same interpretation figures in the completeness argument: It is known how to associate with every formula ϕ another ϕ_{cnf} in 'conjunctive normal form', so that ϕ and ϕ_{cnf} are each derivable from the other in CPC. (A cnf formula is a conjunction of clauses, each of which is a disjunction of propositional variables and negations of propositional variables.) By the previous argument, a formula is provable only if it is constant 0 under the interpretation, which, in the case of a cnf formula, occurs precisely when each of its clauses contains both a positive (unnegated) and negative (negated) occurrence of some propositional variable. Now let ϕ be any unprovable formula. Then its associated formula ϕ_{cnf} must also be underivable and therefore must contain a clause with no propositional variable appearing both positively and negatively. To show that CPC+ϕ (CPC augmented with ϕ as an additional axiom) is inconsistent, let ψ be any formula whatsoever, and label χ the result of substituting, into ϕ_{cnf}, ψ for every variable that occurs positively in c and $\neg\psi$ for every variable that occurs negatively in c. It is easy to show that CPC+$\phi \vdash \phi$, CPC $\vdash \phi \supset \phi_{cnf}$, CPC $\vdash \phi_{cnf} \supset \chi$, and CPC $\vdash \chi \supset \psi$. Thus CPC+$\phi \vdash \psi$ for any formula ψ.

Suppose, now, that some formula ϕ were constant 0 under this interpretation but unprovable in CPC. Then the same consistency argument as before would carry through for CPC+ϕ, contradicting the completeness result just proved. It follows that every formula interpreted as a constant 0 function is a theorem of CPC. This reasoning, reproduced from Hilbert's lectures, establishes that CPC is complete with respect to the functional interpretation and foreshadows the concept of 'semantic completeness' familiar today. It might be surprising initially that these two notions of completeness, the first purely syntactic and the second establishing a bridge between a formal system and its interpretive scheme, mesh so nicely for propositional logic. It might be more surprising, still, that the syntactic criterion held the primary role in Hilbert's thought – his school customarily referred to it, not only as the 'stronger' sense of completeness (which it is), but also as the 'stricter' sense of the word. The influence of the concept of the completeness of mathematical theories is palpable.

The coincidence of these two notions of completeness served the Hilbert school well for their investigations of propositional logic, for even if the primitive notion of logical completeness is the one about the tractability, with one's logical system, of all truths, they always held talk about truth and content at arm's distance for being insufficiently 'formal'. Hilbert preferred to use interpretations as tools for discovering purely mathematical facts and wished to avoid debates about which interpretations are correct. So if the primitive question of logical completeness could be sharpened into one entirely about formal provability, Hilbert viewed this as progress.

As it happens, however, such was not the fate for the concept of completeness as it arises for quantification theory. By the publication of Hilbert and Ackermann's *Grundzüge der theoretischen Logik* in 1928, Ackermann had discovered that unprovable formulas can be consistently added to the classical predicate calculus. To see this, one again begins by verifying an axiom system's consistency with an interpretation: to interpret a formula of first-order quantification theory, first erase all quantifiers. Interpret propositional variables and propositional connectives as before (variables range over $\{0, 1\}$, disjunction is the multiplicative product, etc.) Further, ignore how the argument places of the predicate letters are filled, and interpret these also as variables ranging over $\{0, 1\}$. As before, each axiom gets interpreted as a constant 0 function, and each rule of inference preserves this property. But the negation of any theorem is a constant 1 function and therefore underivable, so the system is consistent. (Unlike the case of propositional logic, however, this interpretation in no way foreshadows a semantic theory. It is *only* a tool for metatheoretical investigations, not an *intended* interpretation.)

The incompleteness, in the strong sense, of the predicate calculus is witnessed by the formula $\exists x F(s) \supset \forall x F(x)$, which gets interpreted as a constant 0 function in the scheme just described. To see that this formula is underivable, one need only observe that in any domain with more than one object, the sentence that results from this formula if we interpret *F* as any predicate true of only one thing is false, and appeal to the soundness of the system under consideration. Hilbert's scruples are evident when he describes this reasoning as merely making the underivability of the formula 'plausible' – he proceeds to present a 'strictly formal proof' of its underivability with no appeal to the system's soundness or matters of truth and falsity.

In any case this result certainly does not establish that there are logically valid formulas of quantification theory that are unprovable in the predicate calculus. Instead, it drives a wedge between the two senses of completeness that coincide in the case of propositional logic. The demonstration that 'any legitimate conclusion may be reached and any fallacious one avoided' so that we are left with no 'absolute privation of results' cannot be 'sharpened' in this case so as to eliminate all talk of truth.

It is well known that Gödel proved the semantic completeness of the predicate calculus in his 1929 thesis. Less well known is that the question he answered in the process was not, despite his remarks, one that 'arises immediately' to everyone who thinks about logic. It could not arise less than a century earlier, when the distinction between logical systems and the truths they are meant to track was completely reversed in the work of Bolzano, and it could barely figure in the thought of most logicians as a respectable problem in the ensuing years, because it had not been shown that such a question could be framed in precise mathematical terms. Things changed rapidly after Hilbert turned his attention to logic. If his attempts to treat the question of quantificational completeness did not materialize, the conceptual clarification ushered in by those attempts paved the way for Gödel's success.

There is little doubt, however, that Hilbert's distrust of semantic notions hindered his research on quantificational completeness as much as it helped him in the case of propositional logic. There is no 'strictly formal proof' of the completeness of quantification theory precisely because the necessary semantics are ineliminably infinitary and therefore not accessible by the methods in which Hilbert aimed to cast all of his metatheoretical investigations. This is witnessed doubly by the existence, on the one hand, of quantificational formulas that can be true but only in an infinite domain and, on the other hand, by the prominent role of the law of excluded middle applied to an infinite domain in Gödel's completeness proof.

Again, it remains a matter of some debate exactly what Hilbert's reasons were for requiring all metatheoretical investigations to be finitary precisely as his most celebrated work in ordinary mathematics is not. But the seeds of this conviction were sown at the very beginning of Hilbert's logical investigations. The 'implicit definition' doctrine that mathematical existence amounts to no more than the consistency of a set of axioms, Gödel pointed out, is hard to reconcile with Hilbert's insistence that the completeness of the predicate calculus should not be believed based on evidence but requires mathematical proof. For the completeness of the predicate calculus is equivalent to the claim that every consistent set of first-order formulas has a model. To see the implication in one direction, assume that if a collection of formulas is consistent, then they are all true in some model. By contraposition, if a formula is false in every model, then a contradiction can be derived from it. Let ϕ be a first-order validity (a formula true in every model). Then $\neg\phi$ is false in every model. Therefore, a contradiction can be derived from $\neg\phi$. So $\neg\neg\phi$ is derivable, as is ϕ by double negation elimination.

The hackneyed story about how Hilbert's logical programme was undermined by Gödel's results must be toned down. To begin with, we have seen that Hilbert's investigations far extend the search for finitistic consistency proofs of mathematical theories and that the maturation of proof theory, in the work of Gentzen, and of the connections between proof theory and model theory, in the work of Gödel, are actually realizations of Hilbert's broader aims. As for Gödel's arithmetical incompleteness theorems, which would seem to refute at least some of Hilbert's more popular statements, their appropriation by the Hilbert school is instructive.

In short time, Hilbert and Bernays applied those same techniques to the problem of logical completeness and showed that if ϕ is a first-order quantificational formula that is not refutable in the predicate calculus, then in any first-order arithmetical theory **T** there is a true interpretation of ϕ. By Gödel's own completeness theorem, it follows that a first-order formula ϕ is valid if, and only if, every sentence of **T** that can be obtained by substituting predicates of **T** for predicate letters in ϕ is true. 'The evident philosophical advantage of resting with this substitutional definition, and not broaching model theory', wrote Quine, 'is that we save on ontology. Sentences suffice, sentences even of the object language, instead of a universe of sets specifiable and unspecifiable' (Quine 1970: 55). Whether a distrust of modern semantics such as Quine's motivated Hilbert can probably not be known. But it is a truly Hilbertian final word on the matter when one observes not only that what Hilbert would have deemed an 'informal notion' is here reduced to a matter of arithmetical truth, but also that an exact relationship to the 'stricter sense' of completeness is hereby salvaged: as a corollary to this arithmetical completeness theorem Hilbert and Bernays showed that the addition of any unprovable formula of quantification theory as a new axiom causes the formal arithmetical theory PA based on the predicate calculus to become ω-inconsistent.

5 Conclusion

In remarks published alongside papers that he, Heyting and von Neumann wrote to articulate the philosophical positions known as logicism, intuitionism and formalism, Rudolf Carnap distinguished the outlook of a typical logician, for whom 'every sign of the language ... must have a definite, specifiable meaning', with that of the mathematician. The attitude of the latter, he thought, was exemplified by Hilbert when he said, 'We feel no obligation to be held accountable for the meaning of mathematical signs; we demand the right to operate axiomatically in freedom, i.e. to set up axioms and operational specifications for a mathematical field and then to find the consequences formalistically' (Hahn et al. 1931: 141). History has shown that the latter cast of mind, though surely not destined to supplant the former in all investigations, has its place in the advancement of logical theory.

Problems

1. Show that the following are equivalent ways of formulating the consistency of CPC:

   (a) For no ϕ is $\vdash \phi$ and $\vdash \neg\phi$
   (b) For some ϕ, $\nvdash \phi$
   (c) $\nvdash p \& \neg p$

2. Show that $\exists x A(x) \equiv A(\varepsilon_x(A(x)))$.

3. Determine of each formula whether it is unsatisfiable, satisfiable in a finite domain, or unsatisfiable in every finite domain but satisfiable:

   (a) $\forall x \forall z \exists y (R(x, y) \& \neg R(x, x) \& (R(y, z) \supset R(x, z)))$
   (b) $\forall x \exists y \forall z (R(x, y) \& \neg R(x, x) \& (R(y, z) \supset R(x, z)))$
   (c) $\exists y \forall x \forall z (R(x, y) \& \neg R(x, x) \& (R(y, z) \supset R(x, z)))$

4. Verify the four claims used in the final step of the proof of strong completeness for CPC.

5. Explain the other direction of the equivalence between 'Every first-order validity is provable' and 'Every consistent collection of first-order formulas has a model'; i.e. show that if every validity is provable, then every formula from which no contradiction can be derived has a model.

References

Ackermann, W. (1924), 'Begründung des "tertium non datur" mittels der Hilbertschen Theorie der Widerspruchsfreiheit'. *Mathematische Annalen* 93: 1–36.

Bernays, P. (1922), 'Hilbert's significance for the philosophy of mathematics'. reprinted in Mancosu 1998, pp. 189–97.

Bernays, P. (1923), 'On Hilbert's thoughts concerning the grounding of arithmetic', reprinted in Mancosu 1998, pp. 215–22.

Bernays, P. (1930), 'The philosophy of mathematics and Hilbert's proof theory', reprinted in Mancosu 1998, pp. 234–65.

De Morgan, A. (1849), 'Trigonometry and Double Algebra', reprinted in Ewald 1996a, pp. 349–61.

Ewald, W. (1996a), *From Kant to Hilbert: a sourcebook in the foundations of mathematics* (Vol. 1), New York: Oxford University Press.

Ewald, W. (1996b), *From Kant to Hilbert: a sourcebook in the foundations of mathematics* (Vol. 2), New York: Oxford University Press.

Ewald, W. and W. Sieg (eds) (2013), *David Hilbert's Lectures on the Foundations of Arithmetic and Logic 1917–1933*, Berlin and New York: Springer.

Feferman, S.J., W. Dawson, Jr., S.C. Kleene, G.H. Moore, R.M. Solovay and J. van Heijenoort (eds) (1986), *Kurt Gödel: Collected Works* (Vol. 1), New York: Oxford University Press.

Frege, G. (1980), *Philosophical and Mathematical Correspondence*, ed. G. Gabriel et al., Oxford: Blackwell.

Gentzen, G. (1938), 'Neue Fassung des Widerspruchefreiheitsbeweises für die reine Zahlentheorie', *Forschungen zur logik und zur Grundlegung der exackten Wissenschaften*, New Series 4, 19–44. Translated as 'New version of the consistency proof for elementary number theory' in Szabo 1969, pp. 252–86.

Hahn, H. et al. (1931), 'Diskussion zur Grundlegung der Mathematik', *Erkinntness* 2, 135–49 (translated by J. Dawson, Jr. 1984).

Helmholtz, H. (1976), 'The origin and meaning of the geometric axioms', reprinted in Ewald 1996b, pp. 663–88.

Hilbert, D. (1899), 'Grundlagen der Geometrie', in *Festschrift zur Feier der Enthüllung des Gauss-Weber-Denkmals in Göttingen*, pp. 1–92. Leipzig: Teubner.

Hilbert, D. (1904), 'On the foundations of logic and arithmetic', reprinted in J. van Heijenoort (ed.) (1967), *From Frege to Gödel: a sourcebook in mathematical logic, 1879–1931*, Cambridge, MA: Harvard University Press.

Hilbert, D. (1905), 'Logische Principien des mathematischen Denkens. Vorlesung, Sommer-Semester 1905'. Lecture notes by Ernst Hellinger. Unpublished manuscript, 277 pp. Bibliothek, Mathematisches Institut, Universität Göttingen.

Hilbert, D. (1918), 'Axiomatic Thought' reprinted in Ewald 1996b, pp. 1105–15.

Hilbert, D. (1922), 'Neubergründung der Mathematik. Erste Mitteilung', translated by William Ewald as 'The new grounding of mathematics: first report' in Mancosu 1998, pp. 198–214.

Hilbert, D. (1929), 'Probleme der Grundlegung der Mathematik', *Mathematische Annalen* 102, pp. 1–9, as translated in B. Dreben and J. van Heijenoort, 'Introductory note to Godel 1929, Godel 1930, and Godel 1930a', in Feferman et al. 1986, pp. 44–59.

Hilbert, D. and W. Ackermann (1928), *Grundzüge der theoretischen Logik*. Berlin: Springer.

Kreisel, G. (2011), 'Logical hygiene, foundations, and abstractions: diversity among aspects and options', in Baaz, M., C.H. Papadimitrou, H.W. Putnam, D.S. Scott and C.L. Harper (eds), *Horizons of Truth*, New York: Cambridge University Press, pp. 27–56.

Mancosu, P. (1998), *From Brouwer to Hilbert: the debate on the foundations of mathematics in the 1920s*, New York: Oxford University Press.

Mancosu, P., R. Zach and C. Badesa (2009), 'The development of mathematical logic from Russell to Tarski, 1900–1935', in Haaparanta, L. (ed.), *The Development of Modern Logic*, New York: Oxford University Press.

Peirce, C.S. (1885), 'On the Algebra of Logic' reprinted in Ewald 1996a, pp. 608–32.

Peirce, C.S. (1976), 'Notes on Benjamin Perice's linear associative algebra', reprinted in Ewald 1996a, pp. 594–5.

Quine, W.V.O. (1970), *Philosophy of Logic*, 2nd edn, Cambridge, MA: Harvard University Press.

Reid, C. (1996), *Hilbert*, Berlin: Springer.

Robinson, A. (1952), 'On the application of symbolic logic to algebra', *Proceedings of the International Congress of Mathematicians*, Providence, RI: American Mathematical Society, pp. 686–94.

Rowe, D.E. (1989), 'Klein, Hilbert, and the Gottingen Mathematical Tradition', *Osiris* 5, 186–213.

Szabo, M.E. (ed.) (1969), *The Collected Papers of Gerhard Gentzen*, London: North Holland.

Part IV

Twentieth-Century Logic

11

Gödel

P.D. Welch

Gödel's achievement in modern logic is singular and monumental . . . a landmark that will remain visible far in space and time . . . The subject of logic will never again be the same.

von Neumann

1 Introduction

Kurt Gödel is claimed by some to be the greatest logician since Aristotle. The ideas that Gödel is associated with in logic are the *Completeness Theorem* which appeared in his 1929 PhD thesis, but more particularly the *Incompleteness Theorem* (actually a pair of theorems), and they have both been crucial in almost all theoretical areas of twentieth century logic since their inception. Whilst Frege's keen insights into the nature of quantifier ensured a great leap forward from the Syllogism, and his attempts to formulate a conception of arithmetic purely as a logical construct were groundbreaking and influenced the course of the philosophy of mathematics in the late nineteenth, and through Russell, in the early twentieth century, and determined much of the discourse of that period, ultimately it is Gödel's work that encapsulated the nature of the relationship between *deductive processes* acting on symbolic systems, and the nature of *truth* (or *satisfaction*), or more widely interpreted *meaning* or *semantics* in the Completeness Theorem. It is often said that the much deeper Incompleteness Theorems that came a year later illustrated a limitation of the axiomatic method, and in particular brought to a halt David Hilbert's programme of putting mathematics on a secure, *finitistically* provable, ground of consistency. It may even be true that more ink and paper has been expended on the Incompleteness Theorem and its consequences (imagined or otherwise) than any other theorem in mathematics.

We shall give an introductory account of these two theorems but one should be aware that Gödel made significant contributions to other areas of logic (notably giving an interpretation of intuitionistic logic in the usual predicate logic) which we do not cover here. Gödel's contributions to set theory (his hierarchy of constructible sets with which he showed the consistency of the Axiom of Choice and the Continuum Hypothesis, one might consider a form of 'ramified' or 'iterated logic') have had almost as much foundational impact in set theory as the logical theorems referred to above have been in all areas of current logic. We do not cover these here either.

2 The Completeness Theorem

We shall describe the Completeness Theorem presently, but to set it in some context we must see what people meant by 'Logic'.

Russell and Whitehead in the *Principia Mathematica* (*PM*) had set up a *deductive system* whereby, as in the axiomatic system of Euclid, the concepts of the subject under discussion, here of logic, and then it was hoped, also of arithmetic, could be codified and reduced to a small number of self-evidently true postulates, and rules of inferring from those postulates. What Russell meant by 'logic' was perhaps not entirely the same as what has come down to us as a 'logic' in the twenty-first century. A line in a deductive proof of the logical calculus of *PM* would be an interpreted formula, about something, but in a modern deductive proof need not be so interpreted. However, Russell was trying to follow Frege and formulate such a system, ultimately from which it was hoped the laws of arithmetic could be derived. This latter aim is not our concern here; merely the idea of a *deductive system* is what is important.

Thus, one might have a collection of axioms, or postulates, P say (which might be *PM*), and one may derive by applying one or more 'rules of deduction' from a collection R of rules, a particular proposition A, say. Now what exactly a 'proposition' is here, we can ignore (although Russell could not) because all that mattered later was that there was some symbolic, or formal language in which the postulates, the proposition A, and the intermediate propositions $B_1, B_2, \ldots, B_n$ could be written. Here, the point was that B_n was the final proposition A and any B_i was either (i) a postulate from the collection P or followed from one or more earlier propositions on the list, by an application of a deductive rule from R. In modern notation this state of affairs is rendered '$\vdash_P A$.'

What is allowed as a 'deductive rule'? This would have had a different answer to different people in different eras. Bolzano took a 'deductive rule' as one that appealed to notions of truth, or something like meaning. For Frege and Russell deductive rules should at least be meaningful and preserve the truth of the consequent *A* from the truth of the axioms *P*.

By the the time Gödel emerged as a graduate student in Vienna in the later 1920s, Hilbert and Ackermann (1929) had codified a system of deduction, the 'restricted functional calculus' which emerged from their deliberations on the deductive system of *PM*. This could be applied to sets of postulates in a fixed type of language which we now call a 'first order language' and consisted of constant symbols, and symbols of both functional and relational type that might be used to express possible functions and relations amongst *variables v_0, v_1,*.... However it is important to note that *what* those variables will be interpreted *as* and what actual functions and relations those functional and relational symbols denote play absolutely no part in this specification whatsoever. The language is to be thought of as merely symbol strings, and the 'correct' or 'well-formed' strings will constitute the relevant 'formulae' which we shall work with. The rules determining the well-formed formulae are thus purely *syntactic*. The set of derivation or deduction rules for determining which sequences of formulae constituted permissible proofs had emerged from *PM* as we have mentioned, but the question of the correct set, or adequate set of rules had not been settled. Hilbert had remarked that empirical experience with the rules then in use seemed to indicate they were indeed adequate. The question was stated explicitly in Hilbert and Ackerman (1929).

Hilbert had, over the previous decades, embarked on an ambitious scheme of proving the consistency of all of mathematics. The motivation for this came from the disturbances caused by the discovery by Russell of a 'paradox' in Frege's system – really a fundamental error or inconsistency in Frege's basic conception – and the similar 'paradoxes' in set theory of Cantor and Burali-Forti. We shall not discuss these here, but only remark that Hilbert had envisaged a thorough-going rethinking of mathematical axioms, and a programme for showing the *consistency* of those axioms: namely that one could not prove both *A* and its negation, $\neg A$, using rules from the given set *R*. The danger had surfaced that set theory might be inconsistent and whilst all of mathematics could be seen to be developed from set theory how could we be sure that mathematics was safe from contradiction? Hilbert's thinking on this evolved over the first two decades of the twentieth century and set out to reassure mathematicians of the logical safety of their field. Hilbert had thus, as part of the programme, axiomatized geometry in a clear modern fashion, and had shown that the problem of establishing the consistency of geometry could be reduced to the problem of the consistency of analysis. Hilbert had thus founded the area which later evolved into *proof theory*, being the mathematical study of proofs themselves, which, as indicated above, were to be regarded as finite strings of marks on paper. It was in this arena that the basic question of completeness of a set of rules had arisen.

What would be needed if a deductive system was to be useful was some reassurance that a) deductive rules themselves could not introduce 'falsity' (in short: only true statements could be deduced using the rules from postulates considered to be true; this is the *'soundness'* of the system), and more pertinently b) that any 'universally valid' formula could in fact deduced. We have referred already to a) above, and for the system derived from *PM* in Hilbert and Ackermann (1929) this was not hard to show. But what about b) and what does it mean?

For a well-formed formula B to be *universally valid* would mean that whatever domain of objects the variables were thought to range over, and whatever *interpretation* was given to the relation and function *symbols* of the language as actual relations and functions on that domain, then the formula B would be seen to be true with that given *meaning*. In modern parlance again, we should say that B is universally valid, or more simply just 'true' in every relevant domain of interpretation. In modern notation, the idea that B is universally valid is written $\models B$.

Given a set of sentences Γ of the language $\mathcal{L}$ one may also define the notion of a formulae B being a *logical consequence* of Γ: in any domain of interpretation in which all of Γ was satisfied or deemed to to be true, then so must also B be true.

Denoting this as $\Gamma \models B$ the Completeness Theorem can be stated thus:

Theorem 1 (*Gödel: The Completeness Theorem (1929)*) (Gödel 1930)

For any first order language $\mathcal{L}$ and any sentence B of that language then:

$$\vdash B \quad \Longleftrightarrow \quad \models B.$$

More generally for any further set of sentences Γ from $\mathcal{L}$:

$$\Gamma \vdash B \quad \Longleftrightarrow \quad \Gamma \models B.$$

The ($\Longrightarrow$) direction of both statements represents the *soundness theorem* of the deductive system's set of rules: if B is provable in the system then B would be universally valid; that is, true in every interpretation. Similarly in the second part, if B were provable from the assumptions Γ, then in any interpretation of $\mathcal{L}$ in which all the sentences of Γ were satisfied, (that is interpreted as true statements), B would also have to be made true in that interpretation. A paraphrase is to regard the rules as being *truth-preserving*. As an example let us take Γ as the set of axioms for group theory in mathematics, with B some assertion in the appropriate language for this theory. The Soundness Theorem states that if B is derivable from the axioms using the rules of inference, then in any structure in which the axioms Γ are true, *i.e.* in any group, B will necessarily be true. This direction of the theorem was essentially known in some form to Hilbert, Ackermann *et al.*

The harder, and novel, part is the implication ($\Longleftarrow$) which sometimes alone is called the *completeness (or adequacy) theorem*. Taking the example of Γ the axioms of group theory, if $\Gamma \vDash B$, which asserts that if in any group B is satisfied, then the conclusion $\Gamma \vdash B$ is read as saying that from the group axioms Γ, the statement B can be *deduced*. This is the sense of 'completeness': the rules of deduction are complete or adequate, they are up to the task of deriving the validities of the system.

If one looks at the proof one can see how it goes beyond a very strictly finitary, syntactically based argument. We shall see that the argument intrinsically involves infinite sets. We give a modern version of the argument due to Henkin, and for the sake of exposition assume first that the set of assumptions Γ is empty and concentrate on the first version. Suppose when trying to prove the ($\Longleftarrow$) direction, we assume that B is not deducible: $\nvdash B$. We wish to show that B is not universally valid and hence we seek an interpretation in which $\neg B$ is satisfied. This suffices, as no interpretation can satisfy both B and $\neg B$. We thus need a structure. In this argument one enlarges the language $\mathcal{L}$ to a language $\mathcal{L}'$ by adding a countable set of new constants $c_0, c_1, \ldots c_n \ldots$ not in $\mathcal{L}$. One enumerates the formulae of the language as $\varphi_0, \varphi_1, \ldots \varphi_k, \ldots$ taking $\neg B$ as φ_0. One then builds up in an infinite series of steps a collection of sentences $\Delta = \bigcup_{n \in \mathbb{N}} \Delta_n$. At the k'th stage, when defining Δ_k one considers whether $\Delta_{k-1} \nvdash \neg\varphi_k$. If this is the case, then φ_k is added to Δ_{k-1} to obtain Δ_k, which by the case assumption, is not inconsistent. If this is not the case then $\neg\varphi_k$ is so added, and consistency is still maintained. Additionally, if φ_k is to be added and it is of the form $\exists v_m \psi(v_m)$ then a new constant, not yet used so far in the construction, c_r say, is chosen and $\psi(c_r)$ is added as well. These are the two essential features. For our discussion the first is notable: what one does is to make an infinite sequence of choices whether to take φ_k or $\neg\varphi_k$ when building Δ. We are thus picking an infinite branch through an implicitly defined infinite binary branching tree: *binary* since we are making yes/no choices as to whether to add φ_k or $\neg\varphi_k$. To argue that such a branch must exist one appeals to *König's Tree Lemma: any finitely branching infinite tree T must contain an infinite branch* *or path through T.* The second feature, the choice of constants c_r allows us from the branch, that is the sequence of formulae that make up Δ, to construct a structure whose domain will be built from sets of constants. Because the set of constants is countably infinite, the structure so built will also be countable. This will be important for consideration below. These details and how the language $\mathcal{L}'$ is interpreted in the resulting structure will be suppressed here.

In the case that one starts from a set of sentences Γ and assumes $\Gamma \nvdash B$ and wishes to show $\Gamma \nvDash B$, one needs a structure in which all of $\Gamma \cup \{\neg B\}$ is satisfied. The process is the same as before but starting with Δ_0 as $\Gamma \cup \{\neg B\}$.

The crucial use of the Tree Lemma argument marks the step Gödel took beyond earlier work of Herbrand and Skolem. He saw that use could be made of this infinitary principle to construct a semantic structure. Two immediate corollaries can be drawn from Gödel's argument:

Theorem 2 *(The Löwenheim-Skolem Theorem)*
If Γ is a set of sentences in $\mathcal{L}$ that is satisfiable in some structure then it is satisfiable in a countable structure.

The argument here is just the proof of the Completeness Theorem itself: first if Γ is satisfiable in some structure then it is consistent. Now build a structure using the proof of the Completeness Theorem starting from $\Delta_0 = \Gamma$. In the resulting countable structure all of Γ will be true.

This theorem had been proven much earlier by the logicians after whom it is named. Skolem's 1923 argument had come quite close to proving a version of the Completeness Theorem. Later Gödel said:

> The Completeness Theorem, mathematically, is indeed an almost trivial consequence of Skolem 1923. However, the fact is that, at that time, nobody (including Skolem himself) drew this conclusion neither from Skolem 1923 nor, as I did, from similar considerations of his own. This blindness (or prejudice, or whatever you may call it) of logicians is indeed surprising. But I think the explanation is not hard to find. It lies in the widespread lack, at that time, of the required epistemological attitude toward metamathematics and toward non-finitary reasoning.
>
> Gödel 2003

The second Corollary is also a simple observation but apparently was unnoticed by Gödel and others for some years before it was explicitly stated.

Theorem 3 (*The Compactness Theorem*)
Suppose a set of sentences Γ of a first order language $\mathcal{L}$ is not satisfiable in any structure. Then there is a finite subset $\Gamma_0 \subseteq \Gamma$ that is inconsistent.

The argument here is that if Γ is not satisfiable, then no structure makes Γ true; this implies 'Γ $\vDash \sigma \wedge \neg \sigma$' (interpretation: any structure that makes Γ true also makes a contradiction true and the latter can never happen). Hence by Completeness $\Gamma \vdash \sigma \wedge \neg \sigma$. But a proof of $\sigma \wedge \neg \sigma$ from assumptions in Γ is a finite list of formulae, and so can only use a finite set Γ_0 of assumptions from Γ. Thus Γ_0 is a finite inconsistent subset.

What we see here is that the inconsistency of the set Γ can always be localized to a finite subset of sentences responsible for an inconsistency (of course there could be infinitely many non-overlapping inconsistent finite subsets depending on what Γ is).

Returning to the example of general theory above: then many such theories Γ require an infinite set of axioms. If $\Gamma \vDash B$, then we know that in any structure M_1 in which all of Γ is true, then B will be true. The Compactness argument shows that we do not have to give one reason why in another structure M_1 B is true, and another reason for being true in structure M_2: because $\Gamma \vdash B$, a finite subset Γ_0 suffices as assumptions to prove B, and the proof $\Gamma_0 \vdash B$ gives us one single reason as to why in any structure in which Γ is satisfied, B will be true.

2.1 In conclusion

To summarize: we now use the idea of a *logic* more generally as a system comprising three components: a syntactic component of a language $\mathcal{L}'$ in some form, a deductive component of rules of inference that acts on the formulae of that language, and a third very different semantic component: the notion of a structure or interpretation of the formulae of the language $\mathcal{L}'$. It has become second nature for logicians when studying the plethora of different logics to define such by reference to these components. However, it was the Completeness Theorem that showed, certainly in the case of standard first order logic, the necessary interconnectedness of these concepts for demonstrating the adequacy of the rules of inference.

Given a logic, one of the first questions one asks, is 'Is it complete? Is there a Completeness Theorem for it?' For a host of logics, modal logics, logics of use to computer science, completeness theorems are provable. For others they are not and the reasons why not are themselves interesting. For so-called *second-order logic* where we allow the language to have quantifiers that range not over just individuals but sets of individuals and relations between individuals, the logic is incomplete: there is a deductive calculus for the logic but the lack of a Completeness Theorem renders the logic intractable (apart from special cases or areas such as in finite model theory) for proving useful theorems. It is partly for such reasons that set theorists followed Skolem into formulating set theory and thinking and reasoning in first order logic, because there is a Completeness Theorem and all the useful model building tools (such as the Corollaries of the Löwenheim–Skolem Theorem and the Compactness Theorem) that come with it.

Whilst the Theorem is nowadays not seen as at all difficult, Gödel's 1929 result can be seen as distilling out exactly the relationship between the different threads or components of first order logic; by answering Hilbert and Ackermann's question he demonstrated that semantical concepts, concepts of structure, satisfiability and of truth in such structures, had to be brought in to answer the drier questions of whether the rules of the deductive calculus which told only how strings of marks on paper could be manipulated, were sufficient for producing all validities in structures satisfying a set of assumptions. It is not insignificant that the Tree Lemma brought out what would otherwise have remained implicit and hidden: the nature of the argument also required infinite sets. Indeed from our present vantage point we know that the Completeness Theorem *must* use the Tree Lemma: if one assumes the Completeness theorem then we can prove the Tree Lemma from it: they are thus equivalent. But these discoveries were to come much later.

3 Incompleteness

To understand the Incompleteness Theorems we need to discuss further Hilbert's programmatic attempt to put mathematics on a consistent footing by returning to the position in the late 1920s.

Hilbert had the belief that mathematics could be made secure from possible paradoxes that dogged the early years of set theory by means of a series of *finitary consistency proofs*. A consistency proof for a theory T stated in a language $\mathcal{L}$ would be some form of proof that one could not have $T \vdash \varphi \wedge \neg\varphi$ for some (or any) formula φ of $\mathcal{L}$. But what should count as a legitimate proof or argument that T was consistent? To be of any value the argument had to use indubitably secure means, that themselves were not open to question. Hence the notion of 'finitary'. What Hilbert meant by this term was never given an absolutely explicit definition by Hilbert or his followers, even though the term was discussed by Hilbert on many occasions. Hilbert divided mathematical thinking into the 'real' and the 'ideal'. The former was essentially the mathematics of number theory, and the subject matter was 'finitist objects' the paradigm being stroke sequences '$||||, \ldots, |$' representing numbers, together with simple repetitive operations performed on them. Hilbert formulated various epistemological constraints on such objects, such as surveyability etc. Operations on them (such as concatenation corresponding to addition) should again be of a simple kind. The truth or otherwise of such finitarily expressed statements was open to inspection as it were.

At a later stage Hilbert and Bernays used the idea of *primitive recursion* (a scheme of building up number functions by simple recursion schemes) and forms of induction that could be expressed in the language of arithmetic $\mathcal{L}_A$ by quantifier-free formulae, stating that such should count as finitary. As a deeper discussion of what constituted finitary methods would take us too far afield, we shall let the idea rest with this version.

Ideal mathematics according to Hilbert could prove for us, for example, *quantified* statements in number theory. But if we really were in possession of finitary means for proving the consistency of that piece of idealized mathematics, we could have confidence in the truth of that quantified number theoretical statement, in a way that we could never have otherwise, because of the complexity involved in surveying all the natural numbers required by the quantifiers. Hilbert is sometimes paraphrased as saying that 'consistency of a theory yields the existence of the mathematical objects about which it speaks'. But his intentions here were more nuanced, and more restricted.

Hilbert had given a thorough-going axiomatization of geometry in *Foundations of Geometry* (1899). The consistency of the axioms of higher dimensional geometry could be reduced to that of plane geometry alone, and in turn the latter could be seen to be consistent by interpreting it in analysis, and thus as reducing the problem to that of the consistency of analysis. Given the emergence of the set theoretical paradoxes at the time, Hilbert wanted a proof of the consistency of analysis that was direct and did not involve a reduction using, say Dedekind cuts of sets of reals (as this might be in danger of importing unsafe methods). In his 1900 problems list, at second place he gave this consistency problem for analysis.

Hilbert's thinking was that the logical system of *Principia Mathematica* was inadequate for their purposes and so developed a new calculus for logical expressions (the ε-calculus). In 1924 Ackermann developed an argument for the consistency of analysis, but von Neumann, who took a deep interest in the foundations of mathematics at that time (formulating an axiomatic set theory, and the notion of 'von Neumann ordinal' number), saw an error. By the late 1920s Ackermann had developed a new ε-substitution method and there was optimism that with this, a new consistency proof for analysis given in this calculus could be given. This was even announced by Hilbert at the 1929 International Congress of Mathematics. But it was to be short-lived.

3.1 Gödel's First Incompleteness Theorem

Gödel worked in Vienna, and quite independently of Hilbert's Göttingen school. He expressed surprise concerning attempts at proving the consistency of analysis.

> It is mysterious why Hilbert wanted to prove directly the consistency of analysis by finitary methods. I saw two distinguishable problems: to prove the consistency of number theory by finitary number theory and to prove the consistency of analysis by number theory ... Since the domain of finitary number theory was not well-defined, I began by tackling the second half ... I represented real numbers by predicates in number theory ... and found that I had to use the concept of truth (for number theory) to verify the axioms of analysis. By an enumeration of symbols, sentences and proofs within the given system, I quickly discovered that the concept of arithmetic truth cannot be defined in arithmetic. If it were possible to define truth in the system itself, we would have something like the liar paradox, showing the system to be inconsistent ... Note that this argument can be formalized to show the existence of undecidable propositions without giving any individual instances. (If there were no undecidable propositions, all (and only) true propositions would be provable within the system. But then we would have a contradiction.) ... In contrast to truth, provability in a given formal system is an explicit combinatorial property of certain sentences of the system, which is formally specifiable by suitable elementary means.
>
> quoted in Wang 1996

In September of 1930 there was to be a joint meeting of several academic societies in Königsberg. Various members of the Wienerkreis, Carnap, Feigl and Waismann would speak at the Conference on Epistemology of Exact Sciences. At the meeting Carnap, Heyting and von Neumann would give hour-long addresses on logicism, intuitionism and formalism respectively. Gödel was to give a short contributed talk on results relating to his thesis. A few days before, Gödel met Carnap in a cafe to discuss the trip and then, out of the blue, related to Carnap his theorem concerning incompleteness of systems similar to *PM*. It seems that although Carnap noted in a memorandum 'Gödel's discovery: incompleteness of the system of PM, difficulty of the consistency proof', he could not have understood exactly what Gödel had achieved. He met Gödel three days later for a further discussion, but a week later, in Königsberg, he would still in the ensuing discussions there emphasize the role of completeness of a system being an overriding criterion for a formal theory.

Let us suppose a formal system *P* has sufficient syntax to talk about numerals '0', '1', ... '*k*', ... (as names for the corresponding actual numbers) as well as symbols for some basic arithmetical operations such as the successor operation of adding one, $x + 1$, addition and multiplication in general. The system embodied in *Principia Mathematica* is such a system. Also the Dedekind-Peano axioms for number theory ('PA') are expressed in such a language and allow the use of such operations with their normal properties, together with the notion of mathematical induction.

A formal theory *P* is called *ω-consistent*, if whenever we have that *P* proves all of $\varphi('0')$, $\varphi('1')$, ..., $\varphi('k')$, ... individually, then it is not the case that *P* proves $\exists v\neg\, \varphi(v)$. Because of the infinite hypothesis here, this is a stronger requirement on a theory *P* than simple consistency alone.

Theorem 4 (*Gödel : The First Incompleteness Theorem (1930)* (Gödel 1931)
Let P be a formal theory such as that of Principia Mathematica expressed in a suitable language L. If the theory P is ω-consistent, then there is a sentence γ_p of $\mathcal{L}$ such that:

$$P \nvdash \gamma_p \text{ and } P \nvdash \neg\gamma_p$$

The existence of such a sentence γ_p (a 'Gödel sentence' for the system *P*) shows that *P* cannot derive any sentence or its negation whatsoever. The system is 'incomplete' for deciding between γ_p and $\neg\gamma_p$. If the sentence γ_p is purely a number-theoretic statement then the conclusion is that there will be sentences which are presumably true or false of the natural number structure (as the case may be) but the system *P* is necessarily incapable of deriving either. If some version of 'ideal' mathematics could decide between the two, then that ideal mathematical argument could not be given within the formal system *P*.

Gödel said nothing about the Incompleteness results during his own talk in Königsberg, and only mentioned them in a rather casual manner during a round-table discussion on the main talks that took place on the last day of the conference. Hilbert was attending the conference and would give his farewell address as President of the German Mathematical Union, but did not attend the session at which Gödel made his remarks. It may well have been the case that, with the exception of von Neumann, no one in the room would have understood Gödel's ideas. However, von Neumann realized immediately the import of Gödel's result.

We discuss here the proof of the theorem, which proceeded via a method of encoding numerals, then formulae, then finite sequences of formulae (which might constitute a proof in the system P) all by numbers. This coding has become known as 'Gödel coding (or numbering)' and when a numeral 'k' for the number k is inserted into a formula $\varphi(v_0)$, resulting in $\varphi('k')$, then the latter can be said to be assigning the property expressed by φ to the number k (the which may encode a certain proof, for example). Thus indirectly formulae within the language can talk about properties of other formulae, and properties of sequences of formulae, and so forth, *via* this coding.

How the coding is arranged is rather unimportant as long as certain simplicity criteria are met. It is common to use prime numbers for this. Suppose the language L is made up from a symbol list: $(,), 0, S, +, \times, =, \neg, \wedge, \rightarrow, \exists, v_0, v_1, \ldots, v_k,$ ... (where S denotes the successor function, and there is an infinite list of variables v_k etc.) To members on the list we respectively assign code numbers: $1, 2, \ldots, 9, 10, 11, 12+k$ (for $k \in \mathbb{N}$). (Hence the variable v_2 receives code number $12 + 2 = 14$.) For the symbol s let $c(s)$ be its code in the above assignment.

A string such as: $\exists v_1(0 = S(v_1))$ expresses (the false) statement that some number's successor is 0. In general a string of symbols $s_1 s_2 \ldots s_k$ from the above list can be coded by a single number:

$$c(s_1 s_2 \cdots s_k) = 2^{c(s_1)}.3^{c(s_2)}. \cdots .p_k^{c(s_k)}$$

where p_m is the m'th prime number.

Given a number, by computing its prime factors we can ascertain whether it is a) a code number of a proof, or b) of a formula, or c) of just a single symbol, and moreover, which symbol, formula, or proof, in a completely algorithmic fashion. The *number* 2 has the *numeral term* or *name*: $S(S(0))$ from $\mathcal{L}$ and we abbreviate the latter name as '2'.

We shall write 'φ' for the numeral of the code number of the formula φ. 'φ' functions thus as a *name* for φ. Then the formula $0 = S(0)$ has as code: $c(0 = S(0))$ $= 2^3.3^7.5^4.7^1.11^3.13^2$. Suppose the latter value is k say, then '$0 = S(0)$' is 'k'. The efficiency of the coding system is entirely irrelevant: we only require the simple algorithmicity of the coding processes that maps the syntax of the language in a $(1-1)$ fashion into $\mathbb{N}$ in a recoverable fashion. Those codes are then named by the appropriate numerals which are terms in $\mathcal{L}$.

A further minimal requirement on the formal system *P* is that it be sufficiently strong to be able to *represent* predicates or properties of natural numbers which are definable over the standard structure. By this is meant the following: let $\varphi(v_0, \ldots, v_k)$ be any formula. *P represents* φ if for all natural numbers $n_0, \ldots, n_k$ both of the following hold:

$$\mathbb{N} \vDash \varphi[n_0, \ldots, n_k] \Rightarrow P \vdash \varphi(`n_0`, \ldots, `n_k`);$$

$$\mathbb{N} \nvDash \varphi[n_0, \ldots, n_k] \Rightarrow P \nvdash \varphi(`n_0`, \ldots, `n_k`).$$

One may show that any primitive recursive (p.r.) predicate, as mentioned above, can be represented in a system such as *PM*. Gödel then developed a series of lemmas that showed that operations on syntax could be mimicked by p.r. operations on their code numbers. For example, there is a p.r. predicate $R_\wedge(v_0, v_1, v_2)$ so that if χ is $\varphi \wedge \psi$, then in *P* we may prove $R_\wedge(`\varphi`, `\psi`, `\chi`)$. This is merely a reflection of the fact that we can calculate a code number for χ once those for φ and ψ are given. Ultimately though, the fact that $R_\wedge(`\varphi`, `\psi`, `\chi`)$ may hold is because of certain arithmetical relationships between the code numbers, not because of any 'meaning' associated to those numbers (which we attribute to them because they code particular formulae).

Similarly if we have three formulae ϕ, ψ, χ and ψ happens to be the formula $\phi \rightarrow \chi$, then we could view this triple if it occurred in a list of formulae which may or may not constitute a derivation in *P*, that they stand in for a correct application of Modus Ponens on the first two formulae yielding the third. Gödel shows that the relation $P_{MP}(v_0, v_1, v_2)$ which holds of a triple of numbers as above if indeed that third follows by application to the first two in the appropriate order, is primitive recursive: then we have:

$$\mathbb{N} \vDash P_{MP}[c(\varphi), c(\varphi \rightarrow \chi), c(\chi)], \text{ and hence } P \vdash P_{MP}(`\varphi`, `\varphi \rightarrow \chi`, `\chi`).$$

In short, syntactic operations, the checking of formulae for correct formation, and substitution of terms for variables, etc., up to the concept of the checking of a number that codes a list of formulae whether that list constitutes a correct proof of the last formula of the list, these are all p.r. relations of the code numbers concerned. For the last then Gödel constructs a p.r. predicate $\text{Prf}(v_0, v_1)$ which is intended to represent in *P* (in the above sense)

'v_0 is the code number of a proof of the last formula which has code number v_1.'

If then, *k* is the code number of a correct proof in *P* of the last formula σ of the proof, then the number relation $\text{Prf}[k, c(\sigma)]$ holds, and indeed is itself a relation between numbers; moreover it is provable in P because P can represent any p.r. predicate: $P \vdash \mathrm{Prf}('k', '\sigma')$. Again, to repeat, the fact that $\mathrm{Prf}(x, y)$ holds just says something about a particular numerical relationship between x and y, which either holds (or does not) irrespective of the interpretation we may put on it in terms of formulae, correct proofs, etc., etc.

Having done this, $\exists v_0 \mathrm{Prf}(v_0, v_1)$ is naturally interpreted as 'There is a proof of the formula with code number v_1.' This existential statement we abbreviate $\mathrm{Prov}(v_1)$. This final relation, due to the existential quantifier turns out not to be p.r., but this does not matter.

Lemma 1 *(The diagonal lemma)*

Given any formula $\varphi(v_0)$ of the number-theoretic language we may find a sentence θ so that $P \vdash \theta \leftrightarrow \varphi('\theta')$.

Proof: We let s_e be the string with code e, thus $c(s_e) = e$. Define the function $r :$ $\mathbb{N} \times \mathbb{N} \to \mathbb{N}$ by:

(1) $r(e, n) = c(\forall v_1 (v_1 = 'e' \to s_n))$.

Then $r(e, n)$ is p.r. being a composition of simple p.r. functions, indeed just multiplications involving some primes, the number n, and the codes for the symbols $s, \forall, =, \to$ etc. occurring in the string $\forall v_1 (v_1 = 'e' \to s_n)$.

This entails, *inter alia*, that r is representable in P. We now define a *diagonal function* $d : \mathbb{N} \to \mathbb{N}$ by $d(e) = r(e, e)$. Then d is p.r. and so representable too: there is a formula $D(v_1, v_0)$ that represents the graph of d as above. Moreover it can be shown:

(2) $P \vdash \forall v_0 (D('n', v_0) \leftrightarrow v_0 = 'd(n)')$.

Given our φ let $\psi(v_1)$ be $\exists v_0 (D(v_1, v_0) \wedge \varphi(v_0))$. Let $h = c(\psi(v_1))$. Then, to spell it out: s_h is $\psi(v_1)$. Let θ be $\forall v_1 (v_1 = 'h' \to s_h)$. Then by our definition of s_h:

$$P \vdash \theta \leftrightarrow \forall v_1 (v_1 = 'h' \to \psi(v_1))$$

by logic: $\leftrightarrow \psi('h')$

Using (2), Def of ψ: $\leftrightarrow \varphi('d(h)')$

But 'θ' is '$d(h)$', so we are done.   Q.E.D.

The lemma, despite its construction, is less mysterious than it seems: it is just a fixed point construction. Indeed there is nothing terribly particular about the choice of θ: one may show for each choice of φ that there are in fact infinitely many different formulae θ' satisfying the lemma: the argument has just provided one of them. One should note, however, that the proof is completely constructive (and can be run in intuitionistic logic): a θ is given, together with a proof that it satisfies the biconditional.

We can immediately derive a corollary which is often referred to as that 'truth is undefinable'. What this means is that there is no formula of the language $\tau(v_1)$ for which we have that for any k: $\mathbb{N} \vDash \tau('k')$ if and only if $\mathbb{N} \vDash \sigma$ where $c(\sigma) = k$. For, assume the axioms of P are true in $\mathbb{N}$. Suppose τ were such a formula, thence we should have by applying the Diagonal Lemma to the formula $\neg\tau(v_1)$, and then Soundness Theorem, that there is some sentence θ:

$$\mathbb{N} \vDash \theta \leftrightarrow \neg \tau('\theta'). \quad (**)$$

However, this θ is like a liar sentence: for if it is true in $\mathbb{N}$, then so is $\neg\tau('\theta')$; but by the assumption on τ then we also have $\mathbb{N} \vDash \tau('\theta')$. Hence $\neg\theta$ is true in $\mathbb{N}$; but this immediately leads to the same form of contradiction. Hence there is no such formula $\tau(v_1)$. We have shown that the set of arithmetical truths is not arithmetically definable:

Corollary 1 *(Tarski: The Undefinability of Truth)*
There is no formula $\tau(v_1)$ of $\mathcal{L}$ for which we have that for any k: $P \vdash \tau('k')$ if and only if $\mathbb{N} \vDash \sigma$ where $c(\sigma) = k$.

This theorem, usually attributed to Tarski, is easier to establish than the Incompleteness Theorem to come, and seems to have been also known to Gödel (see the quotation at the beginning of this section). Gödel seems to have come to the realization that an Incompleteness Theorem would be provable precisely because provability within a formal system such as P was, unlike truth, representable within P. That was the key.

In the proof of Theorem 4 we shall apply it with $\neg\exists v_0 \mathrm{Prf}(v_0, v_1)$ as φ. This yields

$$P \vdash \gamma \leftrightarrow \neg\exists v_0 \mathrm{Prf}(v_0, '\gamma') \quad (*)$$

We emphasize once more that the diagonal lemma says nothing about truth or meaning or satisfaction in the structure $\mathbb{N}$: it says something only about provability of certain formulae in the formal system P, formulae which express certain equivalences between sentences and formulae containing certain numeral terms. And that holds for the expression $(*)$ too.

Proof of Theorem 4

Suppose y is as at ($*$) above. Suppose for a contradiction that $P \vdash y$. Let n be the code number of such a proof. Combining that proof with ($*$) yields that $P \vdash \neg \exists v_0 \operatorname{Prf}(v_0, \lq y\rq)$. However n is after all a code of a proof of y and as P represents Prf, then $P \vdash \operatorname{Prf}(\lq n\rq, \lq y\rq)$. The conclusions of the last two sentences imply that P is inconsistent. This is a contradiction. Hence $P \nvdash y$.

Now from the last statement we conclude that no natural number n is a code of a proof of y in P. Hence, as P represents Prf, we have for all n: $P \vdash \neg\operatorname{Prf}(\lq n\rq, \lq y\rq)$. The assumption of ω-consistency now requires that $P \nvdash \neg y$ Q.E.D.

Note that the assumption of ω-consistency of P is only deployed in the second part of the argument to show $P \nvdash \neg y$. Rosser later showed how to reduce this assumption to that of ordinary consistency by the clever trick of applying the Diagonal Lemma to the formula

$\lq \forall v_0(\neg\operatorname{Prf}(v_0, v_1) \vee \exists v_2(v_2$ is the code of a shorter proof than v_0 of the formula $\neg v_1))\rq.$

Another remark: it is often asserted that the Incompleteness Theorem states that 'there are true sentences (in arithmetic, or in a formal theory, or in ...) that are not provable'. This is not a strictly accurate account of the theorem: the theorem itself mentions only deduction in formal theories and says nothing about truth. However, the Gödel sentence y is indeed true if we assume the consistency of P: by assuming the consistency of P we concluded that $P \nvdash y$, that is $\neg \exists v_0 \operatorname{Prf}(v_0, \lq y\rq)$ is true, which of course is y itself. We thus have '$Con(P) \Rightarrow y$'. But note this is not (yet) an argument *within* the deductive system P.

Yet another remark: the use of the self-referential Gödel sentence y that asserts its own unprovability sometimes leads to the impression that all undecidable statements unprovable in such a theory as *PM* must of necessity have some degree of self-reference. However, this is false. We comment on this again below. Similarly we do not refer to *the* Gödel sentence y for *PM*, since one can show there are infinitely many such.

3.2 The Second Incompleteness Theorem

Von Neumann left the room in Königsberg realizing the import of what Gödel had achieved. He may have been the only person to do so: Hans Hahn, Gödel's thesis supervisor, who was also present, made no mention of the Incompleteness results. Neither the transcript of the session, nor the subsequent summary prepared by Reichenbach for publication made any mention even of Gödel's participation. Although Gödel attended Hilbert's lecture, the two never met (or corresponded later), and the Viennese party then returned home. If von Neumann approached Hilbert whilst at the meeting to appraise him of the results, then it was not recorded.

Von Neumann shortly realized that more could be obtained by these methods. We can express the consistency of the formal system P by the assertion that from P we cannot prove a contradiction, $0 = 1$ say. We thus let $Con(P)$ be the sentence $\neg \exists v_0 \mathrm{Prf}(v_0, \text{‘}0 = 1\text{’})$.

Theorem 5 *(Gödel Second Incompleteness Theorem)*
Let P be a formal system as above. Then $P \nvdash Con(P)$.

Proof: The essence of the argument is that we may formalize the argument of '$Con(P) \Rightarrow \gamma$' at the end of the last section in number theory, and so in a system such as P. We should thus have shown

$$P \nvdash Con(P) \to \gamma. \quad (**)$$

We know from the First Incompleteness Theorem that $P \nvdash \gamma$. Hence $P \nvdash Con(P)$.

Q.E.D.

Von Neumann realized that the something akin to the Second Incompleteness Theorem would follow by the same methods Gödel had used for the First, and, in the November after Königsburg, wrote to Gödel. However, Gödel had himself already realized this and submitted the Second Theorem for publication in October. Of course the above is extremely sketchy: the devil then is in the detail of how to formalize within the theory P, the inference above from $Con(P)$ to $\neg \exists v_0 \mathrm{Prf}(v_0, \text{‘}\gamma\text{’})$, we thus need to show '$P \vdash Con(P)$ implies $P \vdash \exists v_0 \mathrm{Prf}(v_0, \text{‘}\gamma\text{’})$' *within* P itself. In other words we must establish $(**)$ above. Gödel did not publish these rather lengthy details himself, they were first worked out by Hilbert and Bernays in 1939.

4 The sequel

There are many points of interest and possibilities for elaboration in these theorems, and hence the extensive academic literature on them. Gödel left deliberately vague what he meant by 'formal system'. He said at the time that it was not clear what a formal system was or how it could be delineated. He stated his theorems as being true in the system of *PM* and for 'related systems'. It was clear that a similar system that had sufficient strength to prove the arithmetical facts needed in the coding and deduction processes would do. Hence the theorems were more general than had they been restricted to just *PM*. It was left to Alan Turing five years later (1936) to give a mathematical definition of 'computable' that could be used to demarcate what a formal system was: a set of axioms and rules that could be 'recognized' by a Turing machine, and so that a programmed machine could decide whether a derivation in the system was correct. In the intervening period Gödel had speculated regarding on what an 'effectively given' formal system could subsist, and rejected proposals from Church for such. However, he recognized that what Turing proposed was definitive:

> When I first published my paper about undecidable propositions the result could not be pronounced in this generality, because for the notions of mechanical procedure and of formal system no mathematically satisfactory definition had been given at that time ... The essential point is to define what a procedure is.
>
> That this really is the correct definition of mechanical computability was established beyond any doubt by Turing.
>
> Gödel 1995a

We give now a more modern statement of the First Incompleteness Theorem.

Theorem 6 (*Gödel, First Incompleteness Theorem*)

Let P be a computable set of axioms for number theory that contain the axioms PA. Then if P is consistent, it must be incomplete: there is a sentence γ_p so that $P \not\vdash \gamma_p$ and $P \not\vdash \neg\gamma_p$

4.1 Consequences for Hilbert's programme

The most dramatic consequences of the theorems were for Hilbert's programme of establishing the consistency of mathematics, and in particular focussing on arithmetic, by 'finitary means'. As we have discussed above finitary methods were to be of a restricted kind: the writing of, and operations on, finite strings of marks on paper, and using intuitive reasoning that 'includes recursion and intuitive induction for finite existing totalities' (Hilbert in a 1922 lecture). However finitary reasoning was also left somewhat vague, but clearly the usual arithmetical operations on numbers (and this for him included exponentiation) counted as finitary. Hilbert and Bernays (1929) seem to have settled on primitive recursive arithmetic, *PRA*, which allows the definition of functions by primitive recursion schemes, and induction on quantifier-free formulae. If this constituted the 'finitary means' of Hilbert, then indeed the Incompleteness Theorems dealt a death blow to this programme. Von Neumann thought so, and Weyl, in his 1943 obituary of Hilbert, described it as a 'catastrophe'. Gödel was initially more circumspect: he did not consider at that time that it had been argued that all methods of a 'finitary' nature could be formalized in, say, *PM*. At a meeting of the Vienna Circle in January 1931 he said that he thought that von Neumann's assertion that all finitary means could be effected in one formal system (and thus the Incompleteness Theorems should have a devastating effect on Hilbert's programme) was the weak point in von Neumann's argumentation. Again in his 1931 paper Gödel wrote that there might be finitary proofs that could not be written in a formal system such as *PM*. It was hard to bring forward convincing arguments in either direction at this point: there was no clear notion of 'formal system'; this had to wait until 1936 for Turing and there was also something of a confusion about intuitionistic logic: both von Neumann and Gödel thought that intuitionistic logic could count as finitary reasoning. However, this turned not to be the case: in 1933 Gödel showed that classical arithmetic could be interpreted in the intuitionistic version (known as Heyting Arithmetic, *HA*, and which only uses intuitionistic axioms of logic and rules of inference), thus ruling out the idea of using intuitionistic logic to help codify finitary reasoning, since the consistency of *HA* alone would now give the consistency of *PA*.

However, by 1933 (Gödel 1995b) he had changed his mind and acknowledged that all finitary reasoning could indeed be formalized in the axiom system of *Peano Arithmetic* ('*PA*'), which in particular allowed mathematical induction for formulae with quantifiers. He later remarked in several places (as in the quotation above) that Turing's precise definition of a formal system convinced him that the Incompleteness Theorems refuted Hilbert's programme.

4.2 Salvaging Hilbert's programme

It was not recorded when precisely Hilbert learnt of the Incompleteness results. Bernays, when he had previously suggested to Hilbert that after all a completeness proof might not be possible, reported that Hilbert reacted with anger, as he did eventually to the results themselves. Nevertheless, attempts were made to recover as much of the programme as was consistent with the Incompleteness Theorems. Bernays (who in correspondence with Gödel indicated that he was also not convinced that all finitary reasoning could be captured by a single system) in particular sought to discover modes of reasoning that could count as finitary but avoid being captured by the formal systems of the kind Gödel discussed. Hilbert and Bernays soon afterwards reacted positively by trying to see what could be done. By 1931 Hilbert was suggesting that an 'ω-rule' might be deployed where from an infinite set of deductions proving $P(0)$, $P(1)$, ..., $P(n)$, ... one would be allowed to infer $\forall k P(k)$ might be permissible as a form of reasoning. It is unknown whether Hilbert was reacting directly to the hypothesis of ω-consistency in the first version of the First Incompleteness Theorem, since indeed the displayed Gödel sentence was a pure $\forall$ sentence which would be 'proved' if the ω-rule were allowed. But the rule itself was not perceived as being finitary.

However, the major and most striking advance here came from G. Gentzen, who showed that the consistency of Peano Arithmetic could be established after all, if one allowed inductions along well orderings up to the first 'epsilon number' (ε_0 being the first fixed point of the ordinal exponentiation function $\alpha \to \omega^\alpha$). Clearly these are not finitary operations in any strict sense, but nevertheless Gentzen's work opened a whole area of logical investigation of formal systems involving such transfinite inductions thus opening the area of proof theory and 'ordinal notation systems'. (Gentzen also had the result exactly right: inductions bounded below ε_0 would not have sufficed.)

4.3 After Incompleteness

Had the Hilbert programme succeeded, it would have shown that ideal mathematics could be reduced to finitary 'real' mathematics: the consistency of a piece of ideal mathematics could be shown using just real, finitistic mathematical methods. A *relativized Hilbert programme* seeks to reduce an area of classical mathematics to some theory, necessarily stronger than finitary mathematics. Feferman has argued that most of mathematics needed for physics, for example, can be reduced to *predicative* systems which can be proof-theoretically characterized using ordinal notation systems albeit longer than ε_0, but still of a small or manageable length.

As the Second Incompleteness Theorem had shown, given a formal theory T_0 (such as *PA*) we have that $T_0 \nvdash Con(T_0)$. But we may add $Con(T_0)$ as a new axiom itself to T_0 thereby obtaining a somewhat stronger deductive theory. (It is not that the Theorem casts any doubt on the theory T_0 or its consistency, it is only that it demonstrates the impossibility of formalizing a proof of that consistency within T_0.)

Thus setting:

$$T_1 : T_0 + Con(T_0)$$

The thinking is that since we accept *PA* and believe that its axioms are true of the natural number structure, we should also accept that *PA* is consistent. (Whilst a T_0, if consistent, neither proves $Con(T_0)$ nor its negation, it would be presumably perverse to claim that $\neg Con(T_0)$ is the correct choice of the two to make here.)

Continuing, we may define:

$$T_{k+1} : T_k + \mathrm{Con}(T_k) \text{ for } k < \omega, \text{ and then: } T_\omega = \bigcup_{k<\omega} T_k.$$

Having collected all these theories together as T_ω, we might continue:

$$T_{\omega+1} = T_\omega + \mathrm{Con}(T_\omega) \text{ etc.}$$

We thus obtain a transfinite hierarchy of theories. What can one in general prove from a theory in this sequence? Turing called these theories 'Ordinal Logics' and was the first to investigate the question as to what extent such a sequence could be considered complete:

Question: Can it be that for any problem, or arithmetical statement A there might be an ordinal α so that T_α proves A or ¬A? And if so can this lead to new knowledge of arithmetical facts?

Such a question is necessarily somewhat vaguely put, but anyone who has considered the Second Incompleteness Theorem comes around to asking similar or related questions as these. The difficulty with answering this, is that much has been swept under the carpet by talking rather loosely of 'T_α' for $\alpha \geq \omega$. This is a subtle matter, but there seems no really meaningful way to arrive at further arithmetical truths. Such iterated consistency theories have been much studied by Feferman and his school (see Franzén 2004).

Lastly we consider the question of Gödel sentences themselves. Much has been studied and written on this theme alone. However, the use of the diagonal lemma leading to the self-referential nature of such a Gödel sentence gives a contrived feeling to the sentence. (One should also beware the fact that not any fixed point of a formula $\varphi(v_1)$ is necessarily stating that it says of itself that it satisfies φ.) Could there be propositions that were more genuinely mathematical statements, and were not decided by *PA*? Gödel's methods produced only sentences of the diagonal kind, and the problem was remarkably difficult. Some forty years were to pass before the first example was found by Paris and Harrington (concerning so-called Ramsey-like partition principles). Since then many more examples of mathematically interesting sentences independent of *PA* have been discovered.

Further reading

Dawson, J. (1997), *Logical Dilemmas: The Life and Work of Kurt Gödel*, Wellesley, MA: A.K. Peters.

Franzén, T. (2004), *Inexhaustibility: A non-exhaustive treatment*, vol. 16 of *Lecture Notes in Logic*, Wellesley, MA: ASL/A.K. Peters.

Franzén, T. (2005), *Gödel's Theorem: An Incomplete Guide to Its Use and Abuse*, Wellesley, MA: A.K. Peters.

Kennedy, J. (2011), 'Kurt Gödel', *Stanford Encyclopedia of Philosophy*, <http://plato.stanford.edu/entries/goedel/>.

Smullyan, R. (1993), *Gödel's Incompleteness Theorems*, Oxford and New York: Oxford University Press.

Zach, R. (2003), 'Hilbert's program', *Stanford Encyclopedia of Philosophy*, <http://plato.stanford.edu/entries/hilbert-program/>.

References

Franzén, T. (2004), *Inexhaustibility: A non-exhaustive treatment*, volume 16 of *Lecture Notes in Logic.*, Wellesley MA: ASL/A.K.Peters.

Gödel, K. (1930), 'Die Vollständigkeit der Axiome des logischen Functionenkalküls?, Monatshefte für Mathematik und Physik', *Monatsheft für Mathematik und Physik*, 37 (trans. in Gödel (1986)), pp. 349–600.

Gödel, K. (1931), 'Über formal unentscheidbare Sätze der Principia Mathematica und verwandter Systeme. *Monatsheft für Mathematik und Physik*, 38 (transl. in Gödel (1986)), pp. 173–98.

Gödel, K. (1986), *Collected Works: Publications 1929–36*, ed. S. Feferman, J.W. Dawson Jr., S.C. Kleene, G.H. Moore, R.M. Solovay and J. van Heijenoort, pp. 304–23, Oxford: Oxford University Press.

Gödel, K. (1995a), *Collected Works Vol III: Unpublished Essays and Lectures*, ed. S. Feferman, J.W. Dawson Jr., S.C. Kleene, G.H. Moore, R.M. Solovay and J. van Heijenoort, pp. 166–8, Oxford: Oxford University Press.

Gödel, K. (1995b), 'The present situation in the foundation of mathematics', in S. Feferman, J.W. Dawson Jr., S.C. Kleene, G.H. Moore, R.M. Solovay and J. van Heijenoort (eds), *Collected Works Vol III: Unpublished Essays and Lectures*, Oxford: Oxford University Press.

Gödel, K. (2003), *Collected Works Vol V: Correspondence H–Z*, ed. S. Feferman, J.W. Dawson Jr., S.C. Kleene, G.H. Moore, R.M. Solovay and J. van Heijenoort, pp. 304–23, Oxford: Oxford University Press.

Hilbert, D. and W. Ackermann (1929), *Grundzüge der theoretischen Logik*, Berlin: Springer-Verlag.

Hilbert, D. and P. Bernays (1934), *Grundlagen der Mathematik*, vol. I, Berlin: Springer-Verlag, Berlin.

Hilbert, D. and P. Bernays (1939), *Grundlagen der Mathematik*, vol. II, Berlin: Springer-Verlag.

Turing, A.M. (1936), 'On Computable Numbers with an application to the *Entscheidungsproblem*', *Proceedings of the London Mathematical Society*, 42(2).

Wang, H. (1996), *A Logical Journey: From Gödel to Philosophy*, Boston: MIT Press.

Zach, R. (2003), 'Hilbert's program', *Stanford Encyclopedia of Philosophy*, http://plato.stanford.edu/entries/hilbert-program, accessed 12 August 2016.

12

Tarski

Benedict Eastaugh

1 Introduction

It is hard to overstate Alfred Tarski's impact on logic.* Such were the importance and breadth of his results and so influential was the school of logicians he trained that the entire landscape of the field would be radically different without him. In the following chapter we shall focus on three topics: Tarski's work on formal theories of semantic concepts, particularly his definition of truth; set theory and the Banach–Tarski paradox; and finally the study of decidable and undecidable theories, determining which classes of mathematical problems can be solved by a computer and which cannot.

Tarski was born Alfred Tajtelbaum in Warsaw in 1901, to a Jewish couple, Ignacy Tajtelbaum and Rosa Prussak. During his university education, from 1918 to 1924, logic in Poland was flourishing, and Tarski took courses with many famous members of the Lvov–Warsaw school, such as Tadeusz Kotarbiński, Stanisław Leśniewski and Jan Łukasiewicz. Prejudice against Jews was widespread in interwar Poland, and fearing that he would not get a faculty position, the young Alfred Tajtelbaum changed his name to Tarski. An invented name with no history behind it, Alfred hoped it would sound suitably Polish. The papers confirming the change came through just before he completed his doctorate (he was the youngest ever to be awarded one by the University of Warsaw), and he was therefore awarded the degree under his new name of Alfred Tarski.

Struggling to obtain a position in line with his obvious brilliance, Tarski took a series of poorly paid teaching and research jobs at his alma mater, supporting himself by teaching high-school mathematics. It was there that he met the woman who would become his wife, fellow teacher Maria Witkowska. They married in 1929, and had two children: their son Jan was born in 1934, and their daughter Ina followed in 1938. Passed over for a professorship at the University of Lvov in 1930, and another in Poznan in 1937, Tarski was unable to secure the stable employment he craved in Poland.

Despite these professional setbacks, Tarski produced a brilliant series of publications throughout the 1920s and 1930s. His work on the theory of truth laid the ground not only for model theory and a proper understanding of the classical logical consequence relation, but also for research on the concept of truth that is still bearing fruit today. Tarski's decision procedure for elementary algebra and geometry, which he regarded as one of his two most important contributions, was also developed in this period.

In 1939 he embarked for the United States for a lecture tour, with a thought of finding employment there. Seemingly oblivious to the impending conflagration, Tarski nevertheless contrived to escape mere weeks before war with Germany broke out, but leaving his wife and children behind. Working as an itinerant lecturer at Harvard, the City College of New York, Princeton and Berkeley, Tarski spent the war years separated from his family.

Back in Poland, Maria, Jan and Ina were taken into hiding by friends. Despite intermittent reports that they were still alive, Tarski spent long periods without news, and his attempts to extricate them from Poland were all in vain. It was not until the conclusion of the war that he learned that while his wife and children had survived, most of the rest of his family had not. His parents perished in Auschwitz, while his brother Wacław was killed in the Warsaw Uprising of 1944. About thirty of Tarski's close relatives were amongst the more than three million Polish Jews murdered in the Holocaust, along with many of his colleagues and students, including the logician Adolf Lindenbaum and his wife, the philosopher of science Janina Hosiasson-Lindenbaumowa. In 1945, Tarski gained the permanent position he craved at the University of California, Berkeley, where Maria and the children joined him in 1946. Made professor in 1948, Tarski remained in California until his death in 1983. There he built a school in logic and the philosophy of science and mathematics that endures to this day: a testament to his brilliance as a scholar, his inspirational qualities as a teacher, and his sheer force of personality.

The most universally known and acclaimed part of Tarski's career consists of his work on the theory of truth, so it is natural that we begin our journey there. Section 2 starts from the liar paradox, and then turns to Tarski's celebrated definition of truth for formalized languages. This leads us to the undefinability theorem: that no sufficiently expressive formal system can define its own truth predicate.

Much of Tarski's early research was in set theory. Although he remained interested in the area for the rest of his working life, his best-known contribution to the field remains the paradoxical decomposition of the sphere which he developed in collaboration with Stefan Banach, colloquially known as the Banach–Tarski paradox. This striking demonstration of the consequences of the Axiom of Choice is explored in section 3.

As a logician, only Kurt Gödel outshines Tarski in the twentieth century. His incompleteness theorems are the singular achievement around which the story of section 4 pivots. Before Gödel, logicians still held out hope for a general algorithm to decide mathematical problems. Many of this area's successes in the 1920s are due to Tarski and his Warsaw students, such as the discovery that when formulated in a language without the multiplication symbol, the theory of arithmetic is decidable. In 1936, five years after Gödel's discovery of incompleteness, Alonzo Church and Alan Turing showed that the general decision problem for first-order logic was unsolvable. The focus then turned from complete, decidable systems to incomplete, undecidable ones, and once again Tarski and his school were at the forefront. Peano Arithmetic was incomplete and undecidable; how much could it be weakened and retain these properties? What were the lower bounds for undecidability?

This is only intended as a brief introduction to Tarski's life and work, and as such there are many fascinating results, connections and even whole areas of study which must go unaddressed. Fortunately the history of logic has benefited in recent years from some wonderful scholarship. The encyclopaedic *Handbook of the History of Logic* is one such endeavour, and Keith Simmons's chapter on Tarski (Simmons 2009) contains over a hundred pages. Tarski is also the subject of an engrossing biography by Anita Burdman Feferman, together with her husband and Tarski's former student, Solomon Feferman (Feferman and Feferman 2004). Entitled *Alfred Tarski: Life and Logic*, it mixes a traditional biography of Tarski's colourful life with technical interludes explaining some of the highlights of Tarski's work. Finally, in addition to being a logician of the first rank, Tarski was an admirably clear communicator. His books and papers, far from being of merely historical interest, remain stimulating reading for logicians and philosophers. Many of them, including early papers originally published in Polish or German, are collected in the volume *Logic, Semantics, Metamathematics* (Tarski 1983).

2 The theory of truth

Semantic concepts are those which concern the meanings of linguistic expressions, or parts thereof. Amongst the most important of these concepts are *truth*, *logical consequence* and *definability*. All of these concepts were known in Tarski's day to lead to paradoxes. The most famous of these is the *liar paradox*. Consider the sentence 'Snow is white'. Is it true, or false? Snow is white: so the sentence 'Snow is white' is true. If snow were not white then it would be false. Now consider the sentence 'This sentence is false'. Is it true, or false? If it's true, then the sentence is false. But if it's false, then the sentence is true. So we have a contradiction whichever truth value we assign to the sentence. This sentence is known as the *liar sentence*.

In everyday speech and writing, we appear to use truth in a widespread and coherent way. Truth is a foundational semantic concept, and therefore one which we might naively expect to obtain a satisfactory philosophical understanding of. The liar paradox casts doubt on this possibility: it does not seem to require complex or far-fetched assumptions about language in order to manifest itself, but instead arises from commonplace linguistic devices and usage such as our ability to both use and mention parts of speech, the property of bivalence, and the typical properties we ascribe to the truth predicate such as disquotation.

2.1 Tarski's definition of truth

Both their apparent ambiguity and paradoxes like the liar made mathematicians wary of semantic concepts. Tarski's analyses of truth, logical consequence and definability for formal languages were thus major contributions to both logic and philosophy. This paved the way for model theory and much of modern mathematical logic on the one hand; and renewed philosophical interest in these semantic notions – which continues to this day – on the other.

In his seminal 1933 paper on 'The Concept of Truth in Formalized Languages' (1933), Tarski offered an analysis of the liar paradox. To understand Tarski's analysis, we need to make a few conceptual points. The first turns on the distinction between use and mention. If we were to say that Tarski was a logician, we would be *using* the name 'Tarski' – but if we said that 'Tarski' was the name that logician chose for himself, we would be *mentioning* it. In the written forms of natural language we often distinguish between using a term and mentioning it by quotation marks. When we say that 'Snow is white' is true if, and only if, snow is white, we both use and mention the sentence 'Snow is white'.

The liar paradox seems to rely on our ability not merely to use sentences – that is, to assert or deny them – but on our ability to refer to them. The locution 'This sentence' in the liar sentence refers to (that is, mentions) the sentence itself, although it does not use quotation marks to do so. Consider the following variation on the liar paradox, with two sentences named A and B. Sentence A reads 'Sentence B is false', while sentence B reads 'Sentence A is true'. We reason by cases: either sentence A is true, or it is false. If A is true, then B is false, so it is false that A is true – hence A is false, contradicting our assumption. So A must be false. But if A is false, then it is false that B is false, and so B is in fact true. B says that A is true, contradicting our assumption that it is true. So we have a contradiction either way.

In his analysis of the liar paradox, Tarski singles out two key properties which a language must satisfy in order for the paradox to occur in that language. The first consists of three conditions: the language must contain names for its own sentences; it must contain a semantic predicate 'x is true'; and all the sentences that determine the adequate usage of the truth predicate must be able to be stated in the language. These conditions are jointly known as *semantic universality*.

The second property is that the ordinary laws of classical logic apply: every classically valid inference must be valid in that language. Tarski felt that rejecting the ordinary laws of logic would have consequences too drastic to even consider this option, although many philosophers since have entertained the possibility of logical revision; see section 4.1 of Beall and Glanzberg (2014) for an introductory survey. Since a satisfactory analysis of truth cannot be carried out for a language in which the liar paradox occurs – as it is inconsistent – Tarski concluded that we should seek a definition of truth for languages that are not semantically universal.

There are different ways for a language to fail to be semantically universal. Firstly, it could fail to have the expressive resources necessary to make assertions about its own syntax: it could have no names for its own expressions. Secondly, it could fail to contain a truth predicate. Finally, the language might have syntactic restrictions which restrict its ability to express some sentences determining the adequate usage of the truth predicate.

This seems to exclude the possibility of giving a definition of truth for natural languages. Not only are they semantically universal – quotation marks, for instance, allow us to name every sentence of English within the language – but they actually *aim* for universality. If a natural language fails to be semantically universal then it will be expanded with new semantic resources until it regains universality. Tarski goes so far as to say that 'it would not be within the spirit of [a natural language] if in some other language a word occurred which could not be translated into it' (Tarski 1983: 164). When English fails to have an appropriate term to translate a foreign one, in cases like the German *schadenfreude* or the

French *faux pas*, the foreign term is simply borrowed and becomes a loanword in English.

Tarski therefore offered his definition of truth only for *formal languages*. These tend to be simpler than natural languages, and thus they are more amenable to metalinguistic investigation. The particular example that Tarski used was the calculus of classes, but essentially the same approach can be used to define truth for any formal language. As is standard in the current literature on formal theories of truth, we shall use the language of arithmetic.

A formal language is typically constructed by stipulating two main components. The first is the *alphabet*: the collection of symbols from which all expressions in the language are drawn. In the case of a first-order language like that of arithmetic, the alphabet includes (countably infinitely many) variables v_0, v_1, ...; logical constants $\forall$, $\exists$, $\neg$ $\wedge$, $\vee$, $\rightarrow$, $\leftrightarrow$, $=$; punctuation (,). This is then enriched by the addition of nonlogical constants, function symbols and relational predicates. In the case of the first-order language of arithmetic this includes the constant symbols 0 and 1; the two binary function symbols $+$ and $\times$; and the binary relation symbol $<$. The second component of a formal language is the *formation rules*, which state how one may build up well-formed formulas from the symbols of the alphabet. Again, in the case of arithmetic, these are just the standard recursive definitions familiar from first-order logic.[1]

A formal language is generally understood as one which can be expressed in terms of an alphabet and a set of formation rules. These rules are decidable: given a sequence s of symbols drawn from the alphabet, one can always determine in a finite number of steps whether or not the sequence is a well-formed formula of the language or not.

Implicit in the circumscription of a formal system – its syntax, its semantics, its axioms and rules of inference – is the idea of the metatheory in which all of these things are laid down. One of the major innovations in logic during the first part of the twentieth century was the recognition of this fact, and the subsequent results obtained by formalizing the metatheory. Tarski was one of the pioneers in this area.

We call the language for which a definition of truth is to be given the *object language*, and the language in which we do so the *metalanguage*. The metalanguage can simply be an expansion of the object language with the necessary semantic terms, although this is not essential, as long as it contains translations of the terms of the object language. The metatheory is a theory – and as Tarski showed, it can be a formal theory, i.e. a set of sentences in a formal metalanguage – in which to theorize about the object theory.

Here we pause to highlight a change in terminology between Tarski's work and current usage. Tarski uses the term 'language' to denote what we nowadays call a *formal system*: not just a formal language in the sense described above, but also a set of axioms and inference rules associated with that language. In keeping with current practice, and fixing the logic throughout to be first-order classical logic, we shall be concerned with *theories*: sets of sentences of a given formal language, such as Peano Arithmetic or ZFC. When Tarski writes of the 'object language' and the 'metalanguage' he thereby means what we mean when we write *object theory* and *metatheory*.

As we have seen, quotation marks are not the only linguistic device by which we can refer to sentences and their components. Demonstratives and names can both be used, but in his account of truth Tarski settled on *structural-descriptive names*: names for primitive parts of language which can be combined to yield the names of compound expressions. In the particular case of arithmetic, this amounts to providing a formal counterpart of the description of the language of arithmetic given above. It must contain names for variables $x_1, x_2, \ldots$; names for logical vocabulary such as $\neg, \wedge, \forall$; and names for grammatical symbols such as (and). It must also provide names for the nonlogical symbols: 0, 1, +, ×, <. With the referential devices in hand, it must also provide a way to combine them to give the names of complex expressions such as *terms* (denoting expressions such as $1 \times (1 + 1)$), *atomic formulas* like $1 = 1$, and complex formulas like $1 = 0 \rightarrow 1 < 0$.

As Corcoran notes in his introduction to Tarski (1983), Tarski effectively provided the first formal theory of syntax, something which has gone on to become a subject of substantial importance in computer science. Tarski's approach of adding a syntax theory to the object language is currently undergoing a small revival, being used in recent work by Leigh and Nicolai (2013). However, we shall not pursue this method further, since in most applications within logic it has been superseded by an alternative which is available in arithmetic and other suitably expressive formal systems: *Gödel coding*.

So called because it was invented by Kurt Gödel in the course of his proof of the incompleteness theorems, Gödel coding is a way of encoding sentences in the language of arithmetic as particular natural numbers, in such a way that given any number coding a sentence we can determine just what that sentence is. The details of Gödel coding can be found in the previous chapter on Kurt Gödel; for our purposes all we need to know is that for any sentence φ in the language of arithmetic, its Gödel code $\ulcorner \varphi \urcorner$ is a natural number, denoted by a closed term of the language – that is to say by a numeral $\bar{n}$.

Tarski stressed two qualities which any definition of truth must satisfy: *formal correctness* and *material adequacy*. The former concerns the form of the definition, namely whether it provides an explicit definition of the predicate 'is true'; the latter, whether the formal definition captures our informal concept of truth.

Think back to our example: 'Snow is white' is true if snow is white, and false if snow is not white. In other words we have an equivalence: 'Snow is white' is true if, and only if, snow is white. More generally, let S be a sentence and s a name for S. Then s is true if, and only if, S. This is Tarski's T-schema. Using Gödel coding, we can express this scheme in the formal language of arithmetic (plus the truth predicate):

(T) $$T\left(\ulcorner \varphi \urcorner\right) \leftrightarrow \varphi.$$

The material adequacy condition Tarski argued for is called *Convention T*. According to Convention T, a materially adequate theory of truth for a language $\mathcal{L}$ should entail every sentence of the T-schema for that language, and every Gödel code falling under the extension of the truth predicate T should stand for a sentence.

Having determined the properties that a successful definition of truth should satisfy, Tarski proceeded to present his definition. The first thing to note is that Tarski defines truth in terms of another semantic notion: *satisfaction*. For a full formal definition the reader should consult an introductory logic textbook.[2] The crucial idea is that satisfaction is a generalization of truth, from sentences to all well-formed formulas of the language, including those with free variables. A satisfaction relation obtains between three components: a model $\mathfrak{M}$; an assignment s of elements of the domain of $\mathfrak{M}$ to free variables of the language $\mathcal{L}_{\mathfrak{M}}$ of $\mathfrak{M}$; and a formula φ in the language $\mathcal{L}_{\mathfrak{M}}$. In symbols we write this as

$$\mathfrak{M} \models \varphi[s].$$

Satisfaction is defined *recursively*, so for example a model $\mathfrak{M}$ and an assignment s satisfy a conjunction $\varphi \wedge \psi$ if, and only if, φ is satisfied by $\mathfrak{M}$ and s, *and* ψ is satisfied by $\mathfrak{M}$ and s. Consider the following example, where we fix the model to be the standard natural numbers $\mathbb{N}$. Take the formula $\varphi = v_1 < 1 \wedge v_2 = 0$, and a satisfaction function s_1 such that $s_1(v_1) = 0$ and $s_1(v_2) = 0$. Then we can see that the left conjunct '$v_1 < 1$' is satisfied by s_1 (and $\mathbb{N}$), since $s_1(v_1) < 1$, and so is the right conjunct '$v_2 = 0$', since $s_1(v_2) = 0$. Therefore the entire formula φ is satisfied by s_1.

Truth is defined as the limit case where no free variables appear in a formula: given some model $\mathfrak{M}$, a sentence φ is true in $\mathfrak{M}$ if, and only if, for every assignment *s*, $\mathfrak{M}$ and *s* satisfy φ. In the specific case of the language of arithmetic and the standard natural numbers $\mathbb{N}$, a sentence ψ in the language of arithmetic is true in $\mathbb{N}$ if, and only if, every assignment *s* of natural numbers to variables satisfies ψ. In symbols we can write this as

$$T(\ulcorner \varphi \urcorner) \Leftrightarrow (\forall \text{ assignments } s)\ \mathbb{N} \vDash \varphi[s].$$

Tarski constructed definitions of truth, in terms of satisfaction, for several different formal systems. As he noted in his 1933 paper, the method is entirely general. Using it we can define truth for arbitrary models and languages, and indeed this is one of the building blocks of mathematical logic as it stands today – in no small part due to Tarski's contributions.

2.2 Tarski's undefinability theorem

Gödel's incompleteness theorems (see the previous chapter) showed that no sufficiently strong, recursively axiomatizable theory of arithmetic *S* is *complete*, in the sense that there are sentences φ in the language of arithmetic such that neither φ nor its negation $\neg\varphi$ can be proved from the axioms of *S*. At the heart of this result is a sentence in the language of arithmetic, known as the *Gödel sentence*, which is a close relative of the liar sentence. Rather than asserting its own falsity, like the liar sentence, the Gödel sentence asserts its own *unprovability*.

Tarski's undefinability theorem shows something stronger: not only are consistent formal theories of a certain strength incomplete, but they cannot define the truth predicate for the language in which they are written. In other words, they cannot prove all instances of the T-schema for that language. The requirement that such theories be consistent is important: classical logic has a property called *explosion*, which means that if a theory *S* is inconsistent then it proves every sentence in the language of *S*, including every instance of the T-schema.

The following way of stating of Tarski's theorem is quite standard. The theory **Q** mentioned in the statement of the theorem is a very weak theory in the language of arithmetic. It was discovered by Tarski's colleague, Raphael Robinson, and we shall learn more about it in section 4.3.

Undefinability theorem

Let $\mathcal{L}$ be a language that extends the language of arithmetic $\mathcal{L}_{PA}$. Suppose *S* is a consistent, recursively enumerable theory in $\mathcal{L}$ that includes the axioms of Robinson's **Q**. Given a Gödel numbering of the sentences of $\mathcal{L}$, there is no predicate τ definable in the language of arithmetic such that S proves the following equivalence scheme for all sentences φ of $\mathcal{L}$:

$$\tau\left(\ulcorner\varphi\urcorner\right) \leftrightarrow \varphi.$$

This might seem a little contradictory: the previous section spelled out in detail Tarski's definition of truth, but the undefinability theorem shows that truth cannot be defined. The resolution of this apparent conflict may already be evident, lying as it does in the way Tarski resolves the liar paradox: by stipulating that the definition of truth for a language $\mathcal{L}$ is not made in the object theory – this is ruled out by the undefinability theorem – but in the metatheory. To take our standard example, arithmetical truth is not definable in first-order arithmetic, but it is definable in a stronger theory, such as that of set theory or second-order arithmetic.

Tarski emphasizes in the historical notes at the end of Tarski (1933) that his work on truth was done independently and was largely complete, including the definition of truth, by 1929. After Gödel published his incompleteness theorems (Gödel 1931) Tarski realized that Gödel's methods could be used to prove the undefinability theorem.

3 The Banach–Tarski paradox

Tarski's work on the theory of truth was not the first time he had flirted with paradox. In 1924 he published a paper with fellow Polish mathematician Stefan Banach showing that a sphere could be cut up into finitely many pieces, and that those pieces could then be reassembled – using only translations and rotations – into two spheres, each with exactly the same volume as the original sphere.

This is, to say the least, a counterintuitive result. We expect Euclidean geometry to respect our basic physical intuitions (suitably idealized). If we take a knife and cut up an orange, we cannot reassemble it into two oranges with the same size as the original one. The problem is *volume*, which in the case of the orange remains invariant no matter how we cut it up. Bounded sets, such as spheres, are supposed to have fixed, finite volumes: we can't just get a little extra from somewhere.

But the Banach–Tarski theorem shows that we can, after all, do exactly that, as long as we can cut up our sphere into parts which do not have well-defined volumes. These strange objects are called non-measurable sets, since they lack a *measure*: intuitively, a way of assigning a size to a bounded set. In the case of a line, this is just the length of an interval, like the set of all points between

0 and 1. For a plane it's the area which a bounded set encompasses; and in the three-dimensional case, its volume. While there are non-measurable subsets of $\mathbb{R}$ and $\mathbb{R}^2$, the one- and two-dimensional versions of the Banach–Tarski theorem are false, although a weaker version where the bounded set is cut into countably infinitely (rather than finitely) many pieces is true.

Non-measurable sets had been around since well before Tarski; the first proof of their existence was given by Giuseppe Vitali in 1905. Both Vitali's proof and the Banach–Tarski theorem rely on a set theoretic axiom whose use had been controversial ever since its introduction by the German set theorist Ernst Zermelo: the Axiom of Choice, or AC.

Definition. The *Axiom of Choice* is the statement that for every nonempty family of sets $\mathcal{F}$, there is a function f such that $f(S) \in S$ for every $S \in \mathcal{F}$.

Such an f is called a *choice function*, because it 'chooses' an element from every set in the family. For finite families of sets, we can deduce the existence of choice functions from the other axioms of set theory. But once infinite collections are brought into the picture, the Axiom of Choice must be added as an additional postulate to guarantee the existence of choice functions for every nonempty family of sets.

The mathematicians of the day had two main quarrels with the Axiom of Choice. The first was that it allows one to prove a number of puzzling and deeply counterintuitive theorems, of which the Banach–Tarski theorem is the quintessential example. The second addressed the character of the axiom itself. In the presence of Zermelo's other axioms, it allows one to prove the existence of a great many sets, yet gives no way to define them. It is in this sense that the Axiom of Choice is referred to as a non-constructive axiom.

The nature of choice functions therefore remains somewhat mysterious. A classic example can be found by comparing the real numbers $\mathbb{R}$ with the natural numbers $\mathbb{N}$. We first introduce the technical notion of a *wellorder*. A set X is wellordered by an ordering $<$ if and only if every nonempty subset $Y \subseteq X$ has a least element: some $x \in Y$ such that every $y \in Y$ is greater than or equal to x under the ordering $<$. It's easy to see that the natural numbers are wellordered under their natural ordering:

$$0 < 1 < 2 < \ldots < n < n + 1 < \ldots$$

However, the usual ordering on $\mathbb{R}$ is not a wellordering. To see this, consider the open interval $(0, 1) \subseteq \mathbb{R}$, which consists of all real numbers greater than 0 but less than 1. If the reals were wellordered then there would be a smallest real $x \in (0, 1)$.

But $\frac{x}{2}$ is also a real number greater than 0 but less than 1, and $\frac{x}{2} < x$. So x could not be the smallest element of $(0, 1)$ after all.

So much for the usual ordering. But perhaps there is another way we can order the continuum to get a wellorder? After all, the rational numbers under their usual ordering are not wellordered – but there is another ordering on them which is a wellordering. As it turns out, the answer to this is no: the axioms of ZF alone do not imply that the continuum is wellordered. To prove that it is, we require the Axiom of Choice. In the theory obtained by adding AC to the axioms of ZF, known as ZFC, we can prove that there is a relation $<$ on $\mathbb{R}$ which wellorders the continuum. In fact, we can prove a lot more than that: ZFC proves the *Wellordering Principle*, which states that every set can be wellordered. And the relationship between AC and the Wellordering Principle doesn't stop there: if we assume only the axioms of ZF, plus the Wellordering Principle, we can prove the Axiom of Choice; they are equivalent.

But the Wellordering Principle merely says that there exists a wellordering; it doesn't tell us what the ordering is. In other words, it doesn't define it. Even worse, there may not even be such a definition: it's consistent with the axioms of ZFC that there is no formula in the language of set theory which defines a wellordering of the continuum, even though ZFC proves that such a wellordering exists.

Later developments in logic have given us a clearer view of what Banach and Tarski accomplished. Using Cohen's method of forcing, Robert M. Solovay constructed a model of the axioms of ZF plus the assertion that every subset of the real numbers $\mathbb{R}$ is measurable. In Solovay's model the Banach–Tarski theorem is false, showing that the Axiom of Choice is indeed required in order to prove it (Solovay 1970). Raphael Robinson, Tarski's colleague at Berkeley, improved the Banach–Tarski theorem itself by showing that a paradoxical decomposition of the sphere could be achieved by cutting it into just five pieces – and that this is the minimum number possible (Robinson 1947). More recently, Pawlikowski (1991) used work of Foreman and Wehrung (1991) to show that the full strength of the Axiom of Choice is not required in order to prove the Banach–Tarski theorem: it suffices to assume a weaker principle, important in functional analysis, known as the Hahn–Banach theorem.

Giving a complete proof of the Banach–Tarski theorem is, unfortunately, outside the scope of this chapter. The reader interested in a fuller account should consult Jech (1973) for a relatively comprehensive reference. A recent popular account is Wapner (2005).

4 Decidable and undecidable theories

4.1 Mechanical mathematics and the Entscheidungsproblem

The history of the *decision problem*, or *Entscheidungsproblem* – the German name by which it is often known – can be traced back to Leibniz, whose hope it was to devise a mechanical means for deriving the truth or falsity of mathematical statements. The problem lay fallow until 1900, when, in an address to the International Congress of Mathematicians, David Hilbert laid down a series of challenges to the mathematical community; these became known as *Hilbert's problems*. The tenth of these problems concerned the solubility of Diophantine equations:

> Given a Diophantine equation with any number of unknown quantities and with rational integral numerical coefficients: *To devise a process according to which it can be determined by a finite number of operations whether the equation is solvable in rational integers.*
>
> Hilbert 1902: 458, italics in original

Hilbert's tenth problem was not resolved until 1970, when Yuri Matiyasevich put in place the final pieces of a proof begun many years earlier by Julia Robinson (another of Tarski's students), Martin Davis and Hilary Putnam, and which showed that no such finite procedure exists. Developing the theme of Hilbert's tenth problem in a more general and precise way, Hilbert and Wilhelm Ackermann posed the classical version of the Entscheidungsproblem in (Hilbert and Ackermann 1928). The solution to the decision problem would be an algorithm that, given a formal language $\mathcal{L}$ and a theory T written in that language, decided whether or not any particular sentence φ in the language $\mathcal{L}$ was true in all models of T. In other words, the algorithm should determine whether or not φ is a logical consequence of T.

As it stood, almost every part of the Entscheidungsproblem could be stated in formal terms: there were unambiguous mathematical definitions of the notions of a formal language and of a theory formulated in that language. Once Gödel proved his completeness theorem for first-order logic, it was also clear that for a sentence to be a consequence of a particular formal theory was precisely for it to be derivable from that theory in an appropriate formal calculus. However, the concept of an effective procedure or algorithm remained unformalized.

If, in the early 1930s, someone had come along with an algorithm solving the Entscheidungsproblem then it would have been clear to the mathematical community that it was in fact such an algorithm. But since they did not – and with Gödel's incompleteness theorems fresh in their minds – logicians turned their efforts towards proving that there could be no such algorithm. To do this, the fuzzy notion of an effective procedure needed to be given a precise formal definition. Otherwise any purported proof of the impossibility of solving the Entscheidungsproblem would have been vulnerable to the accusation that the proof did not cover all of the cases it needed to.

Various definitions were offered, from the notion of a *recursive function* developed by Jacques Herbrand and Kurt Gödel, to Alonzo Church's property of *λ-definability*. Church proved in 1936 that the Entscheidungsproblem has no solution, if the notion of an effective procedure is identified with recursiveness. This identification, known as Church's Thesis, met with resistance in the logical community, not least from Gödel. In the end it was Alan Turing's conceptual analysis of computation, which led him to develop the idea of the Turing machine, that convinced Gödel to accept what is now known as the Church–Turing thesis: the functions that can be effectively computed are precisely those which can be computed by a Turing machine. As Turing and Stephen Kleene proved, this set of functions is identical to that picked out by the other formal notions of computability: recursiveness, λ-definability and Turing computability all coincide. The scientific consensus since then has sided with Gödel: effective computability is Turing computability, and Hilbert's Entscheidungsproblem is unsolvable.

4.2 Decidable theories

Well before Gödel's incompleteness theorems burst into the startled minds of the logical community in 1931, and almost a full decade before Church and Turing's negative resolution of the decision problem, Tarski had done pioneering work on *decidable* theories: ones where there is an algorithm that determines whether or not a given statement is a consequence of the theory. Decidability is closely linked to *completeness*, and proofs of one are often also proofs of the other.

Definition (completeness and decidability). A theory T in a language $\mathcal{L}$ is *complete* iff for every $\mathcal{L}$-sentence φ, either $T \vdash \varphi$ or $T \vdash \neg\varphi$. T is *decidable* iff there is a decision procedure that determines whether or not an $\mathcal{L}$-sentence φ is a theorem of T.

Many major advances were made during a research seminar at the University of Warsaw which Tarski ran from 1927 to 1929. The topic of the seminar was *quantifier elimination.* This is a technique in the field we now call model theory. It first emerged in Löwenheim's (1915) work, and appeared in its full form in Skolem (1919).

Definition (quantifier elimination). A first-order theory T in a language $\mathcal{L}$ admits of *quantifier elimination* if for every $\mathcal{L}$-formula $\varphi(x_1 \ldots, x_n)$ there is a quantifier-free $\mathcal{L}$-formula $\varphi^*(x_1, \ldots, x_n)$ such that

$$T \vdash \varphi(x_1, \ldots, x_n) \leftrightarrow \varphi^*(x_1, \ldots, x_n).$$

Proving that a theory admits of quantifier elimination usually involves specifying an algorithm by which a formula φ containing quantifiers can be transformed into an equivalent formula φ^* without them. Quantifier-free formulas are built up by boolean combinations from atomic formulas, so if a theory proves or refutes every atomic sentence, then it proves or refutes every quantifier-free sentence too. Typically it is easier to show decidability for atomic sentences, since often this is simply a matter of computation, and if a theory with this property admits of quantifier elimination then a decidability result for the theory follows easily.

Langford (1927a, 1927b) used this technique to solve the decision problem for the first-order theory of dense linear orders. In the seminar on quantifier elimination, Tarski began by extending Langford and Skolem's results, before turning to more ambitious targets. One of these was the decidability of the additive theory of the natural numbers. This theory is formulated in the language consisting of the constant symbols 0 and 1, and the binary function symbol +. Its axioms are the universal closures (that is, every free variable is bound by an outer universal quantifier) of the following formulas:

(P1) $0 \neq n + 1$
(P2) $n + 1 = m + 1 \rightarrow n = m$
(P3) $n + 0 = n$
(P4) $n + (m + 1) = (n + m) + 1$
(P5) $(\varphi(0) \wedge \forall n(\varphi(n) \rightarrow \varphi(n + 1))) \rightarrow \forall n \varphi(n)$

Note that the final axiom is actually a scheme, where $\varphi(n)$ is any formula of this language containing one or more free variables. Tarski's student Mojżesz Presburger proved in 1928 that this theory – now known as Presburger arithmetic, in his honour – is consistent, complete and decidable.[3] These results formed Presburger's Master's thesis at the University of Warsaw, and were his only published results in logic: he left the academy soon after, and like so many other Polish Jews, perished in the Holocaust (Zygmunt 1991).

The centrepiece of Tarski's research on this topic was his proof that the theory of real closed fields admits of quantifier elimination. Van den Dries (1988: 7) goes so far as to say that 'Tarski made a fundamental contribution to our understanding of $\mathbb{R}$, perhaps mathematics' most basic structure.' The theory of real closed fields is formulated in the *language of ordered rings*, $\mathcal{L}_{or}$, which is the language of rings (the constant symbols 0 and 1, and the binary function symbols + and ·) supplemented with the order relation ≤. The *axioms for ordered fields* are the usual definitions of addition and multiplication for fields, with additional axioms governing the order relation:

$$a < b \vee a = b \vee b < a,$$

$$a \leq b \rightarrow a + c \leq b + c,$$

$$0 \leq a \wedge 0 \leq b \rightarrow 0 \leq a \cdot b.$$

A *real closed field* is an ordered field which also obeys the following continuity scheme: for every polynomial term p, if there exist real numbers a and b such that $a < b$ and $p(a) < 0 < p(b)$, then there exists another real number c such that $a < c < b$ and $p(c) = 0$. Tarski proved that given any formula $\varphi(x_1, \ldots, x_m)$ in the language of ordered rings, we can effectively find a quantifier-free formula $\varphi^*(x_1, \ldots, x_m)$ and a proof of the equivalence $\varphi \leftrightarrow \varphi^*$ that uses only the axioms for real closed fields.

Many important and fruitful consequences follow from this result. To begin with, the theory of real closed fields is both complete and decidable. Moreover, since the real numbers $\mathbb{R}$ are a real closed field – indeed, the prototypical one – it follows that the theory of $\mathbb{R}$ is also complete and decidable. More formally, given any sentence φ in the language $\mathcal{L}_{or}$ of ordered rings, there is a finite procedure that determines whether or not $\mathbb{R} \vDash \varphi$. This stands in striking contrast to the theory of the rational numbers $\mathbb{Q}$, which does not have this property. Julia Robinson proved that the integers $\mathbb{Z}$ are definable in the field $\mathbb{Q}$, and thus the theory of the rational numbers is neither complete nor decidable (Robinson 1949).

The solution of the decision problem for the theory of real closed fields was intimately linked to Tarski's work on geometry, and in particular to the axioms he gave for what he called *elementary geometry*: a substantial fragment of Euclidean geometry, formulated in first-order logic with identity, and requiring no set theory. By reducing the theory of elementary geometry to the theory of elementary algebra – that is to say, the theory of real closed fields – Tarski proved that it was decidable.

As with much of Tarski's work, his decision procedure for elementary algebra and geometry was worked out in the 1930s but publication was delayed until much later. An attempt to publish it in a French journal was ruined by the German invasion of 1940. It finally made it into print as a RAND Corporation report and was subsequently reprinted as Tarski (1951); an extensive discussion, with interesting historical as well as mathematical insights, is van den Dries (1988). Tarski and his school proved many other decidability results, which have been surveyed by Doner and Hodges (1988). A more general study of Tarski's work in model theory is Vaught (1986).

4.3 Undecidable theories

The success of Tarski and his students in classifying decidable theories notwithstanding, it was clear that undecidability was a widespread phenomenon. Presburger's theorem showed that one way of weakening Peano Arithmetic, by removing multiplication, resulted in a decidable theory. A natural question to ask was thus: how weak could an undecidable subtheory of Peano Arithmetic be?

A precise answer to this question was provided by Raphael Robinson, who formulated the weak theory of arithmetic **Q** – now known as *Robinson Arithmetic* – and proved its undecidability. Robinson's **Q** is formulated in the language of first-order arithmetic, that is, the language of first-order logic supplemented by the constant symbol 0; the unary function symbol S denoting the successor function; and binary function symbols $+$ and $\cdot$ denoting addition and multiplication respectively.

*Definition (Robinson's **Q**).* The axioms of *Robinson arithmetic* or **Q** are the universal closures of the following.

(Q1) $S_x \neq 0$
(Q2) $S_x = S_y \rightarrow x = y$
(Q3) $y = 0 \lor \exists x (S_x = y)$
(Q4) $x + 0 = x$
(Q5) $x + S_y = S(x + y)$
(Q6) $x \cdot 0 = 0$
(Q7) $x \cdot S_y = (x \cdot y) + x$

Q has many interesting properties. For instance, it proves the commutativity of addition in every individual case: $t + s = s + t$ holds for all closed terms (those containing no free variables) t and s in the language of arithmetic. However, it cannot prove the universal generalization $\forall x \forall y (x + y = y + x)$.

Definition (essential undecidability). A theory T is *decidable* if the set of its provable consequences in the language of T is recursive, and *undecidable* otherwise. A theory S is *essentially undecidable* if S is undecidable and every consistent extension of S is also undecidable.

Theorem (Robinson). **Q** is essentially undecidable.

This result was originally proved in 1939 for a stronger subsystem of first-order Peano Arithmetic by Tarski and Andrzej Mostowski. Raphael Robinson showed in (Robinson 1950) that it also holds for **Q**; for details see Tarski, Mostowski and Robinson (1953: 39–40). Robinson also proved the following intriguing theorem, showing that the essential undecidability of **Q** is in some sense *irreducible*.

Theorem (Robinson). None of the theories obtained by removing one of the 7 axioms of **Q** is essentially undecidable.

Tarski, Mostowski and Robinson collaborated on a book, *Undecidable Theories* (Tarski et al. 1953). The slimness of this volume belies its importance: in it, Tarski not only set out a general and powerful method for proving undecidability results, but he inspired a new wave of research. The first part of the book consists of a general introduction to the issue of undecidability, written by Tarski. In it he uses the notion of an *interpretation* of one theory in another to develop a quite general method of proving undecidability results. This proceeds, as Tarski puts it, in an *indirect* manner: rather than directly demonstrating undecidability, as for example Church did, it proves that a theory T is undecidable (or essentially undecidable) because it interprets a theory S which is already known to be undecidable (or essentially undecidable).

Part II contains detailed proofs of a number of key undecidability results, including Robinson's theorem that **Q** is essentially undecidable, and was co-authored by Tarski, Mostowski and Robinson. One of the striking features of the results is the generality and clarity that Tarski achieved, analysing in great detail the results of the past twenty years and distilling them into a pure and powerful form. The clearest example of this is theorem 1 of this part, which states that no consistent theory T can define both the diagonal function (which should be familiar from the discussion in the preceding chapter of Gödel's incompleteness theorems) and the set of theorems of *T*.

In the final part, Tarski uses the machinery of interpretability developed in Part I, along with the undecidability results of Part II, to show that the first-order theory of groups is undecidable. Here once more we see the unity of Tarski's project, since in 1949 his student Wanda Szmielew had shown that the first-order theory of Abelian groups – formed by adding the commutativity axiom to the theory of groups – is *decidable*. The theory of groups is therefore not essentially undecidable, since it has a consistent decidable extension.

Notes

* The author was funded by an Arts and Humanities Research Council doctoral studentship during the completion of this work.

1 See for example section 2.1 of Enderton (2001: 69–79).

2 For example pp. 80–86 of Enderton (2001).

3 The axioms above are closer to those in Hilbert and Bernays (1968, 1970) than the axioms used by Presburger himself, as noted by Zygmunt (1991: 221). Presburger's original axioms can be found on pp. 218–19 of Zygmunt (1991).

References

Beall, J. and M. Glanzberg (2014), 'Liar Paradox', in E.N. Zalta, ed., *The Stanford Encyclopedia of Philosophy*. Fall 2014 edition, Stanford: Stanford University Press.

Doner, J. and W. Hodges (1988), 'Alfred Tarski and Decidable Theories', *The Journal of Symbolic Logic*, 53(1):20–35.

Enderton, H.B. (2001), *A Mathematical Introduction to Logic*, 2nd edn, San Diego: Harcourt Academic Press.

Feferman, A.B. and S. Feferman (2004), *Alfred Tarski: Life and Logic*, Cambridge: Cambridge University Press.

Feferman, S., J.W. Dawson, Jr, S.C. Kleene, G.H. Moore, R.M. Solovay and J. van Heijenoort (eds) (1986), *Kurt Gödel: Collected Works. I: Publications 1929–1936*, Oxford: Oxford University Press.

Foreman, M. and F. Wehrung (1991), 'The Hahn–Banach theorem implies the existence of a non-Lebesgue measurable set', *Fundamenta Mathematicae*, 138:13–19.

Gödel, K. (1931), 'Über formal unentscheidbare Sätze der Principia Mathematica und verwandter Systeme I'. *Monatshefte für Mathematik Physik*, 38:173–98. (English translation in van Heijenoort (1967), pp. 596–616 and in Feferman et al. (1986), pp. 144–95.)

Hilbert, D. (1902), 'Mathematical problems', *Bulletin of the American Mathematical Society*, 8:437–479. doi: 10.1090/S0002-9904-1902-00923-3. Translated for the Bulletin by Mary Winston Newson.

Hilbert, D. and W. Ackermann (1928), *Grunzuge Der Theoretischen Logik*, Berlin: Springer-Verlag.

Hilbert, D. and P. Bernays (1968, 1970), *Grundlagen der Mathematik*, vols I and II, 2nd edn, Berlin: Springer Verlag.

Jech, T.J. (1973), *The Axiom of Choice*, Amsterdam: North-Holland (republished 2008, Mineola, NY: Dover).

Langford, C.H. (1927a), 'Some theorems on deducibility', *Annals of Mathematics, second series*, 28:16–40.

Langford, C.H. (1927b), 'Theorems on deducibility (second paper)', *Annals of Mathematics, second series*, 28:459–471.

Leigh, G.E. and C. Nicolai (2013), 'Axiomatic truth, syntax and metatheoretic reasoning', *The Review of Symbolic Logic*, 6(4):613–636. doi: 10.1017/S1755020313000233.

Löwenheim, L. (1915), 'Über Möglichkeiten im Relativkalkül', *Mathematische Annalen*, 76:447–70.

Pawlikowski, J. (1991), 'The Hahn–Banach theorem implies the Banach–Tarski paradox', *Fundamenta Mathematicae*, 138:21–2.

Robinson, J. (1949), 'Definability and decision problems in arithmetic', *The Journal of Symbolic Logic*, 14:98–114.

Robinson, R.M. (1947), 'On the decomposition of spheres', *Fundamenta Mathematicae*, 34:246–60.

Robinson, R.M. (1950), 'An essentially undecidable axiom system', *Proceedings of the International Congress of Mathematicians*, 1:729–30.

Simmons, K. (2009), 'Tarski's Logic', in D.M. Gabbay and J. Woods (eds), *Handbook of the History of Logic. Volume 5. Logic from Russell to Church*, pp 511–616, London: Taylor & Francis.

Skolem, T. (1919), 'Untersuchungen über die Axiome des Klassenkalkuls und über Produktations- und Summationsprobleme, welche gewisse Klassen von Aussagen betreffen', *Skrifter utgit av Videnskapsselskapet i Kristiania. I, Matematisk-Naturvidenskabelig Klasse*, 3.

Solovay, R.M. (1970), 'A model of set-theory in which every set of reals is Lebesgue measurable', *Annals of Mathematics, Second Series*, 92(1):1–56.

Tarski, A. (1933), 'The Concept of Truth in Formalized Languages', in *Logic, Semantics, Metamathematics*, ed. J. Corcoran, pp. 152–278, Indianapolis: Hackett, 1983.

Tarski, A (1951), *A Decision Method for Elementary Algebra and Geometry*. Berkeley: University of California Press. Prepared for publication by J.C.C. McKinsey. Originally published in 1948 as RAND report R-109, RAND Corp., Santa Monica, CA.

Tarski, A. (1983), *Logic, Semantics, Metamathematics*, ed. J. Corcoran, 2nd revised edn, Indianapolis: Hackett, Original 1956 edition translated and edited by J.H. Woodger.

Tarski, A., A. Mostowski and R. M. Robinson (1953), *Undecidable Theories*. Amsterdam: North-Holland.

van den Dries, L. (1988), 'Alfred Tarski's Elimination Theory for Real Closed Fields', *The Journal of Symbolic Logic*, 53(1):7–19.

van Heijenoort, J. (ed.) (1967), *From Frege to Gödel: A Source Book in Mathematical Logic, 1879– 1931*, Cambridge MA: Harvard University Press.

Vaught, R.L. (1986), 'Alfred Tarski's Work in Model Theory', *The Journal of Symbolic Logic*, 51(4): 869–82. doi: 10.2307/2273900.

Wapner, L.M. (2005), *The Pea and the Sun: A Mathematical Paradox*, Wellesley, MA: A.K. Peters.

Zygmunt, J. (1991), 'Mojżesz Presburger: Life and Work', *History and Philosophy of Logic*, 12(2):211–23. doi: 10.1080/014453409108837186.

Index